# DESTAPE

**PITT LATIN AMERICAN SERIES**
Catherine M. Conaghan, Editor

NATALIA MILANESIO

# ¡DESTAPE!

## SEX, DEMOCRACY, & FREEDOM IN POSTDICTATORIAL ARGENTINA

UNIVERSITY OF PITTSBURGH PRESS

**Published by the University of Pittsburgh Press, Pittsburgh, Pa., 15260**

Copyright © 2019, University of Pittsburgh Press

All rights reserved

Manufactured in the United States of America

Printed on acid-free paper

10 9 8 7 6 5 4 3 2 1

Cataloging-in-Publication data is available from the Library of Congress

ISBN 13: 978-0-8229-4584-0

ISBN 10: 0-8229-4584-3

Cover art: Detail of cover of *Shock: La Revista Bomba*, issue no. 94.

Cover design: Alex Wolfe

*To César*

# CONTENTS

# ACKNOWLEDGMENTS

**Many people helped me immensely** to complete this book, contributing both their time and archival materials. Without knowing me and with no references, they opened their homes and libraries, provided me with contacts, and responded to my questions about Argentina in the 1980s with an eagerness that matched my own. To all those who agreed to interviews and shared their expertise on sexology, sex education, journalism, feminism, history, films, and literature—along with their personal memories of those years—I want to express my profound gratitude. Our conversations had a great impact on my intellectual growth well beyond this project.

I am very grateful to Marcelo Raimon for sharing his impressive collection of *destape* magazines and his passion and knowledge about the topic. Sara Torres, Mirta Granero, María Luisa Lerer, Walter Barbato, and Laura Caldiz not only sat with me for hours patiently answering my questions but also opened their remarkable personal archives, gave me valuable support, and put me in contact with a network of other people willing to help. Very special thanks to Jorge Fontevecchia for sharing the history of Perfil with me and allowing me access to the Perfil Archives, and to Adriana Lobazo for coordinating it all. At Perfil, many thanks to Omar Arredondo for guiding me in their collections. I am also indebted to Mabel Bellucci for sharing images of feminist militant María Elena Oddone and to Maitena for educating me on comics and their history. I am grateful to Alicia Sanguinetti for her memories of photographer Alicia D'Amico and to María Laura Rosa for discussing D'Amico's images with me. Special thanks to Julia Debernardi, who so kindly gave me access to her amazing collection of the journal *Contribuciones* and to Mabel Bianco for generously sharing the work of her mother, sex educator Liliana Pauluzzi. I want to thank everyone at the Instituto de Estudios Jurídicos Sociales de la Mujer (INDESO Mujer) in Rosario, and especially Betiana Spadillero, for their willingness to help.

I am grateful to Jennifer Adair, Daniel Fridman, Susan Kellogg, Sarah

Fishman, William Walker, Benjamin Cowan, Elizabeth Hutchison, María Elena de las Carreras, and Antonius Robben for contributing with comments and suggestions at different stages of my research. Special thanks to Daniel Fridman for helping me with materials housed at the University of Texas at Austin, and also to Catalina Trebisacce, Karin Grammático, Paula Torricella, Paula Bertúa, Lucía De Leone, Moira Soto, Elsa Meinardi, Daniel Jones, Mónica Gogna, Daniel Merle, Karina Felitti, Gloria Loresi, Mary Helen Spooner, Paulo Menotti, and Bernardo Subercaseaux for guiding me when I was searching for sources, answering my questions, and providing ideas, recommendations, and contacts. I am indebted to Mario Pecheny and Santiago Joaquín Insausti for sharing their work and primary source materials. Many thanks also go to Wendy Gosselin and Rebecca Bender for their willingness and ability to help me convey my ideas better.

At the University of Houston, Philip Howard, Anadeli Bencomo, Sarah Fishman, and Catherine Patterson guided me through grant applications and proposal writings and offered sound advice, and Donna Butler, Gloria Turner, Paul Scott, Daphyne Pitre, and Norma Sides helped me with administrative issues related to research and beyond. Thanks for your assistance. For the funds that were indispensable for the completion of this book, I am very grateful to the University of Houston Department of History, the College of Liberal Arts and Social Sciences, the Office of the Provost, and the Women's, Gender & Sexuality Studies Program. Special thanks are due to the staff of Interlibrary Loan Services at the University of Houston's M. D. Anderson Library for effectively assisting me to find the rarest of materials.

Working with Joshua Shanholtzer at the University of Pittsburgh Press has been a real pleasure. I thank him deeply for his enthusiasm about this project right from the start, his professionalism and accessibility, and his openness to my ideas. I also want to express special thanks to Matthew Karush and Barbara Sutton, who kindly and respectfully provided me with excellent suggestions and constructive comments.

Finally, I thank my husband, César Seveso, for being both the number one fan of the idea for this book since the beginning and the most critical reader of every single draft. When I was undecided about venturing into unknown historical territory, he encouraged me to trust my instincts and then reminded me to enjoy the challenge. His optimism and support made all the difference.

# DESTAPE

# INTRODUCTION

## A Poem and the *Destape*

**One humid winter morning** of August 2016, sexologist Mirta Granero welcomed me to her home in Rosario, Argentina's third largest city and the place where I grew up. Granero, a psychologist and sexologist, was a leading figure in the rise of sexology and sex education after the return to democracy in the 1980s. She was an original member of one of the earliest organizations devoted to the promotion of school-based sex education and the training of sex educators in the country as well as one of the founders, in 1983, of the first institute outside Buenos Aires for the training of clinical sexologists and the treatment of sexual problems. I had contacted Granero a few months earlier to tell her I was conducting research for a book on sexuality in Argentina after 1983, when one of the most repressive military dictatorships in Latin America (1976–83) ended and Argentines rejoiced in a democratic spring that began with the election of Raúl Alfonsín as president (1983–89). Granero was enthusiastic about examining the relation between sexuality and democracy, agreed to an interview, and invited me to work in her library.

The morning we met at her house, Granero walked me to a spacious office packed with bookcases and storage cabinets covering every wall, told me I had free access to everything in the room, asked me to call her if I needed her, and left. She is a fine example of the generosity and trust that I had the fortune to experience during my research. In her big and rich archive I found invaluable and unexpected materials, the type that elevate historians' heart rates and overwhelm them with a proud sense of discovery. I also found a typescript copy of a beautiful poem titled "Una utopía razonable" ("A Reasonable Utopia"), written by Josep Vicent Marqués,[1] a Spanish sociologist who specialized in sexuality and played a fundamental role in the redefinition of modern sexology in Spain after the fall of Francisco Franco's dictatorship in 1975.

> Erotizar la vida.
> Descentrar el coito del placer genital.
> Reconstruir el coito como cópula.
> Airear el sexo guardado en los genitales.
> Honrar, sin embargo, tus genitales como una parte aceptada de tu cuerpo aceptado.
> Desdramatizar los asuntos sexuales sin banalizarlos.
> Aprender a jugar y aprender la importancia del juego.
> Hacer el amor siempre que al menos dos personas quieran.
> No hacer el amor cuando es otra cosa lo que se quiere hacer.
> Hacerlo siempre con, nunca contra.
> Separar el sexo de la procreación, pero también de la machada y la resignación, de la agresividad, la competencia o la compensación de agravios.
> Saber "técnicas sexuales" pero haberlas olvidado como se olvidan los libros que se aprenden bien.
> No hacer de la masturbación un sucedáneo del intercambio.
> No hacer del intercambio un sucedáneo de la masturbación.
> Dinamitar la edad, el tiempo usurpado por el patriarca.
> Hacer en la cama un lugar al humor y a la ternura.
> Probar a hacer el amor para conocerse, pero también probar a conocerse para hacer el amor.
> Olvidar para siempre las inhibiciones y los récords.
> No ser indiferentes al acostarse o no, sin encontrar angustia en ello.
> Inventar por el camino un nuevo lenguaje para hablar de esto llanamente, sin la alternancia de la pomposidad y la burla.[2]

*Eroticize life.*

*Separate coitus from genital pleasure.*

*Rebuild coitus as coupling.*

*Air out the sex tucked in the genitals.*

*Yet honor your genitals as an accepted part of your accepted body.*

*Play down sexual matters without trivializing them.*

*Learn to play and learn the importance of playing.*

*Make love whenever at least two people want to.*

*Don't make love when you really want to do something else.*

*Always do it with, never against.*

*Separate sex from procreation, but also from macho bravado and from resignation, from aggressiveness, competition and revenge.*

*Know "sexual techniques" but then forget them like you forget a book you've studied well.*

*Don't make masturbation a substitute for interaction.*

*Don't make interaction a substitute for masturbation.*

*Blot out age, the time usurped by the patriarch.*

*Make room in bed for humor and tenderness.*

*Try making love to get to know someone, but also try getting to know someone to make love.*

*Forget the inhibitions and the records, forever.*

*Don't be indifferent to whether or not you get laid, but don't agonize over it.*

*Invent a new language for speaking plainly about this as you go, without interjecting bluster or mockery.*

Granero told me she and her colleagues had used the poem in the mid-1980s to jumpstart discussion in the popular sexual enrichment workshops that flourished in those years. She conveyed how relevant this piece was as an invitation to rethink sexuality in the new context of freedom after years of authoritarianism. At the time of our interviews, puzzled by archival finds and my own thrilling but disjointed ideas about how to make sense of it all, I was unable to understand what I realized months later, at my desk in Houston, while rereading the poem aloud. Marqués's work was an effective tool to talk about sex in the return to democracy in Argentina because it perfectly reflected the new meanings and representations of sexuality. The poem separated sex from reproduction, contested fears and ideas of morality and duty, and focused on pleasure, well-being, identity, rights, and choice. These were the central components of the unparalleled sexualization of Argentine culture and society after 1983 that contemporaries called the *destape*. Following cultural and media studies expert Feona Attwood, I understand a "sexualized culture" to be "a contemporary preoccupation with sexual values, practices and identities; the public shift to more permissive sexual attitudes; the proliferation of sexual texts; the emergence of new forms of sexual experience; the apparent breakdown of rules, categories and regulations designed to keep the obscene at bay; our fondness for scandals, controversies and panics around sex."[3]

The destape was the biggest and most explosive sociocultural phenomenon after the fall of the military dictatorship. *Destapar* means "to take the lid off, uncover, expose, or undress," and the destape was, in fact, an avalanche of sexual images and narratives characterized by new levels of visual and discursive explicitness about sex and the body, topics the dictatorship had considered tasteless, immoral, mystifying, and, for all these reasons, dangerous. Scholars of Argentina have traditionally studied the process of redemocratization by focusing on the reconstruction of the public sphere in a postdictatorial context, the reorganization of the state, the emergence of new social movements, and the resurgence of political parties and labor unions—themes that are common in the scholarship of democratic transitions all over the world, from European postcommunist countries to more contemporary experiences in Arab countries.[4] Less attention has been devoted to cultural issues, and nothing has been said about sex or the destape. The omission is interesting because scholars and historians of sexuality have been particularly interested in the relation between sex and politics.[5] Paradigmatically, in the context of the rapid spread of fascism through Europe, Austrian psychoanalyst Wilhelm Reich, who is considered the intellectual father of the sexual revolution, believed that a vibrant sexuality was a precondition for a vibrant democracy. For Reich, on the contrary, sexual repression was a vehicle for the transmission of authoritarian ideologies.[6]

*Destape: Sex, Democracy, and Freedom in Postdictatorial Argentina* is the first history of the destape considered as both a large-scale media phenomenon and a far-reaching process of change in sexual ideologies and practices. The destape timidly emerged in 1981, with the military weakened but still in power, and gained momentum between 1983, with the return to democracy, and 1987. Although it ran out of steam by the end of the decade, when the novelty and the scandal wore off, the destape's influences and legacies have pervaded Argentine culture to this day. This book asks a significant question that historians of democratic transitions in Latin America and beyond have overlooked: How did the restoration of democracy in 1983, after years of repression and censorship, transform sexuality as well as representations and ideas about sexuality? In answering this question, the book is guided by anthropologist Gayle Rubin's argument that although sex is always political, there are "historical periods in which sexuality is more sharply contested and more overtly politicized. In such periods, the domain of erotic life is, in effect, renegotiated."[7] The first history of Argentine sexuality in the 1980s, this study is devoted to understanding the country's transition to democracy as a prime example of these unique historical moments by examining the complex relationship among the fall of political and social authoritarianism, freedom, democracy, and sex. This is a relationship that remains unexplored, although it is relevant to the many Latin American countries in the region that experienced similar transitions to democracy, most notably, Chile, Brazil, and Uruguay.

With the end of the military dictatorship and the return to democracy, nudity and sex became ubiquitous. Sexual images and texts saturated all types of publications, 15 percent of all magazines sold were erotic, soft-porn movies topped the lists of the ten highest-grossing films each year, erotic novels and sexology books became best sellers and quickly sold out, and seminudity and erotic innuendos inundated television shows. Argentina experienced an unprecedented sexual exhibitionism in mainstream culture, or the rise of "on/scenity," as film scholar Linda Williams has described the process by which a society makes public, bringing "on/scene," what was once deemed obscenity and kept off scene.[8] I argue, however, that the destape went beyond the sexualization of media content and was a profound transformation of the way Argentines talked about, understood, and experienced sexuality. In order to reveal the destape as a sweeping change of discourses, representations, manners, and morals that both grew from and reinforced the newborn democracy, this book examines the boom of sex therapy and sexology, the fight for the introduction of sex education in schools, the expansion of family planning services and the emergence of organizations dedicated to sexual health care, and the centrality of discussions on sexuality among feminist as well as gay and lesbian organizations, which reawakened with the return to democracy. Therefore, this book offers a historical analysis of the sexualization of mass media alongside a larger social and cultural history of sex.

While Argentines have commonly used destape as a term to refer exclusively to the new, abundant, and explicit sexual content in the media, I propose a reconceptualization that includes mass media commodities but goes beyond. Here, the destape was not only a market development or a commercial manifestation of popular culture but also a process of individual and collective sexual discovery and liberation as well as the social disclosure of sexism, homophobia, and sexual injustice. There was a destape in films, the press, television, advertising, theater, and literature. There was also a women's destape; a destape of feminist, gay, and lesbian activists; and a destape led by sexologists, sex educators, and sexual health experts. Together, these destapes took the lid off Argentine sexuality. They all emerged from the same postdictatorial conditions and participated in the same cultural and political milieu, but they represented distinctive positions, had differing goals, and engaged with and benefited from democracy and freedom differently. Consequently, they all made contributions to reformulating sexual culture in Argentina but, despite some commonalities and overlapping, in their own very idiosyncratic ways.

This book engages with a scholarship that has drawn attention to the fascinating and intrinsic connection between media representations and sexual culture. Media and cultural studies expert Brian McNair has argued that this connection happens at three different levels. First, media representations reveal sexual and behavioral norms, both lived and aspirational. Second, they are bearers of ideology, disseminating views about sexual roles, rights, and responsibilities from which individuals may learn or find inspiration. In this regard, Linda Williams has asserted that "moving images are surely the most powerful sex education most of us will receive."[9] Finally, media representations are, at the same time, influenced by consumers who may respond unfavorably to images and messages that do not resonate with what they want, what they do, or who they are in a given historical context.[10] This book shows that cultural commodities affect and reflect sexual culture, but consumers have the power to endorse, reject, or alter their messages. This is one reason why the destape emerges as riddled with ambivalences; it was a process in which new and progressive ideas, defiant of the sexual and gender status quo, coexisted with reactionary and conventional ones that reinforced traditional sexual morality. Indeed, this book tests the argument that speaking more about sex necessarily and unconditionally advances the cause of sexual freedom for all. In Argentina, more and more explicit sexual speech and imagery broke a monolithic sexual culture. However, the book asks how, why, and to what extent this break happened to demonstrate that neither the process nor the outcome was mechanical, predictable, or homogenous.[11]

Through different levels of analysis, this study offers a multivocal social and cultural history of sexuality that includes the contributions of movie directors; writers; scholars; educators; sex therapists; journalists; physicians; gay, lesbian, and feminist activists; audiences; readers; family planning experts; the Catholic Church and Catholic organizations—the strongest opponents of the destape—and the state. The analysis is based on a large and diverse body of sources, including untapped magazine collections, films, television shows, sexology books and journals, sex education books, literature, surveys, polls, and statistics. The rich archive of publishing house Perfil provided me with access to some of the most iconic destape publications. I conducted oral interviews with feminists, sexologists, sex educators, and journalists, and explored their personal archives. In addition, bulletins and internal documents of gay, lesbian, and feminist organizations; sex therapists' personal papers; and sex research were invaluable in reconstructing sexuality in the 1980s. The documents and newsletters authored by Catholic organizations and Argentina's episcopal conference provided insights to understand the most important enemies of the destape. To effectively incorporate this broad range of primary sources, I combined the methodological tools and theoretical insights of cultural studies, film and media studies, feminist theory, and oral history.

## FROM DICTATORSHIP TO DEMOCRACY

Legendary populist leader Juan Domingo Perón returned to Argentina in 1973 after being exiled for almost two decades. Upon Perón's return to the country to assume the presidency for the third time, many believed that he would be able to control the leftist forces that had emerged in the 1960s authoritarian context as well as the escalating volatile social and political conditions. Instead, violence increased, particularly when the internecine fighting between left-wing Peronist guerrillas and right-wing Peronists intensified. This conflict worsened when Perón died in July 1974 and the vice president, his widow María Estela Martínez de Perón, also known as Isabel Perón, took power. The combination of an unraveling economic crisis, the lack of leadership, and the violence between the guerrilla organizations and the Alianza Anticomunista Argentina (Argentine Anticommunist Alliance), or Triple A—a right-wing death squad under the orders of José López Rega, the minister of social welfare and a close collaborator of the Peróns—threw the country into chaos, creating the conditions for the 1976 military coup. On March 24, 1976, under the direction of General Jorge Rafael Videla, the military deposed President Isabel Perón and launched the Proceso de Reorganización Nacional (Process of National Reorganization), or *proceso*, which promised to eradicate the revolutionary movement, restore the economy, and protect the so-called Western and Christian way of life.

Instead, the military embarked on a program of ruthless repression. Political and trade union activities were prohibited, the national congress and provincial legislatures were shut down, and the members of the Supreme Court of Justice were removed. Strikes were made illegal, and labor laws were repealed. The press was silenced, and censorship was heavily imposed over the media and the arts. Unequaled levels of state terrorism against the population peaked between 1976 and 1978, when the armed forces abducted, tortured, and executed thousands of civilians. Their bodies were burned, buried in unmarked graves, or thrown from military planes into the sea—the victims became *los desaparecidos* (the disappeared). Operating clandestinely and free from accountability, the military used the argument of confronting and destroying the guerrillas to eliminate all forms of activism, social mobilization, and civic participation. Terror ran without any restrictions throughout a society that became atomized, while individuals were increasingly isolated, fearful, and distrustful. Meanwhile, the financial sector became the heart of the economy, economic concentration increased, and the government dismantled tariff protection, exchange controls, and the regulation of credit and interest rates. Consequently, industrial production declined by 20 percent as many sectors of the national industry were unable to survive foreign competition. To complete the dreadful economic scenario, real income fell, and starting in 1981, inflation and recession caused employment and real wages to also drop dramatically.[12]

By 1982, the defeat in the Malvinas War against Great Britain (a military fiasco driven by an attempt to win popular support through the invasion of the islands occupied by the British since 1833), internal conflicts within the armed forces, and the growing severity of the economic crisis precipitated the beginning of the end of the regime. Equally important, society was becoming defiant, as evident in a series of general strikes, mounting popular mobilization, public demonstrations of discontent, and open criticism. Leading this process of social agitation and censure were the human rights organizations, especially the Madres de Plaza de Mayo (Mothers of Plaza de Mayo), which had attained high national and international visibility. The denunciation of human rights violations and the circulation of information about state violence were now increasingly public. This explosive social, political, and economic climate propelled an agreement between the political parties and the dictatorship for an electoral exit in 1983. Elected in October 1983, lawyer Raúl Alfonsín assumed the presidency on December 10 of that year. The motor behind the renewal of the Unión Cívica Radical, Alfonsín stood out from other politicians during the dictatorship by criticizing the military and demanding explanations for the *desaparecidos*, assuming the legal defense of political prisoners, and proposing the modernization of society and the state. Alfonsín made democracy the banner of his electoral campaign and, as president, proposed it as the key to solving all problems confronting the nation.[13]

The new government identified cultural modernization, political participation, free speech, human rights, and social pluralism as central goals of democracy. However, the road to political and economic recovery and social healing was extremely complicated. Argentina was plagued by rampant inflation, expanding foreign debt, and fiscal deficit, but beyond the economic variables, business, the unions, the Catholic Church, and the military proved to be even more difficult to control and subordinate. The government entered into conflicts with the unions, directed by Peronist leaders, over its attempts to regulate them and over the deteriorating real wages and standard of living. It suffered the opposition of the church for liberal projects like the divorce law passed in 1987 and the secularization of education. And, it faced the resistance of business sectors to the close control the new government imposed on credit, exchange rates, and prices. By setting up the Comisión Nacional sobre la Desaparición de Personas (CONADEP; National Commission on the Disappearance of Persons) in

1983, a truth commission assigned to investigate and report about the violations of human rights during the dictatorship, and by carrying out the trial of the *juntas* in 1985, which succeeded in prosecuting the crimes of the military hierarchy, the Alfonsín administration began to fulfill its promise to bring the perpetrators of crimes against humanity to justice. However, under pressure from the armed forces and challenged by several military uprisings of mutineers called *carapintadas*, the government pulled back. Despite social opposition, in 1986 the Full Stop Law mandated the end of the investigation and prosecution of political violence during the dictatorship. A year later, the Due Obedience Law dictated that officers and their subordinates could not be legally punished for crimes committed during the dictatorship as they were following orders from their superiors.

Between 1987 and 1989, when Alfonsín handed over the government to his successor, Peronist Carlos Menem, the administration's problems increased exponentially to culminate in disaster. Disputes within the Unión Cívica Radical, military uprisings, and the attack of La Tablada military barracks in January 1989 by a poorly armed left-wing group weakened the president and cast doubts on the government. Finally, the inability of the administration to pay the foreign debt, the peso's devaluation that devoured the savings of many Argentines in February 1989, the rise of hyperinflation, and the looting of supermarkets in May 1989, which was harshly repressed by the authorities, forced Alfonsín to resign in order to move the transfer of power forward by six months before the date prescribed by the constitution.[14]

## HISTORICAL CHANGE, DEMOCRATIC TRANSITION, AND THE HISTORY OF SEXUALITY

This book is not a comparative history of sexuality in the dictatorship and in democracy; it is a history of the sexual culture that emerged with the fall of the military regime in 1983. The dictatorship is key to understanding the destape because it provides the immediate historical backdrop to appreciate the nature and the impact of the changes that followed its demise. Therefore, each chapter goes back to the 1970s, and even the 1960s, to provide enough background to put the destape in perspective. Yet the book focuses on the destape in democracy and postulates its historical specificity, identifying it as a particular and unique object of study in its own right—even though scholars have ignored it. The clarification is important because the destape is historically and scholarly placed in an awkward position: it chronologically followed the dictatorship, one of the most studied topics in current Argentine historiography—only comparable to studies on Peronism—and it happened in the return to democracy, a period that has been predominantly addressed from a political science standpoint.

The opulence of the historiography on the 1970s military dictatorship appears more remarkable when considering that the field began developing in the 1990s and is, today, the protagonist of the *historia reciente*, as Argentine historians refer to studies of the recent past. The histories of the military dictatorship have been largely focused on the study of political violence and thus are overwhelmingly centered on social and political analyses of state repression and the guerrillas.[15] In the last decade, historians of the dictatorship have turned to studies of memory, recuperating the reminiscences of leftist militants and victims of state violence, and, more recently, how ordinary Argentines remember living under a military regime. In this way, the scholarship began shifting from an analytical focus on repression and militancy to one on the building of consensus and everyday life.[16] The prominence of these themes led me to a painstaking job of reconstructing in broad terms sexual culture during the military regime. Indeed, despite some insights on sexuality in works on women in radical leftist organizations and in research on gay culture, there is no established, specific body of scholarship on sexuality and the dictatorship from social or cultural histories.[17]

Not long ago, historians began questioning earlier characterizations of the 1970s dictatorship as a historical exception or a rupture, considering instead the continuities between the military regime and the preceding as well as succeeding periods. Still incipient, this approach has uncovered the endurance of earlier repressive institutions and mechanisms, state technocracies, and political cadres during the dictatorship, and, in some cases, their survival afterward, as well as the permanence of dictatorial values and representations in the press in the first years of the transition to democracy.[18] Beyond these cases, which are, in general, interested in understanding the rise of political violence after the 1976 coup as part of a longer historical process, the discussion is still quite speculative. Continuities and changes between two different historical moments are difficult to determine when information is missing on one of the two. The historiography on the 1970s dictatorship intuits rather than proves continuities with the subsequent democratic period for the simple reason that, from a historical perspective, the 1980s are still uncharted territory. As Marina Franco and Daniel Lvovich have suggested in a thorough assessment of the *historia reciente*, historians of the military dictatorship have been more comfortable going back in time to place the regime in a continuum but have not yet disputed the monopoly of political scientists over the 1980s.[19]

This is where this book engages with the emerging debate. A history of the destape that goes back to the dictatorship to put 1980s sexuality in historical perspective tacitly poses questions about permanence and discontinuity. I argue that the destape was synonymous with a profound change. People had sex, talked about sex, and consumed cultural products with some sexual content during the dictatorship, but sex was socially and culturally marginal, censored, purged, and silenced. As fear, violence, and incertitude reigned all around, sex was infused with negative, frightening, and dark connotations or was associated with social and political responsibilities that had little to do with selfhood and desire. Sex was infantilized for adults while demeaned for the young; it was homogenized, sanitized, and institutionally, culturally, and legally controlled for all, but fundamentally for women. Many of these characteristics predated the dictatorship as part of a longer tradition of a conservative sexual culture that "treated sex with suspicion."[20]

In contrast, with the return to the democracy, the end of censorship, and the new freedom, sex captured the social imagination and became the biggest star of popular culture in the democratic transition. This was both a qualitative and quantitative transformation with significant social consequences: sex was everywhere and everything was about sex, and culture and society experienced historically unparalleled levels of sexual explicitness. Sexual frankness pervaded the media, the streets, schools, health clinics, consciousness-raising groups, sex workshops, political marches, and bedrooms. Society became eroticized. Omnipresent, sex was not only about fantasies, eroticism, indulgence, and libido but was also imbued with a myriad of social-, political-, and cultural-positive, thought-provoking meanings—including citizenship, social progress, national development, and modernity—that made sexual culture into a powerful metaphor for democracy and the reconstruction of Argentine society. In fact, in openly addressing sex, different social sectors proposed their own visions for a new democratic nation. Democracy freed sexual images and discourses while allowing for the open politicization of sexuality as women and sexual minorities organized to fight for their sexual rights.

If the destape appears as a vast transformation against the background of the dictatorship, placed in a larger historical continuum, its singularity and significance are even more remarkable and its historical roots longer. Historian Isabella Cosse has argued that Argentina experienced a "discreet sexual revolution" in the 1960s that was primarily centered on the new social acceptability of premarital sex and the challenge to female virginity as a requirement for women's respectability and access to matrimony. The "revolution" was made even more discreet by the fact that premarital sex was still framed by traditional values and was thus legitimate only as a part of formal dating—a test and preparation before marriage—and as an expression of love, especially for women. Equally important, these very contained changes in the sexual culture of the 1960s did not question heterosexuality, the nuclear family, power imbalances, or sexism. Neither did they liberate sex from domesticity, responsibility, and love. In fact, love was the prerequisite and the justification for sex, and the public discussion of pleasure was glaringly absent. Given the predominantly authoritarian and conservative ethos of the 1960s and 1970s—during both military and democratic regimes—the "discreet sexual revolution" had no opportunity to become a full-blown transformation of sexual values and conduct during those decades. Sexual modernization may have happened inconspicuously and gradually over this period, but it was not until the 1980s that the process of change that had begun two decades earlier came to fruition stridently. The destape drove sex from the private realm to the public sphere and made it the epicenter of social debate, propelling a profound change in content as well as in the levels of display.[21]

Because of the destape's contradictions and limitations, this book does not postulate that it was a sexual revolution—although some contemporaries believed so. Still, the sexual bombardment was loud, public, intense, and unsettling enough to make the destape close to a revolutionary upheaval, and even more so when considered in the light of the prudent 1960s historical precursor and the immediately preceding 1970s dictatorial context of sex censorship and public prudishness. In fact, historians have been questioning how representative the model of the sexual revolution as a short and radical phase born in the 1960s really is. Rather than generalizing the conclusions made from iconic cases in Western Europe and the United States—and associated with emblematic historical events such as the 1967 Summer of Love in England or 1969's Stonewall in New York—scholars are now favoring a specific assessment of local conditions and historical contexts to understand the differences in scope and timing of diverse experiences. As a consequence, historians are arguing that major changes in sexual culture also happened after the 1960s and that, in many cases, these changes were the outcome of a long-term process of sexual modernization, suggesting a "long" history of the sexual revolution. Like this scholarship, this book challenges established chronologies of sexual history by reconsidering the timing, context, history, and conditions of the sexual explosion in 1980s Argentina.[22]

This book also intervenes in the scholarship of democratic transitions, opening up uncharted territory both methodologically and thematically. The traditional periodization of the transition to democracy in Argentina generally includes the time between 1982 and 1983, the last phase of the military dictatorship, which opened with the defeat in the Malvinas War, and between 1983 and 1989, the years of the Alfonsín administration. The study of this historical period, called "transitology," has mostly been the realm of political scientists, not historians.[23] Classic studies from the 1980s and early 1990s were interested in differentiating the moment of transition from the "consolidation" of democracy, understanding the structural conditions for the return to democracy, and discussing whether the transition—conceptualized as a stage of negotiation between the military forces and the political parties to agree on the terms of the military retreat—was, in reality, the "collapse" of the dictatorship.[24] Alongside these works devoted to periodization, typologies, political elites, and the construction of comparative models, new approaches emerged in the 1990s that were focused on the reintroduction of electoral practices, the institutional reconstruction of the state, the role and reorganization of political parties, the rise of human rights organizations and new social movements, and the concept of the public sphere as an intermediary space between the state and society—a set of thematic interests that have characterized the field to this day.[25] Notably, historians who in the past few years began exploring the democratic transition have kept an interest in politics and the institutional approach—in many cases applied to regional and local contexts—while social and cultural issues remain largely unexamined.[26]

Despite these emphases, political scientist Guillermo O'Donnell drew attention, early on, to the fact that "the problem of consolidation and expansion of democracy in Argentina is linked as much to society as it is to state and macropolitics."[27] This book follows on this argument from a cultural history perspective to demonstrate that beyond paradigmatic democratic practices such as elections, the restoration of civil and political rights, and the restructuring of government institutions, Argentines experienced and resignified democracy through new ideas about sex and changes in sexual expression. In sending letters to the editors for sex columns, submitting erotic photos and short stories to magazines for publication, buying erotic magazines, attending sex therapy sessions and workshops, denouncing sexual violence against women, organizing for the right to abortion, protesting police repression against gay people, and advocating for sex education in schools, different groups of Argentines productively linked sexual culture with democratic values such as participation, activism, openness, accessibility, and self-expression. This study enriches our understanding of the transition to democracy by showing that for Argentines, sex as discourse and practice was a sphere in which democracy was experienced as powerfully as in the voting booth. In other words, making and consuming the destape in its different manifestations was a concrete form of participation in the democratization of the country and the reconceptualization of citizenship.

Finally, this book introduces new questions and new social actors to the history of sexuality in modern Latin America. This field is difficult to categorize because it is thematically and methodologically heterogeneous, including histories of sex work, reproductive rights, sexuality and the state, and sexual minorities, especially gay men.[28] In recent years, new studies have emerged, on the one hand, revealing the connections among sexuality, youth culture, and counterculture in the 1960s, and, on the other, exploring the relation between politics and sexual cultures—the attempts of the Right and the Left to control sexualities, and, especially, the experience in revolutionary contexts in the 1960s and 1970s, mainly in Cuba and Nicaragua. Similarly, Argentine historiography has begun to examine sexual politics in radical leftist organizations in those same decades.[29] For its part, this book delves into a historical period and a theme overlooked by historians, and analyzes largely ignored subjects in the Latin American history of sexuality, like sex in media culture, soft porn, erotic comics, sex therapy, personal ads, and sexual enrichment groups. This study also shows that the search for pleasure, associated with life and indulgence, was a central mechanism for social and individual healing in the new democratic context after a period marked by death, pain, and brutality. Thus, the book moves the traditional focus of the history of sexuality toward subjects quite uncommon in the current Latin American historiography, such as recreational sex, eroticism, pornography, and sexual desire. The book also recovers towering figures such as feminist María Elena Oddone, gay militant Carlos Jáuregui, and lesbian activist Ilse Fuskova, all key contributors to the destape who asserted that sexual freedom in democracy remained an unfulfilled goal for many social sectors. Moreover, this analysis expands the history of feminism, the gay movement, family planning, and sex education through a novel perspective that foregrounds the historical significance of a discourse of human rights and sexual rights in the achievement of sexual citizenship and national development after 1983.

## BOOK STRUCTURE AND A NOTE ON LANGUAGE

Chapter 1 examines the characteristics and ideological foundations of the censorship and repression of sexual content in the media during the dictatorship. It then moves to an analysis of the destape, exploring this historically unrivaled sexualization of culture in different media forms and excavating the meanings contemporaries assigned to it. The chapter argues that while ultra-Catholics and conservatives condemned the destape as a symbol of social corruption and perversion, and a grave threat to the moral order, for most Argentines, it was synonymous with freedom, modernity, self-expression, the enjoyment of life, and, ultimately, democracy. In fact, the destape was a way to enjoy democracy in the simple, everyday life experience of purchasing an erotic novel or attending the screening of an adult movie that had once been banned. In turn, with these choices, audiences and consumers reaffirmed the new democratic order and showed they supported it.

Chapter 2 provides a cultural analysis of destape images and discourses. With an emphasis on the print press and film as well as examples from television, radio, comics, literature, theater, and advertising, the chapter analyzes the hypersexualization of women, the use of nudity, the exaltation of heterosexuality, the silence about alternative sexualities, and the depiction of sexual violence. It also examines audience participation in new sex fora in the print press that included polls and surveys, letters to the editor, and short sex stories and erotic photos submitted by the general public for publication. The chapter argues that rather than being ideologically consistent, the commercial destape in the media was a complex, contradictory combination of both redeeming, progressive messages and detrimental, anachronistic notions. The destape simultaneously subverted and endorsed traditional representations of female sexuality, stimulated a democratic debate about heterosexuality and heterosexual pleasure while muting expressions of queer desire, and erased from the press but addressed in films sexual violence against women during the dictatorship.

Chapter 3 characterizes the sexual practices and concerns of Argentine adults in the new democracy and traces the institutional, social, and cultural consolidation of sexology. The chapter argues that the boom of sexology—the emergence of sex experts and the increasing dissemination of and popular access to sex information and sex treatment—was not only a central component of the destape in the media but also the engine driving a heterosexual destape in bedrooms, therapists' offices, and sex workshops, especially for women. The expansion of sex knowledge and sex therapy was simultaneously a cause and an effect of the decline in the personal and social repressive mechanisms that consciously or unconsciously had restrained sexual desires in the past period. Sexology promoted sexual literacy and legitimized the search for pleasure as the main goal of sexuality, sanctioning a sexual ideology that defied the emphasis on duty and reproduction promoted by the military dictatorship and the Left in the previous decade.

Chapter 4 sets the stage by delineating the obstacles to and repression of sexual and reproductive health care in the 1960s and 1970s, when sex education in schools was suppressed and all activities directly and indirectly related to family planning were prohibited by law. It then characterizes the changes in youth sexuality during the dictatorship and in the transition to democracy. Central to this chapter is the rise of nongovernmental organizations devoted to sexual health, which, facing the opposition of the Catholic Church, contested the idea upheld by the dictatorship that school-based sex education and family planning were threats to demographic growth, affronts to morality, and a challenge to the rights of parents. The chapter argues that after 1983, advocates and experts conceptualized family planning and school-based sex education as human rights and as legitimate means to achieve social well-being and personal fulfillment. Furthermore, they proposed both as major factors for the construction and strengthening of the newborn democracy. In the midst of the destape, when sex was all about pleasure, family planning and sex education specialists fueled an alternative debate focused on health, economic progress, individual fulfillment, and national development.

Chapter 5 investigates the fundamental contribution of feminists and gay and lesbian activists to the debate on sexuality after the return of democracy. Taking to the streets alongside human rights organizations, political parties, and different civil associations, feminist, gay, and lesbian advocates became vital participants in "the resurrection of civil society" after the profound depoliticization and atomization of the previous years.[30] The chapter argues that those advocates not only criticized the destape but also produced one of their own. If destape means to take the lid off, by becoming public, active, organized, and assertive, these sectors revealed themselves, exposing to society sexual and gender discrimination as well as uncovering and denouncing the extent of male power. A language of sexual rights allowed feminist and gay and lesbian organizations to articulate a powerful agenda centered on the defense of nonheterosexual identities and practices, the fight for sexual and reproductive self-determination, the protection of sexual freedom, the denunciation of violence, and a critique of motherhood and heterosexuality. In their fight for sexual rights, activists redefined the idea of citizenship and condemned the limited inclusiveness of the new democracy.

The epilogue examines some of the most relevant developments in sexual culture and politics in Argentina today and problematizes the legacies of the destape.

Finally, a brief note on terminology. In translating the sources and in some instances of my analysis, I decided to use the prevalent language of the 1980s to refer to sexual and gender identities, behaviors, orientations, and expressions despite the fact that, in many cases, such language is now anachronistic and does not abide by current conventions and sensitivities. For example, "homosexual," used as a noun to refer to a gay man, was the common term of choice in 1980s Argentina. My decisions for usage are based on the fact that I did not want to betray the language of the historical sources or the voice of the historical subjects by arbitrarily imposing a terminology that is culturally and historically extraneous and would end up conveying my own personal semantic choices rather than the spirit and meanings of the period. In cases in which clarity, accuracy, and cultural idiosyncrasy could be compromised by attempts at translation to English, I used the terms in Spanish and offered descriptions and explanations in endnotes and the text.

# 1

# THE RETURN TO DEMOCRACY AND THE

# SEXUALIZATION OF MEDIA CULTURE

**In 1982, journalist Rolando Hanglin** asserted with a humorous tone that "we live in the most moralistic country in the world. Here you can be a thief, rip-off artist, liar, slanderer, hypocrite, and even murderer. You can do anything. Anything! Except show your rear. Because that's when things get serious."[1] Hanglin was referring to how the military dictatorship, while embracing the titles of guardian of the nation and protector of the family, censored sexual content in mass culture, misinforming and infantilizing the citizenry, and curtailing freedoms of choice and of expression as a result. Only in the last two years of the dictatorship, with the regime in crisis and restrictions weakened, were critics like Hanglin able to more or less openly bring attention to the contradiction between the social decay unleashed by an anticonstitutional regime that persecuted and killed its citizens and that regime's public moralistic views on sex and nakedness.

Cultural censorship did not begin after the 1976 military coup; it had been a common practice in the twentieth century despite evident historical periods of liberality. However, cultural critics agree that it is difficult to identify the birthdate of censorship in the country. Instead, they suggest that it built up over time, in both democratic and military governments, into a repertoire of practices, institutions, and laws with different degrees of application and different goals, notably involving the control of sexual content in culture.[2] In his classic study, Andrés Avellaneda maintains that cultural censorship reached new heights with the military regimes of the 1960s that, for example, launched "moralizing campaigns" against sex and nudity, banning magazines and cutting movies. Yet, Avellaneda argues, it was the 1970s dictatorship that expanded and perfected censorship; this was a period when "the loose ends of the two previous decades were tied tight."[3] The most original aspect of this censorship, and one of the reasons for its efficacy, was that it operated in a historically unparalleled context of state terror and violence that both overtly and tacitly empowered cultural censors and terrorized creators. Pilar Calveiro condensed this idea best when she asserted that "the *proceso* did not simply take existing elements to a whole new level but instead reorganized them and added others, thus giving rise to new forms of power circulation within society."[4]

The profusion of sexual images and discourses in television, radio, literature, advertising, theater, cinema, and the print media in the transition to democracy called the destape was a powerful reaction to the censorship, prohibition, and self-control imposed by the 1970s dictatorship. It was also the result of the cravings and active support of the audiences; business acumen; creative choices based on artistic, economic, and ideological reasons; and in some cases, like in cinema, the financial support of the state. This chapter explores the censorship of sexual content during the dictatorship and the subsequent sexual bombardment brought about by the destape in the return to democracy. In so doing, it demonstrates the fundamental role of the mass media in bringing sex from the discreet, private realm of the bedroom, where the dictatorship wanted to keep it hidden, into the public sphere—what had been only suggested and implied was now openly showed and discussed to an unprecedented level.

However, I argue that the destape was more than a commercial spectacle of sex and nudity; it was a vehicle for experiencing and defending values and ideals obliterated during the dictatorship. Thus, while ultra-Catholics and conservatives denounced the destape as a symbol of social decline and moral degeneration, for most Argentines, including journalists, cultural critics, writers, sex educators, and government officials, it became a metaphor for democracy, freedom, modernity, national adulthood, self-expression, and the exuberant enjoyment of life. In showing that the destape was both a field of ideological construction and confrontation connected to broader political, cultural, and social discussions as well as a cultural symptom of larger historical transformations, I elaborate on historian Dagmar Herzog's suggestion that "the value of the history of sexuality lies just as much in what it can teach us about how meaning-making happens in quite diverse political circumstances—and how it is shaped by and shaped those circumstances."[5] Although this chapter focuses on the media rather than the audiences, an exploration of meanings contributes to our understanding of why Argentines became fervent consumers and participants of the destape.

## SEX AND CENSORSHIP

The 1970s dictatorship considered culture and education to be fields of "ideological infiltration" that were vulnerable to "foreign influences" ranging from Marxism, Communism, and atheism to nihilism and hedonism. In fact, sex and revolution were twinned concerns in Cold War counter-subversion. In 1977, Admiral Emilio Massera declared that the adoption of the "terrorist faith" among the young was the culmination of an "*escalada sensorial*" (sensual escalation) that was preceded by sexual promiscuity.[6] Therefore, the war against Communist infiltration required fighting moral dissolution and the decline of civilization.[7] The military regime argued that in spheres such as the arts and the media, which were "unruly" by nature, that fight would be longer and harder than the armed struggle against the guerrillas. Appropriately, anthropologist Antonius Robben has defined the mission of the military in Argentina as a cultural war that legitimized the use of inadmissible violence to reap victory. In addition to annihilating the opposition and demobilizing society, the cultural war waged by the dictatorship required the "conquest of the mind."[8]

Ultimately, the goal of the military dictatorship was to subordinate culture and all forms of creative expression to a certain type of morality that extolled Christianity, family, modesty, children, the fatherland, order, and tradition. Morality was so central to the military's social and political project that a few months after the coup, the Ministry of Education developed a new subject, moral and civic education, that became a mandatory course in high schools and aimed to teach students the characteristics of "a moral order based on God's will." This order was centered on the Christian family, where the father, as the "natural holder of reason and authori-ty," commanded, and the mother, "the epitome of love and tenderness," and the children obeyed.[9] This moral order was, however, under attack. Government authorities used metaphors of disease and war prolifically to emphasize contamination and the destruction of morality as well as the military's fundamental mission as rescuers. Sexual content in the arts and the media was considered a serious danger by moral technocrats—from state officials to right-wing and ultra-Catholic interest groups—who were concerned with the corruption of propriety, excess, perversion, obscenity, and debauchery.[10]

The Ministry of Interior identified obscenity, immorality, and sub-versive immorality as the most serious threats to the moral order and formulated a division of labor to face them, although in practice, zealous-ness and resources blurred the lines among agencies, powers overlapped, and implementation was uneven. Obscenity or pornography extolled eroticism, excited *bajos apetitos sexuales* (depraved sexual urges), offended *pudor público* (public modesty) and *buenas costumbres* (good manners), and fell under the realm of criminal courts. Immorality promoted hedonism, exacerbated indulgence and the enjoyment of the senses, displayed licen-tiousness, and encouraged "pleasure for pleasure's sake," and should be repressed by city and state governments. Finally, subversive immorali-ty showed contempt for life, society, the family, ethical values, and the national tradition, and should be the target of the national government and particularly the Ministry of Interior.[11] Morality, then, functioned as a malleable and all-encompassing banner that justified censorship and prohibition. Censors at different levels condemned writers, journalists, researchers, movie directors, and artists for producing works with sex and nudity, which they considered a menace to rectitude, and thus banned, cut, purged, and publicly devalued these creations.[12]

For ideological validation of this project, the military authorities especially turned to ultra-Catholic and right-wing sectors that had been demanding an end to excessive cultural and social permissiveness and the restoration of a Christian way of life.[13] In 1976, for example, eight months after the coup, a communiqué by the Liga de Padres de Familia (Fathers League) and the Liga de Madres de Familia (Mothers League)—organizations founded in the 1950s and committed to the defense and promotion of the family and Catholic values—maintained that "grand

Figure 1.1. Emilio Massera, Rafael Videla, and Orlando Ramón Agosti, members of the military junta that took power in 1976. Courtesy Archivo General de la Nación, Buenos Aires.

economic, political, and social plans to support family and community will be futile unless we fight immorality on all fronts, driving out eroticism, pornography, and violence from the media."[14] This is what Avellaneda has called the "*discurso de apoyo*" (supporting discourse), an efficient and ideologically analogous complement to the military's official discourse. The dictatorship capitalized on these allies—as the allies made the most of the new context—appointing, for example, representatives of different Catholic organizations as members of the film censorship board and, in 1978, naming a prominent member of the Liga de Padres de Familia as the board's director.[15]

In addition to creating new institutional and legal censorship mechanisms, the military dictatorship made full use of existing ones, such as the 1966 law that prohibited the post office from carrying "immoral materials," and reactivated dormant agencies such as municipal commissions and the police "morality squads" employed to monitor and prohibit publications and shows.[16] With no central agency entrusted with policy and implementation, and lacking clear guidelines—except in cinema and broadcasting—censorship was not always consistent but was more strict, comprehensive, and effective than in previous repressive contexts.[17] In 1981, writer Héctor Lastra affirmed that "the censorship that plagues our country must be one of the toughest and most virulent, fundamentally because it is applied without any attempt to conceal it, with bluster and with arrogance, and with the intention to make it noticed and felt at first sight. It is the typical censorship that serves as punishment and as a clear form of intimidation."[18] For this reason, and because of deep fear in the face of increasing state violence, self-censorship rapidly became the norm among those determined to protect themselves and survive.[19]

On the day of the 1976 coup, communiqué 19 announced that publication of statements or images from those involved in "subversive activities" would be penalized with an indefinite prison sentence, while the printing of news or images that could harm or discredit the armed forces was punishable with up to ten years in jail. Thus, all periodicals had to submit their content to the Servicio Gratuito de Lectura Previa (Free Prior Reading Service), housed in the Casa Rosada—where the President's Office is—for government approval. Although this requirement lasted only a month, it set the tone for the strict print media censorship that the new government enforced.[20]

The Secretaría de Prensa y Difusión (Press and Publishing Office) compelled publications to uphold "the fundamental values of Christian morality" against "subversive ideologies"—a wide-ranging and flexible concept that encompassed everything from liberation theology and syndicalism to sexual freedom and abortion, all considered threats to the "Christian way of life." As a result, treatment of sex matters in the press was scarce, dated, and reactionary, condemning audiences to misinformation. In 1985, sexologist León Roberto Gindin argued that during the dictatorship, the press dedicated three times less space to issues related to sexuality than it would after the return to democracy. Furthermore, Gindin maintained that the quality of the content was substantially different during these two periods. During the dictatorship, the discussion of sexual matters in the media was oblique, ominous, and demonizing; the emphasis was on the dangers, threats, and problems related to sex.[21]

To control sex content, the Secretaría de Prensa y Difusión demanded that the media adhere to a series of "Principles and Procedures" that included "defending the family," "striving to reduce and eventually eradicate any sexual stimulus," "working continuously and decisively to battle vice in all of its manifestations," and "fully eliminating words and images that are obscene, lewd, troubling, or risqué, erotic suggestions or double entendres."[22] The resulting overall tone was so puritanical that articles on sexual matters usually referred to "wife" and "husband," to emphasize marital sex, instead of "women" and "men," which could imply sex outside marriage. In the same way, journalist Alcira Bas recalled how, to illustrate its articles, health magazine *Vivir* only published photos of couples wearing wedding rings.[23] Tomás Sanz, one of the founders of the legendary humor magazine *Humor*, created in 1978, confirmed that especially during the first three years, the magazine refrained from publishing about sex to prevent government confiscation and closure—even though its political satire made *Humor* the most critical media voice against the dictatorship.[24]

The "Principles and Procedures" were also effective tools for persecuting editors, confiscating materials, and shutting down magazines. This was the case, for example, for *Padres*, a magazine about parenting and health whose chief editor Mario Muchnik was kidnapped and forced to leave the country. Similarly, women's magazine *Emanuelle* was closed down "to protect the moral health of the population and preserve the values at the core of our nationality," and its editor in chief Oskar Blotta, who had already been forced to shut down the bold humor magazine *Satiricón*, also left Argentina after being briefly detained.[25] *Satiricón*, first published in 1972, offers a good example of the qualitative change in cultural repression that took place during the 1970s dictatorship. Purged and banned because of its irreverent sexual humor, *Satiricón* survived the repressive Peronist years but was unable to endure after the 1976 coup.[26]

In many instances, state agencies and courts of law responded to formal complaints and accusations by institutions and individuals who singled out periodicals, publications, plays, and movies for challenging the standards of appropriateness. In other cases, the regime manipulated accusations of immorality to ban publications for transgressing more than the limits on eroticism. In December 1980, for example, the city of Buenos Aires confiscated and prohibited an issue of *La Semana*, contending that a cover featuring American actress Bo Derek—dressed in a tunic and showing only her shoulder and part of her covered breast—and an article illustrated with several pictures of Derek in a bikini "were an attack on morality and good manners." Yet the same issue had a piece criticizing the government for canceling a public transportation discount for media workers and another about hardships in a Buenos Aires slum, content as provocative as Derek on the beach.[27]

In one way or another, the use of erotic and nude images became a grueling task, and publications had to find creative ways to include them. Journalist and writer Cecilia Absatz remembered that while she was working at *Status*, a magazine devoted to travel, exotic cuisine, and art that targeted a sophisticated readership, nude models were deliberately placed behind fabrics, curtains, and furnishings.[28] But even these strategies could be ineffective, such as when in September 1980 the city of Buenos Aires banned the circulation and sale of general interest magazine *Siete Días* for a cover featuring the famous Italian actress Stefania Sandrelli clad in a bikini and a five-page article about fashion trends and modesty illustrated with women in miniskirts, shorts, and two-piece swimsuits.[29] The sanction was in line with the idea, explained in an article in the army's *Revista de Educación del Ejército*, that bikinis and miniskirts not only undermined a traditional decorous dress code but also unleashed hidden passions, promoted disrespect and immodesty, and dissolved moral values, which ultimately subverted people's defenses against Marxism.[30]

Sex and nudity were also targets of film censorship. The Instituto Nacional de Cinematografía (INC; National Film Institute), the most important state source of financing for film production, was subjected to military intervention after the coup, dampening an industry that was profoundly dependent on state funding.[31] In 1976, Captain Jorge Bitleston, the first INC military interventor, declared that support would only be granted to "[national] films that exalt the spiritual, moral, and Christian values of nationality, be these current or historic, or that reaffirm the concepts of family, order, respect, work, healthy efforts, and social responsibility, striving to create an optimistic attitude towards the future, and avoiding lewd scenes or dialogues."[32] To aid the INC in controlling national film production and censoring both Argentine and foreign films prior to their theatrical release, the military regime employed the Ente de Calificación Cinematográfica (ECC; Board of Film Ratings). In addition to rating, expurgating, and prohibiting films and scripts, the ECC regulated titles, trailers, and movie posters; ensured that theaters only showed films that had received an exhibition permit; and verified that the version of the film showed was the one approved by the board.[33]

The ECC was created by law 18,019, passed under the military government of Juan Carlos Onganía in 1968 and inspired by Spanish censorship legislation during Francisco Franco's dictatorship. The law remained in place during the democratically elected governments of Héctor Cámpora (1973), Juan Domingo Perón (1973–74), and Isabel Perón (1974–76), and continued throughout the military dictatorship. Upon its creation in 1968, the ECC was part of the Secretaría de Educación y Cultura (Department of Education and Culture), but after the 1976 coup, it was placed under the influence of the Secretaría de Información Pública (Department of Public Information) and thus under direct control of the presidency. Miguel Paulino Tato, a film critic who had been appointed as ECC director in 1974 and would become an icon of censorship, remained in the post. During his four-year tenure—he retired in 1978—Tato censored 1,200 films and prohibited 337 in the name of "cinematic prophylaxis and hygiene."[34] After his departure and until the dissolution of the ECC by the democratic government in 1984, the director was Alberto León, a lawyer and board member of the Liga de Padres de Familia. During León's tenure, an average of ninety films were banned annually.[35]

In addition to the director, two adjunct directors, and a secretary, the ECC comprised an honorary advisory council of fifteen members; nine were representatives of state agencies such as the Ministry of Interior, the Ministry of Defense, and the Department of Culture and Education, and six were members of private institutions "known for their work in defending the family and the moral values of the community," most notably Catholic organizations such as the Liga de Padres de Familia, the Liga de Madres de Familia, and the Liga por la Decencia (Decency League).[36] There were also occasional external advisors, most famously Bishop Justo Oscar Laguna, but the ECC lacked representatives from the film industry, film scholars, academics, script writers, or experts in the field.[37]

All national and international films required an exhibition permit for theatrical release. Local film producers submitted their screenplays—which was necessary to receive state funds—and later, their finished films, and distributors submitted foreign films for approval before screening. In his report, Jorge Miguel Couselo, the film critic appointed by the Alfonsín administration to shut down the ECC, listed 725 national and foreign films prohibited in the country between 1969 and 1983. During the 1970s dictatorship, Argentine audiences were particularly deprived of international cinema since foreign directors rarely approved the cuts and modifications imposed by the ECC, and as a result the films were not released. Some famous exceptions were *Casanova* (1976), directed by Federico Fellini; *The Postman Always Rings Twice* (1981), by director Bob Rafelson; and Bruno Barreto's *Dona Flor e Seus Dois Maridos* (1976), steamy films that were only screened in Argentina because the ECC-mandated cuts had been made.[38]

The ECC issued ratings for films based on five categories: recommended for children, suitable for all audiences, forbidden for minors under fourteen, forbidden for minors under eighteen, and banned. In numerous cases, the ECC simply opted to not classify a film, resulting in an unofficial ban as films could not be screened without a rating. Sex figured prominently on the list of subjects that law 18,019 banned in movies. Justification of adultery or affronts to matrimony and the family; justification of abortion, prostitution, and sexual perversions; and lascivious scenes (violence, drugs, vice, and cruelty) against morality and *buenas costumbres* were completely prohibited. The ECC embodied the cultural and social mission of the military as the self-proclaimed defender of the moral order and custodian of good taste, and, in so doing, contributed to impoverishing culture while grossly violating the freedoms and rights of audiences, artists, and the film industry. The agency operated under the premise that cinema unilaterally and uncritically influenced behaviors and ideas, and that audiences lacked proper discernment and were intellectually and ethically unprepared for certain films or types of content. In this regard, Miguel Paulino Tato, the ECC director, declared that "we Argentines are not mature enough for many films that could cause us harm" while overpraising censors for "defending people who do not know how to defend themselves."[39]

With sex at the core of the censorship law, most cuts and modifications targeted sex scenes, and most banned films were erotic or pornographic or included prominent or exceedingly graphic depictions of sex.[40] The ECC ruling against director Armando Bó's film *Insaciable* (1984), starring Isabel Sarli, illustrates the new, more stringent position of the agency during the 1970s dictatorship. Although Bó's sexploitation films—a genre characterized by erotic content and nudity—had been censored and objects of legal battles in the 1960s, they had always been exhibited in the country. In 1976, in contrast, the ECC prohibited the theatrical release of *Insaciable*—even after the director maintained he was willing to cut or change the most problematic scenes—making it Bó's first film to be banned. *Insaciable*, the story of a nymphomaniac, was only screened in 1984 after the return to democracy and was the first of Bó's movies to be shown without state-mandated cuts.[41]

Despite rigid censorship, the *comedias picarescas*, a genre comparable to the Spanish *landismo* and the Brazilian *pornochanchadas*, allowed for a mild treatment of sexuality and of otherwise forbidden topics such as infidelity and the dissociation between sex and love.[42] Starring popular comedians Jorge Porcel and Alberto Olmedo, these movies—banned for audiences under eighteen—relied on a repetitive and sexist formula that combined double entendres with unfaithful men and objectified women in skimpy clothes. Yet because they lacked nudity and sexuality was never explicit, the comedias picarescas were tolerated under the dictatorship. Furthermore, the films were conservative, as most ended by exalting marriage, traditional gender roles, and respectability while punishing any sexually liberated characters. Additionally, humor mitigated the potential "threats" of sex.[43] When asked why the government was more permissive toward this genre, a censor responded: "We don't prohibit it because it ridicules sex, making it look clumsy, ugly, and vulgar."[44] Consequently, the screening of comedias picarescas contributed to a false image of ideological and sexual openness and served as an escape valve while censorship deprived spectators of "real" sexual content, nudity, and eroticism. Moreover, although popular, the comedias picarescas represented just 17 percent of all films produced in the country during the dictatorship. Restricted to adults in the movie theaters of mainly big cities, their reach was small and thus their cultural impact more limited than television or press content.[45] As with all film genres, the destape liberated the comedia picaresca in democracy: sexual content became unrestricted, humor was more irreverent, and women wore way less.[46]

Like film, television and radio were also under stringent control during the dictatorship. After the coup, the three armed forces divvied up state television and radio stations for intervention and empowered state institutions such as the Secretaría de Información Pública, the Secretaría de Comunicaciones (Department of Communications), and the Comité

Federal de Radiodifusión (COMFER; Federal Radiobroadcasting Committee)—which were also staffed by members of the military—to mandate and zealously guard content and penalize public and private broadcasting entities for violations.[47] In 1977, the COMFER sent TV stations a long list of themes that were banned from the air, including material that

> undermines the meaning of marriage in sexual relations; presents divorce as a solution to marital troubles; treats adultery or infidelity as a legitimate way out; deals with the subject of abortion . . . ; includes actual scenes of labor, birth and caesarean sections; contains any reference to birth control; subverts the real concept of sex; includes scenes that reveal the underworld of prostitution, in any of its aspects; includes scenes of rape or incest; uses sexual deviance as a core plot theme; includes love scenes, dance scenes, and dialogues or theatrical props that do not fit within a framework of decency or that connote lewdness, impropriety or compulsive exaggeration; or proposes sexual lifestyles that do not fit with our idea of community.[48]

The Secretaría de Información Pública was the most inflexible, especially censoring *telenovelas* (soap operas) that had been approved by the COMFER but were still considered inappropriate for content such as love triangles and adultery. It also limited the number of telenovelas that could be on the air and, more than once, moved them to late-night time slots—despite their being traditionally televised in the early afternoon—to protect children.[49] In a 1979 interview, the famous scriptwriter Abel Santa Cruz avowed that the limits were so rigid that "a married man shouldn't look at a single woman," reducing all storytelling to "the good girl and the good boy, nothing else."[50] Only in the last two years of the dictatorship were TV shows able to introduce some "explicit" sexy content when the Dirección General de Radio y Televisión (Radio and Television Authority) allowed "decorous" bed scenes and "relaxed" the restrictions on formerly unacceptable themes.[51]

The publishing industry also experienced years of firm control after the 1976 coup. Under the jurisdiction of the Ministry of Interior, the Dirección General de Publicaciones (Publications General Authority) not only evaluated books and periodicals but also monitored and impounded prohibited materials from bookstores and libraries all over the country, ordering interventions and raids on publishing houses as well as the destruction of banned books, all with the assistance of the police and the army. Municipalities also played a central role in censoring and confiscating "immoral" books. Between 1976 and 1982, for example, the Secretaría de Cultura (Department of Culture) of the city of Buenos Aires—an agency particularly zealous and effective in this endeavor—objected to 560 books: 433 were classified as "limited display," which meant they had to be shelved in the back of bookstores, and 127 were deemed "immoral" and thus prohibited.[52] Censorship and prohibition had a profound impact on the publishing industry, reducing the number of novels and poetry books printed in the country from five million in 1976 to 1.3 million in 1980.[53]

Although publishing houses requested clarification about censorship criteria, military-controlled agencies kept the definitions of "obscenity" and "immorality" elusive, and as a result, comprehensive. The range of works banned included erotic fiction such as Reina Roffé's *Monte de Venus* (1976), about life in a boarding school for girls and with a prominent lesbian character; social drama such as Enrique Medina's *Perros de la noche* (1977), in which a marginal young man forces his destitute sister into prostitution; sex instruction books such as Graham Masterton's *1,001 Erotic Dreams Interpreted* (1976); heavily illustrated art books such as Phyllis and Eberhard Kronhausen's *The Complete Book of Erotic Art* (1978); and best-selling sexology books such as *Sexual Honesty* (1974) and *The Hite Report on Female Sexuality* (1976), both by feminist sex educator Shere Hite.[54]

Sex became more apparent in public life in the last two years of the dictatorship. A number of factors—the 1981 financial and economic crisis, the political weakening of the regime due to increasing social mobilization and protest, the national and international attention to human rights violations brought by the Madres de Plaza de Mayo, and the country's defeat in the Malvinas War in 1982—contributed to a slight loosening of control over the media and artistic expression as the government struggled on other fronts. Regulation over cinema, radio, and television remained firm, especially until the Malvinas War, but the new flexibility was more evident in magazines and newspapers, allowing for sexual humor in comic strips as well as humorous—but still quite innocuous—articles about sex. There was also an increasing tolerance of provocative images of bikini-clad models and actresses on magazine covers and in pieces devoted to summer fashion trends.

The most notable examples of the new acceptance of sexuality and nudity on television were episodes of a soap opera and a miniseries, respectively, where two different actresses appeared kissing their partners "as if naked," with one of the actresses showing her bared upper back and the other, Edda Bustamante—who would become an icon of the destape for her half-naked, racy pictures and sexy film performances—completely covered by a bedsheet. Bustamante declared that the Channel 11 authorities had agreed to the suggested nakedness because "there was nothing that could be taken as erotic."[55] Yet as late as 1982, the regime prohibited a TV commercial for Hitachi television sets just three days after it aired. Depicting young women dancing and strolling along the beach in two-piece bathing suits, the ad was banned because the "images were an affront to morality."[56]

In the last years of the dictatorship, tolerance toward nudity was most evident in the theater, probably because it was less popular and less influential among audiences than movies and television, and because with the exception of Buenos Aires, the country did not have prominent commercial or fringe theaters. A precedent was *La lección de anatomía* by Carlos Mathus, which opened in 1972 and remained on stage during the dictatorship. The play explored themes such as loneliness, suicide, and parenthood, and offered a few minutes of full frontal male and female nudity—but devoid of sexual content. Although the play ran throughout the military regime, it suffered some notorious episodes of intimidation, such as an incident when police officers stormed the theater after the play had begun, jumped onto the stage, and requested identity cards from all the actors and actresses as they were performing . . . naked.[57] Additionally, dancers and *vedettes* with skimpy clothes had always been the main attraction at the *teatro de revistas* (revues), and the military government did not interfere with this tradition, although full strip tease and naked torsos, which became widespread later, were not common in those years.[58]

Outside the revues, nudity became more accepted on stage between 1980 and 1982, though always in nonerotic contexts. Popular plays that opened in those years, such as *La señorita de Tacna* by Mario Vargas Llosa, *The Elephant Man* by Bernard Pomerance, and *White Wedding* by Tadeusz Różewicz, required actresses to undress for their roles, but like in *La lección de anatomía*, most nude scenes were asexual, depicted partial and nonfrontal nudity, and were thus allowed by the government. Although the new lax standards were a stark contrast to those of the early years of the regime, government control, fear, and self-censorship continued to impose clear boundaries. After the opening of *Violines y trompetas*, a comedy about two musicians, authorities demanded that an actress who undressed for a scene remain clothed. The director and performers obliged.[59] In addition to suffering government censorship, theaters, as well as movie theaters, were targets of right-wing groups that used bombs and arson as a "means to fight against pornography," destroying facilities, demoralizing and scaring performers, and terrifying and driving away audiences—crimes that continued for some time after the return to democracy.[60]

Therefore, in quantity and quality, the process of liberalization that began under the dictatorship was just a preamble to the erotic explosion that occurred months later. On the one hand, coverage of the incipient destape in the military-controlled press was more of a convenient distraction from other, more pressing news—the humiliating defeat in the Malvinas War, increasing social upheaval—than the cultural menace and threat to morality that the media attempted to convey. On the other hand, even in the last year of the military regime, numerous examples of censorship show that the government was not ready to relinquish control over cultural and media content and that this domain was still important for the display of power, especially when power was rapidly being eroded on other fronts.[61]

In addition, the most conservative and ultra-Catholic allies pushed for more control, complaining about "the alarming wave of permissiveness." In 1981, the Catholic magazine *Esquiú* argued that the incipient sexual content in the media was "pure subversion" and urged the dictatorship to combat those sectors leading the trend as they had done with the "subversives armed with machine guns." *Esquiú*, in fact, vehemently clamored for the application of article 128 of the Penal Code, which mandated jail sentences of between two months and two years for those charged with obscenity. The reporter affirmed, "Not only must the government protect sovereignty: it must also protect the individual rights, which go beyond property, freedom, health, and knowledge and encompass the right to faith, the right to become aware of God and put that awareness into practice. And if the State has taken note of this situation, then it must give the courts its approval to safeguard the right that all men have to a better life, but in the sense of rescuing the spiritual values whose absence in society is the cause of this destape."[62]

Figure 1.2. President Raúl Alfonsín delivering a speech in 1987. Courtesy Archivo General de la Nación, Buenos Aires.

Despite these demands, change was unstoppable. Defeat in the Malvinas War in June 1982 signaled the imminent demise of the military government, and when General Leopoldo Galtieri, who had ordered the invasion and occupation of the islands, was removed from power just a few days after the British victory and replaced by Reynaldo Bignone, the impending end to the regime was all the more evident. The second half of 1982 saw increasing negotiations between the regime and political parties to agree on the terms for the military's departure, mostly centered on amnesty and immunity from criminal charges once democracy was restored. In the meantime, social protests, political mobilization, strikes, and public discussion about the desaparecidos spread rapidly. The democratic transition was now under way. In April 1983, Bignone at last announced elections for October, and when Raúl Alfonsín assumed the presidency on December 10 that year, the destape blew the lid off sexual matters.[63]

## THE DESTAPE: SEX AS THE STAR OF THE DEMOCRATIC STAGE

Whatever changes in sexual behaviors and ideas occurred in the bedroom, the classroom, and the offices of doctors and therapists, the first and most spectacular transformation when the dictatorship fell was the rise of "sex as a spectator sport"—that is, the expansion of what audiences could see, read, and hear about sexuality.[64] Theater offers a paradigmatic case of how the destape amplified sexual explicitness to an all-new level. The timid liberalization during the last two years of the dictatorship burst with the return to democracy, when nudity and sex became ubiquitous on the stages of Corrientes Avenue, "the Broadway of Buenos Aires." Plays that had been shut down and banned during the dictatorship became emblematic of the destape, such as *Doña Flor y sus dos maridos*, directed by José María Paolantonio and based on the famous novel by Jorge Amado, with its female and male nudity and bed scenes, and *Camino negro*, written by Oscar Viale and directed by Laura Yusem, with its explicit depiction of sexual harassment.[65] Off-Corrientes, revamped strip-tease clubs and burlesque performances advertised themselves as the "school of destape" or "the only place with total destape," while the new *pornoshows*, erotic and explicit sex shows, promised "sex with total freedom" and emphasized that "now everything means everything."[66]

In the print media, all publications, old and new, engaged in the open and vivid discussion of sex. Women's magazines such as the well-established *Para Ti* and the newly created *Mujer 10*, general interest publications such as *Somos* (which had openly supported the dictatorship) and newcomer *La Semana*, humor magazines such as *Humor* (combative during the dictatorship) and *Satiricón* (closed in 1976 after the military coup and reopened in 1982), cultural magazines such as recently founded *El Porteño*, feminist publications such as *La Mujer* (the women's supplement of newspaper *Tiempo Argentino*), health magazines such as *Vivir*, and all newspapers, from *La Nación* (established in the late nineteenth century) to *Página/12* (published for the first time in 1987), avidly engaged with the new topic. Moreover, many publications issued popular supplements specifically focused on female sexuality and sex education. There were differences in tone, purpose, and quality, but the mood was festive and joyful. In an editorial in its second issue after the return to democracy,

*Eroticón*, for example, defined sex as enjoyment, gratification, ecstasy, and a celebration of the body, and proposed the magazine as a means to fight "the somber depiction of sexual life as morbid, pathetic, and shameful."[67]

Female and male genitalia, orgasm, sexual pleasure, sex positions, pregnancy and birth control methods, sex education, sexual fantasies, sexual dysfunctions, sexual abstinence and virginity, eroticism, abortion, orgies, and pornography are part of an illustrative but by no means exhaustive list of subjects now open for discussion. The arenas for such discussion were equally diverse: medical, scientific, and pseudoscientific articles; editorials; investigative reports; humorous pieces; comic strips; short stories; letters to the editor; personal accounts; and interviews with sexologists, sociologists, educators, actresses and actors, writers, and government authorities. In fact, any interviewee was asked about sex in those years, and almost everything was about sex. Publications were filled with articles on the sexual lives of such varying groups as lifeguards, butchers, and blind people; histories of sexuality and sexual repression in Argentina since colonial times; "investigative reporting" on nineteenth-century sex trafficking and cemeteries for prostitutes; and pieces on how diet affected sexual performance and which sex positions contributed most to weight loss. A prototypical example is a 1984 interview published in *Libre* with eighty-eight-year-old Doña Petrona de Gandulfo, the most important culinary referent of the country and the embodiment of middle-class female respectability. In the article, suggestively titled "Doña Petrona Has Lived a Great Life because She's Got a Recipe That Turns Men On," the cook offers a recipe for an aphrodisiac stew.[68]

Additionally, the print media devoted countless pages to reflecting on, criticizing, and celebrating the destape in television, theater, advertising, radio, and cinema. By describing sex scenes and sexual language in movies, television shows, plays, and novels, and by publishing explicit photos to illustrate those descriptions, the press added more sexual content to publications already teeming with sexual matters, amplifying and propelling the destape forward. Even periodicals such as *Esquiú*, which fought the destape bitterly, contributed indirectly to its propagation. While its reporting lacked the graphicness of other publications, it provided free publicity for the films, television shows, and plays it severely criticized.[69]

With the outburst of discourses came an eruption of provocative images that the Argentine media had never printed before. From fashion and general interest publications to health magazines and comic books, the destape brought unparalleled levels of nudity and sensuality. Just as a few years earlier nobody would have expected Doña Petrona's advice on how to make men better lovers, many unexpected candidates bared all in the return to democracy, such as actress Cristina Lemercier, who played the sweet and chaste primary school teacher Jacinta Pichimahuida in the popular children's television show *Señorita maestra*.[70]

Equally remarkable was the boom of new publications exclusively devoted to sex and graphic sexual images, with formerly banned frontal nudity included. Many appeared between 1983 and 1984, some of them reaching the newsstands only a few days after Alfonsín's inauguration and thus literally born of democracy. The editor of *Hombre* magazine equated this boom to "opening an ice cream parlor in the desert. The thirsty arrive in flocks."[71] An investigative report published by *Somos* magazine revealed that twenty-four erotic publications had been launched in 1984, distributing 1.2 million issues monthly in the city of Buenos Aires and its metro area alone (a region with 9.5 million inhabitants, according to the 1980 census); these publications made up 13 percent of all periodicals distributed in the area. Corroborating this boom, Norberto Chab, who worked as a writer for *Destape*, affirmed that in their first six months, *Destape* and *Shock* together sold 300,000 issues weekly. *Hombre* sold a similar number each month as well.[72] Furthermore, a deluge of previously banned erotic magazines from Spain, Brazil, and the United States entered the country with the destape. In 1984, for example, customs authorities seized twenty thousand issues of American *Penthouse* in the port of Buenos Aires because they lacked import permits.[73]

The flurry of local sex publications included humor magazines such as *Eroticón* and *Sex Humor*, the sex-centered equivalents of *Satiricón* and *Humor*, respectively; comics such as *Fierro* and *Historietas Sex*; *Playboy*-inspired[74] publications such as *Hombre*; erotic magazines of mostly graphic photographic content such as *Mundo Erótico*, *Shock*, *Viva*, *Climax*, *Prohibida*, *Testigo*, and *Don, la revista para Juan*, mostly conceived for a male readership; *Adultos*, a monthly with a strong component of sexology; and *Libre*, *Dar la cara en entrevista*, and *Destape*, which combined general interest articles, sensationalism, and sexual and nude or seminude images. The editor of *Dar la cara en entrevista* explained this formula as "mixing water and oil," but the final product was a spectacular success among readers.

Although far from exhaustive, this list shows a target segmentation of the consumer magazine market that suggests how massive and socially inclusive the destape was. *Hombre* and *Adultos*, for example, directed toward a sophisticated readership interested in intellectual and scientific discussions of sex, were intended for middle- and upper-class consumers, while *Viva* and *Shock*, characterized by vulgar language and devoid of "serious" journalism or reporting, targeted a "less-discerning" reader.[75]

The destape in cinema was as explosive as it was in the print media. In February 1984, two months after Alfonsín's inauguration, Congress passed law 23,052, revoking law 18,019 and effectively abolishing film censorship along with the ECC. This had been one of the one hundred proposed measures of Alfonsín's platform "to change your life."[76] Law 23,052 assigned film rating to the INC, with the goal of establishing appropriateness for minors and warning adults about content. President Alfonsín granted the INC a generous budget to be allocated as production loans and appointed Manuel Antín, a film director and screenwriter identified with the 1960s Argentine New Wave, as the agency's director.[77] Antín believed that a free Argentine cinema was a symbol of a new era, "an open window abroad that demonstrates the democracy we have established."[78]

Like in the press, despite differences in degree, tone, and quality, sex became present, more prominent, and more explicit across the cinematic spectrum, extending to all genres and to well-known veteran directors— many recently back from exile—as well as newcomers. The destape became a stylistic trend that, based on the use of strong sex and erotic scenes, deeply pervaded domestic productions. Within the group of destape films was a large number of comedies, such as *Las colegialas se divierten* (Fernando Siro, 1986), about the escapades of a group of students faced with a new disciplinarian headmistress; *Las lobas* (Aníbal Di Salvo, 1986), which focused on two sisters forced to pay a huge debt left by their father by attracting one suitor after another; and *Camarero nocturno en Mar del Plata* (Gerardo Sofovich, 1986), chronicling the adventures of a waiter working in a luxury hotel. The emblematic destape movies, however, have the typical attributes of softcore pornography or sexploitation, that is, simulated sex acts and female nudity, quite often gratuitous.[79] They are dramas with flimsy plots, violence, and a tone of timely denunciation of social problems such as prostitution, drug trafficking, poverty, and crime. Some of the most representative films that flawlessly combine these components are

*Atrapadas* (Aníbal Di Salvo, 1984) and *Correccional de mujeres* (Emilio Vieyra, 1986), both focused on life in a women's prison; *Los gatos (Prostitución de alto nivel)* (Carlos Borcosque, 1985), about a prostitution ring; and *Sucedió en el internado* (Emillio Vieyra, 1985), which tells the story of a series of murders at an all-girls boarding school.

The end of censorship and the active promotion and economic support of national film productions by the new democratic government played a significant role in the making of these films. However, filmmakers could have wagered on other types of movies and taken different creative choices given the same financial assistance and freedom. Like the publishing houses, the movie industry chose to ride the wave of the destape because it was, in commercial terms, the wisest decision. Evidence of audience preferences is that between 1983 and 1987, destape movies figured prominently on the annual list of the ten top-grossing Argentine films. In fact, *Atrapadas* was the third most successful movie at the box office in 1984. These films did not introduce the sexploitation genre in Argentina—pioneered by Armando Bó—but took it to a different level in terms of both content and popularity. Entertainment magazine *Variety* maintained that *Atrapadas* included the most daring softcore sex scenes in the history of Argentine films, "helping it sell nearly 1,000,000 tickets its first weeks of general release."[80] In 1985, *Sucedió en el internado* and *Los gatos* occupied the fourth and fifth place in the list of top-ten grossing films, respectively. That same year, the last six films on the top-ten list were destape movies, even though all were rated as only suitable for adults and most had received unenthusiastic or negative reviews in the press.[81]

Without censorship, Argentine audiences were also able to enjoy films long banned in the country, such as the controversial erotic dramas *Last Tango in Paris* (1972), directed by Bernardo Bertolucci, and Nagisa Oshima's *In the Realm of the Senses* (1976).[82] Similarly, the increasing number of adult movie theaters—despite the municipal legal requirements about location, facilities, and operation that made them difficult to open and run—gave local spectators unrestricted access to foreign X-rated films, as the genre was not yet produced locally.[83] Furthermore, with the arrival of VHS technology, local audiences could easily and legally rent foreign pornography in neighborhood *videoclubes* (video rental stores) nationwide to watch at home. In 1985—when there were only 114 videoclubes in the country and almost half were located in Buenos Aires city—only 3 percent of consumers rented porn; two years later, the market had expanded to 10 percent. As confirmation of the growing trend, the company that monopolized porn distribution in the country claimed that in 1987 there were 3,500 legal video cassettes of *Cicciolina Number One* (1986), starring the internationally renowned Italian porn star Cicciolina, and 3,300 tapes of *Top Gun* (1986), the hit military action drama with Tom Cruise.[84]

With the return to democracy, television content also experienced the radical transformation of the destape. Audiences could now watch open discussions of sexual matters on talk shows and the news. For the first time, comedies such as *Matrimonios y algo más* (1982–89), *Sexcitante* (1984–85), *No toca botón* (1981–87), *Operación Ja-Já* (1981–84; 1987–91), *Monumental Moria* (1986–89), and *Las gatitas y los ratones de Porcel* (1987–90) were able to combine an unparalleled number of seminaked women with sexist and sexual humor. And, telenovelas such as *Amo y señor* (1984) defied all genre conventions to date by showing ardent bed scenes. Innovatively, shows such as *Polémica del amor* (1988) and *¿Qué sabe usted de sexo?* (1988) were exclusively devoted to discussing sexuality with experts and answering questions and taking "explicit sexual confessions" from the audience. A television critic praised *¿Qué sabe usted de sexo?* for the casualness with which the panelists addressed sexual matters, "as if they were discussing cooking recipes."[85] This trend began when *Veinte mujeres* (1986), a show with a panel of twenty women from the audience and special guests debating different topics, made the popular sexologist María Luisa Lerer a regular. The same openness characterized radio programming, where previously taboo issues were discussed in clear language and sexologists occupied important segments in general interest shows and even had their own hit shows entirely on sex. For their part, advertising agents filled ads and commercials with suggestive scenes and a lot of women's skin to sell everything from jeans to sodas to television sets. Fittingly, Hitachi returned to the screen the day of Alfonsín's inauguration with a new version of the commercial the dictatorship had banned just a year earlier, this one more provocative and fixated on women's backsides.[86]

Similarly, the new freedom triggered great interest in classic erotic literature such as *Justine* and *Juliette* by the Marquis de Sade and a surge in the sales of Argentine works in the genre.[87] Erotic books were quite a heterogeneous mix. Poorly written second-rate novels with predictable plots, widely available on newspaper stands, boomed in these years—

such as *Taxi dormitorio* (1984), about the sexual escapades of a cabdriver, or *Boutique todo servicio* (1984), about sensual saleswomen in a male clothing store. Bookstore best sellers also flourished—such as Mempo Giardinelli's *Luna caliente* (1983), about a young man's obsession with a thirteen-year-old girl he rapes; *Los amores de Laurita* (1984), a novel by Ana María Shua about the sexual experiences of a young woman; and *Dueña y señora* (1983), a collection of short erotic tales by Susana Torres Molina. In fact, the return to democracy provided the background for the rise of a powerful erotic narrative by women, further exemplified by Tununa Mercado's *Canon de alcoba* (1988), Cristina Peri Rossi's *La nave de los locos* (1984), Griselda Gambaro's *Lo impenetrable* (1984), and Liliana Heer's *Bloyd* (1984), among others.[88] Meanwhile, sexology books thrived, in keeping with the unparalleled growth of the field in the country. Between 1986 and 1987, the four most popular Argentine sexologists published books that rapidly sold out—María Luisa Lerer's *Sexualidad femenina: Mitos, realidades y el sentido de ser mujer* (1986) was reprinted three times in two months—and important publishing houses such as Grijalbo and Horme launched sexology collections that featured iconic works in the discipline by William Masters and Virginia Johnson, Helen Kaplan, and Benjamin Karpman.[89]

## THE MEANINGS OF THE DESTAPE

The emblematic publishing house Perfil released iconic publications such as *Libre*, *Hombre*, *La Semana*, and *Mujer 10* in the return to democracy. In a 2016 interview, Perfil's owner Jorge Fontevecchia explained that censorship during the dictatorship had brought Argentine culture to a halt and submerged the country in a state of underdevelopment. Fontevecchia affirmed that it was as if the dictatorship had stopped time in 1976, impeding progress, and as a result, a foreigner visiting in 1984 actually encountered the Argentina of the mid-1970s. The destape, on the contrary, represented a jump forward toward the future.[90] Sergio Sinay, the chief editor of *Hombre*, summarized this idea well when he contended that the mission of his magazine was "a small contribution to the effort of moving the country into the twentieth century."[91] With the destape, supporters agreed, Argentina was belatedly joining in international cultural trends that had started in the previous decades. *Mujer 10* was thus inspired by the American *Cosmopolitan*, which revolutionized women's magazines in the mid-1960s; *Hombre* by *Playboy*, created in the United States in the 1950s; and *Libre*, a mix of sensationalism, investigative reporting, and nude models, by Spanish *Interviú*, first published in 1976. Spain, in fact, which experienced its own destape after the end of Francisco Franco's dictatorship in 1975, offered the perfect blueprint. Many Argentine journalists and writers experienced the Spanish destape firsthand when they arrived in the country in the mid-1970s, fleeing the Argentine dictatorship; later, many of these exiles brought the destape lessons with them when they came back to Argentina after 1983.[92]

Fontevecchia's statement about time standing still during the military dictatorship suggests an intrinsic relationship between the destape and the achievement of modernity, an idea that circulated widely in the return to democracy. In 1984, for example, a *Libre* editorial argued that the discussion around the destape was ultimately about the type of nation Argentines aspired to be. The editorial explained that France and the United States, which exemplified the most advanced Christian Western societies, were strong democracies with solid economies in which citizens had the freedom to enjoy what some groups in Argentina were labeling "obscene." In contrast, Iran and the Soviet Union, nations torn by broken economies and totalitarianism, revealed the equation of sexual censorship with social backwardness. Destape defenders contended that in essence, the discussion about explicit sexual content in mass culture was about defining a "way of life."[93] Those against the destape were, in fact, "damning Argentina to remain a dinky, undeveloped republic," while freedom to talk, show, or write openly about sex was a sign of the development and progress of "civilized" nations, an example the newly democratic Argentina was set to follow.[94]

In this new Argentina, the destape delivered on the promise of freedom of expression with a vengeance because sex was associated with the secret, the private, and the primal, and in the context of the military dictatorship, it had also been the prohibited, the expurgated, and the unspoken. Furthermore, what made sex the perfect subject for epic liberation in the media was its potential to disrupt themes considered "sacred," such as family, childhood, and religion. Popular magazines *Sex Humor* and *Eroticón* represent two of the most extreme examples.[95] They both offered historically unmatched, irreverent, "profane" humor that depicted such things as women who, surrounded by unruly toddlers, regretted not having had an abortion; pregnant nuns; and priests who participated in orgies. Similarly, the newly created adult comic magazines *Historietas Sex* and *Fierro*—the latter advertised as "the comic strip that was not possible in the past"— published sexually explicit cartoons with never-before-seen close-ups; detailed images of sexual organs; and rape, oral sex, and group sex scenes. These images and humor represented a cry of emancipation after years of state-imposed prudishness and crushed freedoms of the press and of speech even when some considered them to be gross, raw, and brutal.[96]

In fact, even progressive artists, journalists, and thinkers who endorsed the destape began discussing issues of taste, limits, and discernment. This was a conversation about the uses of freedom, the acceptance of excesses and risks, and the search for balance. In this discussion, the difference between pornography and eroticism was central but remained largely unresolved as there was no universal, ahistorical, and objective definition of obscenity people could agree on.[97] "Who says that a naked breast is erotic and a pubis is pornographic?" asked journalist Daniel Pliner, director of the weekly *El Observador*. Pliner maintained that questions like this had no objective answers and that they could dangerously reintroduce the issue of censorship.[98] This possibility made progressive sectors extremely uncomfortable. Therefore, they ultimately justified the "excesses" of the destape—on which there was no agreement—in the name of freedom and using the Spanish destape as an example, explained those excesses as the "natural" and temporary reaction to past repression. Many foretold that audiences would start experiencing a "destape fatigue" that would make them more discerning about content. As a consequence, the crudest components of the destape would vanish and only its fine expressions would remain.[99] Others, such as pioneering pediatrician and sex educator Florencio Escardó, held that the new freedom was entirely positive and that the destape should not be reduced to merely its excesses because this was "as absurd as protesting against sugar because a child got an upset stomach from eating candy."[100]

For their part, general audiences embraced the different manifestations of the destape, making it a huge commercial success. According to a poll published in *La Semana*, only 10 percent of the respondents believed that censorship should be introduced to restrain the unwanted aspects of the destape.[101] Like writers, comic artists, and journalists who were free to create without constraints, audiences reveled in the freedom to choose what to consume. Throughout his campaign, Alfonsín had emphasized the importance of this right for true democracy, arguing that "censorship represents a direct attack on freedom and an affront to the spectator. The existence of censorship suggests that as audiences, we are incapable of distinguishing between good and bad and of choosing accordingly."[102] In fact, the government explained that past censorship agencies represented "an elite group that takes it upon itself to think so that the rest of the population does not have to."[103] With the end of a paternalistic view of audiences that highlighted their lack of standards, taste, morals, and education, the public regained its right to choose—even if what they chose caused dismay among some movie, theater, and literature critics and members of the intellectual elite.[104]

This freedom of choice proposed by the destape implied recovering the self. Censorship and self-censorship prompted by anxiety and violence had annulled the capacity of individuals to decide for themselves, crushing the feelings of autonomy that are essential for the creation of personhood. After the return to democracy, "I decide" meant "I exist," a strong sentiment that given the violence of the dictatorship many people might have easily reformulated as "I survived." The content of the destape added another layer of complexity to the repossession of the self because sex involved issues of conscience, intimacy, and private responsibility that reinforced feelings of self-determination. At the most basic level, then, the destape provided Argentines the opportunity to overcome the "culture of fear" that had made violence, torture, and death "the gods" that determined behavior.[105] Now audiences could conquer the fear of exploring and accepting subjects that censors had previously demonized, the fear of personal responsibility, the fear of facing the "excesses" of freedom, and the fear of accepting who they were and what they liked. Indeed, the right to read an erotic magazine or watch a pornographic movie was more than an expression of sexual freedom—it was an assertion of sexual identity. In those acts, subjects defined themselves as free consumers and readers but also expressed themselves as sexual beings.[106]

Because of these effects, the destape powerfully symbolized the age of adulthood. In a 1979 essay published in the newspaper *Clarín*, writer and poet María Elena Walsh bravely denounced how censorship infantilized audiences by calling Argentina "a kindergarten country" inhabited by "children" with "a broken pencil and an enormous eraser already encrusted in their brains" that prevented them from thinking or articulating their thoughts. Censors, Walsh suggested, claimed to preserve purity but were actually producing backwardness. The writer pointed out that in democratic regimes around the world, free choice did not destroy families, pervert youth, or disintegrate the community. Frustrated, she called for the end of censorship by urging military authorities to "let us grow up." Yet Walsh's plea was ignored because as political scientist Guillermo O'Donnell has affirmed, turning citizens into "obedient infants" was central to the military's plan of subjugation.[107]

"Adulthood," understood as the freedom to decide what to read, watch, and listen to, would only be attained after 1983, making the destape the ultimate metaphor of a national coming of age. Openness about sexual matters, the traditional realm of mature individuals, confirmed Argentines in their new grown-up status. The magazine *Adultos* put this symbolic association to work when laying out its goals in its first issue: "To discuss what we've never discussed before. To allow ourselves what we've never allowed ourselves before. To stop believing that sex is something ugly and understand, once and for all, that it is something beautiful. To hear the world's foremost experts on the subject. . . . To cease to be what María Elena Walsh referred to as a 'kindergarten country,' especially in terms of sex. Today, we launch *Adultos*. We hope to be *Adultos* [adults] together."[108]

Celebration of adulthood notwithstanding, some intellectual sectors criticized the destape for its commercial nature. These commentators disagreed with the sexualization of culture as just "good business" and maintained that sexual freedom and sexual well-being were different from the commodification of sex for profit. These critics believed that money-making tainted the enterprise when it interfered with or distracted from higher goals such as sexual liberation or sex education. Yet writer Marcos Aguinis argued that disapproving of the economic motivations behind the destape was different from defending censorship, which he vehemently opposed. Aguinis asserted that "sex is something too valuable and worthy for it to be handled by neurotic dictators or for it to be exploited by slaves to money."[109]

The most extreme remark on the commercial nature of the destape came from Minister of Interior Antonio Tróccoli, who suggested it was a spurious business by using the word "mafia"—a comment that he soon dismissed due to the negative reaction in the media and its rapid appropriation by conservative and ultra-Catholic sectors. Journalists and editors were the first to reject these types of criticisms by arguing that profit was the motivation and condition of survival for all types of businesses operating in a market economy, and publishing houses functioned under the same terms. "Should the government pass a law to ban publishers for making money?" some asked with sarcasm. The destape industry was no different from the textile or food industries; they all manufactured and sold products for profit. Erotic magazines or erotic movies were unique merchandise but consumer goods nonetheless. Most importantly, advocates agreed, the destape industry was simply responding to an insatiable demand.[110]

This demand might explain why of all the taboo media topics that were unleashed after the fall of the dictatorship, sex was the first, the rawest, and the most ubiquitous. It might also clarify its pioneering role in suggesting and facilitating public discussions about other previously prohibited and painful subjects such as political violence and the desaparecidos. Early on, indeed, several voices argued that the sexual destape should only be the beginning of a larger process of openness. Ultimately, the destape was "talking about everything, writing about everything, filming everything, painting everything"—an "everything" that unquestionably included the crimes committed by the military.[111] Yet once this started happening, the treatment of sensitive topics such as clandestine detention centers, kidnapped babies, and death flights[112] took on a sinister, distasteful, and macabre tone. The hyperrealistic news that proliferated about human rights violations was labeled "the horror show." Even more so than in the case of the sexual destape, critics condemned the profit-making nature of "corpse trafficking"—as one journalist summarized the morbid reports that crudely commodified human suffering.[113]

In this context, sex did not fall into the background but instead became a bizarre complement prompting critical commentators to denounce a "race" between the sexual destape and the "destape of tombs."[114] The press was plagued by an uneasy mix of images of provocative nude women and unidentified dead bodies, articles about orgasm and explicit sex shows followed by exposés on torture in illegal prisons, and comics about sex positions next to editorials about unmarked graves. *Libre*, the magazine that best exemplified this trend, was the third best-selling weekly in the country, showing that there was an eager audience for this formula.[115]

Many progressive sectors of the media, which otherwise oscillated between supporting and tolerating the destape, criticized the grotesque pairing "of the tiniest bikini and the biggest crime" because it had transformed serious and disturbing news into something frivolous, vulgar, and puerile.[116] Furthermore, critics warned that this offensive pairing would desensitize the public toward sex and, most importantly, toward death and suffering.[117]

While also being critical, others saw a deep-set, significant connection between the two realms. Florencio Escardó affirmed that both sex and crimes against humanity shared a common past as invisible subjects. Argentines had developed a gigantic scotoma, a blind spot, to avoid seeing what they did not want to see, when in most cases, it was in plain sight. It is no coincidence that the dictatorship turned its victims into desaparecidos, rendering them "invisible" to their families and to the nation as a whole. Escardó explained that in the midst of the destape, the obsession with sex and the morbid exposure of the military's violent crimes were a collective strategy of acceptance. Argentines had consciously rejected both subjects because they were too chaotic, complicated, dangerous, and painful to acknowledge, but now they were coming to terms with past denial. Like the destape of state violence, the sexual destape was a reaffirmation of the right and the ability to see, and, consequently, to know and to accept. The sexual destape also represented an empowering, voluptuous recovery of all senses. Escardó maintained that as a symbol of pleasure and amusement, the destape provided a profound "sense of relief" from the suffering and death people had witnessed, suspected, experienced, or denied, and that now, increasingly disclosed in the press and socially acknowledged, all had to cope with.[118]

Along these lines, writer Susana Torres Molina explained the success of her best-selling book of erotic tales by asserting that eroticism connects us to uninhibited pleasure and in so doing teaches us to deal with guilt. In a society plagued by remorse about the recent past, the destape as a celebration of exuberant sensuality may have served as a soothing tonic to process the grim previous years and the uncertainty about the future and to help contend with personal responsibilities. Yet the destape was more than a cheap thrill cobbled together by opportunistic movie directors, magazine editors, and writers. Griselda Gambaro argued that in the new democratic context, books like her erotic novel *Lo impenetrable* (1984) were "a place where imagination, nonchalance, and irreverence are but small contributions to a more playful, permissive society."[119] It was French philosopher Georges Bataille who equated eroticism with an experience of life in all its intensity and exuberance, the embracement of existence in its richest manifestation. Gambaro was, in effect, drawing attention to the urgent need of Argentines to recover the joy of being and the role of a light-hearted, bright, healthy eroticism in doing so.[120] This type of eroticism was the opposite of the eroticized violence of the military that, according to Frank Graziano, derived pleasure from another's pain. Furthermore, the military, Diana Taylor has suggested, relocated "the masculinist desire for domination onto the feminized population," which was rhetorically and literally violated with impunity.[121] In Argentina, after years of the rule of death and terror, the destape was a celebration of eroticism that represented, even in its most unrefined and profit-driven versions, an unrepentant collective enactment of self-indulgence as well as the right of life enjoyed to the fullest.[122]

## THE CATHOLIC CHURCH, ULTRA-CATHOLICS, AND THE *CONTRADESTAPE*

The Catholic Church became a vocal enemy of the destape, especially the Conferencia Episcopal Argentina (CEA; Argentine Episcopal Conference)—the official assembly of all bishops in the country—and its Comisión Episcopal para los Medios de Comunicación (Episcopal Media Commission), which filed lawsuits and actively protested against media content. For their part, figures such as Rosario archbishop Jorge Manuel López, priest Julio Triviño, and San Juan archbishop Italo Di Stéfano became nationally known for their vociferous positions. Most importantly, ultra-Catholic sectors joined a myriad of local and national institutions, both long-lived and newly founded, that worked in a coordinated and very visible fashion against the destape, such as the Liga de Madres de Familia, the Liga de Padres de Familia, the Liga por la Decencia, Acción Católica, the Movimiento de Afirmación de los Valores Morales, the Federación de Entidades para la Defensa de la Dignidad Humana, the Liga de Amas de Casa, el Movimiento Familiar Cristiano, la Asociación de Abogados Católicos, Fuerza Moral, and the Coordinadora Nacional de Defensa de la Familia (CONADEFA).

Among these, the Liga por la Decencia, created in Rosario in 1963 under the motto "For a more decent society for our children," was one of the strongest and most reactionary, prompting a journalist to equate it to "the destape of Rosario's far right."[123] The Liga was also a fundamental planner and organizer of concerted nationwide efforts that earned it a reputation across Argentina. Presided over by Pedro García and with a board of directors almost entirely composed of men, the Liga enthusiastically supported the dictatorship. As early as July 1976, four months after the coup, the Liga welcomed key new national and local military authorities in its anniversary celebrations while foreseeing a shared future working for the same goals, morality being the most coveted. García affirmed that "we are hopeful and optimistic, but also convinced that unless we achieve the moral recovery of our people, all economic, political and other efforts we make will have been built on sand."[124]

When the dictatorship was unofficially over after the Malvinas War and the call for elections, conservative, ultra-Catholic sectors profoundly lamented and protested the increasing sexualization of culture. But when the destape actually began, it represented for them the coming of apocalyptic times. It was considered a constant, all-encompassing, and violent perversion that overran culture and everyday life, threatening to destroy Christian values, innocent children, and the family. Ultra-Catholic associations compared the destape to "uncovering garbage" (el destape de basura), and thus an open, smelly trash can became a common graffiti on city walls. For the CEA, the destape was a form of obscene exhibitionism that produced an incapacity to feel, depriving individuals of their emotions. The media—labeled the "medios de corrupción social" (mediums of social corruption)—was causing an "alienating extroversion" that profoundly degraded culture. The destape rendered society insensitive; the sexualization of culture hardened the heart.[125]

The CEA equated the destape with pornography, understood as "expressions that undermine modesty and good manners, distorting sexuality and extolling sexual impulse in an uncontrolled manner."[126] While journalists and scholars were debating the difference between eroticism and pornography with no definite resolution, ultra-Catholic associations condemned all sexual content for threatening pudor (modesty) and used the term "pornographic" liberally. With no tolerance for even the most innocuous manifestations of the new openness toward sexual matters, no challenge to morality was too small for these "stoic modesty soldiers," as an article in *Sex Humor* sarcastically nicknamed the Liga por la Decencia.[127] For the league, pornography included hardcore porn movies and arthouse films featuring bed scenes, sexually provocative frontal nudity and short shorts, naughty dialogues brimming with double entendres on theater stages, and the most infantile versions of off-color humor on television shows. A warning in the newsletter published by the Liga por la Decencia against the increasingly popular use of the term *pareja* (couple) because of its associations with *aparearse* (to mate)—"like animals do"—is an illustrative example.[128] Similarly, they denounced the "sexually aggressive" dialogues on television shows, such as a scene on the popular adult show *No toca botón* where a male character tells his love interest on the phone: "I'd like you to come over and pose naked for me tonight. . . . What do you mean, you're not a professional model?! . . . That doesn't matter . . . I'm not a painter, either."[129]

Ultra-Catholics pointed to democracy as the enabling factor for the new culture of sexual frankness and thus criticized its freedoms. In 1984, the Comisión Episcopal para los Medios de Comunicación declared that all aspects of life had to be subordinated to morality and that this was the only possible path to true freedom. The bishop of Jujuy Raúl Casado summarized this view by arguing that "morality should inform politics and economics, professional and domestic life, the world of culture and work, the sphere of the family and school, artistic expressions and social communications. Morality is the exercise of freedom."[130] With these arguments, ultra-Catholic sectors walked a thin line between attacking the sexualization of culture and contesting the new democratic order that allowed it. By questioning the value of voting for causing "moral degradation," emphasizing how easily freedom became licentiousness, affirming that happiness could never result from a type of liberty that involved obscenity and attacks on family and religion, and insisting that permissiveness endangered political stability, the Catholic Church eroded confidence in democracy among its congregation. The process reached its boiling point when in October 1984, during a mass for military officers, Father Julio Triviño coined the infamous term "pornographic democracy," which severely vilified the new political order.[131]

Many different voices strongly condemned this position, openly rejected the equation between the destape and pornography, defended freedom of expression, and attacked priests for being "falsely moralistic" and "sexually repressed."[132] Florencio Escardó criticized the "scandalized hypocrites" who "believe they've got the monopoly on morality and judge everyone else" for using the destape as an excuse to send the dreadful message that democracy was corrupt. Escardó further asserted that the true sources of corruption were the denial, hypocrisy, and concealment that had prevailed during the dictatorship and that the contradestape was zealously advocating now.[133] For his part, Buenos Aires Secretary of Culture Mario O'Donnell, who was otherwise inclined to place limits on the destape, such as ordering that erotic magazines should be displayed in black plastic covers, argued that Argentines, the church included, had to treat democracy as if it were a "fragile crystal." Pampered minorities, O'Donnell declared, should refrain from endangering the new political order with demands and accusations only they believed to be important, as most citizens were focused on coping with the nefarious legacies of the dictatorship. O'Donnell insisted, "We cannot risk our democracy over trifling matters. We are immersed in very basic situations such as hunger, trying to figure out whether our country can continue as a nation, and whether we'll be asphyxiated by the rope of our foreign debt. So quit whining about porno films, a topic that only interests a very small sector of the middle class and is of no interest to the average Joe, who can barely make it from paycheck to paycheck."[134]

While ultra-Catholics relativized democracy and highlighted the limits of freedom, they used both concepts to defend their position when attacked. Bishops, for example, differentiated between the "false freedom" of the destape and the "true freedom" and the "common good" resulting from limiting freedom of expression. Santa Fe Archbishop Eduardo Storni explained that the battle of the church against the destape was not motivated by censorship but by the need to protect Catholics from damaging influences. In a democracy, Storni affirmed, the rights of Catholics should be respected.[135] The CEA even compared the Catholics' affliction to the infringement of human rights by arguing that in a context in which there was "extreme sensitivity" in relation to this issue, it was important to understand that the destape was, in fact, a violation of body and spirit. In this way, ultra-Catholics conveniently alternated religious discourses that defined the destape as "sins against culture" and "the devil's market" with a political language of rights.[136]

These sectors drew on this language to defend themselves from a cultural trend they experienced as compulsory and inescapable. During their campaign "For freedom, against imposed pornography," CONADEFA argued that "we are not asking for censorship but we are asking for respect for our right to choose, without any imposition, what we want to watch and what we want our children to watch. We appeal to your responsibility as the government so that in each of your respective departments, you take the measures necessary to defend family and ensure that the laws are upheld."[137] Rather than turning off the TV and freely choosing the movies they wanted to watch and the books and magazines they wanted to read, ultra-Catholic sectors proposed to eliminate or censor those movies, television shows, books, and magazines they disapproved of, curtailing the right of choice and the freedom of expression of the rest of society in the process. Ultimately, in the name of morality, the freedoms of others should be restricted.

Also in the name of morality, where others saw modernity and liberation, ultra-Catholics viewed corruption, underdevelopment, and slavery. According to this view, the destape was synonymous not with emancipation but with oppression, turning audiences into slaves to their most basic instincts. Furthermore, an editorial in the Catholic magazine *Criterio* contested claims that the destape was a sign of national maturity and independence by charging that Argentines had made hedonism their tyrannical master and were "a community of spoiled children incapable of looking beyond pleasure."[138] With regard to the "so-called modernization" propelled by the destape, the Catholic magazine *Esquiú* declared that in reality, it was a "form of plagiarism" that entailed the reproduction of undesirable foreign models in Argentine media and culture.[139] Similarly, the episcopate affirmed that the destape was a shift in national culture, in the values and the lifestyle that represented the true Argentine identity, "a foreign cultural invasion."[140] Interestingly, international influences notwithstanding, the destape was predominantly composed of cultural products—from magazines and movies to television shows and sexology books—created in Argentina by Argentines.

Ultra-Catholics lamented that by naturalizing sex content in culture, "we gradually learn to live with evil, to tolerate it." Like in the case of illegal drugs, they argued, "the social body grows accustomed and then requires increasingly higher and frequent doses."[141] This "addiction" had devastating consequences. Ultra-Catholics denounced the destape for the "perversion of sexuality" evident in "immoral practices" such as premarital sex, same-sex relations, and autoerotism, all of which they believed to be on the rise. In an otherwise uneasy alliance, ultra-Catholics cited American radical feminist Robin Morgan's famous quote "Pornography is the theory, and rape is the practice" to support claims that the destape was the main cause of sexual violence against women and children. Yet the destructive effects of the destape were not limited to sexuality. The Catholic Church considered that Argentines were facing a doomsday scenario and that the destape was the cause of all evils, including the dissolution of the family, crime, drug addiction, declining patriotism, and, ultimately, the collapse of the nation.[142] Comparing the current situation in which "the leprosy of pornography spreads slowly" to the depravity that caused the destruction of Sodom and Gomorrah by divine judgment, ultra-Catholics warned of the consequences of the destape in ominous terms: "If we examine the national context, we can see that sentence has been passed and our punishment is now being imposed: hyperinflation, the worst that any country in the world is suffering; unemployment; scarcity; hatred among brothers; violence. . . . Punishment for a people who have turned their back on God worshipping the false idols of pleasure and decadence, a country that continues down the wrong path towards the wrong objective."[143]

The Catholic Church identified the culprits clearly. It blamed the media—"the merchants of sexual degradation"—for its lack of morals and thirst for profits, the people for their weakness, and the government for its permissiveness.[144] In fact, the church profoundly resented the national government for relaxing the control of agencies such as the COMFER and, most importantly, for eliminating infamous censorship bodies such as the ECC, an agency they had controlled tightly. These acts represented a terrible blow: "the triumph of *pornocracia*" enabled by a government that was viewed as a "patron of obscenity."[145] As a response, ultra-Catholics forcefully pushed for stringent censorship, which the bishopric of Posadas, Misiones, likened to an umbrella against the rain or a muzzle that prevented a dog from biting.[146] In this view, censorship was inevitable because pornography was as violent as "armed terrorism." The state, endowed with the duty to preserve public morality and social order, was thus expected to effectively use "police force to safeguard the physical and moral integrity of the nation's inhabitants."[147]

To transform a reality they despised and feared, and to counteract an "indolent" federal government they accused of imposing "moral liberalism," ultra-Catholic organizations and individuals acted with resolve and persistence, particularly at the municipal and provincial levels. Here, even in the midst of the destape and in the face of the democratically elected government working hard to deliver on its electoral promise of freedom of expression and the right of choice, they found some trusted allies in judges, prosecutors, mayors, governors, and councilmen. An extreme illustration of this collaboration for its political and symbolic meanings is the Eucharistic Congress in San Juan province in 1984, when several mayors participated in the mass celebrated by Archbishop Di Stéfano by carrying up the offerings. The gifts rendered at the altar were approved municipal ordinances and decrees against the destape and aimed at monitoring, prohibiting, closing down, and fining publications, establishments, forms of entertainment, and individuals who were considered threats to morality.[148]

In order to reach their goals, ultra-Catholic sectors printed and broadly circulated newsletters and bulletins; met with government authorities and representatives of television channels, film industry figures, editors, publishers, advertising agents, and newspaper and magazine distributors to discuss their demands; and organized popular petitions, hunger strikes, demonstrations, protests, talks, and conferences all over the country. They denounced movie theaters for the film posters on display; filed complaints against different intercity coach companies for the movies they showed on their buses; and even monitored the Boletín Oficial de Marcas, where brand names were registered, to hunt down sex-related products and lascivious labels.[149] Ultra-Catholics also intensely employed the court system by filing criminal complaints against movies, magazines, and television shows. In fact, when Minister of Interior Antonio Tróccoli dismissed the creation of censorship government agencies and argued that "justice will be entrusted with handling the excesses," ultra-Catholics took note.[150] In 1985, an editorial in Sex Humor expressed frustration and contempt over the manner in which the judiciary was being used against the media, maintaining that "the same old guys have now assumed the censor's role, those who continue to believe that sex should be silenced because it is ugly: the clergy, different leagues, sanctimonious oddballs who go running off to court when they spot a derrière."[151]

Article 128 of the Penal Code against obscenity became an effective tool invoked in legal actions. This strategy rapidly brought different sectors of the film industry, the media, and congressmen together to work toward reforming the law because in the hands of sympathetic judges, its application represented seizures, closures, and prison for magazine editors in chief and newsstand and movie theater owners and managers, the most common targets.[152] Yet, in other cases, ultra-Catholics favored dialogue. Fuerza Moral, for example, suggested taking advantage of personal relations whenever possible. Residents of big cities only had recourse to the law, but those who lived in a small town were advised to gather a group of neighbors "and amicably convince the theater owner that what he is doing is bad for the community and its future."[153]

It is difficult to assess the popular support for these ultra-Catholic sectors and to what extent Argentines either publicly or privately shared or sympathized with their position and criticisms, regardless of the commercial success of the destape. However, reporting on demonstrations, marches, and petitions by the Liga por la Decencia reveals its scarce convening power. In 1984, in Rosario, a city of 800,000 inhabitants, only 14,600 citizens (less than 2 percent of the city population) signed a petition against the destape, and a year later, only 2,000 rosarinos attended a demonstration in front of the cathedral. That same year, 3,000 people assembled in a demonstration against the destape in Mendoza, a city of 120,000. Suddenly, a Catholic nation that had accepted sex censorship and sexual conservatism imposed by the military dictatorship ignored or flatout rejected the ultra-Catholic contradestape and actively consumed the products of the destape.[154]

An explanation for this apparent contradiction must take into consideration the increasing discredit of the Catholic Church—whose complicity with the military regime was becoming apparent—and the clashes between the bishops and the Alfonsín administration due to its liberal policies on education, human rights, and divorce.[155] Most importantly, accepting and celebrating the destape, and contesting the contradestape, may have reaffirmed the identity of many Argentines as true opponents of the dictatorship. In a now classic study, political scientist Guillermo O'Donnell showed an almost "instantaneous conversion" among individuals who were acquiescent, acritical, and even supporters of the regime when interviewed during the dictatorship but who, after the return to democracy, denied they had espoused those previous positions, claimed they had been completely unaware of the repression in the previous years, and now energetically condemned the military. Similarly, in the late 2000s, historian Sebastián Carassai's interviewees changed the register of their stories from the personal "I" to the impersonal "one" or "it" ("one thought" or "it was said") when answering his questions about state terrorism during the dictatorship. Carassai explains this as a mechanism to dilute personal responsibility for the past by attributing blame to an "anonymous being." Thus, despite the reasons for and the genuineness of the change-over, embracing or tolerating the destape and rejecting or ignoring the contradestape might have been one more way to pledge commitment to democracy and repudiate the recent past.[156]

Although most Argentines refrained from participating in ultra-Catholic events and continued enjoying destape trends that made them modern, liberated, and democratic subjects, the mobilization of ultra-Catholic sectors resulted in key achievements. Ultra-Catholics successfully blocked the opening of adult cinemas, forced the COMFER to more strictly control television content and to prohibit the airing of films unsuitable for viewers under eighteen, achieved city ordinances for the creation of municipal boards of film rating and "moral committees" to supervise publications and entertainment and impose fines, closed down movie theaters and erotic shows, and impounded films and magazines. Just a few weeks after Alfonsín's victory, the city of Buenos Aires mandated that magazines such as *Shock*, *Destape*, and *Viva* could not be sold at the traditional sidewalk newsstands—where magazines were hung or displayed for the passersby to see and leaf through—but only in stores where they could not be openly displayed.[157] Alluding to the regulation, comic magazine *Sex* announced in its ads that "though you may not see it, *Sex* is always there." Later, these types of publications had to be sold in a black plastic bag, prompting *Adultos*'s editor in chief to wonder if the prohibition of the magazine for readers under eighteen was not enough protection for youth in a free country.[158]

The local victories of ultra-Catholics produced a very uneven national cultural map where the same or comparable films or magazines were available in some cities and prohibited in others. In 1984, for example, a judge in Rosario rejected a claim against *Last Tango in Paris* (1972), ruling

Figure 1.3. The progressive press criticized the attempts of the Catholic Church to control sexual practices and discourses. "What Is the Church Doing in My Bed?" *El Porteño*, August 1986.

in favor of its screening because he considered that the sex scenes were not obscene, while two years later, in San Juan, a judge impounded and prohibited the screening of *Emmanuelle* (1974) and sentenced the owner of the movie theater to prison based on charges of obscenity. In the verdict, the judge explained that "obscene is anything which tends to stimulate vulgar instincts and basic sexual desires, offending public modesty and good manners."[159] Likewise, early in 1985, Oskar Blotta, chief editor of *Eroticón* and *Satiricón*, was prosecuted in Buenos Aires for obscenity, and several issues of the magazines were seized and banned, even though they were being sold freely in the rest of the country. *Destape*, *Libre*, and *Shock*, for their part, were often confiscated in the city of San Juan.[160] The managing editor of *Sex Humor*, which was banned in some cities, confirmed that some regional distributors refused to deliver publications, drawing attention to the fact that the church had collaborators beyond the court-rooms. Indeed, contradestape demonstrations and signed petitions may not have attracted much support, but the church found adherents outside ultra-Catholic organizations. In November 1985, for example, the subway company in Buenos Aires and the newspaper vendors inside most of the stations boycotted some publications in a campaign against "imposed pornography."[161]

Progressive sectors condemned the church harshly for its defense of censorship, its denunciation of the government's commitment to free-dom, and its attacks on the new cultural and political order, highlighting the obscurantism and totalitarianism of the ultra-Catholic sectors. The church, for its part, minimized criticism by arguing that the media char-acterization of Catholics as "pious," "moralistic," and "old-fashioned" was merely an unsuccessful attempt to ridicule an urgent and noble cause.[162] Yet animadversion was more complex and serious than the church wanted to accept. As information about the horror of life and death in clandestine detention centers and the church's complicity with the dictatorship be-came public, detractors equated censorship with a form of torture inflicted on the intellectual abilities of society, a dangerous and painful remnant of the preceding times. They also posed an important question: "What is more corrupt, a movie or 30,000 disappeared?"[163] Similarly, an editorial in *Sex Humor* pointed to the contradiction between the church's crusade against the destape in the name of decency and "the seven years of mur-ders and tortures we went through without a single episcopal document on the matter."[164] *Sex Humor* was echoing critics who drew attention to how the church condemned the destape as immoral and evil, even calling it a violation of human rights, but had remained silent about the obscene violence that the military perpetrated against the people during the dictatorship.[165]

As the triumph of "spectator sex," the destape made sexuality a valid entertainment choice for audiences long deprived of erotic content in the arts and media. As such, it revolutionized visual culture, transformed social scripts about sex, and pushed the limits of taste and tolerance to unprecedented levels. It also repositioned sex on-scene, in the public sphere, open to discussion and to view. From being banned and obscured in the dictatorship, sex became the star of the democratic stage. Rather than asking whether the destape was an opportunistic commercial trend imposed on the audiences by the media or a media response to the authentic demands of eager consumers—a question that leads to circular reasoning more than to a stimulating inquiry and helpful conclusions—this chapter examines why the destape was such a spectacular commercial success and the most explosive cultural trend after the fall of the dictatorship. The answer lies in its social meanings and its social function: the destape was at the same time a cause and an effect of the democratization process. If democracy allowed for the liberalization and commodification of sex, the new culture of sexual frankness rendered democracy a lived experience as much as practices such as voting and protest marches did.

The commodification of sex propelled by the destape was in itself a concrete example of democratization that moved sex away from the sole control of governmental and religious forces and placed it in the market for massive consumption. This shift in influence left the traditional arbiters of sexuality feeling vulnerable and aggravated, and thus for some ultra-Catholic, conservative sectors, the destape represented the rise of a "pornographic democracy." However, for most social sectors, the destape was associated with the recuperation of the rights and liberties lost during the dictatorship and, perhaps, was even a means to reaffirm loyalty to democracy. As a sphere for practicing choice, becoming modern, experiencing adulthood as an individual and as a nation, feeling pleasure, and enjoying life, the destape became a fundamental component of democratic life for both creators and audiences. For many Argentines, the destape was an everyday reminder that living in a democracy was quietly but effectively present in the act of buying a sex manual or watching an erotic movie. And, in these acts, individuals simultaneously reaffirmed their allegiance to the new democratic order. The destape also disclosed the role of sex, and more specifically, the role of talking about, reading, watching, writing about, filming, and showing sex, as a powerful metaphor for personal and social liberation, and consequently, as a sphere for the rise of discerning and fearless subjects and a modern and forward-thinking society.

# 2

## A REAL CHALLENGE TO
## TRADITIONAL SEXUAL CULTURE?

The Conflicting Messages of the *Destape*

**The most iconic image** of the destape is a seminaked woman. Even today, when Argentines remember the destape, the first idea that comes to mind, the prime examples, are the beautiful actresses and models in provocative poses that filled the magazine covers or played the lead in destape blockbusters. The destape confirmed the feminist argument that the woman displayed as sexual object and signifying male desire "is the *leitmotif* of erotic spectacle."[1] The *chicas del destape* (the destape girls), moreover, played out heterosexual fantasies. While heterosexual pleasure and eroticism colonized the mainstream media—from television comedies and print ads to health magazines and comics—the silence about male and female homoeroticism was almost total. Thus, as bold, shocking, and unshackling as the media destape might have been perceived to be after years of censorship, and regardless of celebratory discourses that emphasized its novelty and defiance of sexual conventions, it objectified women for male viewers and erased same-sex desire, reproducing central components of the traditional sexual culture.

This chapter explores these two prominent features of the destape but goes deeper into advertisement, literature, television, and particularly films and the print press to achieve a more rounded and exhaustive characterization based on the analysis of three other remarkable traits: the unprecedented attention to female sexuality and the vindication of women's pleasure, the depiction of the otherwise silenced subject of sexual violence against women, and the new role of the press as a space for the participation of common people in discussions about sex. By examining these components, the analysis reveals an unexpected, original, and quite productive facet of the destape while it excavates sources such as sexploitation films, erotic cartoons, personal ad sections, and sexy photo contests that have been ignored and quite often trivialized by historians of Latin America. The chapter argues that the destape in the media was not a singular or homogenous process but a highly ambiguous cultural phenomenon full of stimulating contradictions that challenge facile classifications as either completely liberating and enriching or utterly restraining and offensive. As the destape commodified hypersexualized images of the female body to sell sexual fictions mainly to men, it also contributed to an open and more honest discussion and understanding of women's sexual needs, fears, and desires, a destape by women and for women. The destape transformed female sexuality into a common topic in general interest publications and the pivot of women's magazines, reversing a long tradition of silence and denial or unsophisticated, timorous treatment. Targeted magazine audiences went from being imagined and appealed to as asexual housekeepers, mothers, wives, professionals, and consumers to being reconceived as sexual subjects—not objects—actively battling past taboos that prevented them from freely addressing their fears, frustrations, questions, and wants in the bedroom.[2] Therefore, images of sexual objectification coexisted with a new "sexual subjectification," a term cultural critic Rosalind Gill has coined to refer to a process that promotes women as knowledgeable, active, and desiring sexual subjects.[3]

At the same time, destape films exposed sexual violence against women in an unprecedented fashion, and although they relied on misogynistic conventions of traditional sexploitation such as women's objectification and submission, they also defied the genre by portraying them as powerful avengers. Thus, female characters are not merely objects of violence but also use violence as an empowering mechanism to survive and get justice. Most importantly, destape movies unexpectedly revealed sexual violence against women during the dictatorship in a context in which the public discussion of sexual crimes committed by the military in the previous years was absent. Thus, enabled by the conventions of sexploitation, de-stape films were the first, and in the return to democracy the only, vehicles to openly show rape and sexual abuse of women in clandestine detention centers, drawing attention to the otherwise ignored female experience of illegal imprisonment.

Finally, the destape not only liberated periodicals to publish profusely and bluntly about sex matters, but it also freed heterosexual readers to express themselves unreservedly in and through this form of media. Echoing the appetite for communication and communion that the restoration of democracy provoked among Argentines, newspapers and especially magazines from all over the editorial spectrum provided a safe space for readers to ask questions, answer surveys, share their testimonies, publish short stories and personal photos, connect with others, and debate and exchange ideas about sex, thus making a fundamental contribution to the participatory ethos of the nascent democracy. Furthermore, the 1980s democratic hetero sex fora and their enthusiastic contributors pioneered in Argentina the sex confessional imperatives of the twentieth century, the rise of what sociologist Ken Plummer has defined as a culture of sexual storytelling in which ordinary people publicly disclose details of their sex lives and desires in different stages, from talk shows to sex tapes.[4]

## THE CHICAS DEL DESTAPE

Women on display were central to the media in the return to democracy, but their prominence was even more stunning when compared to the imagery of the previous decade. Diana Taylor has revealed the symbolic absence of the feminine in the masculinist imaginary imposed by the dictatorship and the extent to which a system dominated by male self-representation made women "unrepresentable." Taylor argues that while the military dictatorship feminized the enemy and the nation, it concealed, scorned, and repressed real women behind a mythic image of ethereal, self-sacrificing, and pure womanhood. Furthermore, the dictatorship fetishized male virility into the model of authentic Argentineness and colonized the public space with a display of rigid, disciplined, and controlled military male bodies. In the spectacle starring the armed forces, women were physically and symbolically disappeared from the scenario while the "glorious leaders, as objects of the look, inspire both desire and identification."[5] For their part, Argentine left-wing militants, intellectuals, and guerrillas extolled masculinity and the male body with the same fervor as their rivals. Historian Valeria Manzano has shown that these sectors exalted the male, heterosexual, ascetic, young body as the one most suitable to carry out the Revolution. At the same time, they figuratively and literally marginalized the female body as "less resilient," "too sexy," and the vehicle of a commercial bourgeois eroticism they despised.[6]

Conversely, when democracy returned to Argentina in the 1980s, it had a woman's body. It was the resilient and selfless body of the Madres de Plaza de Mayo but also the young, eroticized, seminaked body of the chicas del destape, the centerpiece of a variety of erotic and soft-pornographic magazines, such as *Shock*, *Climax*, *Viva*, and *Dar la cara en entrevista*, that boomed after 1983.[7] These publications combined collections of explicit nude photos of, for the most part, unknown models and crude and sensationalist articles on mostly sex matters. If this was a true novelty after years of censorship, the most original innovation of the destape was the rise of general interest publications such as *Libre* and *Destape*, which mixed images of seminaked women with sober political and social news. Most of the women in these magazines were well-known actresses and models or ascending starlets in films and television shows. In comparison to the current homogenous beauty standards in the print media, dominated by digitally enhanced photos, silicone breasts, and buttock implants, the destape images depicted "natural" women with traits that now would be considered "imperfections"—a small belly, small breasts, stretch marks, or a less-defined waistline. This suggests less standardized, more diverse, fresher beauty models that allowed for a variety of body types, although they were all young, white, heterosexual, middle-class, thin, and conventionally attractive.[8]

As an icon of the destape, this female body on display was a metaphor for modernity, freedom of expression, pleasure, life, and, ultimately, democracy, meanings examined in the previous chapter. But it was also sexualized, objectified, and commodified to sell magazines, consumer goods, television shows, and movie tickets. The female body was, in other words, "democracy's best *negocio*" (business).[9] The most apparent example was in advertising, where female nudity and a profound fixation on women's behinds marketed everything from TV sets—such as the famous Hitachi commercials, banned during the dictatorship and then aired right after the

Figure 2.1. *Libre* featured the most popular *chicas del destape* on its covers. *Libre*, December 17, 1985.

return to democracy—to cigarettes and anything in between, including, quite peculiarly, the traditional sweet bread eaten during Christmas.[10] What a reporter described as the "new collective obsession" was further propelled by the rapid adoption of "*colaless*," a micro bikini bottom or thong that became a fashion craze starting in the summer of 1983 and received voluminous media attention.[11]

An article in *La Mujer*, the women's supplement of the newspaper *Tiempo Argentino*, affirmed that a comparative analysis of international advertising festivals made evident that the overwhelming presence of backsides in advertisements was "an Argentine invention."[12] As in the case of the Hitachi commercials, where the camera zoomed in on the bikini-clad bottoms of women walking, running, or riding horses on the beach or playing a soccer match in tight, revealing shorts, the commercials of the destape had a marked preference for reducing the woman to her highly eroticized derriere, both a sexual fetish and a taboo associated with nonreproductive sex. Journalist Moira Soto noticed that this new sexual objectification of women in commercials and ads rigidly polarized the female universe into vamps on one side versus abnegated and asexual housewives and mothers on the other. These stereotypes were also extensively present on television comedies and telenovelas obsessed with the dichotomy between "prostitutes" and "virgins." Physician and sex educator Florencio Escardó argued that Argentine women were tyrannically categorized as either "repressed" or "sinners."[13]

In this universe, the *carnazas* (fleshy, carnal women), rather than the *electrodomésticas* (household-appliance women)—as an advertising agent called the two main character types in Argentine commercials and print ads—had a body (or buttocks), were sexy, and had fun.[14] Still, many advertising agents maintained that despite the fixation on the female body, Argentine advertising was not as erotic as its European counterpart, a result of local social conservatism and the recent history of severe censorship. The new democratic freedom allowed for the introduction of erotic references, but slowly, timidly, and inadequately, using messages and images that lacked subtlety and imagination. Thus, experts agreed, the focus on the female backside was an easy creative shortcut while copywriters were learning to use sensuality more ably and effectively.[15]

In their many incarnations, the destape girls reaffirmed female sexual subordination to men, silenced female pleasure, and emphasized women's sexual availability for and accommodation of male desires. This echoes feminist film theorist Laura Mulvey's now classic argument about how pleasure in looking had been traditionally divided between men as the active bearers of the look and women as the passive image; the male gaze projects its fantasy onto the female figure, which is at the same time shaped to meet men's expectations.[16] A good example is the photo published in *Shock* of a seminaked woman on all fours, seductively gazing at the camera with an inset that reads: "Laura knows what part turns on men and she strikes a pose that ups the eroticism for our photographer. 'Note the look of pleasure on my face and the white panty pressing into my thighs. Isn't it hot?' asks Laura."[17] Critics lamented that with these types of images, women were so objectified for male consumption—as a result of their body postures, the nudity, the textual cues—that they could be easily replaced by inflatable sex dolls.[18]

On television, the female body on display became a fundamental characteristic of humor shows, where seminaked women operated as props that were paraded, often groped, and had little to no participation in the script. As in commercials and men's magazines, women on television shows were mainly a body with little voice. Indeed, the most successful shows in the second half of the 1980s owed their popularity to celebrated comic figures such as Jorge Porcel, Alberto Olmedo, and Mario Sapag, but also to the beautiful actresses and models who were the objects of the lascivious look, the not-always-welcome bold caress, or the vulgar comment made by their male counterpart.[19] Like the images circulating in the press, these actresses played roles that underlined traditional stereotypes of the sexy and sexually treacherous but ultimately easily dominated and gullible women, such as the lolita, the gold digger, the *femme fatale*, and the incredulous sex bomb. Actresses Adriana Brodsky, Silvia Pérez, Susana Romero, and Susana Traverso, for example, iconically played these parts in Olmedo's *No toca botón*: Brodsky (the star of the Hitachi commercials) as a naive young girl brought by her father to a lecherous *manosanta* (quack) for discipline and advice; Pérez both as the opportunist and self-interested lover of her married and older boss or the unfaithful, egocentric wife; Romero as the simple-minded countess deceived by the cunning butler who has sex with her in a dark bedroom, making her believe she is actually with her husband; and Traverso as the ingenuous patient who reenacts her dreams to her lustful psychoanalyst.

Female nudity was also essential to the cinematic destape. The comedias picarescas, starring Porcel and Olmedo, reproduced the same dynamics seen in their television shows where seminaked women were merely props. In dramas, while the male body remained clothed—even in sex scenes that would have allowed for a more prominent display—women's bodies were disproportionally exposed, and female nudity was quite gratuitous. In most cases, neither the narrative nor the part called for women's nakedness, but they always ended up with the blouse unbuttoned, the dress opened, and the skirt lifted. This abundance of female nudity was related to the fact that classic destape films had an overwhelmingly female cast—for example, *Correccional de mujeres*, *Sucedió en el internado*, and *Atrapadas*. Most of the stories developed in all-women settings such as prisons, prostitution rings, and boarding schools, where filmmakers overplayed nude scenes in communal showers, dormitories, brothels, massage parlors, and cabarets. Since the two most emblematic characters of destape films are the victim of sex trafficking and the female prisoner, the lack of freedom and the subjugation are unequivocally expressed in the objectification of women's bodies. The female body is an instrument for male pleasure—displayed, controlled, manipulated, vulnerable, and abused. Here again, films echo the dichotomy between the asexual mother and housewife, absent from these movies, and the hypersexualized body of the woman who does not conform to social expectations or "the bad woman"—the drug mule, the rebel teenager who sleeps with the chauffer, the porn actress, the young student who seduces the male teacher, the housekeeper who killed her employer, or the "villain lesbian," an uncommon character that reveals the purging of narratives centered on same-sex desire.

## AN INCOMPLETE DESTAPE

The destape in the mainstream media was essentially heterosexual. After the censorship and the persecution and repression of sexual minorities during the dictatorship, and given the new climate of sexual openness and the new activism of the gay community and its incipient visibility in the press, the absence of homoeroticism in the destape is somehow perplexing. Ignorance, discrimination, and aversion, which had contributed to the ostracism and concealment of homosexuality in the previous decade, were not automatically reversed because democracy had returned, but the media attention devoted to sexuality and the new frankness and boldness in discussing sexual matters after 1983 could have introduced nonheteronormative sexualities, cautiously but determinedly, as a topic of consideration in mass culture. Yet this was not the case, revealing the limits of a commercial phenomenon such as the destape to challenge heteronormativity, test the power of convention, and bring down the legacy of bigotry and obscurantism bequeathed by the dictatorship. The limitations of the destape also signal the cultural and media marginality of sexual minorities, even though gay and lesbian activism was gaining considerable momentum—the Comunidad Homosexual Argentina (CHA) was founded in 1984, and Carlos Jáuregui, its articulate and visible leader until 1987, published *La homosexualidad en Argentina* that same year.[20]

The media was unwilling to unleash a more profound, accurate, and intelligent exploration of sexuality in the country, probably more because of business acumen and conservatism—both in the media itself and in society—than due to external pressures. In fact, the silence of the Catholic Church on homoeroticism shows how little space it had in the popular media. While the weekly bulletin of the Catholic Church news agency was saturated with complaints, activities, and legal actions against the destape, there were no denunciations against gay content in the media. Catholic institutions fought the war against "*pornocracia*" on many fronts, but disturbing as they might have found magazines such as *Eroticón* and television shows such as *No toca botón*, all their targets reinforced heteronormativity.

In the midst of complete silence on lesbianism, quintessential destape magazines such as *Libre* and *Destape* along with the sensationalist press reported on crimes against gay men. Seventeen gay men were murdered in Buenos Aires between 1982 and 1983, fueling the most startling speculations in the media, including a serial killer and a "gay hunter," in articles that underlined gay promiscuity and abnormality.[21] Early in the transition to democracy, the press even continued using the term *amorales* ("the amoral ones"), which was commonly applied to gay people during the dictatorship, and the concept of *submundo homosexual* ("a homosexual underworld"), which emphasized illegal and criminal connotations of the gay culture. By the mid-1980s, iconic destape magazines oscillated between candid and informative interviews with gay militants and ridiculing as well as quite openly reproving portrayals of gay men. Other nonnormative identities continued, as in the past, to be mostly absent from the press.[22] For their part, cultural magazines such as *El Porteño* or *El Periodista* reported on the repression and discrimination experienced by the gay community, almost exclusively focusing on men, as well as on the organizing efforts and political activism of the CHA, with a particular emphasis on Carlos Jáuregui.[23]

General interest publications approached the topic only sporadically, and even when they did it sympathetically, the tone tended to be ominous and worrying. The groundbreaking image of Jáuregui embracing another CHA activist on the cover of *Siete Días* in 1984, for example, was titled "El riesgo de ser homosexual en la Argentina" ("The Risks of Being Homosexual in Argentina"). And although the article recuperated the voices and experiences of gay men (mostly anonymously) and interviewed supportive experts, discussions of double lives, "abnormality," and danger more or less inadvertently reinforced stereotypical and pathological views. There were, indeed, many risks for gay people in 1980s Argentina, but a unilateral portrayal of gay culture based on discrimination, violence, and marginalization buttressed stigmatization and images of deviation.[24] Similarly, in 1985, during one of Jáuregui's first interviews as president of the CHA, a reporter from the magazine *Ahora* affirmed that homosexuality "might be normal" but questioned if it was "natural." He further asked Jáuregui if gays "respected" heterosexuals, suggesting gays could "force," "indoctrinate," and "harass" heterosexual men. The journalist also pondered if gays were "faithful" and if there were gays among priests and military men. When Jáuregui declared that people incorrectly viewed gays as "the devil," the journalist mockingly asked if, instead, they should be considered "angels."[25]

In the second half of the decade, the HIV crisis created a new interest in homosexuality, but the discourses became heavily medicalized and frequently condemning. An editorial in the CHA bulletin affirmed that AIDS represented for gays a double threat because it was not only a disease but also "an excellent excuse to put the crudest prejudice on display."[26] Honest press reports on the lives and suffering of gay people were scarce, while sensationalist accounts of death and isolation as well as panicky and reprimanding views on the role of the gay community in contracting and spreading the disease proliferated. The CHA complained that news titles like "Los normales también lo contraen" ("Normal People Catch It, Too") reaffirmed a pathological view of homosexuality that, connected to the HIV epidemic, categorized gays as a public danger.[27]

Figure 2.2. Carlos Jáuregui and Raúl Soria of the CHA on the cover of *Siete Días*, May 23–29, 1984.

Thus, throughout this period, there was nothing in the print press about homoeroticism comparable to the exploration of desire and the celebration of pleasure that was taking place in relation to heterosexuality. There was no real liberation, no equivalent honesty, and absolutely no joyfulness, only cautioned tolerance, nervous interest, and biased questions at best. Even more liberal publications were far from trusted and supportive allies. For example, the review in the magazine *Humor* of openly gay author Hermes Villordo's *La brasa en la mano* (1983), a novel about gay culture in the 1950s, maintained that the story was "hard to swallow" because of its graphic nature. And while the critic commended Villordo's bravery, he underlined that "he did not share his tastes."[28]

The CHA reacted by openly criticizing the press, even irreverent and alternative publications like *El Expreso Imaginario* and *Eroticón*, the latter of which featured itself as "the magazine that revolutionized sex in Argentina." The CHA argued that superficial discourses of tolerance, freedom, and modernity as well as unprecedented reporting on sex taboos could not really hide the fact that defamation and bias against gay people were as strong as in the recent past: "The common currency of 'liberated' media outlets consists of mixing up homosexuality, drugs, perversions and illness; they say they accept us, but the truth is they're just one step away from accusing us of being terrorists and clamoring for us to be taken away to concentration camps, just the way the press controlled by [José] López Rega was doing 10 years ago."[29] Furthermore, gay activists demanded not only objectivity and respect from the press but also social responsibility. The CHA affirmed that when covering police raids in gay bars and discos or the indiscriminate detention of gay men on the streets—which continued unchanged after the return to democracy, as examined in chapter 5—newspapers should openly condemn, not merely report, this form of unjustified persecution and harassment that only reinforced authoritarianism. Only then would the press be a true defender of democracy for all.[30]

For their part, publications such as health and men's magazines and adult comics ignored lesbianism and homosexuality completely. Even those periodicals that most profoundly defied conventions and propriety avoided same-sex relations. In fact, the silence was so profound that it spread to sections that could have more easily incorporated the subject, such as short fictional stories and readers' letters. Comic magazines occasionally published some stories with lesbian content, but this was done quite sporadically. Humor magazines such as *Sex Humor* followed the same trend. They showed extreme temerity in satirizing the sexuality of priests, pedophilia, zoophilia, and abortion among other taboo topics, but they disregarded homosexuality entirely. The absence of lesbianism reigned also in women's magazines, even those that most openly addressed risqué topics. When many readers condemned an exceptional article about lesbianism in *Mujer 10* and accused the staff of being lesbians, the editorial that followed was less focused on defending the article—and even less so on supporting lesbianism—and was instead more interested in vehemently clarifying that there were no lesbians on the staff.[31]

Lesbophobia and the consequent invisibility of lesbianism in mass culture was indeed stronger than in the case of homophobia. When in 1989, for example, gay singers Sandra Mihanovich and Celeste Carballo announced their tour with street posters that featured the cover of their LP—an innocuous portrayal of both women with Carballo resting her chin on Mihanovich's cheek—conservative critics blasted what they called "unhealthy exhibitionism," "an apology of lesbianism," "an invasion," "a glorification of deviation as a right," and "a proselytizing campaign that promotes wretchedness." Although the image was unexceptional, the sexual orientation of the singers made it a provocation. The author of a column in *La Prensa* affirmed that "although pathology has to do with this matter, those affected by it are far from unaccountable and certainly have no right to make a show of their suffering by throwing it in our faces and trying to make us believe that their abnormality is normal."[32]

Lesbophobia helps explain why even though women were the center of the cinematic *destape*, there were no movies on lesbianism or featuring prominent lesbian characters. Lesbian scenes were part of some of the classic *destape* movies but were infrequent and much less explicit than heterosexual sex scenes.[33] Same-sex scenes between women are more prevalent in emblematic *destape* films depicting life in women's prisons and all-girl boarding schools, such as *Sucedió en el internado* and *Correccional de mujeres*. These types of films reproduced common stereotypes in which lesbian sex is the result of women's forced socialization and coexistence rather than conscious choice. While the film heroines never engage in same-sex intercourse, the handful of lesbian secondary characters are always villains, manipulative, and otherwise vicious—the abusive jail guard, the sadistic prisoner, the cruel student, the perverted teacher—suggesting

Figure 2.3. Singers Marilina Ross and Sandra Mihanovich on the cover of
*Revista 10*, October 8, 1982.

Figure 2.4. Roberto (Carlos Calvo) begins a romantic relationship with his roommate Marcelo (Víctor Laplace) in *Adiós Roberto* (1985). Courtesy Museo del Cine Pablo Ducrós Hicken, Buenos Aires.

that even in an environment characterized by extreme maladjusted female behavior, only the most deviant engaged in same-sex relations. Remarkably, despite the predominant content of sexual violence against women that characterized these movies, lesbian sex is always consensual.

Although the cinematic portrayal of male homosexuality during the peak of the destape was also minimal, two movies focused on the subject. Yet contrary to the typical Argentine destape cinema, saturated with steamy heterosexual scenes, both were visually and discursively chaste. *Adiós Roberto* (Enrique Dawi, 1985) follows a newly separated young father of a small child who moves in with a gay writer with whom he starts a romantic and sexual relation that fills him with guilt. Roberto has visions about the disapproval of his parents, friends, former female lovers, and even the neighborhood priest. Although the film is centered on the relation between the two men, they never embrace, touch, or kiss in a sexual or romantic way, and the first sexual encounter is only obliquely implied. The end suggests that Roberto returns to his wife.[34]

*Otra historia de amor* (Américo Ortiz de Zárate, 1986) tells the story of a married business executive who develops feelings and later a clandestine relationship with a new employee. The film is a melodrama with a happy ending—although they lose their jobs and are socially condemned and discriminated against for their sexual orientation, the couple stays happily together. *Otra historia de amor* has only one kiss scene, in which the kiss is actually hidden by the close-up of a wine bottle. Interestingly, the scene with the most sexually suggestive content shows two female coworkers who are reading aloud a very graphic magazine article about techniques for performing oral sex on men. Sex between the main characters is only suggested, and although the men lay together naked, there is no openly sexual content in these scenes nor frontal nudity. This approach secured praise from critics, who applauded the "absolute elegance" of the film that addressed a "risqué topic" with "good taste and no outbursts," while Jáuregui celebrated it as "a dignified film" that showed gay men—educated, middle-class, and masculine—leading honorable lives.[35] Yet in 1988 the INC prohibited *Otra historia de amor* from being aired on national television. One of the members of the committee, which included representatives of Catholic and Jewish institutions, explained that the decision was based on the fact that "the issue of homosexuality and bisexuality is presented not as an anomaly but as a life choice." The film director Américo Ortiz de Zárate responded that, indeed, the reason for censorship was that the movie portrayed gay characters who lived their sexuality without restraint and guilt, and that homosexuality was not punished by disease, loneliness, or exile.[36]

On television, the absence of gay characters was prevalent. In telenovelas, which was one of the most oversexualized genres on television, for example, there were no gay characters or relations.[37] Comedies were an exception, most notably *Matrimonios y algo más*, a set of sketches about marital life populated by lascivious male characters and beautiful women in underwear. The most popular gay character, Huguito Araña, played by actor Hugo Arana, acted mostly as a presenter of the skits and interviewer of famous guests on the show. Huguito Araña was an over-the-top, glamorous, effeminate type who, despite mannerisms and constantly putting his foot in his mouth about his sexual preferences, denied being gay. Gay militants opposed these characters, arguing that television went from forbidding to ridiculing gay men, reducing them to stereotypical figures that homogenized and denigrated gay identity. The CHA argued that "the fag is a laughable creature: he did not exist, but now he does. That leads one to conclude that he is an offshoot of modernity, of new times; it could be said that he is the daughter of the *destape*, of degeneracy."[38] Interestingly, Arana also played *el groncho*,[39] the most popular character on the show, who happened to be the absolute opposite of Huguito. The *groncho* was an extremely *machista*, hypermasculine, and unrefined mechanic who, married to a high-class woman, boasted about his past conquests and sexual escapades as a bachelor when the couple fought. Therefore, *Matrimonio y algo más* distinctly reveals the contradiction, even in the "safe" context provided by humor and satire, between "the asexual sissy gay character" and "the extreme hypersexual heterosexual male character." Yet the over-population of Casanovas preying on stereotypical naive female characters that abounded in television comedies and soap operas did not reflect the new open and active discussion of female sexuality and women's sexual pleasure that was taking place in other spheres.[40]

## WOMEN'S SEXUAL SUBJECTIFICATION

In June 1983—six months before Alfonsín's inauguration—the magazine *La Semana* published a piece aptly titled "¿Argentinas siglo 19 o siglo 21?" ("Argentine Women, 19th or 21st century?"), by best-selling author Silvina Bullrich. Bullrich contended that Argentine women were still condemned to Hitler's three Ks—children, kitchen, and church (*kinder, küche, kirche*)—and correspondingly lacked any education or information on sexual matters. The writer, publicly defiant of gender conventions since her youth, asserted: "I remain heartbroken over the fact that anything related to sex gets censored," even marital sexuality.[41] Reflecting on her own experience, Bullrich affirmed: "What kept my first marriage going was our mutual intelligence and our love for culture. It was destroyed by what those phonies, hypocrites, and perverters of youth never even mention: our sexual incompatibility. It is, on the other hand, what brings normal men and women together, and what pulls them apart. Marriage is the only union, the only feeling based on physical attraction. No one marries their sibling."[42]

Bullrich argued that censorship and prejudices conspired against the achievement of a satisfying sex life, which was not only a fundamental requirement for the personal fulfillment of men and women but also the key to a happy marriage, and lamented the misinformation and silence that prevented individuals, and fundamentally women and the young, from enjoying their bodies and, ultimately, their lives to the fullest. Women, the writer concluded, were still reduced to dull domestic roles, and men were taught to "look for plump women who know how to make *milanesas*, not a partner both in the bedroom and in life's struggle."[43]

In fact, as a historian whose first book was on mid-twentieth-century Argentina, I was stunned by the resilience of extremely antiquated views on female sexuality in the 1980s and the long-standing suppression of sexual freedoms, sexual modernization, and women's rights in the country.[44] In the 1970s, the military continued an existing tradition that extolled the role of women as mothers—"good mothers" who raised supporters of the regime—to the detriment of all other identities, while repression, false moralism, and overimposed prudishness in the name of "Christian and Occidental" values substantially delayed and obscured the revelations, achievements, and conundrums of the sexual revolution.[45] This obscurantism pervaded most of the two thousand interviews about sexuality that sociologist Julio Mafud conducted with men and women between 1966 and 1988. In his volume on female sexuality, Mafud explained that Argentine women's sexual conduct had been traditionally determined by a "psychology of modesty," resulting from very conservative, informal sex information and principles that emphasized sex for reproductive purposes, equated virginity with perfection, and rejected and vilified female masturbation.[46] Correspondingly, sexologists in the return to democracy agreed that the average Argentine woman lacked knowledge of her anatomy and was inhibited by feelings of shame, embarrassed to explore her sexuality and express openly what she found pleasurable.[47]

Yet the destape changed public perceptions of female sexuality as well as women's access to sex information, launching a distinct women's destape. The print media employed the new freedom of expression to overtly portray heterosexual women as sexual beings entitled to and pursuers of sexual gratification while questioning deep-rooted and common stereotypes in the popular imagination, such as women experiencing sex as a chore, being exclusively motivated by reproductive goals, feeling anxious about their bodies, and being conformist and uninformed in the bedroom. In 1985, for example, actress and vedette Moria Casán made an argument quite different from Bullrich's two years earlier by affirming: "In the past, for example, the press used to say: 'How to keep your husband from falling in love with his secretary' and now it teaches you 'How to have six orgasms in half an hour.'" Casán suggested the middle-class status of the intended audience and referred to a recent past where women depended on men— both sexually and otherwise—and competed with one another for male attention, and where sex was present only implicitly in arguments about gender relations. In fact, the discussion of men's infidelity was framed in terms of love instead of sex. Casán revealed that, in contrast, after the return to democracy, the media focused on female sexual gratification, erased husbands, recuperated autoeroticism, and provided women with information in order to take action in the service of their sexual desires. The new female sexuality endorsed by the women's press was vibrant, goal-oriented, and venturesome, and the new woman who materialized from this process of sexual subjectification was confident, resourceful, and actively invested in her own pleasure more than in performing to keep men happy.[48]

Sex experts agreed that censorship in the media as well as the public emphasis on procreative sex in previous years had forced women into an "intuitive learning process" without access to accurate and honest information that would "teach them to like sex." As a case in point, journalist Alcira Bas recalled the criminal complaint against the newspaper *Diario Popular* during the last year of the dictatorship because it had published an article about women's sexual fantasies. In a meeting with the Ministry of Interior, the editor in chief responded to accusations of pornography—a crime under the penal code—by explaining that the piece was based on scientific evidence and had been written in consultation with psychologists.[49] Reflecting on this recent past, in 1984 an article about female orgasm in *Mujer 10* affirmed that women had been dependent on men to learn about sex and even about their own bodies, and thus men had imposed their own model of pleasure on women. Forced to trust men as sources of sexual knowledge, women had been left passive, ignorant, frustrated, and feeling unjustly inadequate.[50] Significantly, a poll conducted among women between twenty and fifty years of age revealed that more than 40 percent had problems reaching an orgasm.[51]

With a tone that was educational, nonjudgmental, encouraging, and open yet authoritative, the media promised to help heterosexual female readers be proud, happy, and accomplished in their sexuality. In the process, women's magazines contributed to a widespread "feminization of sex," reversing the traditional paradigm in which public discussion of sexual desires, performance, and agency almost exclusively pertained to men. Publications such as *Mujer 10*, *La mujer*, and *Claudia* filled their pages with a variety of sex topics as well as blunt photos and illustrations, thus transforming an editorial tradition dedicated to recipes, fashion, children, and occasional medical advice on "female health problems." *Vivir en pareja* (a supplement of health magazine *Vivir*) devoted each issue to themes such as preorgasmia, sex positions, and sex education, discussed by local sexologists, psychologists, and physicians. *Vivir* also published the popular *Diccionario del sexo*, which was not explicitly devoted to female sexuality but might have found its largest audience among women, who were the typical readers of the magazine. Similarly, *Adultos* published translations of classic sexology research by renowned foreign authors such as Helen Kaplan and Shere Hite as well as contributions by Argentine specialists, while *Sex Humor* issued "Investigación Especial," a popular serious thematic booklet in collaboration with the most important sexologists in the country.

Women's magazines celebrated sexual gratification as a significant component of women's personal realization. Sexual pleasure, an article in *Mujer 10* argued, was indeed as important for human life as food. Yet women had to fight archaic sexual ideologies that placed them as an object of pleasure expected to fulfill men's desires rather than as a desiring subject entitled to sexual satisfaction. Moreover, women had to contend with their lack of sex information and a traditional education that positioned the needs of others, in and out of bed, first. Thus, whether the article was on sex during pregnancy, body types, sex positions and sexual fantasies, anatomy, masturbation, or changes in sexual desire, women's search for— and, most importantly, the right to experience—pleasure dominated the discussion. An amusing symptom of this major trend is the way *Sex Humor* mocked traditional women's magazine *Para Ti* by publishing *Para Vos*, a parody of the popular publication in which the articles in all sections, from recipes and pets to horoscope and beauty, were about sex. Similarly, in 1986 *Sex Humor* laughed at the new fixation on female orgasm by arguing that *orgasmar*—an invented word that means to orgasm—had become a new and popular verb in everyday language.[52]

Indeed, orgasm became the central topic in women's magazines, contributing to make the 1980s the "decade of orgasmic preoccupation," to use the famous expression that American sexologist William Masters had coined to describe the 1960s in the United States.[53] In Argentina, the clitoris and the G-spot—which captured the popular imagination after the publication of the controversial international best seller *The G Spot and Other Recent Discoveries about Human Sexuality* (1982) by Alice Kahn Ladas, Beverly Whipple, and John D. Perry—became the most cited terms.[54] The vindication of clitoral orgasm that thrived in the press was a direct response to the misinformation and ignorance that still made it abnormal in the mid-1980s. In the film *Flores robadas en los jardines de Quilmes* (Antonio Ottone, 1985), for example, based on Jorge Asís's best-selling novel of the same name published in 1980 and set in the 1970s, Angélica (Alicia Zanca) apologizes to Rodolfo (Víctor Laplace) for having clitoral orgasms and confides in him that she has consulted several doctors to find a solution to "her problem." In another scene that similarly reaffirms her "deviancy," a former boyfriend calls her "frigid" and "a dyke" because of how she reaches climax.[55]

All women's magazines focused on sexuality extensively, but *Mujer 10*, born out of democracy in 1983, openly connected a full expression of female sexuality and a satisfying sex life with the new democratic context. The magazine asked women, "¿Es usted democrática consigo misma?" ("Are you Treating Yourself Democratically?") and affirmed that it was time women transferred the openness of postauthoritarian Argentina to themselves—to their minds, bodies, and hearts—to eradicate preconceptions and become free to fulfill their wishes, from work to sex.[56] *Mujer 10*, which promoted a campaign and signature petition in favor of the divorce law, spoke to modern women who materialized as a result of the newly gained freedoms and whose modernity was largely determined by their uninhibited sexuality. These were women who declared: "We talk about sex. We say clitoris out loud and try not to flush. We are concerned with the orgasm, with a fulfilling sexual relationship, with masturbation, and with pleasure."[57]

# MUJER ES PODER

Poder pensar. Poder hablar. Poder modificar la realidad.
Poder equivocarse. Poder empezar de nuevo. Poder gozar. Poder crecer.
Querer. Querer es poder.

Estamos en el decenio de la mujer, y se celebra, este 8 de marzo, el Día Internacional de la Mujer. La mujer, en el mundo y en la Argentina, está ocupando un espacio distinto del que le habían adjudicado. Está peleando por ese espacio nuevo. Para hacerlo, en nuestro país tuvo que vencer muchos obstáculos: primero, junto a los hombres, quebró la dictadura militar; después encaró la lucha contra la represión en todos sus niveles, finalmente no cedió a la censura y tampoco eligió el esnobismo, ni el político ni el farandulero ni el social. Eligió, simplemente, la democracia. De esa elección, de ese querer, de ese crecer, de ese poder, nació MUJER. Que en el número de esta semana le propone:

## La convivencia: ¿arruina el amor o lo enriquece?

Una profunda investigación con reportajes a especialistas y a parejas, con testimonios y análisis. Los peligros y las ventajas de convivir. ¿Se puede en realidad ir hacia una nueva forma de pareja?

## La depresión se cura

Excepcional nota científica. Médicos y psicólogos coinciden en afirmar que la enfermedad que afecta a un gran número de mujeres puede curarse con los tratamientos adecuados, neurológicos y psicológicos.

## Súper ofertas para escolares

Todo lo que necesitan sus hijos para empezar las clases, a los mejores precios, en todo el país.

Aparece los martes y se agota

## El sexo y la Iglesia

Las relaciones prematrimoniales, la masturbación, las relaciones extramatrimoniales. Cómo analizan teólogos y sacerdotes estos temas. La Iglesia es, a veces, mucho más permisiva que los laicos.

### ORGASMO MASCULINO

## Los gritos sexuales del hombre

Escrita por un hombre, esta nota intenta describir un fenómeno hasta ahora poco investigado. ¿Cómo es el orgasmo masculino? ¿Qué siente el hombre durante la eyaculación? ¿Qué significan sus gritos, si se anima a gritar?

Una publicacion de ⊙Editorial Perfil

Figure 2.5. "Woman Is Power." *Mujer 10* ads celebrated the new empowerment of women. *Libre*, March 6, 1984.

*Mujer 10*'s discourse was implicitly empowering: it promoted women's entitlement and ability to experience sexual pleasure and desire, portrayed as a long overdue privilege women should now advocate for and achieve, and endorsed knowledge of the body and sex education as personal responsibilities. The magazine commended sexual women who were informed, proactive, and had initiative in the bedroom because this was an indication that they possessed these traits, which were fundamental in the new democratic spring, in life and in politics. A 1984 article argued that men felt disoriented when women communicated and experienced their sexual desires freely as much as when they asserted their rights in the public sphere. Moreover, the author equated a sexually liberated and active woman with "an intellectually advanced woman" but warned readers that this was a social type easily perceived as a threat by most men.[58] For example, *Mujer 10* argued that many men prohibited their wives from buying the magazine. Yet women did not give in; not only did they purchase it, but they also shared it with girlfriends and daughters.[59]

In an article in feminist journal *alfonsina*, journalist María Moreno argued that, in contrast to traditional women's magazines such as *Para Ti* and *Vosotras*, newcomer *Mujer 10* "has managed to imagine a woman with a vocation other than pushing the pedal on the Singer [sewing machine] until her death. Or maybe they have realized that a female worker is more productive if they are looking out for her orgasms." Moreno affirmed that the most important contribution of *Mujer 10*, with its numerous articles on female pleasure, orgasm, and sexual fantasies—content that the military regime would have considered "subversive"—was not only positioning sex over home life, fashion, and motherhood as the central topic of its pages but also liberating female readers from guilt over their sexuality and from ideas of sexual abnormality and deviation.[60]

Publications like *Mujer 10* also contributed to denounce the double moral standard, common in the destape press, and the stereotyping of the new sexual woman as a menace. A satisfying, active sex life and sexual experimentation outside marriage was not only expected of a man but also turned him into a "Don Juan," experienced and proficient in bed and thus desirable among women. In contrast, the same sex life and experimentation made a woman *descocada* ("loose") and ultimately socially condemned and unwanted, stigmatized by fantasies of hypersexuality based on her multiorgasmic capacity and sexual endurance.[61] This double standard was openly evident in *Libre*, an icon of the destape press, whose articles on the sex lives of celebrities wholeheartedly celebrated men for their womanizing, infidelities, and even for fathering children they did not recognize; extolled their sexual potency and reputation as irresistible lovers; and discussed their conquests as collectible trophies. Yet *Libre* vulgarly condemned and ridiculed women known or suspected of having had several partners, labeling them as "sexual predators." One of those articles, for example, praised world middleweight boxing champion Carlos Monzón, defined as "an Argentina stud" because he "leaves women up against the ropes, knocked out by his virility or who knows what," while describing singer Ruth Durante as a "devourer" and "voracious," and crudely disparaging her because she "had more soccer players than the AFA [Argentine Soccer Association]."[62]

*Libre* extended this characterization to ordinary women. Lifeguards complained that women "used" them as "sex toys" and affirmed that "pretty chicks are easier because they have had a longer career in love"; a butcher maintained that married women harassed him and that one "raped" him at her home when he was making a delivery; and an article about "summer trends" argued that female adolescents were promiscuous and their middle-aged mothers vacationing on the coast seduced underaged boys while their husbands stayed in the city to work. Given the double standards regularly advocated in the magazine, if these had been men, the tone would have been triumphant, but being women, it was condemning and demeaning.[63] *Sex Humor* caricatured what *Libre* reported as "serious news" by portraying women as "man-eaters," sexually aggressive and manipulative, and eager readers of manuals that taught them how to seduce, "exploit," and "discard" men who, in turn, felt quite dumbfounded by the *destape femenino* (the female destape) and their own new status as "sexual objects."[64]

A sign of the changing times was the film *Los amores de Laurita* (Antonio Ottone, 1986), which, based on the best-selling novel of the same name by Ana María Shua (1984), would have been unthinkable just a few years earlier. By placing a pregnant woman as the main character of an erotic narrative, Shua not only challenged the silence on pregnancy that had characterized classic erotic literature but also the social, cultural, and gender canons that considered pregnancy and sexual desire to be incompatible and the pregnant body as taboo.[65] In an interview in 1984, Shua affirmed that despite the immediate and remarkable success of the book and the way women identified themselves with the protagonist in the new context of open discussion of female sexuality, many readers expressed that they found the presence and description of an orgy, an abortion, a rape, and a scene of autoeroticism involving the eight-month-pregnant protagonist truly "repugnant."[66]

A tale of Laura's sexual and romantic relations since her teen years and of her search for erotic fulfillment at distinct moments of her life and with different partners, the movie ends with a pregnant Laura (Alicia Zanca) masturbating naked in the bathroom while saying aloud phrases like "mothers don't fuck" and "girls who screw a lot don't get married." These were, in fact, the types of archaic sexual ideologies that *Mujer 10* determinedly contested by proposing that sex was different from love and reproduction; women could be both good mothers and sexual, defying the traditional dichotomy between "saintly mothers" and "sexy women"; and sexual gratification was important for a strong marriage and during pregnancy. Equally important, *Mujer 10* underlined that there was no typical recipe for sexual pleasure, thus "women have to ask for what they want, what they like best. It is up to every woman to discover her own timing, rhythm, body, and degree of excitement."[67] According to Susana Torres Molina, author of *Dueña y Señora* (1983), this vision was, in fact, the reason why her collection of short erotic tales about women and narrated by female characters became an instant best seller. In the stories—including the experience of a dark-room orgy and sex with a stranger on a beach— Torres Molina argued that "female characters enjoy true pleasure, without inhibitions, joyfully. . . . These are stories where a woman decides what will happen; she is no longer a passive being to whom things happen."[68]

This new sexual woman also found a place in the humor magazine *Sex Humor* and comic magazine *Sex Humor Ilustrado*, both of which offer fine examples of how the destape redefined traditional understandings of female sexuality and incorporated a novel women's perspective. "La fiera" (*Sex Humor*, 1987–89), a beast or wild animal and also slang for "the ugly one," was a parody that broke with several conventions at once. Against traditional female stereotypes for whom female beauty was the measure of social and personal worth, a means of success and of a gratifying sex life, and a weapon for attracting men, la fiera has an unpleasant face and a well-proportioned but average body. In the world of adult comics, populated by statuesque, voluptuous, glamorous, and sexy characters, her unattractiveness made her quite peculiar. Most importantly, la fiera is all about sex. Yet she humorously challenged stereotypical characters in adult comics that depicted women as sexual objects, always ready, willing, docile, silent, more props than subjects. La fiera, always aroused, upfront, and determined in her endeavor, seduces all men—the mailman, the doctor, the electrician, the hairdresser, the fireman, the new neighbor—who cross her path. Like traditional male cartoon characters, she only cares about sex, and like them, she is uninterested in dating, promises, or love. La fiera is a desiring subject for whom sex is fun, casual, free, adventurous, and noncommittal. She is assertive, outspoken, and resolute even in the most bizarre situations, such as her sexual experiences with a tightrope walker, an alien, and Santa Claus! Interestingly, her varied sexual adventures never included a female partner.[69]

Finally, la fiera was original because she was authored by a woman in a world dominated by men. Maitena Burundarena, better known as Maitena, was one of only a handful of women cartoonists in the 1980s and one of the few who wrote her own scripts.[70] In an interview in 2016, Maitena affirmed that la fiera was her reaction against the machismo of the comic world in which female characters were sexually "used and discarded"; her "horny female hunter," only motivated by pleasure, was an anomaly. As much as the character, the artist was, in turn, accused of being a "*hembrista*," a "man-hater" who objectified and disdained men.[71]

During this period, Maitena created two other characters that similarly altered conventional sexual stereotypes. "Coramina" (*Sex Humor Ilustrado*, 1986–87), an erotic comic strip based on the sexual escapades of a beautiful young woman, lacks the humor and caricaturesque tone of "La fiera," but her protagonist is as sexually assertive, uninhibited, and audacious. Maitena offers her version of female eroticism by repositioning the heterosexual woman as the one who desires and whose fantasies dominate the story. The stories always revolve around Coramina's sexual experiences—exciting, satisfying, and heterosexual with the exception of some threesomes—and focus on female desire and pleasure. With "El langa" (*Sex Humor Ilustrado*, 1988)—a *lunfardo* term that means *galán*, a handsome man—Maitena parodied traditional male stereotypes but without the crude content or eroticism of the stories led by her unconventional female characters. An office worker, el langa is overconfident, a bit arrogant but

Figure 2.6. In "La fiera," Maitena challenged stereotypical views of female sexuality in adult comics. *Sex Humor*, May 1988.

kind, and always chasing women and trying to have sex with them. Despite the tales of conquests he tells his friends, and his numerous and frantic attempts to seduce women, el langa is a complete failure. He always ends up conned and manipulated by the beautiful women who successfully resist his sexual advancements but make him pay for expensive nights out, rob him, and sell him things he does not need. Thus, "El langa" wittingly reverses the classic stereotypes in adult comics: the irresistible, dominant, and unbeatable lothario and the sexually available woman, both of which overwhelmingly characterized *Fierro* and *Historietas Sex*, the two most popular comic magazines of erotic and sexually explicit content in the return to democracy.[72]

Maitena's portrayal of sex was cheerful, pleasant, and fun, with the exception of "Barrio Chino" (1989), a six-part story published in magazine *Fierro* that includes a brutal scene of the rape of a woman who was abducted by a gang. In 2016, Maitena believed that the violence she portrayed in "Barrio Chino"—and that was not a requirement of the script authored by Juan Marini—was an instinctive, not totally intentional, way of processing the information about human rights violations during the dictatorship that had begun circulating in the media. With her work, Maitena was engaging with the darkness and savagery of the previous years that were now becoming more and more apparent. However, despite its motivations, "Barrio Chino" did not address sexual violence against women kidnapped and imprisoned by the military dictatorship. In this, it was part of a common, larger cultural pattern since the subject was largely purged from the media in the return to democracy. Unexpectedly, though, the destape offered a remarkable means to help it surface in the collective imagination.[73]

## SEXUAL VIOLENCE AGAINST WOMEN

At first sight, the common denominator of the cinematic destape is sex, but a closer look reveals that the most pervasive element of destape movies is sexual violence against women. Although sexual violence is a usual component of sexploitation cinema, in destape films, it is intrinsically connected to the specific cultural and historical conditions of production. Furthermore, because of sexual violence, the cinematic destape was essentially different in tone from the destape in the print press and on television, where sex was festive and liberating, and in women's maga-zines, where it was occasionally empowering. Even though women in magazines and on television shows were usually objectified, they were rarely violated. When present, violence was frequently masked under the veil of humor, innocence, or double meaning. In 1984, for example, Tía María liqueur shocked audiences with a commercial that showed a semi-naked couple in bed (the woman older than the man) who erotically called themselves "stupid." A year later, the same advertising agency upped the ante in a much-debated—and finally canceled—commercial of American Club piña colada that showed several attractive women with a black eye saying suggestively to the camera, "*dame otra piña*" (throw me other punch / give me another *piña*), an allusion to the beverage as well as to a blow to the face. The commercial was heavily criticized by the progressive and feminist press for its depiction of women asking to be physically abused in a sexualized context and thus for suggesting that violence is a requirement for female pleasure.[74]

On television, the most significant illustration of sexualized violence was *Amo y señor*, the most iconic destape telenovela, which told the story of Alonso Miranda (Arnaldo André), a powerful and rich man of humble origins, the big shot of the imaginary town suitably named Puerto Caliente (Hot Port), who falls for Victoria Escalante (Luisa Kuliok), the beautiful daughter of an aristocratic but broke family. Compared with *Rosa de lejos* (1980), the most successful telenovela aired during the dictatorship, which achieved record audience numbers, *Amo y señor* seems even more incendi-ary. In *Rosa de lejos*, Rosa María Ramos (Leonor Benedetto), an illiterate young woman from the provinces who comes to Buenos Aires to work as a housekeeper, becomes pregnant early on in the story, but the tenor was extremely prudish, and the story lacked any sexual or erotic components. Remarkably, just a few years later, Benedetto would become one of the emblematic stars of the destape for her leading role in the iconic destape blockbuster *Atrapadas*.

Radically departing from *Rosa de lejos*, *Amo y señor* drew record ratings for the unprecedented bed scenes, the erotic content, and the skimpily clad actresses who appeared at 1:00 p.m. daily. The opening credits, for example, showed Kuliok bathing in nothing but a see-through short white shirt. Most importantly, *Amo y señor* scandalized audiences for the fre-quency with which Alonso slapped Victoria strongly across the face. These slaps cannot be likened with the extreme and sadistic violence of destape movies, but they were a shocking novelty for the genre and for television. Furthermore, they naturalized and played down men's use of physical force to discipline and control women. This, according to the magazine *Somos*'s television critic, was not a deterrent for female viewers. In his review, the critic affirmed that "any woman (whether she is an electronic engineer or a maid by the hour) is dying to know what will happen tomorrow between Victoria Escalante and Alonso Miranda," an argument that infantilizes the female audience and portrays female viewers as dismissive and uncritical of the mistreatment of women.[75]

Television and advertising depictions of cruelty against women paled in comparison with those found in films. The cinematic destape is the most notable illustration of the violent sexual objectification and victimization of women in the media. Verbal aggression such as the manager calling his secretary *putita* (little whore) in *Los gatos* or Laurita's (Alicia Zanca) boyfriend calling her *puta* (whore) as he assaults her in *Los amores de Laurita*; the groping, molestation, and beating of prostitutes and showgirls in *Tacos altos* (Sergio Renán, 1985), *El desquite* (Juan Carlos Desanzo, 1983), and *Correccional de mujeres* (Emilio Vieyra, 1986); the sexual abuse of mother and daughter in front of their family in *La búsqueda* (Juan Carlos Desanzo, 1985); and the vicious torture and rape of Cecilia (Edda Bustamante) by an ex-boyfriend in *En retirada* (Juan Carlos Desanzo, 1984) are just a few examples of the brutal violence against women depicted in destape blockbusters. The films underline the powerlessness of women and their vulnerability but also the horrifying fate of "bad women," that is, prostitutes, criminals (murderers, robbers, drug mules), drug addicts, and unruly teenagers, who were the prototypical female characters in destape movies, and even the sexually liberated and adventurer protagonist of *Los amores de Laurita* and the "seductive" lolita in *Luna caliente* (Roberto Denis, 1985).

Despite the thin story lines, the clichés, the trite villains, and the absurd plot twists that populated most destape movies, sexual violence against women follows a recurring pattern. It may be, depending on the plot, based on retribution, punishment, opportunity, or pure hatred, but ultimately, it is always meant to break the women's spirits, to put them in their "proper place," to set standards of control over newcomers. In destape films, violence is, first, a method for teaching women a lesson and, second, is the lesson itself. Yet the lesson is ampler than the plot requirements of the particular films, exceeds them, and expresses the voice of the perpe- trators articulating a simple but sinister claim: "We do this because we can." Furthermore, there is no state nor social institutions to protect and impart justice, which becomes the task of victims who turn to retaliation.

Sexual violence in these films is the rawest expression of male dom- inance over women, an engulfing, inescapable menace in suffocating and dispiriting scenarios. As crude, primal mechanisms of male power, rape, abuse, torture, and molestation are essential forms of what Car- ole Sheffield has called "sexual terrorism," a system based on a type of hostile masculinity that maintains male supremacy through actual or implied violence.[76] Both the reality and the threat of force, humiliation, and pain uphold men's systematic control and domination over women. This is evident, for example, in the violent rape of a drug mule before she is forced into a prostitution ring in *Los gatos*; the brutal gang rape—led by her former boyfriend—of Luisa (Susú Pecoraro), a prostitute visiting her family after leaving for Buenos Aires with dreams, soon shattered, of becoming a singer in *Tacos altos*; and the sadistic gang rapes of a new teacher and another young woman in front of her boyfriend in *Sucedió en el internado*. It is also represented in films such as *Correccional de mujeres*, *Los corruptores* (Teo Kofman, 1987), and *Las esclavas* (Carlos Borcosque, 1987), which center on sex trafficking and sex slavery. Interestingly, in a context of cheerful and festive sexuality, destape films were the only realm in which depiction of sexual violence against women was significant. As a result and even though they were far from being feminist projects, these films peculiarly intersected with feminists, the only social sector drawing attention to the subject and openly mobilizing against it in the return to democracy, a theme analyzed in chapter 5.

Remarkably, abused and sexually objectified female characters in de- stape films retaliate. Whether this somehow resonated with the rise of local feminism is difficult to assess, but film theorists such as Carol Clover, Jacinta Reed, and Hilary Neroni have argued that 1970s and 1980s Amer- ican horror and rape-revenge films, where women turned from victims to avengers, can be seen as a historical result of the empowering messages of second-wave feminism, or, as Mary Ann Doane has affirmed, "as a symp- tom of male fears about feminism."[77] In any case, the female leads in these destape blockbusters refuse to live in fear and danger, or to let rapists, killers, and torturers go unpunished. Silvia (Leonor Benedetto) kills all members of the band that smuggled drugs into the prison and women out, and that murdered her sister in *Atrapadas*; Laura (Edda Bustamante) kills the drug traffickers who murdered her boyfriend and forced her and other inmates into prostitution in *Correccional de mujeres*; the students in *Sucedió en el internado* use hot coals to burn the genitals of the gang of rapists; and Patricia (Andrea Tenuta), the young woman abused by the same gang that destroyed her family, brutally kills all of them in *La búsqueda*. The scenes are gory, extravagant, and overdone, but they translate the humiliation and suffering experienced by the women at the hands of their tormentors. Although the female characters end up empowered, revenge is not only in their name but also, and most frequently, in the name of others. It is not necessarily retaliation because they have been raped, tortured, and abused, but in most cases, the women are avenging someone else—a boyfriend, a sister, their family, a friend. Yet, in so doing, they challenge traditional scripts of female victimhood and conventional representations of violence as extraneous to femininity.[78]

In destape films, there are instances in which women inflict violence over other women, but they mostly do it on behalf of or in collaboration with men, as shown by the women who control the prostitutes in *Los gatos* and *Las esclavas*, the prison guards in *Atrapadas* and *Correccional de mujeres*, or the group of female students who help the gang abuse their victims in *Sucedió en el internado*. Yet in the cases in which violence by women against women happens independent from male intervention, it is never sexual. There are no destape films in which women are sexually abused by other women. The absence is remarkable in the case of classic destape blockbusters such as *Atrapadas* and *Correccional de mujeres*. Although both are populated by numerous clichés of traditional sexploitation depictions of sexual violence against women in prison, the occasional scene of lesbian sex is always consensual. And while sex between women is sometimes contrived by needs of a vulnerable inmate for protection or material benefits, it is never violent or sadistic. The most famous scene in *Atrapadas*—and repetitively commented on by the press at that time—shows the prison bigshot Susana (Camila Perissé), who is a lesbian, leading a group of women who take newcomer Silvia (Leonor Benedetto) to the showers in the middle of the night where they savagely beat her. After the attack, Susana urinates, standing over Silvia. The act reproduces a clichéd gesture

Figure 2.7. *Atrapadas* (1984), starring Leonor Benedetto, was one of the most iconic *destape* films. Film poster from author's personal collection.

of male humiliation over other men and reinforces the masculine side of the lesbian character. Yet Susana, who is otherwise cruel and ferocious, never sexually assaults Silvia nor any other inmate. Similarly, the lesbian characters in *Sucedió en el internado*, a malicious student and a wicked teacher who terrorize and plot against faculty and students alike, never perpetrate sexual violence over women, and the lesbian prison guard who trades drugs for sex in *Correcional de mujeres* never forces or bullies inmates into the exchange.

If sexual violence is a common component of sexploitation and thus destape movies abide by genre expectations, there is an element that is distinct and speaks of Argentina's postdictatorial context. Iconic destape movies relate to the dictatorship and, implicitly or explicitly, deliberately or unintentionally, address or echo the sexual violence experienced by female prisoners in clandestine detention centers.[79] Diana Taylor has drawn attention to the extreme sexualization of torture in these centers—suffered by both male and female prisoners—and how torturers rehearsed on the individual bodies, which were made docile and easily "penetrable," the violence and feminization that the regime was inflicting upon the entire social body. Frank Graziano has explained this eroticization of the Argentine military's repression as an aberration of the Christian interrelation of sin, the flesh, and violent atonement. Graziano argues that in defense of the Christian canon, the military regime denied psychosexual impulses—evident, for example, in the censorship of sex content in the media, the opposition of sex education, and the condemnation and prohibition of contraception. These impulses, however, did not disappear but were diverted through torture. In its crusade for Western civilization, the regime ignored the extreme contradiction between the supposed defense of Christian values and the systematic abduction, torture, rape, and execution of citizens.[80]

In the return to democracy, the "horror show" saturated the press with its explicit and disturbing narratives about the torture and murder of prisoners during the dictatorship, but sexual violence against women and men was eschewed. The sexual abuse and rape of detainees was revealed in 1984 by *Nunca Más*, the report elaborated by the CONADEP (Comisión Nacional sobre la Desaparición de Personas) after an investigation on human rights violations, and once again in 1985, when it was uncovered in testimonies during the trial of the *juntas*. However, sexual violence in clandestine detention centers remained somehow buried. In many cases, victims themselves silenced their suffering and denunciations to priori-tize the fight to do justice for the desaparecidos, due to feelings of shame and guilt, the fear that they would bear the burden of proof, and because they had not yet come to terms with their particular experiences.[81] The inadequacies of the Argentine legal system to prosecute sexual crimes and the lack of recognition that, in the context of the dictatorship, they were indeed human rights violations—rape was codified as part of the definition of crimes against humanity in the Rome Statute of the Interna-tional Criminal Court in 1998—further discouraged victims from coming forward. Furthermore, the Full Stop Law (1986), which mandated the end of the investigation and prosecution of individuals accused of political violence during the dictatorship; the Law of Due Obedience (1987), which exempted military subordinates from prosecution under the assumption that they were only carrying out orders; and the *indultos* (1989–90), the executive pardons granted by President Carlos Menem to those previous-ly convicted, paralyzed all attempts to gain justice until the laws were annulled by Congress in 2003. For these reasons, women survivors have started to openly relate their stories of sexual abuse in clandestine deten-tion only in the past decade, followed by scholars who have just recently begun to explore the subject from legal, gender, historical, sociological, and psychoanalytical perspectives.[82]

Compared with the academic, public, and media silence on sexual violence in clandestine detention centers that characterized the 1980s, the references, associations, and allusions to the subject in destape films are quite unanticipated, and perhaps for this reason largely ignored by film scholars studying cinematic narratives about the dictatorship. In some way, the exploitation genre, based on lurid content and freed from censorship, allowed for the explicit and crude portrayal of sexualized vio-lence, content that other film genres only approached indirectly and more discreetly, if approached at all. As film scholar Eric Schaefer has affirmed, adult films that have been traditionally disparaged and marginalized be-cause of their display of "deviant" subjects are, in many contexts, the only motion pictures that deal with controversial topics in a direct fashion.[83] In Argentina, both commercial and auteur postdictatorial films that specifi-cally focused on the repression during the military regime barely depicted life and death in detention camps. And, when they did, films generally refrained from direct references or explicit depictions of sexual violence against women, or men for that matter. A clear example is *La noche de los lápices* (Héctor Olivera, 1986), which tells the real-life story of the abduction and confinement of ten students from La Plata in 1976, six of whom were disappeared. The film, the first and only one from the period to locate the story almost completely in a detention center, graphically portrays the ruthless torture of the male detainees, particularly the protagonist, but only slightly conveys the rape and sexual abuse of the women. In one scene, one of the abducted young women is groped by a guard; in another, a young woman briefly reveals she had been raped.[84]

A few months before the opening of the Oscar-winning drama *La historia oficial* (Luis Puenzo, 1985), about the illegal adoption of the child of desaparecidos, *En retirada* was not only the first film about the dictatorship but also the first to depict its viciousness by exposing the rape and torture of a woman. *En retirada* is the ultimate example of what film scholars have identified as the *policial post-proceso*, a genre that portrays the paramilitary as protagonist. The film examines the retreat of Ricardo "el oso" (Rodolfo Ranni), a member of a *grupo de tareas* (task force) "unemployed" after the return to democracy.[85] In the most brutal scene of the movie, Ricardo viciously beats, rapes, and tortures his ex-girlfriend Cecilia (Edda Bustamante). In the attack—triggered by jealousy—Ricardo recreates a torture session to extract information from detainees in clandestine detention centers during the dictatorship, a terrifying combination of sexual and state terrorism. When Cecilia, naked and severely hurt from the bashing, almost faints due to the pain and does not respond to his questions, Ricardo uses the bed metal frame as a *parrilla* for torture, ties Cecilia's feet and hands to the bars of the bed, and improvises an electric prod with a table lamp in the room. "So you don't want to talk, you goddamn slut," shouts Ricardo over the loud music he plays to cover Cecilia's screams, and then he rapes her. Similarly, the gang that robs, beats, kills, and rapes in *La búsqueda* is also made up of former paramilitaries, this time operating as guns-for-hire in the new democracy. The band destroys a family by murdering the father, traumatizing the young son, and sexually abusing the mother and daughter. In these films, as in the cases of victims kidnapped by the military during the dictatorship, "torture happens not because it must but because it can."[86]

Both *Atrapadas*, which is set in 1980 and refers explicitly to the military in power, and *Correccional de mujeres* also resonate with the crimes against women during the dictatorship. In clear reference to the military regime, the criminal band in *Atrapadas* kidnaps, molests, and kills the protagonist's teenage sister and leaves her dead body on the street while affirming: "No problem. They'll blame the subversives." Focused on life in women's prisons, both films depict sex traffickers smuggling women outside the penitentiary and then back in. The women are forced to attend parties and nightclubs, socialize at dinners, and have sex with men, and are then returned to prison afterward. This echoes a common and surreal practice that the military had in the clandestine detention centers, most infamously the one housed in the Escuela Superior de Mecánica de la Armada (ESMA; Mechanics School of the Navy), where repressors took female prisoners whom they tortured and abused out for dinner and to nightclubs. Victims recall the upsetting effects that this extremely disturbing form of psychological torment had on them, as they were obliged to feign compliance while hanging out with the very same men who mistreated them on a daily basis.[87] In representing or alluding to the sexual crimes of the dictatorship, destape films appear quite similar to the way feminist cultural critic Laura Kipnis has defined pornography, that is, as a historically constructed medium for "confronting audiences with exactly those contents that are exiled from sanctioned speech, from mainstream culture and political discourse."[88] For all other sex contents that Argentines were willing and ready to discuss without euphemisms, vastly and in the open, they had the press.

## SEX FORA

Reflecting on the state-enforced and self-inflicted silence that prevailed during the dictatorship, journalist and writer Marcos Aguinis maintained that "we had grown accustomed to getting by on little air, to read what the censors had authorized, to watch tedious television, to stay quiet. Above all else, to stay quiet."[89] With the redemocratization, Argentines recovered their lost voice and used it to talk about topics that had been expunged from public debate. Regarding sex, they talked with sexologists, psychologists, friends, and partners, as well as on radio programs and television shows such as *Veinte Mujeres*, *Polémica del amor*, and *¿Qué sabe usted de sexo?*, where they could openly ask questions and get information.

Yet the print press experienced the most radical transformation by becoming a prevalent public platform for the exploration of sex matters. Periodicals offered different spheres of participation for readers: polls; letters to the editor; the *consultorio sexológico* (sexology clinic), where readers sent their questions; personal testimonies about sex experiences; as well as erotic short stories, personal ads, and the photos section, to which individuals contributed their own suggestive images.[90] At the most basic level, these readers' sections established sex as an important, debatable, and popular topic of social interest. They also confirmed a demand for sex knowledge from the audience and naturalized sex information and education, making it both proper and unthreatening. Furthermore, they ratified publications' new status as an arena for participation, dissemination, and convergence, one that listened to ordinary people and endorsed their interests. Just four months after the magazine's launch, and stunned by the popular response, *Adultos*'s editor in chief thanked readers for the voluminous correspondence and affirmed:

> This overwhelming desire to communicate reveals something more than the end to a period in which our sexuality was repressed. It is also indicative of a serious and genuine interest in this fundamental topic. Our readers—as the letters they send prove—comprise an ample social spectrum that includes adults of all ages. They are notably frank, something we never would have suspected, and show true enthusiasm and willingness to learn and teach— questions, suggestions, queries, testimonies of experiences of their own and those of others, things they have lived and dreamed—all of you have provided *Adultos* with rich material that we have done our best to condense into these pages and those to come.[91]

Publications further reaffirmed and celebrated a climate of democracy and freedom when, beyond their pages, they organized face-to-face events for the discussion of sexuality. *La Mujer* is a good example of the sponsoring and organization of talks, movie exhibits followed by Q&A sessions, roundtable talks, debates, and lectures about different aspects of women's lives with a particular emphasis on female sexuality. Later, the supplement reported on the events in detailed articles.[92] Publications thus provided citizens with public platforms to reclaim their right to speak out, communicate, reach out, ask questions, and share opinions and experiences about sex, reversing the passivity and indifference that had flourished during the military dictatorship. These new fora facilitated the rise of what media and communication expert Brian McNair has termed "striptease culture," which involves common people talking about sex and revealing details of their sexual conduct, feelings, and bodies—a form of confession that, as Michel Foucault showed, has been the most prominent mechanism for the production of discourses and knowledge of sex.[93]

Because it was mainly created by ordinary individuals rather than professionals, this striptease culture was highly democratic and nonhierarchical. Although most publications relied on sex therapists and sexologists to answer questions and conduct and interpret surveys, the main components of the striptease culture—the inquiries from readers, their answers to polls, the fiction they wrote, the anecdotes they told, and the photos they shared—promoted the construction of a collective and nonspecialized sex archive powered by the winds of egalitarianism and openness that picked up after the fall of the dictatorship. This sex archive resulted from what Guillermo O'Donnell called "horizontal voice," which surfaced when, in the return to democracy, individuals recuperated the right to freely and fearlessly address others, frequently based on the belief of shared interests, ideas, or goals. Although O'Donnell used "horizontal voice" as a precondition to explain the rise of political collective identities, it is also a useful category to describe the type of egalitarian social communication on sex issues taking place in the media. Collaborative and uncensored, this horizontal voice that spoke about sexuality is a remarkable example of the reversal of the extreme privatization of personal concerns and life under the military dictatorship.[94]

One of the most ubiquitous tools of the striptease culture promoted by the destape were polls. From conservative general interest magazines such as *Somos* to the feminist *La Mujer*; from the audacious *Sex Humor* and *Destape* to the cultural journal *El Porteño*; from men's and women's magazines such as *Hombre* and *Mujer 10* to the sex journal *Adultos*, periodicals were obsessed with surveying what Argentines thought about sex and did in their bedrooms. Local surveys provided the necessary material for homegrown conclusions about local sexual behavior anchored to the particularities of recent Argentine history, especially the last dictatorship. This was truly a novelty when compared to the translated articles and sex poll results from Europe and the United States published especially in the 1960s.[95]

For sexologists, who were eager to ride the wave of sexual awakening promoted by the destape in order to carve out a differentiated professional space and boost social recognition, local polls were key to their contribution to a "national diagnosis" of sexuality, that is, the identification of "specific Argentine" problems and concerns, and their educational role among ordinary readers. Polls promoted a nationalistic redefinition of the country's sexual culture through a process of collective self-discovery and emancipation from sex knowledge elaborated abroad. In his introduction to *1ra Encuesta sobre Sexualidad y Pareja,* a book that published the results of a poll sponsored by *Sex Humor* and conducted by the Centro de Educación, Terapia e Investigación en Sexualidad (CETIS; Center for Education, Therapy, and Research on Sexuality), a pioneering research, educational, and treatment center founded in the return to democracy, its codirector sexologist León Roberto Gindin affirmed:

> Why is a survey on sexuality necessary in our country? We know that there has not been a serious, reliable survey on sexual habits and behaviors among couples in Argentina in the past few years—and probably never. We have based our knowledge on "old reports"—which is not to underestimate them, they are simply old: Kinsey (1950s), Hite (end of the 1960s)—that belong to another culture, a different path, and other possibilities for sexual development. And with a particular difference: these were done in countries where there was no repression of the media, no media outlets forced to go underground in order to convey information on sexuality.[96]

Topics, methods, and the depth of the studies varied to include general polls asking men and women questions ranging from the age of first sexual encounter to number of sexual intercourses per week; surveys focusing specifically on male, female, or teen sexualities; thematically oriented queries delving into topics such as infidelity, orgasm, pornography, and sexuality and morality; and large, rigorous, and systematic examinations as well as informal enquiries of small groups of people. The subjects were interviewed on the streets and in their homes, but more frequently, they submitted the questionnaires found in the publications. Although there was certainly social diversity, the general demographic and sociological information provided by participants reveals that the majority of them belonged to an urban educated middle class who could afford the magazines where the questionnaires were published. Describing *1ra Encuesta sobre Sexualidad y Pareja*, for example, Gindin argued that "this is the sexuality of our middle class. . . . It is likely that workers either do not have money to buy the magazine or to pay postage to send in their responses, or are not accustomed to answering questions of this sort."[97] With regard to the presentation of results, it ranged from the publication of the quantitative data and interpretative essays to the elaborate transcription of answers and opinions that more directly illustrated the views of the respondents.[98]

Magazines employed members of the staff to create, conduct, and summarize the surveys, or requested the help of professionals. *Sex Humor*, for example, regularly published numerous polls devised, conducted, and interpreted by diverse academic and scientific centers dedicated to the study of sexuality and the treatment of sexual disorders, which, run by sexologists, physicians, psychologists, and sociologists, boomed during those years. These surveys as well as the supplement "Investigación Especial" were the only two regular serious sections of the magazine and the most popular ones. In fact, readers' enthusiastic and immediate response to the polls encouraged Ediciones de la Urraca, the publishing house behind *Sex Humor*, to publish *1ra Encuesta sobre Sexualidad y Pareja*, conducted by the CETIS. The book, which was an editorial success, presented the results of seventy-five questions directed exclusively at heterosexual individuals who mailed in the completed questionnaires originally published in *Sex Humor*. Forty percent of the respondents discovered the questionnaire by reading the magazine; 31 percent were radio listeners of the show *Sexualidad y pareja*, hosted by Gindin and broadcasted on Radio Belgrano; and 29 percent were told about the survey by friends and colleagues. Based on the responses of more than three hundred participants, the quantitative results were complemented by a thorough discussion and interpretation by the specialists, as well as essays on the most relevant topics addressed in the questions, including female pleasure, sexual desire, sexual pathologies, and monogamy.[99]

The abundance of surveys in the print press conveys a historical urgency for discovery. After the censorship of information about sex and the people's retreat from public debate, periodicals employed polls to both encourage and echo the appetite of readers who wanted to know more about sexual practices, to identify with others, and to express themselves openly. *Sex Humor* argued that "during years of repression, we have become mute, deaf, and dumb before our bodies and those of others. Hidden and denied, sexuality has been absent from the media, making analysis and research impossible. Democracy urgently requires a survey that allows us to approach the state of Argentine sexuality."[100] In having access to the results of these polls, magazine readers were able to recognize themselves as part of trends and practices; in answering the polls, respondents engaged in an individual exercise of introspection, "a brief coming to terms with oneself," and in a form of selfless involvement in a collective cause. Participating in a survey also prompted individuals to confront guilt, shame, and prejudices, embarking on a project of normalization of sexuality and of liberation that replicated similar processes taking place in other spheres of life in postdictatorial Argentina.[101]

Given the prejudices and misconceptions around female sexuality, the voice of women manifested in surveys was even more profoundly associated with freedom and defiance, making poll results a striking find. In fact, *La Mujer* typically published small excerpts of these women's answers—a strategy to recuperate subjectivity behind percentages, to name the women, to affirm their identities as sexual beings without biases, regardless of age, marital status, and occupation.[102] The appeal to use one's voice to talk about sex without guilt was so strong that women often included their names and contact information when submitting the completed questionnaires, even when the instructions required anonymity—a fact the editor of *Sex Humor* interpreted as a strategy of self-affirmation as well as a way to establish a personal channel of communication. Publications explained that after a dark period of silence and the enforcement of traditional gender stereotypes that misrepresented, ridiculed, and stigmatized female sexuality, listening to and knowing "the Argentine women who came of age in the years of the dictatorship" was of vital importance.[103] To this effect, for example, *Mujer 10* prepared in 1983—three months before its launch and at the peak of the democratic transition—"La mujer, hoy," a poll of 1,500 women whose results were published in the first few issues of the magazine. Sex and sexually related matters comprised 60 percent of all the questions.[104]

Women were also the uncontested protagonists of the magazine sections devoted to photos sent by readers. The gender assumptions behind the production of these images are evident in the instructions for the magazine *Destape*'s "1984 First Photographic Contest of Sensual Photos," which took for granted that the photography enthusiasts would be men and the amateur models would be women.[105] This was generally the case for the pictures published in the section "Y fueron protagonistas" ("And They Played a Leading Role") of *Pareja*, the personal ads supplement of *Dar la cara en entrevista*. The section comprised several pages of black-and-white nonprofessional close-ups of naked or seminaked young women in suggestive but never too risqué or crude poses.[106] The brief information included with the photos often stated that they were taken by boyfriends and husbands, and only rarely by a female friend. As evident in its title, the section emphasized that displaying their bodies for the consumption of a mostly male audience was a source of agency for ordinary women and a medium to take center stage. The magazine celebrated the pictures of these teachers, secretaries, and university students as an act of sensual liberation, made possible by the new political and social climate.[107] An ad inviting submissions affirmed: "Today it's time for freedom, time to set free the desires repressed for so many years. Time to leave aside the old biases that only did us a disservice. For that reason, friends and readers, we invite you to play a leading role in *Pareja*."[108]

Like polls and photo sections, *consultorios sexológicos* and personal ads also opened new channels of expression and communication. Personal ad sections with an emphasis on sexual encounters became extremely popular in the magazines born during the destape. *Pareja*, for example, rapidly became an independent supplement for *Dar la cara en entrevista*, and "Los clasificados del sexo" ("Sex Classified Ads") in *Destape* grew from a few pages to occupy 25 percent of the magazine. Journalist Norberto Chab, who worked at *Destape*, argued that after repressive times when people had withdrawn, suppressing social and sexual contact due to fear or shame, "Los clasificados del sexo" had a true social function. Chab affirmed that the destape reawakened a yearning for sexual experimentation, a desire to connect, to find others who shared one's interests and wants, and magazines like *Destape* offered a platform that made it all possible. Chab further remembered that readers were so appreciative that they mailed in cash and sent small presents.[109]

Readers also wrote letters to thank the magazines for the people they had met and the experiences they had had as a result of the personal ads. A woman who had met her boyfriend through the personal ads of *Dar la cara en entrevista* wrote a letter to the magazine conveying her sense of personal realization: "Because we all should understand that utopias are not impossible if we dare to try what appears impossible. Because I would like to send my thanks to *Dar la cara en entrevista*. Because today, on this winter morning, in spite of the cold and the inflation, I can say that I am happy. And coming from someone who has not said that in a long time, that is important . . . very important indeed."[110] Yet gratitude went well beyond the personal ad section. In 1984, a young man wrote to *Dar la cara en entrevista* to express how during the military dictatorship, he had felt intellectually disempowered and emasculated due to the lack of sex information. The reader celebrated the magazine as a source of unrestricted information that was helping him defeat those past feelings and was fundamental to achieving a rewarding sex life. In his letter, the man stated: "I condemn all forms of censorship and I thank you for breathing life into my youth after eight years of psychological and physical castration. I swear that without you, I would have ended up in the nuthouse or the grave."[111]

Notably, if these magazines played a social role, they overwhelmingly served a heterosexual audience. Sections devoted to readers appear, at first sight, to be largely democratic, expressing the views of men and women, single and married individuals, the young and the old, inhabitants of big cities and small towns, experienced and adventurous lovers and sexual novices, the rich and the poor. But a closer look reveals, in line with the essence of the destape, the prevalence of the heterosexual experience and a profound silence of queer sexualities. Even in the personal ads the voices of sexual minorities were uncommon. Whether writers were looking for casual sex or a serious relationship, the vast majority were young heterosexuals—largely between eighteen and thirty-five years of age, that is, individuals who were teenagers and young adults during the dictatorship—whose ads emphasized socially appropriate attributes such as education, culture, status, and politeness; underlined safety and respectability; and avoided any suggestions of kinky sex.

Interestingly, *Pareja* personal ads were divided into three sections: "For men," "For women," and "For all," which, despite its promise of diversification and inclusion, basically published ads that could be found in the other two sections. On occasion, a couple was looking for a young woman, a young man was looking for a bisexual woman, or a lesbian was looking for a partner, but these ads were scarce. Gay men were remarkably absent.[112] This could be one more manifestation of the heterosexual character of the destape as a mainstream media phenomenon no different from, for example, television content that ignored gays. However, it could also be an indication of the limits of the destape as social experience, a reflection of the silences and fears that profoundly pervaded the lives of sexual minorities. The incipient, new, social visibility of gay culture and of the CHA could not wipe out overnight the repression and persecution of the previous years nor the legacy of fear and the prejudices that still characterized Argentine society after the return to democracy. Thus, gay people might have been rightly cautious or uninterested in attempting to connect with others using the same channels that heterosexuals so effortlessly enjoyed, when they still suffered extortion, discrimination, and violence, as chapter 5 discusses in detail.

The destape meant an unprecedented sexualization of media culture endowed with heterogeneous, quite often differing, messages. Contradictions were evident across different destape texts, such as women's magazines promoting orgasm as a form of female sexual empowerment, while commercials commodified women's backsides. They even flourished within the same genre, such as the destape films that objectified and hypersexualized women while also portraying them as powerful avengers. In this context, women were simultaneously sexual objects and sexual subjects; sexual liberation was a metaphor for democracy, yet homoeroticism was suppressed; and heterosexuals found a voice and spaces for exchange and debate of their sexuality, but gay people were mostly excluded from mainstream media representations and participation. Similarly, a festive search for sexual pleasure and a celebration of sexual desire was the norm in the press and on television, but the reality of sexual violence leaked into destape blockbusters, and the experience of everyday sexual discrimination was exposed through investigative journalism.

These contradictions reveal that the destape was only a partial process of the democratization of desire, which Brian McNair has defined as, on the one hand, an expanded popular access to means of sexual expression and, on the other hand, the emergence of a more pluralistic sexual culture.[113] The destape in the media made discussions and representations of sex more open, extroverted, and unashamed, but far from being an absolute and unapologetic democratization of desire, it was plagued with the unequivocal tensions of a transitional moment that wanted to claim total rupture with the past and yet did not totally reject its legacies. The destape allowed for the emergence of Maitena's *la fiera* but made the female characters of Alberto Olmedo's *No toca botón* the iconic 1980s models of femininity. *Otra historia de amor*, a realistic and thoughtful pioneering portrayal of gay love, and a cartoonish television character like Huguito Araña were both born from the destape; magazines *Mujer 10* and *Shock*, one catering to the new sexual woman, the other portraying women as sexual objects, appeared at the same time. Magazine personal ad sections and sex polls boomed in the return to democracy yet only for heterosexuals. In other words, the destape imagined and marketed itself as transforming media culture by radically subverting traditional sexual morality and sexual conventions, and many times it did, but was unable or unwilling to fully denounce and radically break with prejudice and discrimination against sexual minorities, sexism, and machismo.

# 3

## SEX IN DEMOCRACY

The *Destape*, Sexology, and the Search for Pleasure

**The 1970s dictatorship championed discourses** of morality and the Christian way of life, and supported a Catholic agenda of reproductive sex within marriage to prevent the rise of sexuality as a field of disruption. The regime inhibited sexuality and postulated the Catholic family as the baseline of social stability because it associated sexual freedom with other forms of freedom and believed that nonconformity and a lack of restrictions regarding sex could easily spread out to other areas of social life. Ideas considered "subversive"—whether about sex or anything else—were viewed as dangerously inspirational if let to circulate and grow, posing a serious threat to the final goal of the regime, that is, the absolute control of a society organized under the essential principles of discipline and hierarchy.[1] A "liberated sexuality"—premarital, extramarital, pleasure-seeking, nonreproductive, nonheterosexual, and that the dictatorship broadly labeled "promiscuous," "deviant," and on occasion "animal"—was considered part of a process of radicalization with serious social and political consequences, as it would ultimately lead to the adoption of Communism. As was common in Cold War projects in different parts of the world, containment of both political and sexual liberation was a response to the idea that the "Red Scare" and "deviant sexuality" were coexisting and mutually reinforcing. Consequently, repression of sexual matters was an important preventive measure for the maintenance of the status quo as well as an effective pedagogical tool since censorship and restraint of sexuality taught citizens norms such as silence, compliance, and passivity, which the dictatorship expected them to apply to all spheres of life.[2]

The radical Left was, for different reasons, as conservative in their views on sexuality as the military, opposing the sexual revolution as a "false" revolution, a distraction that diverted energies away from the political and social fight for a new society. In 1972, the Marxist guerrilla Partido Revolucionario de los Trabajadores–Ejército Revolucionario del Pueblo (PRT-ERP; Workers' Revolutionary Party–People's Revolutionary Army) crafted *Moral y proletarización*, a programmatic document for shaping the ideal militant based on Friedrich Engel's *The Origin of Family, Private Property, and the State*. *Moral y proletarización* advocated the heterosexual couple, the monogamous family, and sex for reproductive purposes, and censured the sexual revolution for its objectification of women, subjection of women to men, erotization of culture, and promotion of the "animal instincts of sex" over love. The document further proposed that partners consecrate the making of the Revolution as the epicenter of their relationship and postulated motherhood as women's "natural destiny." Similarly, leftist Peronist guerrilla group Montoneros encouraged formal and stable couples, and condemned and even penalized unfaithfulness and adultery based on the idea that romantic fidelity and political loyalty were two sides of the same revolutionary moral—the duties owed to the party and the revolution were conflated to those owed to one's spouse. Montoneros also disapproved of casual and nonmonogamous sex, same-sex relations, and abortion, and endorsed a view of marriage for procreation since militants were required to produce children for the revolution.[3]

By highlighting the political effects of starting a relationship, getting married, and having a child, the guerrillas made the sex and love lives of militants into spheres in which the leadership could intervene actively and directly—such as demanding a six-month dating period before a couple could move in together or demoting members for sexual misconduct—and where a rigid revolutionary morality based on sexual self-restraint was promoted, demanded, and policed. In addition to ideological reasons, sexual debauchery was opposed to preserve the internal order and security of the organizations. Indeed, both the PRT-ERP and Montoneros increased control over sex and relationships when the expansion of military repression and the consolidation of state terrorism forced members underground. And although in theory, expectations and rules about sexual behavior and punishments for transgressions were the same for men and women, testimonies of female militants show the maintenance of sexual double standards; women's behavior was measured with a different yardstick, and they were controlled more thoroughly and punished more harshly than men.[4]

From the far Right to the radical Left, then, sexuality in the 1970s was expected to be conformist, discreet, responsible, reproductive, and connected to either the political and ideological needs of the nation, as interpreted by the military in power, or the needs of the revolution. There was a discursive divorce between self and sex since, for both the dictatorship and the guerrillas, sexuality was a sphere of life to be regulated and controlled so pervasively that it seemed more dictated by extraneous purposes than commanded by personal motives. Sex was also intrinsically connected to love. As historian Isabella Cosse has argued, the 1960s sexual revolution in Argentina severed the tie between sex and marriage, and contested traditional expectations of female virginity, but premarital sex only became socially acceptable if it was concomitant to love.[5] Thus, in the 1970s, sex was prominently correlated with family, love, loyalty, responsibility, and morality, while associations of sex with free experimentation, individual expression, happiness, and fulfillment were silenced or demonized. The period was pervaded by sex negativity, a concept that feminist anthropologist Gayle Rubin has employed to describe a common ideological trend in Western Christian cultures in which sex is generally considered a dangerous and destructive force. To be exempted from this characterization, sex must be linked to "acceptable excuses" such as marriage, reproduction, and love.[6]

This chapter reveals that in the context of redemocratization, the destape and sexology—the study and clinical treatment of human sexuality—radically changed the meanings of sex by placing the search for pleasure at the center of its definition. As Argentines recovered political and social freedom, sex and the satisfaction of heterosexual desire were equated with collective and personal liberation. In turn, the overemphasis on pleasure confronted many with the fears and frustrations they experienced in the bedroom. This chapter argues that while the destape in the media endorsed and naturalized the search for heterosexual pleasure, sexology legitimized and channeled it. The popularity and public prominence of sexology and the boom of sex therapy and sexual enrichment groups were both causes and effects of the destape. They were also mechanisms of rectification that addressed and attempted to remedy the anxieties—from sexual underperformance to feelings of abnormality—triggered by the destape. Sexology banished the emphases on obligation, procreation, and conformism endorsed by the sexual ideologies of the previous decade and promoted and legitimized new meanings of hetero sex centered on joy and indulgence—messages appealing to all but particularly to women.

## THE DESTAPE AND THE BEDROOM

In a short story about the destape published in *Mujer 10*, Doña Rosa tells her neighbor Doña María that she was shocked by the content of a women's magazine:

> You have no idea. Blow by blow. Everything, everything you could ever imagine! Those things you never talk about or even think about. I read some couples get bored in bed. And they give tips to make it . . . well, entertaining! . . . And the words they use . . . It's shocking! I'm embarrassed to even repeat them. . . . And she added in a whisper: Orgasm. For a moment both women remained silent. And then it mentioned, added Rosa, giggling naughtily: Certain games. You won't believe this! The man pretends to be a doctor and he gives her a checkup. Or a different one: she's the teacher and he's the student. . . . What do you think? It must be the destape, murmured Doña María.[7]

Amazed and puzzled, María asked Rosa the name of the magazine, then went to the newsstand and bought it. When Rosa saw her with the magazine later that day, María told her she had purchased it for a pie recipe. Yet that night, María waited for her husband dressed in nothing but a traditional *guardapolvo* worn by teachers and ready for some bedroom role-play.

This story is an interesting reflection of the press's overconfidence in measuring the social impact of the destape it was propelling. After years of silence, censorship, and in some cases, complicity with the dictatorship, the press was eager to recover its credibility and social influence and to reclaim its position as an independent power that shaped reality, and the destape appeared as an effective instrument to achieve this goal. Polls, sections such as the *consultorio sexológico*, and the personal ads offered a new and open platform for participation and discussion of sex, allowing the press to proclaim its fundamental role in providing a timely social service. Yet the tale of the two neighbors reveals that the media saw itself as not only opening the debate about sex and sexualizing popular culture but also making a decisive and direct intervention in one of the most intimate spheres of people's lives by changing sex practices.

Both sexologists and the press underlined the pedagogical character of the destape. Sexologist León Roberto Gindin asserted that the destape was the most widely available form of sex information without reproductive purposes—in other words, sex education for pleasure. Magazines in particular, Gindin argued, "took the lids off" people's minds, showing them that sex was a field for experimentation and encouraging them to be adventurous.[8] In fact, magazines underlined the educational purposes of their articles on sex. A piece on female orgasm in *Mujer 10*, for example, promised to instruct women about their anatomy and eroticism with simple but scientific knowledge, bringing to light a subject traditionally silenced in the media and that women understood (when they did) as a consequence of an intuitive learning process. Others noted that the eye-opening nature of the destape went beyond the circulation of medical science, psychology, and sexology.[9] Psychoanalyst Mauricio Abadi argued that the destape was helping to reduce personal repressive mechanisms that consciously or unconsciously operated over sexual desires. Thus, individuals were now becoming aware of their internal conflicts and prejudices as well as of their most intimate fantasies. Similarly, journalist Sergio Sinay, subdirector of the magazine *Perfil*, affirmed that the destape movies, press, literature, images, and television were teaching Argentines to see and appreciate the beauty and marvel of bodies and sex. Learning to see, Sinay maintained, was the first step toward learning to talk, to listen, and to think about sex differently, and, ultimately, to transform it.[10]

This emphasis exposes a deliberate self-aggrandizing and self-legitimizing image of the press mission, but surveys reveal that the impact was real, confirming the conclusion of media scholars that people increasingly have come to live their sexualities through, and with the help of, film, television, and the press.[11] A 1986 poll among Argentine women ages eighteen to forty showed that 61 percent of the interviewees read magazines as their main and most reliable source of information about sex. Most important, women maintained that these readings had a profound effect in freeing their sexuality, for example, by legitimizing masturbation as a normal sexual practice for grown-up and married women, a source of self-knowledge, and the most reliable method to achieve an orgasm. To deepen this process of liberation, survey respondents demanded even more openness and information, more public exchanges about sexuality "to downsize the enormous pillars of taboo and shame."[12] Similarly, in a survey conducted among women and published in *La Semana*, 74 percent of the respondents declared that the destape had inspired them to change their sex lives. The younger the women, the more impact they recognized the destape was having on their sexuality, even within the previous year. Thus, 29 percent of all respondents argued that the sexual content in the media encouraged them to reexamine their sexual conduct, and 23 percent attested that media content had influenced them to experiment sexually.[13]

These testimonies notwithstanding, some critics expressed disbelief and questioned the extent and the speed with which the destape was transforming sex habits. For these critics, more information and inspiration from the media did not automatically and immediately translate into practice. Most agreed that the destape was a "pedagogical revolution," but many were disinclined to equate it to a "sexual revolution."[14] Even in an engulfing climate of new sexual ideas, people could resist them in private due to education, religion, health and psychological problems, and other factors. Those who were more restrained in celebrating the impact of the destape in the bedroom thought that Argentines watched, talked, and read more about sex but were unsure that people had more sex and more fulfilling sex lives than in the past. Even if they said they did, were they telling the truth? And if so, how objectively were they evaluating the changes? Sociologist Julio Mafud, for example, argued that the destape was more "verbal than real" because sexual practices were more difficult and slower to modify than discourses. This difference was evident even for those who considered the destape a true motor of sexual change. While the press kept pushing the idea of a sexual revolution, some skeptics were cautious to embrace it, arguing that transformations in sexuality were significant, but a true revolution required a profound shift in mentalities that was just beginning. If a meaningful sexual revolution was under way, it was too early to tell.[15]

Furthermore, commentators agreed that a sudden, radical upheaval in the way people viewed and experienced their sexuality was a challenge for a society just awakening after a period of repression. As Florencio Escardó explained it: "We are evolving, that is, doing better. But growth is difficult and it hurts; it is distressing."[16] Some critics were particularly concerned about what they considered an "apology for loveless sex" and a new culture of "*sexo y suma*," where individuals were expected to accumulate sexual experiences in order to explore sexual possibilities and face both their fears and their desires. Yet this conduct ended up generating competition, anxiety, and alienation. Mafud believed that the sex information and images of the destape constituted an avalanche that many people were unprepared to confront, creating a state of shock, instability, and uncertainty.[17] Sexologists, for their part, offered evidence of these feelings by citing the frequent case of female patients who felt discouraged and "defective" because they had read in magazines that women could have many orgasms but that was not their experience.[18] In fact, a poll published in *Mujer 10* showed that some women found the destape's popularized standards of satisfying sex difficult to meet, thus arousing feelings of inferiority and disappointment. Similarly, another poll revealed that the destape made women doubt whether their sex life was indeed as fulfilling as they thought it was.[19] With a humorous tone, a female journalist writing for *Sex Humor* echoed this sentiment by asserting that destape magazines featuring erotic photos and overloaded with sex information had led women into severe depression and low libido by making them realize that in order to truly experience "boundless passion," they must have had sex in "elevators, buses, atop the washer, at the kitchen sink, under each and every desk they passed, in dressing rooms, in parks, on tennis courts, in cars, on subways, on boats, on yachts, in vestries, on top of carpets and underneath them, on top of nightstands and underneath them, and as an absolute exception, even in a bed."[20]

For women, the destape was simultaneously inspirational, and even empowering, as well as a source of frustrations and disruption, a mirror that painfully reflected deficits and fears. In *Las argentinas y el amor*, published in 1985, journalist Haydée Jofre Barroso concluded that most Argentine women were sexually unsatisfied, bored by unimaginative and

inconsiderate partners, and frustrated with monotonous sex that felt like
a tedious task.[21] Surveys revealed that, surrounded by public discourses
on the importance of orgasms, the power of sexual fantasies, and the centrality of good sex for a happy life, women reported feeling uncomfortable
and unfamiliar with their own bodies, refusing to appear naked in front
of their husbands, and disliking to have sexual intercourse with the lights
on.[22] Most women affirmed they complied with the sexual requests of their
partners because they felt a sense of "duty," even when they loathed those
requests, considered them "abnormal," or viewed them as a clear symptom
of machismo. One woman explained this acquiescence by arguing that she
had grown up believing a saying popular among her friends: "Saying no [in
bed] sinks love into the grave."[23] However, a poll showed that 77 percent of
surveyed women did not feel comfortable telling their partners what they
wanted sexually, although they recognized this would make their sex lives
more fulfilling. Moreover, close to 70 percent of the women admitted they
lacked sexual initiative. Sexologists explained these behaviors by pointing
to traditional gender ideologies that emphasized women had to gratify
men, disregarding their own desires, usually as a consequence of considering them improper. Those ideologies were so pervasive that change was
extremely difficult for women. Yet the new sexual discourses circulating
in the media were not only confronting women with their own insecurities
and dissatisfaction but also encouraging them to take action and resolve
them. Polls revealed that women believed they had a right to pleasure, and
90 percent identified seeking professional help to overcome their fears as
the most effective way to improve their sex lives.[24]

Some critics considered that "women's new obsessive search for orgasm," fueled by the destape, had profound, damaging effects for men.
Mafud affirmed that "in a time of sexual change like the one Argentine
society is experiencing, it is logical that a woman might think she is 'a late
sexual bloomer.' This attitude can lead her to make sexual demands on
a man, and this has its dangers."[25] For commentators like Mafud, these
"dangers" included the frustration and declining self-esteem of men
who felt overburdened, exploited, and ultimately inadequate because of
women's "new sexual demands." In this view, the media, workshops, and
therapy promoted a more satisfactory sexuality for women but without
paying the same attention to men, who were beginning to disregard their
own needs and worry exclusively about their "performance" to make their

partners happy. Mafud claimed that for men, going to bed with a woman was increasingly like taking an exam. This caused men to depend on women for the affirmation of their virility—a new, disquieting experience.[26]

Because women were becoming more sexually assertive and demanding and men were feeling discouraged and insecure, couples were plagued with frictions. Based on a survey of seven hundred respondents published in 1984, the magazine *Hombre* concluded that Argentine men and women were sexually *desencontrados* ("at odds"). Indeed, women rated men 6 out of 10 as lovers, and men rated their partners 5 out of 10. While 83 percent of men responded that they considered themselves good lovers, only 47 percent of their partners defined them in this way. Moreover, 92 percent of men answered that women were sexually repressed, and 76 percent stated that women were unimaginative in bed. For their part, 67 percent of women believed men were sexually repressed, and 71 percent thought their partners lacked inventiveness in the bedroom. In this regard, the influence of the media over women as a source of both frustration and inspiration is evident in the testimony of a woman who affirmed that she felt disappointed that her husband did not want to incorporate sex games that were advised "in all the magazines."[27]

While the press and the polls linked tensions in the bedroom with the destape, some commentators connected them more broadly to the new democratic context, viewing them as the quite unanticipated results of the fall of authoritarianism. According to this argument, fear and distrust during the repressive years of the dictatorship had constrained social relations and social interaction, thus forcing individuals to retreat into the safe, dependable, and predictable world of married life. With social and public life restricted, the family and the couple became the most important spheres where subjects could claim membership, experience a sense of belonging, and cultivate connection with fewer risks and more certainty. Having a partner became an antidote to collective and personal sadness, a lack of alternative social relationships, declining socialization, and patrolled cities. Critics noticed that "couples spun around like tops, sometimes drawing close to others, but always in tight circles."[28] The return to democracy, in contrast, fueled social interaction, opened public spaces, promoted new personal relations, and encouraged new encounters and activities. A predictable world was changed into one full of novelty, calls for experimentation, and potential temptations, creating clashes and disputes in couples now opened to external influences. Sexuality was one of the many spheres of life that couples had to renegotiate because of the new freedom. An article in *Mujer 10* maintained: "Democracy brought a higher degree of freedom. And freedom, when you are out of practice, brings a vertigo akin to fear. The fear of losing what is solidly bound and meticulously designed."[29] Thus, previous agreements and past beliefs were easily put to the test, generating suspicions, jealousy, and self-doubt.

For others, the problems faced by Argentine women and men in the return to democracy were less related to outer stimuli and more to pent-up personal frustrations. Psychologist Ana Quiroga suggested that living under the dictatorship promoted a form of "couple symbiosis" character-ized by unrealistic expectations. Without alternative forms of social and personal fulfillment, both men and women clung to high hopes of success, happiness, and achievement related to their romantic and sexual relations as well as to married life. At the same time, they suppressed dissatisfac-tion and regrets about their partners, since the prevailing conditions of social isolation prevented the search for alternatives and solutions, and discouraged criticism and conflict. Compelled by the authoritarian con-text, couples buried their problems, refrained from addressing strains, and forced themselves to be content. The process of democratization, with its emphasis on free expression, personal liberation, and fulfillment, abruptly empowered individuals to challenge the status quo, question their relationships and partners, and openly express personal and sexual dissatisfaction and complaints. For Quiroga, in the new context of per-missiveness and self-gratification that promoted the search for happiness after a period of repressive darkness, couples would struggle to regain a balance that, contrived and based on silence and denial in the past, now required more dialogue and accommodation. And to achieve these, both men and women would probably need the help of experts.[30]

## THE BOOM OF SEXOLOGY

The explosive rise of sexology was a timely response to the transformation of sexuality, to the new desires and promises and the consequent conflicts, tensions, and doubts triggered by the destape, democracy, and freedom. The discipline had appeared in the country in the midcentury, but that version had little in common with the one born out of the redemocratization process in the 1980s. In 1953, Dr. José Opizzo created the first Department of Sexology in Argentina as part of the Urology Clinic in the Cosme Argerich Hospital in Buenos Aires, with the main goal of studying and treating sexual pathologies and "deviant" sexualities, particularly homosexuality. In 1969, Dr. Armando Domenech founded the Sociedad Argentina de Sexología y Educación Sexual (Argentine Society of Sexology and Sex Education), and a year later, gynecologist and psychoanalyst Sergio Segú created the Escuela Argentina de Sexología (Argentine School of Sexology).[31]

This early sexology was invisible in the media and lacked social presence and cultural influence. It privileged a physical and biological interpretation of and approach to sexual disorders that tended to neglect psychosomatic factors, most probably because its practitioners worked largely within the medical field, mostly gynecology. Yet sexology was not part of the curricula in medical schools. Additionally, there were almost no women practitioners, except for psychologist Eva Giberti, who is usually credited with the dissemination of psychoanalytic interpretations of sexuality in the 1960s, especially in relation to children, but who is currently disregarded by sexologists as a true precursor in clinical sexology. Like pediatrician Florencio Escardó, the author of *Sexología de la familia* (1961), considered the first manual of modern sexology published in Argentina, Giberti contributed to sexology as an educator, rather than as a clinician.[32]

Some of these early predecessors supported very conservative views of sexuality and gender roles: Segú, for example, was a fervent Catholic. They understood sex as intrinsically linked to marriage, family, and love; considered men as "natural experts" and "proficient teachers" in sex matters; and defined sexual intercourse as "a moral obligation"—ideas that even Giberti and Escardó, the most liberal experts, espoused. Furthermore, many disapproved of the sexual revolution that, according to an editorial published in 1970 in the *Revista Argentina de Sexología y Educación Sexual*, headed by Armando Domenech, was stretching the limits of sexual morality to the point of anarchy.[33] This type of sexology did not disappear when the new school born with the return to democracy took the field, the media, and the social imagination by storm; rather, it endured, quite unchanged, on the fringes. Paradigmatically, in 1983, Segú presided over a congress organized by obstetricians and gynecologists titled "Educación Sexual para la Vida Familiar" ("Sex Education for Family Life").[34]

In light of this history, the sexology that vibrantly erupted in the 1980s seems an orphan for which establishing local lineage is difficult. Yet this "orphan" successfully seized the subject of sexuality from physicians and psychoanalysts who had been the predominant representatives of scientific sex discourses.[35] The sexology that arose in the return to democracy was as much a cultural, media, and social phenomenon as a scientific and therapeutic one. It was, simultaneously, a cause and an effect of the destape—both a clear symptom and a propeller of the free, liberated atmosphere in which it was born. Thus, this new sexology was a fundamental component of the social imaginary of the democratic transition, and its advocates were as well known by audiences as television stars. It also grew and consolidated institutionally, professionally, and socially in a precipitous fashion while popularizing a therapeutic approach to sex problems that rapidly met with pent-up needs and an increasing demand and acceptance among the public. The 1980s sexology incorporated an increasing number of female practitioners—in fact, some observers argued that they were the majority of sexology students in the decade—and privileged a psychological approach to the study and treatment of sexuality that attracted large numbers of mental health providers, usually surpassing the number of physicians.[36]

Finally, the most unprecedented characteristic of the sexology born with the destape was its unashamed emphasis on sexual pleasure as an absolute value unconditioned by love, family, morality, and convention, and purged of notions of abnormality, failure, and remorse. As sexologist María Luisa Lerer argued: "One of the tasks of our job is to grant permission and free people from guilt, which conveys the few privileges and the enormous shame that characterize us."[37] Yet the search for pleasure promoted by sexologists was not a "one-size-fits-all" approach but an individual process that required professional guidance as much as personal introspection and communication between partners. Sexologists contended that pleasure was not a universal experience for which sex therapists had a "magic" standard formula but a profoundly individual, subjective, and changing sensation that required retraining the mind—questioning beliefs, eliminating prejudices, confronting fears, and challenging social mandates—as much as the body.[38]

Embracing the definition proposed by the World Health Organization (WHO) in the mid-1970s, the new Argentine sexology claimed that "sexual health is the integration of the somatic, emotional, intellectual, and social aspects of sexual being, in ways that are positively enriching and that enhance personality, communication, and love."[39] The right to information and the right to pleasure, the two fundamental aspects of this concept, resonated profoundly with the context of Argentine redemocratization and destape. Argentine sexologists emphasized that this new notion of sexual health implied a positive approach to human sexuality and that their professional contribution was helping individuals to make life and personal relations richer and more fulfilling. This goal involved more than merely treating sexual diseases and dysfunctions and remedying procreation problems. In fact, sexual health went beyond the capacity to enjoy and control reproductive functions free from disorders. It also encompassed individual freedom from "fear, shame, guilt, false beliefs, and other psychological factors inhibiting sexual response and impairing sexual relationship."[40]

These principles, however, were only promoted for heterosexuals. Even in a context in which one of the most evident changes in grassroots mobilization was the emergence and increasing visibility of gay organizations, queer sexualities continued to be silenced, condemned, and pathologized among professionals who otherwise celebrated the new heterosexual "liberation." In 1985, for example, twelve years after the American Psychiatric Association removed homosexuality from the *Diagnostic and Statistical Manual of Mental Disorders*, psychiatrist Mauricio Abadi—who had been the president of the Asociación Psicoanalítica Argentina (Argentine Psychoanalytic Association) in the 1970s—declared in *La Semana* that homosexuality was a mental disease just like schizophrenia. Even some of those who were more accepting of homosexuality contended that it should remained "closeted" and out of the public eye, thus inhibiting the types of discussions that were held about heterosexuality. Many apparent defenses of the right to privacy of gay people were indeed attempts to silence them and to suppress debates about their sexuality.[41] Even when they were genuinely accepting of and interested in same-sex relations, sexologists still focused on and specialized in heterosexuality because, according to their own accounts, they had no gay patients. Reflecting specifically on lesbianism, a sexologist affirmed in a conference that "from the point of view of clinical sexology, female homosexuality does not exist because lesbians never come in for consultations."[42]

Focused on the search for heterosexual pleasure, the emergence of the new sexology in postauthoritarian Argentina was anchored in the larger story of exile of young professionals who left the country during the dictatorship in search of a life of freedom and away from fear.[43] Laura Caldiz was a young psychologist who specialized in juvenile psychosis when she left Argentina in 1976 and moved to the United States. Living in the effervescent San Francisco of the late 1970s—which, with the election of Harvey Milk, became the first city in California to elect an openly gay person to public office—Caldiz was fascinated by the exultant, liberated sexuality in the city that was the cornerstone of the sexual revolution and the LGBTQ rights movement. Increasingly interested in sexuality, Caldiz began reading the work of sexologists William Masters, Virginia Johnson, and Helen Singer Kaplan—she met Johnson and Kaplan in different seminars and talks she attended while in the United States—while pondering the absence of discussion of sexual problems in her own professional education, the timidity with which patients brought sex as a matter of concern to their psychotherapy sessions, and the lack of preparation of Argentine psychologists and psychiatrists to deal with these issues.[44]

Moved by these questions, Caldiz decided to enter the pioneering and recently created Institute for Advanced Study of Human Sexuality (IASHS) in San Francisco. The IASHS evolved from the National Sex Forum (NSF), a service of San Francisco's Methodist-oriented Glide Foundation created in 1968 to address the lack of knowledge on sexuality among the religious and social service professionals who worked in the gay community. The IASHS, which was formally incorporated as a graduate program in 1976, played a fundamental role in the development of humanistic sexology. While scientific, empirical sexologists such as Masters and Johnson focused on rigorous research, quantification, and experimentation, humanist sexology focused on experiential exercises, such as encounter groups, couples treatment, and sensory awareness, designed to explore sexual feelings, fears, and desires. Humanist sexologists were less interested in the empirical understanding of sexuality than in the enhancement of sexual functioning as a major therapeutic enterprise and cultivated a simple and engaging communication style. Caldiz was trained by humanistic sexologists who placed sexual pleasure and sexual enhancement, both as emotional and physical well-being, at the center of their practice and emphasized health and wholeness over sickness and dysfunction.[45]

In September 1979, just a few months after her return to Argentina, Caldiz attended the First Latin American Congress of Psychology and Group Psychotherapy. There she met León Roberto Gindin, a physician and psychoanalyst who was immediately captivated by the exciting field of sexology Caldiz described as well as by her experiences and training abroad.[46] Under Caldiz's guidance, the pair began to research, study, and discuss sexology materials, and in 1981, they started organizing free sexual enrichment groups with friends and colleagues. This was a novelty in the Argentine context, and although they were small at first, they became extremely popular among participants—mostly physicians, psychologists, and psychoanalysts—and very useful for Caldiz and Gindin, who employed them to test, apply, and experiment with what they had been learning. With the dictatorship weakened and retreating, neither Caldiz nor Gindin believed their activities might put them or the participants in danger, yet they kept them discreet and restricted attendance only to people they knew. Just a few years earlier, the culture of silence and fear had been palpable in discussion groups of psychologists and physicians interested in sexuality who met regularly to debate readings and share experiences from their private practices; in fact, the minutes of the meetings refrained from identifying attendees by name.[47]

Caldiz's and Gindin's first experiences with sexual enrichment groups were the beginning of the Centro de Educación, Terapia e Investigación en Sexualidad (CETIS; Center for Education, Therapy, and Research on Sexuality), which became the first institution in the country to offer a postgraduate degree in sexology and was a popular center for the clinical treatment of sexual problems. By following American leading institutions in the field, CETIS incorporated a variety of unheard-of techniques to train sexologists, such as the Sexual Attitude Re-assessment Workshop created by the NSF in the late 1960s and also known as "Fuckarama" or "Sexarama." In the first meeting of the workshop, unwarned participants gathered in a room to watch explicit sex films—porn movies and professional sex films produced by the NSF—that were run simultaneously on several different screens. The goal was to desensitize participants—many of whom, after years of censorship, had never watched a sexually explicit movie. Later, they were encouraged to share their emotional responses to the experience in small discussion groups and in front of the whole class. As part of its curricula, CETIS also included exercise, relaxation techniques, and movement awareness and hired special guests to teach certain classes; CHA president Carlos Jáuregui was frequently invited to talk about homosexuality, as were sex workers to discuss their experiences.[48]

At the peak of the destape, CETIS was attracting professionals from all over the country and employed some of its own graduates in the Buenos Aires clinic. In those first years of collective training and experimentation, Gindin and Caldiz conducted interviews with patients and led the team of therapists, and all appointments were recorded and shared with the group for educational and supervision purposes. These newly trained sexologists applied mostly cognitive behavioral therapy, a set of techniques aimed at changing the patient's thinking and belief system to ultimately modify dysfunctional thoughts and behaviors and bring enduring emotional change. Goal-oriented, problem-focused, and with an emphasis on the present, these therapies departed from psychoanalysis, which is based on the search for unconscious meanings behind conduct and explores the patient's development, fundamentally in childhood.[49]

However, psychoanalysis was not eradicated from sex therapy. Today, Argentine sexologists agree that psychiatrist Helen Singer Kaplan, who in 1970 founded the Human Sexuality Program at the Payne Whitney Clinic in the New York Presbyterian Hospital–Weill Cornell Medical Center, the first clinic for sexual disorders established at a medical school in the United States, was one of the most influential figures in sex therapy in the country in the 1980s. Kaplan's new sex therapy was a combination of William Masters and Virginia Johnson's program with some elements of psychoanalysis. This was a very attractive recipe for Argentine psychotherapists and other mental health professionals in a country with a long and strong psychoanalytic tradition that, in fact, had legitimized a nonthreatening discussion of sexuality in the name of science in the past.[50] Masters and Johnson's brief and symptomatic treatment was an amalgam of behavioral therapy and sex advice and education that considered sex as a form of learned conduct and sexual dysfunctions as "bad habits" that could be altered or unlearned through information and experiential sex exercises. Kaplan followed this model, but unlike Masters and Johnson, she did not view sexual disorders only in the context of the present and always having superficial origins, instead arguing that, in many cases, there were problems with more remote, deeper determinants that could be effectively addressed with the help of psychosexual therapy.[51]

The success of CETIS in drawing an interdisciplinary audience of psychologists, gynecologists, urologists, and other professionals in the medical sciences from all over the country to specialize in sexology brought a rapid increase in private practice in the field as well as the emergence of new training centers. In 1983, for example, members of the Asociación Rosarina de Educación Sexual y Sexología (ARESS; Rosario's Association of Sex Education and Sexology)—a pioneering organization devoted to sex education and the training of sex educators founded in 1976—created the Instituto Kinsey (Kinsey Institute), led by CETIS-trained psychologist Mirta Granero. Replicating the CETIS model and enjoying the same popularity, demand, and success, the Instituto Kinsey was the first school for the training of sexologists outside of Buenos Aires. Postgraduate education in sexual therapy at the Instituto Kinsey was a two-year program, with a monthly meeting for a whole day open only to university graduates. The program of study consisted of fifteen subjects, including biology and anatomy, therapeutic techniques to treat different sexual disorders, the principles of sex education, the creation of educational materials, sex research, sexual orientations, human sexual development, and the ethical aspects of sex therapy. Also like CETIS, the Instituto Kinsey promptly opened a clinic for the treatment of patients. Later in the decade, Eduardo Arnedo, another CETIS graduate, founded the Centro de Asistencia, Investigación y Educación en Sexualidad (CAIES; Center for Sexuality Treatment, Research, and Education) in Córdoba.[52]

In 1982, Caldiz and Gindin founded the Sociedad Argentina de Sexualidad Humana (SASH; Argentine Society of Human Sexuality), the first professional association for Argentine sexologists. The SASH is an indication that the expected growth in the number of practitioners required an organization to support, represent, and connect them, and to further disseminate sex knowledge through conferences and professional meetings. In 1986, for example, the SASH organized its inaugural biannual conference, and a year later began publishing its journal *Revista Argentina de Sexualidad Humana*. Collaborative, extensive research was uncommon in Argentine sexology in this period due to the incipient state of the field, the lack of economic resources, the strong clinical focus, and the absence of affiliation with universities—the most important loci of research in the country. Yet sexologists used their clinical practice with patients to formulate small research projects and conducted polls and surveys that allowed them to maintain active participation in congresses and conferences and to publish locally and internationally.

The development and consolidation of educational institutions, the growth of treatment centers, the establishment of professional associations, the organization of national and international meetings and conferences (e.g., the First Latin American Congress of Sexology and Sex Education in Buenos Aires in 1988), and the publication of specialized journals attest to the stimulating moment for sexology in the country. In addition, the visits of some of the most renowned worldwide specialists in the field, such as sex therapists Helen Singer Kaplan and Joseph Lopiccolo and gender sexologist John Money, reveal the rapid and fruitful connections that local sexologists established with key figures abroad. Equally important, Argentine sexologists became an active part of a dynamic Latin American network of specialists that established the Federación Latinoamericana de Sociedades de Sexología y Educación Sexual (FLASSES; Latin American Federation of Sexology and Sex Education Societies) in 1980 and the journal *Revista Lationamericana de Sexología* in 1986. That year, the first edition of *International Who's Who in Sexology* listed only thirty-five professionals from Latin America, and five, including Caldiz and Gindin, were from Argentina.[53] In fact, Argentina's sexology occupied a remarkable position in Latin America. Although by 1986, Colombia was the only Latin American country where several universities had sexology incorporated in their core curriculum, Argentina and Venezuela—where only occasional sexology classes and seminars were offered in some universities—were the only two Latin American countries with private institutions for the training of sexologists.[54]

Sexologists and their organizations also had a very active role in disseminating the discipline among physicians. Dr. Walter Barbato, an ob-gyn, a professor in the School of Medicine at the Universidad Nacional de Rosario, and the chair of the Obstetrics Department of the Hospital Centenario in Rosario, where medical students completed their residency to obtain their degree, explained that a combination of conservative and Catholic views and a lack of sexology training in medical programs all over the country left physicians—even those in obstetrics, gynecology, and urology—completely unprepared to answer simple and recurrent questions that patients, particularly women, asked about sex.[55] Educated to address mainly reproductive issues, these doctors were unable, disinclined, or uninformed to discuss with their patients concerns about sexuality and sexual pleasure. In 1985, for example, the chair of the Gynecology Department of the Hospital Durand in Buenos Aires claimed that masturbation was not a "proper" means for women to obtain sexual pleasure and that heterosexual vaginal intercourse was the "perfect sex act" for women to achieve sexual gratification.[56]

Some members of the medical profession resisted sexology when hospitals and universities began to invite experts for talks and seminars. In an interview in 1987, CETIS-trained psychiatrist Adrián Sapetti recounted that he had been invited by a teaching hospital to give a series of seminars, and although physicians from different departments enthusiastically attended, the director of the residency program prohibited residents from taking the seminars. Still, sexology talks, workshops, and conferences at medical schools and teaching hospitals became increasingly frequent and very popular and contributed to awakening curiosity about and appreciation for the field in the profession. These types of events also offered sexologists the opportunity to reach a broader audience, including nurses and social workers, and to interest medical students who could only train in sexology after getting their university degrees.[57] A prototypical monthly seminar offered by the Asociación Argentina de Sexualidad Humana (AASH; Argentine Association of Human Sexuality), founded by pioneering sexologist María Luisa Lerer in 1981 at the Hospital Británico in Buenos Aires, consisted of four two-hour classes, led by a staff of mostly sexology-trained psychologists, that covered a list of topics including the history, anthropology, and sociology of sexuality; sexuality and the life cycle; couple development; male and female sexual disorders; diagnosis and common treatments; and the role of the medical team with patients suffering from sexual disorders.[58]

Beyond talks, seminars, and conferences in hospitals and medical schools, institutions such as CETIS and the Instituto Kinsey provided medical doctors a new space for formal training and specialization in sexology. Although it was encouraged and welcome, the presence of doctors among the sexology ranks prompted some psychologists and psychiatrists, who made up the majority of students and practitioners, to pose questions about competence. This group privileged and defended a psychological approach that viewed sexuality and sexual disorders as fields that exceeded genitality and physiology and were connected to mental, emotional, and cognitive issues. Thus, they questioned whether the institutions' training was indeed sufficient for physicians without previous education in psycho-somatic disorders. Critics never denied the advantages of medical doctors' training in sexology as a complement for their practices but expressed reservations when the doctors acted as sex therapists. Clinical sexologists also opposed what they viewed as the overmedicalization of sexual disorders promoted by clinicians, who, for their part, defended themselves by emphasizing that many disorders had organic causes. In the mid-to-late 1980s—a period before the boom of Viagra—sex therapists argued that overmedicalization was evident, for example, in the increase and overuse of penile prosthesis to correct erectile dysfunction. These critics claimed that the practice was not only expensive and risky but also ineffective in the numerous cases in which erectile disorders were not rooted in organic or physiological causes but rather in psychological ones. In these cases, the goal of sexology was to help individuals find their voice and express themselves freely, without constraints.[59]

## SEX IN DEMOCRACY

If talk about sexuality was inhibited by authoritarianism, democracy freed it. An article in *Somos* magazine about sex polls in the return to democracy asserted that researchers were stunned by the enthusiastic participation of interviewees, their candor when answering questions, and the very direct, honest, and almost crude language they used in sharing their opinions about sex and their sexual experiences.[60] Beyond the media, an unexpected but fascinating sign of the new climate of free expression and personal liberation appeared right on the streets. The emergence of sexual graffiti during the destape, which had been previously relegated, on a smaller scale, to hidden places and public restrooms, is a clear indication of how people were more open to talking about sex, bringing it from the private to the public sphere.

In 1983, Adrián Helién, a young doctor who had just graduated from the School of Medicine, began to notice the appearance of graffiti with sexual content in the very same streets of Buenos Aires that he had been walking for years. Camera in hand, Helién documented the large rise of sexual writings on walls all over the city over the next three years, an interest that naturally deepened as he was studying to become a sexologist. He later partnered with sexologist Mario Huguet to systematize and analyze a collection of more than five hundred sexual graffiti—a project they turned into a short documentary they exhibited in 1987.[61]

Sexual graffiti shows how socially comprehensive this new openness about sex was, as they were present in upper-, middle-, and working-class neighborhoods. The graffiti were an act of defiance and liberation not only in terms of form, since graffitists were engaging in an illegal act that just a few years earlier would have had serious consequences, but also in terms of content. Though anonymously and surreptitiously, graffitists joined the media destape, connecting sex with humor, politics, and the recent past. Graffiti expressed sexual views crudely ("Long live jerking off"); used sex to ridicule and condemn the military, the state, and the church ("Obscenity today isn't porn, it's generals showing off their war medals"; "To err is human, to get it on is divine"); challenged "sexual correctness" ("Virginity is an illness, get your vaccination here"); and showed the connection between sexual and political liberation ("Pleasure is revolutionary"; "Orgasms for the people").[62]

This new openness was also manifest in the popularity of sexual enrichment groups that began to be offered by new sexology research and therapeutic centers such as the CETIS and the Instituto Kinsey. In the midst of the destape, sexual experts diagnosed Argentines as suffering a profound and paralyzing "sexual illiteracy," a complete ignorance about anatomy and the sexual response cycle—the physiological responses to sexual stimulation—that inhibited sexual desire and behavior, prevented the achievement of pleasure, and caused deep pain, frustration, and feelings of inadequacy.[63] Sexologists remembered, for example, that many women had no knowledge of their own genitalia, found it "ugly," and felt embarrassed by it, which profoundly hindered healthy and fulfilling sexual encounters. Sexologist Mirta Granero recalled that she always approached this common concern by asking patients why they insisted their vulvas were unappealing or anomalous if they barely knew them and had never seen others to compare. Sexologists found out that women had been taught that looking at and touching their bodies was wrong, inappropriate, impure, and foul, and that they only talked about their genital organs more or less comfortably when discussing reproductive diseases or childbirth. The historical absence of sex education in schools and in the family, the power of Catholicism in silencing and stigmatizing nonreproductive sexual gratification, and the censorship imposed by the last dictatorship had left Argentines, especially women, uneducated and discontented. The local medical and psychoanalytic professions had also contributed to this outcome, frequently reproving and denying the clitoral orgasm and female masturbation.[64]

Sex therapists argued that self-knowledge and education were the first steps toward self-appreciation, healing, and sexual joy, and promoted sexual enrichment groups as an efficient tool to achieve these goals. Sexual enrichment groups offered participants—mostly urban, middle- and upper-class, and educated individuals—a safe, communal, and receptive space to learn about sexuality and their bodies, recognize and normalize sexual preferences, and explore and share sexual fears and prejudices, thus ending sexual illiteracy and improving their sex lives. A typical sexual enrichment group for women (men gathered separately) met four times monthly for three hours each session. During the sessions, the female sex therapist lectured about anatomy and physiological responses to sexual stimulation, led simple physical exercises to improve relaxation and body comfort, and employed images and movie clips to pose questions and debate ideas, but her main role was to facilitate discussion among the participants. In fact, sexual enrichment groups operated as intensive workshops where people talked publicly about their past, current, and ideal sex lives; described sexual fantasies; asked and responded to personal questions about orgasm and sexual arousal; explained their experiences with masturbation; and shared their homework.

Participants were asked to complete a series of tasks at home, both alone and with their partners, and then present the results and discuss their feelings, difficulties, and accomplishments with the whole group the following week. Individual chores included completing assigned erotic and scientific readings, doing breathing exercises and Kegel exercises (the contraction and relaxation of the muscle of the pelvic floor), performing a vaginal and vulval self-exam with the help of a hand mirror and drawing detailed sketches, performing self-stimulation, and keeping a diary of sexual experiences and the emotions and thoughts triggered by the encounters. The intersection between sexual enrichment groups and the destape in the press is evident in assignments that required participants to bring to the session a print advertisement they considered sexy, a photo from a magazine they viewed as sexually stimulating, or an article for discussion. Homework with their partners required couples to discuss their sexual preferences, feelings, and possible changes in their sex lives—for example, by sharing three things they would like the other to do or change in bed. Additionally, home assignments directed participants to give and receive sexual and nonsexual massages, experiment with new sex positions, and enact sexual fantasies with their partners.[65]

Other popular activities led by sexologists were workshops called *talleres de reflexión e información en sexualidad* (TRIS). Men, women, and couples could attend these workshops, which were co-led by male and female therapists. TRIS were not conceived to treat particular problems or concerns of individuals and couples, and thus they did not include a personal exploration of sexual practices, as proposed in sexual enrichment groups. TRIS were designed to demystify sexuality while correcting ignorance on sexual issues, assisting to ease anxiety and confusion caused by misinformation, and helping participants approach and understand sexuality, both as knowledge and practice, without guilt. The rules of the workshop recognized that speaking and learning about sexuality among strangers was challenging, and therefore asked participants for confidentiality, authenticity, and straightforwardness. Equally significant, participation guidelines stressed that silence as an act of contemplation was allowed but would be openly reproved when it denoted a negative attitude or criticism.[66]

For many, speaking out was a challenge. In their study published in 1988, psychologists Diana Kordon and Lucila Edelman argued that two of the most important psychological effects of political repression during the dictatorship were silence and feelings of guilt.[67] Sex group workshops contributed to erasing these effects by offering a space where people could alter the profound inhibition, reservation, and self-restraint that had dominated interpersonal relations in the previous decade. Reflecting on their experiences leading group sessions, sexologists agreed that sexual enrichment groups and workshops provided more than information and techniques to improve the sex lives of participants. Indeed, they were platforms to inspire and teach individuals to speak openly, listen, discuss, share, cultivate an open mind, and avoid judgmental attitudes—an antidote to the culture of shame and introversion developed in the recent past years.[68]

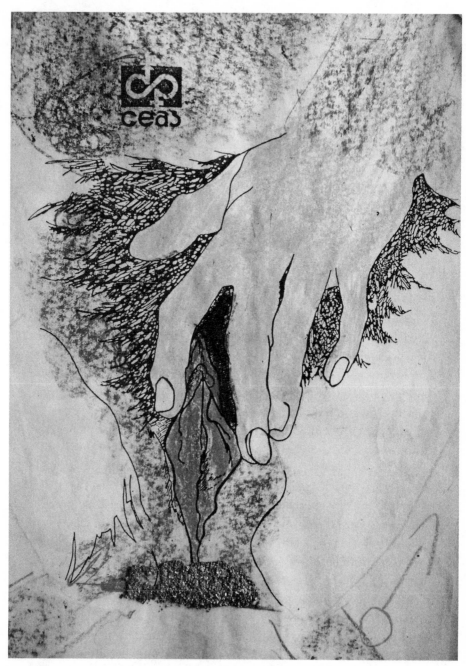

Figure 3.1. In sexual enrichment groups, sexologists invited women to learn about their bodies by coloring drawings. Courtesy María Luisa Lerer.

Just like the success of the sexual enrichment groups, the boom in sex therapy was intrinsically related to the same search for healing and pleasure. Sexologists working in the return to democracy remembered that initially there was a slight majority of male over female patients in sex therapy, while women were the majority and the most enthusiastic attendants in sexual enrichment groups. After those initial years, the number of female patients in sex therapy increased. During this period, couples looking for help were a minority. Patients were middle- and upper-class individuals with economic and cultural resources, and the majority lived in cities, although people from small towns in the provinces traveled to Buenos Aires and Rosario for consultations. This patient profile is related to the fact that there were only a handful of sexology specialists in public (free) hospitals, and the overwhelming majority of sexologists worked in private practice. Furthermore, most health insurance plans did not recognize sexual dysfunctions and thus did not cover sexology treatment, forcing sexologists to disguise diagnostics to help patients obtain some coverage and, most frequently, leaving patients responsible for payment.[69]

Still, the institutional and educational consolidation of sexology, its media prominence, the widening group of professionals in the field, the new personal and social disinhibition to talk about sex, and the perception of sexual pleasure as an important component of life increased the numbers of patients in sex therapy. While some commentators viewed these numbers as evidence of the appearance of new sexual dysfunctions, experts had a more satisfactory explanation. Sex therapist Adrián Sapetti affirmed that the disorders he and his colleagues were treating in the 1980s were not new but had always existed; what had changed was that "people used to repress their problems but now they understand that there is a place to talk about them with no shame and with the hope of change."[70]

The main concerns of women doing sex therapy were preorgasmia and lack of sexual desire, while among men, the main problems were premature ejaculation and erectile dysfunction. There was also a group of men, women, and couples who looked for help after years of unconsummated marriages, in many cases due to vaginismus, an involuntary tightening of the muscles around the vagina that prevents penetration. Pioneering sexologist Laura Caldiz explained that the smaller number of female patients at the beginning was primarily caused by their lack of information about female pleasure. Many women, Caldiz stated, "had no idea they were supposed to experience pleasure; some felt it and some didn't, but for these women, the lack of pleasure was not a reason for consultation."[71] Sex therapists agreed that many women did not know what to ask and how to ask their partners. In many cases, this was directly related to the fact that women knew very little about their own bodies and had seldom explored their reactions to sexual stimulation. In 1984, sexologist León Roberto Gindin affirmed that 80 percent of female patients consulting sexologists for preorgasmia had never masturbated. Similarly, many cases of premature ejaculation in adult men were the result of inadequate ejaculatory control that had started when they were teenagers and continued due to shame, lack of information, and absence of advice; it was "a problem of someone who learned things the wrong way."[72]

And then, the destape happened and all Argentines, but particularly women, were inundated with information about genitalia, sexual satisfaction, and orgasm, creating fertile ground where they could reassess the meanings of "normal." Surveys revealed that women were particularly concerned about this issue, consulting specialists with the goal of either reaffirming "normalcy" or correcting perceived "abnormality." Laura Caldiz gave a clear example of the media's role in encouraging women to look for professional advice and help with their sex lives: when press coverage about the G-spot (an erogenous area of the vagina believed to lead to orgasm when stimulated) exploded, appointments about the G-spot and where and how to find it rose markedly. Interestingly, sexologist Mirta Granero remembered that by the end of the 1980s, exposure to sex information was palpable, as patients were more knowledgeable and came better prepared to their appointments.[73]

For these audiences, articles, advice columns, and interviews with sexologists in the press were empowering and assuring, as specialists promised solutions and promoted their expertise with a tone that positively emphasized the capacity of individuals to change and the availability of means and knowledge to produce new outcomes. A good example of this tone is the more frequent use of the term "preorgasmia"—coined by American sex therapist Lonnie Barbach in the mid-1970s—instead of "anorgasmia," which moved attention away from female inability and failure to the real possibility for all women to reach orgasm under the right conditions. Similarly, "erectile dysfunction" was commonly used instead of "impotence." Furthermore, sexologists argued that pleasure was larger and richer than orgasm and was attainable for all. Rather than proposing pleasure as an obligation, sex specialists defined it as a right and a choice while still highlighting the equation between sexual pleasure and happiness that the media, with their help, so persistently portrayed.[74]

## SEXOLOGISTS AND THE MEDIA

The relationship between the destape and sexologists was profoundly symbiotic. The rise and boom of the field was connected to the omnipresence of sexologists in the media, which secured their popularity, attracted patients, and ensured publishers and readers for their books. Sexologist Adrián Sapetti remembered that when he, as a first-time author, approached the publishing house Galerna—which was printing translations of American sexologists—with his manuscript on male sexuality, the editor signed him a contract on the spot without reading the material. The editor explained to the amazed author that in the current context the book would be a success because all people wanted to talk and read about was sex; sexologists were everywhere, and, naturally, audiences were interested in what they had to say. The editor was right. *La sexualidad masculina* (1986) sold out in a month and was reedited just three months after its first edition. Equally important, it produced for Sapetti the first patient for his private sexology clinic.[75] Between 1985 and 1987, Sapetti, Gindin, Caldiz, and Lerer, the leaders in the field, published books that became instant best sellers—for Sapetti and Lerer, two each during this two-year period—and had numerous editions. In 1986, the owners of a famous bookstore in Buenos Aires observed that sexology books accounted for 10 percent of the daily sales.[76]

The books rapidly sold out because through ubiquitous interviews, articles in the press, sexology sections like "Investigación Especial" in *Sex Humor*, *consultorios sexológicos*, and television and radio appearances, these experts were well known. This was both a national and a local phenomenon. In Rosario, for example, sexologist Mirta Granero had two weekly segments on the most popular local television news show as well as a segment on a radio show every weekend. Predictably, strangers greeted her on the streets. Sexologists had such prominence in the media that they were the most consistent force in propelling the destape forward. Indeed, because of their decisive cultural and social influence, sexologists embodied the destape as effectively as the nude starlets that populated magazines and movies.[77]

Sexologist María Luisa Lerer provides a good example. Although she was a regular figure in the print press, Lerer owed most of her reputation to television, where she participated in different shows and was a frequent guest on *Veinte Mujeres* on the ATC channel, Argentina's principal public broadcast television station. *Veinte Mujeres* was hosted by Fernando Bravo and Mónica Gutierrez and consisted of a panel of twenty women who asked special guests questions and debated different themes. When producers noticed that rating figures grew every time Lerer was on the air, they invited her to a regular space every Thursday. Young, attractive, and soft-spoken, Lerer discussed topics that had never been discussed on television in such a way before. Her emphasis on female pleasure and the importance of the clitoris as women's most sensitive erogenous zone—which prompted a female journalist to call her "Ms. Best Sex"—earned her the support of the female audience and, on occasion, triggered the condescension and scorn of some men.[78] Lerer remembered that one of the first times she talked about female masturbation on television, naturalizing and encouraging its practice, a teary sixty-year-old woman who was part of the cleaning staff in the channel building approached her after the show and thanked her because now she realized she "was normal." Television allowed Lerer to help large numbers of women and men concretely while also boosting her own clinical practice. The week after she talked about the noncon-summation of marriage, her office scheduled close to forty appointments related to this problem.[79]

Television greatly popularized sexology, but it was here where the new democratic government most effectively controlled the "excesses" of the destape and ultra-Catholic sectors most successfully fought back against the new openness in the public discussion of sexuality. In 1986, for example, the COMFER "preventively" suspended for two months the treatment of sexual topics on television after the show *Cable a Tierra* asked people on the streets their opinion on the relation between the size of a penis and sexual pleasure. Ultra-Catholic sectors actively petitioned the government for sanctions against the show, arguing that the topic and the explicit use of "penis" were inappropriate and offensive. They also asserted that the timing made it even more insulting since the day the show aired, Catholics were participating in the procession of the Virgin of Luján in Buenos Aires. The show was canceled a couple months later, and its host was indicted for "an affront to public modesty," the most severe disciplining of television content after the return to democracy.[80]

In addition to censorship, there were other reasons for being careful. In October 1983, two months before Alfonsín's inauguration, an anonymous bomb destroyed the offices of the Asociación Argentina de Protección Familiar (AAPF; Argentine Association for Family Protection), an institution devoted to sex education and family planning with a strong presence in the media. A year later, *Sexualmente hablando*, a radio show hosted by León Roberto Gindin that ran every day from Monday to Friday at midnight on Radio Splendid, received numerous threats signed by the Comando Giovenco—a right-wing Peronist organization—including death threats against Gindin. The popular show had special guests—writers, philosophers, historians—who discussed different themes connected to sexuality and received about forty calls every night from radio listeners who asked questions to Gindin and guest therapists. When Gindin decided to persist despite the threatening phone calls and letters, the extremist group began targeting the show's guests—most of whom continued to contribute. Yet, when the threats began to be directed to the advertisers, most of them withdrew their support and the show had to be canceled. A reporter, reflecting on the reasons behind the end of the radio show, argued that "it died from fear, not from censorship."[81]

Gindin found a home for a new show, *Sexualidad y Pareja*, with the same format in Radio Belgrano and continued successfully for many years. However, the threats in 1984 confirm that the open discussion of sex was resisted by some minorities, even at the peak of the destape and the euphoric democratic context. Further, they corroborate the palpable legacy of authoritarianism and intolerance that employed terror and intimidation to silence and conquer. This resistance notwithstanding, Laura Caldiz, who participated in *Sexualidad y Pareja*, remembered that the show was extremely successful among audiences and an important tool to promote CETIS; many professionals looking for training in the field as well as patients had been show listeners before coming to the center.[82]

## SEXOLOGY FOR WOMEN

Alongside Caldiz and Gindin, psychologist María Luisa Lerer was not only a pioneering figure during the boom of sexology in the 1980s but also the most popular because of her strong presence in the media, especially her weekly appearances on television. Frustrated with the lack of attention and effectiveness of therapy in addressing and solving sexual problems, Lerer immediately connected with Caldiz, whom she met right after her return to the country. Soon after, Lerer also left for training at the IASHS and traveled to New York, where she met Helen Singer Kaplan, establishing a friendly relationship that prompted Kaplan's first and only visit to Argentina (and to Latin America) for a series of seminars in 1984. An active organizer and mentor of the early activities that would lead to the foundation of CETIS, Lerer left her association with Gindin and Caldiz quite early and in 1981 founded the AASH, an institution devoted to sex knowledge dissemination, and the Centro de Estudios y Educación de Asistencia en Sexualidad (CEAS; Center for the Study, Education, and Treatment of Sexuality), which organized educational activities and offered clinical services.

In an interview, Lerer explained that she parted ways with Caldiz and Gindin because she publicly and openly identified herself as a feminist and emphatically defended women's rights in and out of the bedroom. Lerer argued that her colleagues thought her views and profile might alienate potential male and female audiences—both patients and professionals looking for specialization in the field—in a context in which feminism was the object of prejudice and misconception. In fact, a poll among 1,500 women published by *Mujer 10* showed that 87 percent of the respondents disliked women who identified themselves as feminists.[83] This backdrop did not deter Lerer from openly embracing her ideas and joining a revitalized feminism that, in the new democratic context, was experiencing electrifying times. In 1983, she was one of the founders of Lugar de Mujer, a feminist institution devoted to education, consciousness raising, and legal counseling, and later in the decade, of the Grupo Interdisciplinario de Estudios de la Mujer (GIEM; Interdisciplinary Group for the Study of Women), composed of women scholars interested in the study of women and gender issues.[84]

Lerer's *Sexualidad femenina: Mitos, realidades y el sentido de ser mujer* (1986) was probably the most successful sexology book written by an Argentine expert in the 1980s—in a context in which all local sexologists experienced notable editorial success. A best seller for three years, *Sexualidad femenina* had four editions in four months. As in her television and

Figure 3.2. Sexologists Laura Caldiz, León Roberto Gindin, and María Luisa Lerer. Courtesy María Luisa Lerer.

press appearances, in her book, Lerer broadened the scope of discussion by linking female sexuality to the life and experiences of women more generally, highlighting the importance of education for women ("You can't be free if you're ignorant"), celebrating women's independence from men, embracing the idea that the personal is political, and demanding democracy not only on the streets but at home. Lerer applauded feminism for fighting for these goals, voicing women's needs and demands, and questioning motherhood as women's ultimate social role. She emphasized women's commonalities over their numerous differences and imagined a female universe where social class was irrelevant. Lerer affirmed, "We, the women—independently of the social class in which we were born into and belong—share sensations, emotions, feelings, and problems with regards to our role in life, to the dangers involved in deciding, dissenting, and owning our body and our sexuality."[85] As in her appearances in the media, in the book, Lerer refrained from explicitly denouncing patriarchy and machismo, and rather than discussing the role of men in women's sexual, social, and cultural oppression, she identified the "bearers of culture"— parents, political and community leaders, and educators—as those who "always had a thou-shalt-not on the tip of their tongue."[86]

Lerer's book is less a sex manual than a pedagogical consciousness-raising book that employs historical, philosophical, and sociological reflections as much as sex science to educate women, or better yet, to help women "unlearn" what they have been taught wrong. The chapters are organized around myths about masturbation, menstruation, orgasm, birth control, and desire, among other topics. This didactic approach had already proved to be successful for Lerer, as she employed myths in her early television appearances to talk to an audience unaccustomed to hearing a woman publicly discuss such provocative themes. The myths analyzed in the book powerfully reflect the profound misconceptions surrounding female sexuality in the 1980s, which were also revealed in the surveys conducted in those years: women are sexually passive, female masturbation is abnormal and a poor substitute for sex with a man, women are the only ones responsible for birth control, religious women cannot experience sexual pleasure, and women from the lower classes enjoy sex the most. Lerer also debunked myths such as wives must always comply with the sexual requests of their husbands, older and menopausal women are not sexual, women experience pleasure emotionally rather than corporeally, "real" women are multiorgasmic, and women do not have sexual fantasies—just to name a few. In so doing, Lerer rejected common misrepresentations about oral and anal sex, nymphomania, preorgasmia, libido, sexual violence, the vagina and the clitoris, and virginity.

In her book, Lerer celebrated sex for pleasure while recognizing women's rights to enjoy sex independent from reproduction and free from the risk of pregnancy. Lerer was the only sex expert during this period who explicitly declared that maternal instinct is a myth and motherhood is an option. Furthermore, she moved the discussion of motherhood away from common themes such as birth control and family planning. Her argument was less about women's right to decide the number of children they wanted and more about recognizing women's right to remain child-free by choice—a theme both sexologists and family planning experts ignored. Lerer maintained that feminism is not antimotherhood but wants to educate women to be better mothers, to empower them to be more than mothers, and to support women who refuse to be mothers if they so choose.[87] Equally significant, Lerer challenged traditional understandings of women as caregivers by debunking the myth that the self-realization of older women depends on having grandchildren. Lerer proposed seniority as a period of freedom, self-indulgence, and personal achievements that should go beyond taking care of grandchildren and during which a fulfilling, exciting sex life was as feasible and important as in other periods of life.[88]

In line with the overall silence on same-sex relations in the Argentine sexology of the period, Lerer wrote for heterosexual women and called into question myths related to heterosexual sex. She only addressed lesbianism briefly when countering the myth that "homosexual women are different and no integration is possible." She opposed this notion by arguing that homosexuality is not a disease and by drawing attention to the contradiction of those who admire the creations of gay artists—the examples she offered were men—but ridicule and mistreat their gay neighbors. Lerer further asked readers to reject discrimination and intolerance, which cause so much suffering and pain for the victims. Bringing the historical context into the discussion, Lerer argued that defending democracy should not be a discursive exercise but that democracy should be lived and supported concretely by rejecting prejudices and embracing equality for all. Interestingly, and consistent with the overall desexualization and de-erotization of gays and lesbians during the destape, this is the only section in a book about sexuality where there is no discussion of sex.[89]

Against the predictions of Lerer's colleagues, it was probably her emphasis on women's rights that made her extremely popular. In interviews, articles, and essays with several feminist experts—sociologists, activists, lawyers, artists—Lerer was always "the feminist sexologist."[90] Still, she was conscientious to tailor her feminism to make it unthreatening and to differentiate it from "radical" versions that the press stigmatized as "anti-men" and "anti-motherhood." A reporter told Lerer that when she revealed to an acquaintance that she would interview her, he replied: "That feminist that talks nonsense on television must be an old maid, a divorcee, or one of those free-minded lunatics who wants to try absolutely everything." Interestingly, Lerer did not question the stereotype and merely answered by declaring that she was very much in love with her husband

and adored her son.[91] Similarly, in an interview on the popular humorous show *La noticia rebelde* in 1987, the hosts asked Lerer if she was good in bed because she knew so much about sex; expressed disapproval of her talking about sex on *Veinte Mujeres* in the early afternoon, when those topics should only be aired at midnight; and asked whether she studied and wrote about sexuality because she felt sexually unsatisfied with her husband. The interview was jokey and guests of the show knew they would be teased. Yet it is revealing because the show hosts, who were contributors to *Sex Humor*, exposed and ridiculed antiquated assumptions still prevalent even at the peak of the destape—about the propriety of sexology, the sex lives of women therapists, and the pertinence of debating about sex, particularly female sexuality, on television.[92]

Lerer neutralized the characterization of sexology as a discourse that enabled licentiousness and unrestraint by linking women's right to pleasure with a healthy sexuality that was essential for a harmonic, overall state of well-being. Lerer asserted that "a healthier sex life will contribute to more spirited human beings, individuals with a balance between body, mind and spirit, and with a solid identity."[93] The goal, she explained, was to have a happy life away from prejudices and external pressures. Lerer argued that she was a feminist because she believed in the right of women to lead this life and encouraged and educated women so they could succeed. In an interview, for example, she recognized the importance of sexual liberation and experimentation promoted by the destape but praised the young women who wanted to remain a virgin until getting married. Lerer emphasized the importance of personal decisions—especially those that seemed to run against current social, cultural, and sexual trends—and prompted women to listen to their feelings, follow their convictions, share knowledge and experiences with other women, and educate themselves "to put an end to the conspiracy of silence surrounding sex."[94] Thus, she underlined messages of self-knowledge and self-acceptance while encouraging female audiences to liberate their voice and stop silencing emotions and desires.[95]

At the same time, and even in the receptive context of the destape, Lerer also dealt with disapproval. Several listeners complained to the radio station where she used the term "coitus" in an interview, and she was frequently confronted in public by men who told her "she did not know what she was talking about," while strangers shouted at her and called her *tortillera* (dyke) on the streets. In an interview, Lerer explained that at that moment, some sectors associated a woman who talked about female pleasure with a lesbian, and that hostility resulted because men felt challenged when she insisted that many were unable to sexually please a woman. Lerer responded to disparagement by arguing that being called a lesbian was not an insult and lesbianism was not a disease—this was a topic that was rarely discussed in the media and that she addressed only succinctly as she continued talking exclusively to heterosexual women. Her most effective response was to educate heterosexual women about their bodies and sexuality by openly contesting stereotypical models of masculinity and femininity. Lerer supported wives who avoided sex with their husbands, arguing that men lacked imagination and patience; celebrated older women who dated younger men; backed men who wanted to remain a virgin until their marriage; argued that, against male bragging about uninterrupted sexual potency and unending desire, all men suffered from erectile dysfunction on occasion; and promoted women's sexual fantasies with men other than their partners and the open admission of and conversation about these fantasies by the couple.[96]

Maria Helena Moreira Alves and Guillermo O'Donnell have described the culture of fear that pervaded life under the military dictatorships in Latin America by highlighting the silence caused by strict censorship, the frustration resulting from the suppression of most channels of free communication and exchange, a deep sense of isolation and solitude, and a feeling of complete hopelessness in the face of the power of the state. As a result, individuals experienced a profound impoverishment of personal and social life. For most citizens, life was lonely, cold, and dark and infused by an authoritarian ethos that forced them to embrace homogeneity, acquiescence, and an oppressive sense of duty. Sexual ideologies reproduced these dictates: sex information was censured, sex experimentation was curtailed, and sexual freedom was repressed. Sex was imbued with meanings such as allegiance, morality, family, tradition, and the common good, which, ironically, erased subjectivity and individuality from one of the most intimate and personal spheres of life, and with them, any trace of desire, sensuality, and delight.[97]

The return to democracy renewed social and personal interactions, liberated individual expression, invigorated inclusion and companionship, and instilled new doses of courage and optimism. Feelings of individual and collective survival awakened a new hunger for life, for new experiences and sensations, and for excitement. And sex, the destape media assured audiences, was the key to make up for lost time and satisfy that appetite. Yet, in freeing burning desires, the new sexual openness also revealed much sexual misery, confronting many Argentines with frustrations and limitations. As both a cause and an effect of the destape, sexology fueled and channeled a search for sexual pleasure to remedy this deprivation while establishing and legitimizing itself as a profession almost from scratch. Sex experts disseminated sex knowledge in the media; naturalized discussions about sex; popularized sex therapy, sex manuals, and sex workshops; and promoted an unapologetic view of heterosexual gratification and eroticism. Sexology positioned the heterosexual individual at the center of a sexual narrative that, in contrast to the recent past, championed self-discovery, self-expression, personal liberation, and happiness—a promise enticing for all but especially for women, who had been historically repressed in their search for a gratifying sexuality.

# 4

# FAMILY PLANNING, SEX EDUCATION, AND
# THE REBUILDING OF DEMOCRACY

**Personal liberation, the recovery of self,** pleasure, and the satisfaction of desire were the most prominent and tantalizing values embedded in sex discourses in the return to democracy, omnipresent in magazines, erotic literature, films, sex therapy, and sex manuals. However, the cultural relevance of those values fostered by the destape coexisted alongside a different conversation proposed by family planning experts and sex educators who moved the discussion from the bedroom to hospitals and schools and linked sexuality to social progress and the development of the nation. This chapter analyzes the characteristics and goals of family planning and sex education in the 1980s and examines the role of experts in both fields in disseminating an alternative view of sexuality at the peak of the destape. Instead of using a language of sex fantasies and sexual gratification, family planning and sex education specialists and advocates reframed the discussion of sex in relation to health, economic progress, and social well-being; focused on human rights and the social consequences of individual and government decisions; and underlined the roles of the state, the community, and parents in the achievement of a healthy sexuality. This chapter argues that in so doing, experts effectively connected the consolidation and the success of the newborn democracy to popular access to family planning and school-based sex education.

Because of their social prominence, two institutions lie at the core of the analysis. One, the Asociación Argentina de Protección Familiar (AAPF; Argentine Association for Family Protection), was founded in Buenos Aires in 1966 by a group of obstetricians and gynecologists with the support of the International Planned Parenthood Federation (IPPF), which incorporated the AAPF within its network three years later. The two goals of the AAPF were the extension of sex education and the promotion, among both physicians and the general public, of family planning—that is, the practice of controlling the number of children in a family and the intervals between their births through contraception. Given the absence of both private intervention and state policy in the field, the AAPF was a true pioneering institution. In fact, troubled by the consistently small population in a vast and depopulated territory, low fertility rates, and the potential consequences of both for economic development and defense, the Argentine state had historically ignored, reproved, or censured family planning while embracing a pronatalist discourse. The fertility rate, which had been declining since the early twentieth century, reached its lowest point in the 1960s, when the national number of children per woman was 2.93 and in the city of Buenos Aires was 1.69—the lowest among capital cities in Latin America.[1]

The other leading institution was the Asociación Rosarina de Educación Sexual y Sexología (ARESS; Sex Education and Sexology Association of Rosario). Devoted to the promotion of school-based sex education and the training of sex educators, ARESS began informally in Rosario, Santa Fe, in 1976 with a small interdisciplinary group of professionals. In addition to physicians and psychologists, historians and sociologists helped the organization craft its pedagogical style and contributed a social and cultural outlook to discussions, strategies, and teaching materials. Officially founded two years later, ARESS became a fundamental collaborator with the AAPF in the return to democracy, an important organ for the promotion and dissemination of sex education outside Buenos Aires, and a key component of a significant Latin American network of sex educators.[2]

To excavate the social and cultural impact of family planning and sex education in the 1980s and to understand the profound transformations that the arrival of democracy produced in both fields, the chapter first considers the state of family planning and sex education in the 1960s and the 1970s, the restraints imposed by the dictatorship, and how youth sexuality changed in the process of redemocratization. The analysis then moves to exploring the rise of family planning and school-based sex education in the 1980s and the expansion of institutionalization and advocacy while examining the emergent public debate and the opposition of the Catholic Church and Catholic sectors. This chapter reveals how family planning and sex education advocates legitimized their fields by emphasizing their contributions to democracy and discusses the major silences and absences in their proposals.

## FAMILY PLANNING IN THE 1960S AND 1970S

Walter Barbato, an early member of the AAPF, and Luis María Aller Atucha, AAPF director of communication and information in the early 1970s and later the editor of its journal, *Contribuciones*, agreed that the rising maternal mortality rate due to abortion was the main motivation for the founders of the organization. This was a major preoccupation for physicians all over the country and the reason why, from its beginning, the AAPF had representatives from Córdoba, Rosario, and Mendoza in addition to Buenos Aires.[3] The institution was not entirely alone in its endeavors. In 1960, the Universidad Nacional de Buenos Aires (UBA; National University of Buenos Aires) began a family planning program for very-low-income sectors in the Isla Maciel that ended after a few years due to lack of institutional support, dwindling economic resources, and political opposition. In 1964, pastor Luis Parrilla founded the Centro de Orientación para la Vida Familiar y Comunitaria (COVIFAC; Orientation Center for Family and Community Life) in Villa Mitre, Buenos Aires. COVIFAC, which ran a school that pioneered sex education in its curricula and a reproductive health care center that actively promoted family planning, was an important ally of the AAPF. However, original as the COVIFAC's and the UBA's programs were, they did not share the AAPF's national scope and influence nor its endurance over decades.[4]

In its first years, the AAPF's emphasis was on the professional training of doctors, psychologists, educators, and social workers on reproductive health through talks, seminars, and workshops. In the early 1970s, the AAPF began creating educational materials for children and teenagers and expanding the outreach to schools and other institutions interested in sex education. In 1977, the AAPF launched *Contribuciones*, a journal on reproductive health that was distributed among physicians, sex educators, sexologists, and health institutions all over the country, and served as its organ for the dissemination of news and activities. Although Catholic, right-wing, and left-wing sectors alike asserted that the AAPF promoted antinatalism, threatened the moral order, and was an agent of foreign imperialism—one that sought to "sterilize" the country to deplete it demographically in the face of a future of food scarcity—the organization supported family and celebrated children. The institution logo was, in fact, a couple with two children and a baby. Yet the AAPF emphasized the social, economic, and personal importance of controlling the number of children and the intervals between births for the well-being of the family, the individual, and the nation.[5]

From the beginning, the AAPF underlined the role of family planning—which they called "protection" to avoid direct controversial references to contraception—as the best antidote to increasing numbers of abortions. A survey conducted by the AAPF between 1966 and 1969 among more than 10,000 women showed that 30 percent had had at least one abortion. Statistics suggested that there were between 300,000 and 400,000 abortions annually—equaling one abortion for every two births—and that abortion was a main cause of maternal mortality. Polls revealed that half of all women had never used any contraception method before getting pregnant for the first time and that coitus interruptus was the privileged contraception method. Moreover, against common assumptions, surveys showed high numbers of abortions among married women.[6]

Since most of the AAPF's founders and members worked in public health centers and many headed residency programs in public teaching hospitals, the first AAPF-supported family planning programs, which began in the early 1970s, took place in these institutions mainly serving low-income patients. Later, the AAPF opened its own private clinics in different cities around the country, where patients were charged a small fee for services. The AAPF was able to offer affordable reproductive care because it received economic support from the IPPF, and pharmaceutical companies either donated birth control pills (produced in Argentina since 1961 by international laboratories operating in the country), intrauterine devices (IUDs), and condoms or offered them at lower prices. Laboratories were particularly interested in promoting their birth control pills given their novelty, the lack of information about them among physicians and patients alike, and the initial resistance and negative reviews of gynecologists who, based on religious beliefs and lack of experience and knowledge, refrained from prescribing them to their patients.[7] In fact, opposition within the profession was quite strong. In 1982, AAPF president Héctor Peña remembered the difficult beginnings in the 1960s and how resistance still existed two decades later. Peña recalled that "we had to fight against fear, ignorance, incomprehension, indifference, biases, egoism, miserly interests at all hospital levels, especially among those who one would have expected to be more understanding, like directors, chiefs of service, and doctors who even today—though it's hard to believe—we have not yet won over."[8]

In 1974, the slow consolidation of the AAPF and the uneasy expansion of family planning faced the most serious challenge to date, when the government of Juan Domingo Perón passed decree 659. The decree expressed the government's concern about the "alarming demographic crisis" and pointed to family planning as a threat to the nation and the family as well as an obstacle to women assuming their maternal roles. The decree further identified family planning as a factor that "distracted" the young in the fulfillment of their "natural obligation" to secure the future of the country. It instructed the Department of Public Health to research the current demographic situation of the country and mandated control over the commercialization of the birth control pill by requiring a prescription in triplicate—for the patient, the pharmacy, and the Department of Public Health. Most important, the decree prohibited all activities directly and indirectly related to family planning and demanded the development of a popular campaign to inform the population about the "risks" of birth control methods and practices.[9]

After the 1976 coup, the military not only kept decree 659 unchanged but also reinforced it with decree 3,938, which, signed in 1977, aimed at expanding the population—seen as a means to ensure national security and development—by increasing the fertility rate. To achieve this goal, the decree reconfirmed the elimination of all activities promoting family planning.[10] These legal measures and the overall context of fear, repression, and censorship during the dictatorship reversed the slow but consistent development of family planning that had been taking place in the previous decade. However, the precise application and impact of the decrees is difficult to measure—whether physicians and pharmacies, for example, followed regulations on prescribing and selling the birth control pill is hard to assess. Studies do show that between 1970 and 1981, sales of the pill grew only 47 percent—that is, an annual growth rate of merely 3.6 percent. In contrast, in the same period, annual sales in Brazil grew 419 percent and in Mexico 320 percent.[11]

After the 1974 and 1977 decrees, the AAPF-sponsored clinics in public hospitals closed, and although most of the AAPF private clinics continued operating, they did so quietly. These were tough years. Throughout the 1970s, economic hardships for the IPPF meant declining financial support for the AAPF, prompting institutional retreat and a consequent decrease in activities and public visibility. Equally important, during the Peronist government, the AAPF central office in Buenos Aires was vandalized and its archives destroyed.[12] The AAPF suffered the most severe attack in October 1983—a week before the elections that marked the return of constitutional rule—when a bomb destroyed the main office in Buenos Aires. Because the explosion occurred on a Saturday, when the office was closed, there were no casualties. Despite the violence, the fear, and the extensive material damages, and encouraged by public support, AAPF director Domingo Olivares declared that the members of the organization would continue moving forward with "their morale intact." He further reflected that the attack showed how, for "the enemies of democracy," family planning was a profoundly destabilizing and destructive agent against the social status quo.[13]

Despite prohibitions and tight monitoring during the dictatorship, access to all types of contraception was easier—as it had always been—for middle- and upper-class women, who could afford birth control and visits to doctors' private practices. In contrast, women from low-income sectors, who relied on public hospitals to receive reproductive health care, were in the most disadvantageous position since legal measures were more effectively imposed and implemented in those institutions, which were dependent on state funds and under the jurisdiction of the federal and local governments. In some cases, powerful department directors committed to the cause fought to keep the sector in operation under the radar, almost underground, but were unable to offer patients free birth control methods as they had in the past. Less devoted or sympathetic administrators or those who had always opposed family planning abided by the law, and reproductive health clinics in public hospitals were shut down. This did not mean that when the office doors closed, individual physicians did not discuss birth control with their patients, but the legal, institutional, political, and social climate profoundly stigmatized family planning, discouraging both practitioners and patients. Even textbooks for high school students asserted that "any use of contraception is against nature and could thus be considered a wrongdoing, a crime, turmoil in married life."[14]

## FAMILY PLANNING AFTER THE RETURN TO DEMOCRACY

The return to democracy inaugurated a golden period for institutions such as the AAPF and professionals devoted to family planning, as the new climate of freedom, liberalization, and destape invigorated discussions about the subject, giving it unprecedented visibility. After years of silence, the press actively reported about family planning, covered activities sponsored by the AAPF, and interviewed professionals working in the field. The reversal of the restricting legal measures was not immediate, though. In 1984, the Argentine government signed the recommendations of the United Nations International Conference on Population held in Mexico City that declared that "unwanted high fertility adversely affects the health and welfare of individuals and families, especially among the poor, and seriously impedes social and economic progress in many countries." It also maintained that women and children were the main victims of unregulated fertility and pointed to pregnancy as a major cause of maternal, infant, and childhood mortality and morbidity.[15]

Yet Alfonsín's government took two more years to abolish decree 659; decree 3,938 was revoked in 1992. This represented an important triumph for the AAPF, whose director, Domingo Olivares, was part of the Comisión Nacional de Políticas Familiares y de Población (National Commission for Family and Population Policy), organized by the Alfonsín government. The commission, entrusted to develop a program on family planning, recommended the revocation of decree 659 and conceptualized decree 2,274, which, passed in 1986, recognized that the public health system should provide citizens information about and assistance with family planning so they could exercise their right to decide their number of children effectively.[16]

Democracy brought important changes in how the AAPF conceptualized family planning. After 1983, fueled by an atmosphere permeated by
the recognition and defense of human rights, the AAPF fully embraced
the definition of family planning as a human right proposed by the United
Nations in the 1968 Conference on Human Rights in Tehran. The conference declared that "parents have a basic human right to decide freely
and responsibly on the number and spacing of children and a right to
adequate education and information in this respect."[17] The concept of
family planning as a human right expanded and enriched the discussion
about contraception and its benefits. In the repressive and conservative
climate of the dictatorship, the AAPF had mainly proposed family planning as a preventative measure against abortion, as it was more effective,
more acceptable, and safer to represent it as the lesser of two evils. In the
new context of freedom and an uninhibited approach to sexuality fueled
by the destape, the AAPF more significantly linked family planning to
personal choice, responsible parenthood, and individual well-being. The
AAPF also prominently addressed dangers, problems, and tensions that
had only timidly, if at all, been debated in the previous years, such as
the reality of unintended pregnancies in middle-class and upper-class
married couples; female anxiety about motherhood; the physical but also
the psychological mistreatment of unwanted children; the negative effects
of unwanted pregnancies on individuals, couples, and families; and the
power imbalances between men and women in deciding when and how
many children they wanted to have.[18]

A good example of this turn is evident in the AAPF educational and
promotional short films in support of family planning. Made during the
dictatorship, *Dulce espera* (Javier Szerman, 1983) proposes family planning
and sex education as the antidotes to abortion. The film tells the story of
a teenage couple who decide to terminate an unwanted pregnancy, depicting the tensions between the adolescents, their fears of having an illegal
abortion, their problems getting the money for the procedure, the loneliness and frustration experienced by the girl, and the failure of family and
school as means of support and guidance.[19] A year later, the AAPF released
*Los ambiguos sentimientos de las frutillas con crema*, a film also directed by
Szerman that received a lot of attention in the media because it aired on
national television.[20] Unlike its previous films with specific educational
and training purposes, the AAPF explicitly made *Los ambiguos sentimientos*

as a tool to promote sex education and family planning among government authorities, physicians, teachers, and politicians, broadening its bases of support among those who made or influenced state decisions. *Los ambiguos sentimientos* portrays the suffering of a young girl who is mistreated, ignored, and neglected by her emotionless and frustrated young single mother, whose behavior turns her daughter into a sad, hostile, and aloof child. With this film, the AAPF revealed the distressing and yet silenced experience of unfulfilled and regretful parents—in particular single mothers—and unwanted, abused children while underlining how both became powerless victims. As a response, the narrative proposes family planning as crucial for responsible and gratifying parenthood; happy parents make for happy children.[21]

*Los ambiguos sentimientos* was appropriately released a few months after Channel 13 aired *The Silent Scream*, a 1984 antiabortion educational film narrated by American abortion provider turned pro-life activist Bernard Nathanson. Celebrated by Catholic organizations—which organized screenings in schools—the film depicts an abortion process via ultrasound and shows the fetus as opening its mouth "in a silent scream" of pain and supposedly reacting to "imminent destruction," as Nathanson described it.[22] The progressive press in Argentina reacted unanimously against the film, reporting that experts and the impartial media in the United States—they quoted largely from articles published in *Time* and *Newsweek*—had vastly refuted the interpretation of the images shown in the film by explaining, for example, that a twelve-week fetus cannot experience pain and that the movements were reflex, avoidance reactions. Argentine experts also forcefully condemned the film for its unscientific and biased approach. Domingo Olivares affirmed that *The Silent Scream* employed horror, fear, and deception to fight against abortion, while the only effective and fair strategy to suppress it was providing accurate sex education and unrestricted access to contraception. In the midst of the controversy about *The Silent Scream*, *Los ambiguos sentimientos* relocated the discussion away from abortion into the equally dramatic narrative of the "orphans of living parents," an approach the local press praised for its honesty and integrity, in contrast to the American film.[23]

Though women were at the center of family planning, the AAPF did not espouse an explicit pro-women or pro-feminist discourse. Institutional publications, educational literature, and booklets had only scarce references to women's rights; the subject was not even mentioned in the discussion of abortion, which has the female body at the center of it, or in the debate on single teen mothers. Parents, teenagers, couples, and families, rather than women—the actual clients of the AAPF clinics—were identified as the main subjects of family planning and as the AAPF's intended audience. Furthermore, the silence in different types of AAPF documents about feminism and feminists' own fight for contraception is puzzling—even more so because in March 1983, a group of female volunteers created the Comité de Mujeres Voluntarias de la AAPF (AAPF Women Volunteers Committee), whose goal was to connect the institution with feminist and women's organizations.[24] The volunteers recognized the significance of collaborating with these organizations toward common objectives as well as the importance of promoting the AAPF and its services among them.[25] Yet it was also the case that the majority of AAPF members were male, and women in executive positions were only incorporated at the end of the 1980s. Furthermore, the institution historically had presented its actions as prompted by scientific and social rather than "ideological" motivations, and its traditional quest for legitimacy and social recognition would have been further complicated by association with the highly contested and publicly vilified local feminism. These factors combined might explain the reluctance to adopt an explicitly feminist position.

Although the language of the AAPF did not openly support feminism, some promotional and educational materials, such as short films for adults, do suggest the AAPF connected family planning to gender relations and women's rights, especially in middle-class settings. In *La elección*, for example, a woman defends her right to an abortion to her disapproving husband by referring to the sacrifices she had made to raise the couple's child, the postponement of her studies, and his lack of participation in parental and domestic responsibilities. The film exposes the importance of family planning to avoid abortion and to preserve a happy family as it depicts the tensions that an unplanned pregnancy brings to the couple. It also shows women as having the right to control their own bodies. The film reflects on the burden of motherhood, exposes men who demand women to become mothers when they poorly assume their obligations as fathers, and highlights the significance of education as a sphere of women's personal growth as highly valued as motherhood itself. *La mujer de Oscar* offers a similar reflection. In the short film, a young mother defends her choice of having an IUD to a skeptical friend by arguing that children should be planned and that she is currently devoted to her career. The woman also underlines that children are a responsibility of both parents and men should actively collaborate at home. In the short film, the woman defends her right to be independent, to work outside the home, and to share domestic tasks with her husband. Here, contraception is a means to allow women personal development outside the home and to maintain family harmony.[26]

For the AAPF, social well-being and personal fulfillment were the two most important contributions that family planning could make to strengthen the newborn democracy. Like the destape in the media, family planning advocates brought to the forefront a discussion that had been publicly silenced during the dictatorship. In an open letter to Congress published in 1984, the AAPF maintained that "the persistence of illness, death and family discontent, failure and with it, disillusion, weariness and incredulity are the conditions conducive to another authoritarian adventure."[27] In addition to describing family planning as an antidote to authoritarianism, the AAPF openly connected demographic growth to so-cial and economic factors by claiming that poverty and underdevelopment, rather than contraception, were the main causes of a declining population. Domingo Olivares affirmed that the best evidence in support of this argu-ment was the statistics of the past decade: with contraception prohibited and unavailable in public hospitals, the birth rate was still declining rather than growing. In contrast to the idea that banning family planning was an effective way to achieve population growth, the AAPF identified free education, housing, food security, employment, and living wages as the determining bases of a successful pronatalist policy. The argument timely and effectively connected family planning to a definition of democracy anchored in social rights, summarized in Alfonsín's famous quote: "With democracy, you are healed, you eat, and you learn."[28]

In the new political and cultural postdictatorial context, the AAPF's fight was less an ideological defense—which was still important given the opposition of conservative, Catholic, and right-wing sectors—than a plea for state intervention. To be effective, decree 2,274, passed in 1986, required real legal implementation. Freedom to opt for contraception was just the first step; the next step required the state to guarantee access to and information about birth control in order to achieve "the happiness

Figure 4.1. The AAPF educational materials on family planning encouraged a discussion about the importance of maternal health, the support of
men, stable relationships, parental responsibilities, and economic
resources. AAPF, *El mejor momento para tener hijos*, c. 1986. Courtesy
Mirta Granero.

and the dignity of families, the eradication of abortion, the physical and
mental health of children, and social justice for everyone, not only for the
well-to-do who can afford private medicine." To accomplish this goal, the
AAPF emphatically demanded a law that would establish state-funded reproductive health clinics in all public hospitals and health centers around
the country, making family planning genuinely accessible and safe.[29]

This was a battle that the AAPF fought tenaciously but unsuccessfully.
Between the mid-1980s and the mid-1990s, ten law projects—including
one by the AAPF—were presented and discussed in Congress, to no avail.
The first national law that made family planning a matter of state policy

was finally approved in 2002.[30] Despite the pro–family planning rhetoric, by 1987, the Alfonsín government was engaged in other urgent battles, including a rising economic crisis, threats by the military, and increasing tensions with the Catholic Church due to the approval of the divorce law in June, after two years of vigorous public debate. And while polls showed profound public support for family planning, resistance among political sectors, lawmakers, and medical professionals—based on the same geopolitical and demographic pronatalist arguments popular since the 1960s—was sizable. In 1984, the AAPF denounced the opposition to family planning in Congress and equated it to a veiled affront to the new democratic order: "The castrating dictatorship has come to an end. Light is shining on this new and commendable democracy. But those who are against family planning remain and one senses them to be strategically distributed among government officials and within certain political parties. Right now, a coup d'état against democracy seems impossible, a coup from the outside. But let's focus on the coup from within."[31]

Within the opposition, the Catholic Church was an important force. In 1968, Pope Paul VI's encyclical *Humanae Vitae* reaffirmed the traditional rejection of all forms of artificial contraception, allowing only for sexual abstinence to control reproduction. *Humanae Vitae* caused open dissent within and outside the church, especially amid current debates about the demographic explosion and how to prevent it. Although theologians and priests who disagreed with *Humanae Vitae* advised Catholics to follow their conscience in the matter, the most orthodox sectors openly condemned this position as a form of resistance to papal authority and actively defended the encyclical. In Argentina, despite some dissenting voices, this was the official position of the Catholic hierarchy and the national government.[32]

By the early 1980s, Pope John Paul II reaffirmed *Humanae Vitae* and continued rejecting artificial contraception while favoring natural family planning, in which no drugs, surgeries, or devices are employed to avoid pregnancy. In the 1970s, Catholics who followed the doctrine began to replace the Ogino-Knaus or rhythm method, a calendar-based technique to predict ovulation, with the Billings ovulation method, in which women monitor their fertility by learning to identify cervical mucus at different stages in the menstrual cycle. The AAPF disapproved of the Ogino-Knaus method for its inaccuracy and thus criticized the Catholic Church for demanding responsible parenthood among its congregation but without offering them effective means to control the size of their families. At the same time, the AAPF applauded the Catholic Church for its increasing support for the Billings method. Although the AAPF was critical of the method's precision and its difficulties for effective implementation, it included it in its educational literature and booklets and provided advice to interested patients. Yet the AAPF favored artificial contraception based on its effectiveness and extended scientific verification. Furthermore, in the AAPF's central clinic in Buenos Aires, where doctors promoted and discussed natural contraception with their patients, a report summarizing data from 1983 to almost the end of the decade indicates that women were completely disinclined to adopt it. As a consequence, the clinic had no patients who used natural methods.[33]

Ultra-Catholic organizations such as the Liga por la Decencia were outspoken against contraception and, based on the AAPF's goals and relationship with the IPPF, accused the organization of being part of a "worldwide conspiracy" aimed at promoting "castrating family planning."[34] By mixing traditional geopolitical arguments about the dangers of a depopulated country, 1960s and 1970s ideas about foreign intervention through population control and "forced sterilization," and moral claims—"anyone who respects the life of their son or daughter could never take a birth control pill"—the Liga forcefully opposed the position of the democratic government in favor of family planning, calling it "suicidal policy."[35] Consequently, the Liga condemned the opening of family planning clinics in public hospitals and later, when this process was expanding and became irreversible, demanded the government require the clinics to promote the Billings method. At the same time, the Liga denounced artificial contraception for its supposedly negative health consequences for women. The campaign particularly targeted the birth control pill by publicizing a long, inaccurate list of side effects that included pulmonary conditions, venereal diseases, psychological problems, and guilt. These scare tactics were combined with an apocalyptic view of the consequences for teenagers. The Liga por la Decencia anticipated a scenario of indiscriminate access to contraception among the young, even children, that would further denigrate parental authority and condemn the nation to social and moral decay.[36]

Despite this opposition and government inertia, the AAPF flourished after the return to democracy. It organized conferences, talks, seminars, and workshops for both professionals and university students as well as for the general public, and was frequently invited by labor unions, cooperatives such as El Hogar Obrero, schools, and city halls. It trained physicians, sex educators, social workers, and other health care practitioners; organized different cultural activities—such as photographic and essay contests—to promote the institution among broader audiences; and collaborated extensively with institutions such as CETIS, SASH, and the Instituto Kinsey. The AAPF also had a significant presence in the press and on television and the radio. The scope of these activities was truly national, taking place in both big cities and small municipalities all over the country.[37] The expansion of the AAPF initiatives demonstrates the high unmet need for information on family planning. This was palpable, for example, among women metalworkers and wives of metallurgy workers in Quilmes, Buenos Aires, who organized Mujeres Metalúrgicas para la Salud (Metallurgy Women for Health) with the goal of meeting and discussing issues of sexuality and reproduction. The organization sponsored talks and educational activities about contraception, offered support groups, and published a bulletin with information about women's sexual health and contraception. This appetite for change and empowerment secured for the AAPF an enthusiastic public response and the extension of their educational activities.[38]

The growth of AAPF clinics was even more impressive. By the end of the 1980s, the AAPF had sixty-four private clinics as well as clinics operating in hospitals, health care centers, and community centers in Río Negro, Catamarca, Santa Fe, Neuquén, Formosa, Misiones, Chubut, Santiago del Estero, Buenos Aires, Córdoba, Salta, Entre Ríos, and Mendoza. Although provinces such as Misiones, Salta, and Catamarca had only one clinic, whereas Buenos Aires had twenty-eight (six in the capital), Río Negro had thirteen, and Santa Fe had ten, the AAPF was proud it was beginning to extend its reach into poor neighborhoods, small towns, and rural areas. The AAPF was also extremely pleased with its new collaboration with labor unions, which resulted in family planning programs in clinics for metalworkers and railroad workers.[39]

Statistics from the AAPF central clinic that opened in Buenos Aires city in 1982 offer an interesting glimpse into the patient population and their choices. The AAPF central clinic served mainly young, educated women who worked outside the home, with only a small number of teenagers among its patients. This social profile could be connected to the clinic location in a central, upper-class neighborhood—which could be difficult to reach for women from poor, distant neighborhoods—and to the small fee collected from patients, which was not required in public hospitals. Forty percent of AAPF central clinic patients were twenty-four years old and younger, and 46 percent of the patients were women between twenty-five and thirty-four years of age. Half of all patients were single, and the average age for first sexual intercourse was eighteen years old. Eighty-five percent of the women had a high school education and 35 percent had a university education, although in both cases, not all had completed their studies. Almost half of the patients worked outside the home, while 30 percent were housewives and 20 percent were students.[40]

Between 1983 and 1988, about 23,000 women received contraception services in the AAPF central clinic. Half of these patients adopted a birth control method for the first time under AAPF supervision. Within the other half, some women had come to the clinic with previous experience with contraception, while others did not adopt or continue with any contraceptive method or follow up after the initial consultation. Only 9 percent of the AAPF central clinic patients opted for the birth control pill, 24 percent used a diaphragm, and 67 percent used an IUD. There were no patients using natural birth control methods. These numbers are consistent with those of a poll among three hundred middle-class respondents showing that out of the 82 percent in the survey who employed a birth control method, only 9 percent used the pill. Among these respondents, the most commonly used method was the IUD (30 percent), followed by condoms (14 percent) and the diaphragm (13 percent).[41]

The AAPF explained the limited adoption of the pill among its patients by identifying two opposite factors. It pointed to the legacy of years of stigmatization of the method while also arguing that since the government had repealed decree 659 and the triplicate prescription for the birth control pill was no longer required, women did not see a doctor to get advice and obtain a prescription because they could easily purchase it in a pharmacy. The AAPF actively fought against this practice by emphasizing the importance of medical intervention and guidance for the adoption of any contraceptive method.[42] Although the popularity of the pill did not increase immediately, the reversal of the previous constraining legal measures transformed past patterns. Between 1981 and 1986, local production of oral contraceptives grew 43 percent. This represented an annual growth rate of 7.4 percent. In 1986, 12 percent of women of reproductive age used the birth control pill; in 1970, the users were merely 4.9 percent.[43]

Based on a sample of 2,500 patients who attended the central clinic during a five-month period in 1986, the AAPF drew attention to the fact that before their visits, only 4 percent of these sexually active women had adopted a birth control method. For the AAPF, the implication of this data was extremely concerning: if only 4 percent of these educated, urban, and young adult women who did not want to become pregnant used contraception while being sexually active, what was the percentage among a poor, rural, marginal, uneducated, and much younger female population? That 4 percent provided the AAPF with solid evidence to argue for extending and increasing the availability of family planning to all women.[44]

The opening of CO.PLA.FA (Consultorio de Planificación Familiar; Family Planning Clinic), an AAPF clinic in the hospital of San Justo in the Santa Fe province, in 1988 was part of this growing trend and offers an interesting example of a clinic oriented toward a different population. In the first six months of operation, CO.PLA.FA—serving a local population of 9,800 women—saw 371 patients, which represented 22 percent of all patients who visited the ob-gyn department in the initial period after the opening. The clinic analyzed a small sample of all its patients to create a basic profile. In comparison with the patient population of the central clinic in Buenos Aires, the patients in San Justo were younger; in fact, 25 percent were teenagers and 65 percent were ages twenty to twenty-four. Forty percent of all patients were using some sort of contraceptive method—although sporadically—at the time of the appointment, and the other 60 percent were sexually active without using any birth control method, despite the fact that they wanted to avoid pregnancy. Most patients had had an abortion in the past and had children, and within this group of mothers, 60 percent had had a baby when they were teenagers. After visiting CO.PLA.FA, 80 percent of women opted for the birth control pill, and the rest chose an IUD. The prevalence of the pill in comparison with the low percentage of users in the Buenos Aires central clinic earlier in the 1980s reveals the increasing popularity and availability of the method by late in the decade.[45]

While the AAPF prospered and grew, the government retreated. The legal changes had unlocked family planning, but the state, against its initial declarations, remained uninvolved. By the end of the decade, the only exception was the Programa de Procreación Responsable (Program of Responsible Procreation), which the city government of Buenos Aires implemented in three hospitals. In hospitals where management did not explicitly authorize family clinics, daily operation of ob-gyn departments did not change immediately after the revocation of decree 659 in 1986. Ethnographic research conducted in 1988 shows that many physicians had no knowledge of the legal changes and pointed to the hospital authorities as responsible for keeping the staff uninformed. Many doctors, indeed, had learned about the new policy from the media. Two years after the new legal measures were passed, the lack of a systematic institutional policy of general application left professionals operating at their discretion, some incorporating family planning into their practice and some avoiding it because of misinformation, neglect, or disagreement.[46]

Objection to family planning clinics among physicians and hospital authorities was based on many factors, including the absence of professional interest in the subject, religious beliefs, and lack of knowledge and training. In 1985, the head of the Department of Gynecology at the Hospital Durand in Buenos Aires, for example, maintained that "I do not accept [birth control] for those 15-year-old girls who want to have sex with their little boyfriends, only for couples with Christian principles."[47] Other Catholic physicians went even further, affirming that artificial contraception was more than an attack on the gift of procreation; it was an assault on the sanctity of marriage that threatened its constitution and stability.[48] Domingo Olivares of the AAPF argued that in addition to the opposition of Catholic practitioners, some hospital directors defied decree 2,274 based on their political affiliation, refusing to implement family planning because they opposed the Alfonsín administration. Others distrusted the continuity of decree 2,274 beyond the current political climate and believed that with a new government, the legal changes would be reversed and the new clinic would be closed. Some claimed their hospitals had more pressing needs. When an AAPF representative approached the director of a small hospital in the Buenos Aires metropolitan area to offer him assistance to start family planning services, the director replied that he would prefer to receive resources for more hospital beds rather than for that clinic. The AAPF representative responded that with a family clinic in operation, the hospital would not need more beds in the future.[49]

The most successful organization of family planning clinics in public hospitals after the return to democracy happened in those institutions in which the clinics had already been operating covertly during the previous years, generally because the director of the ob-gyn department or a group of physicians were committed to the cause. However, even in these cases, a lack of resources and institutional support negatively impacted their functioning. Most of these clinics operated only two or three days a week with restricted hours because they lacked full-time physicians. Furthermore, available contraceptive methods to provide patients for free were restricted—although the clinics received some at no cost from pharmaceutical companies, this was not enough to satisfy the demand. In addition, without a systematic institutional plan to legitimize and effectively include family planning clinics within the integral operation of the hospitals, getting patients was complicated because most often they were referred to the clinics by other specialists and other departments.[50]

Most women ignored the existence of family planning clinics, and thus, in general, they discussed contraceptive concerns with other specialists. These specialists, in turn, would only refer the patients for proper contraceptive advice if they were well informed and supportive of the family planning clinics operating in their institutions. Family planning doctors working in public hospitals agreed that because of misinformation, lack of spousal support, guilt, and shame, women from low-income sectors had difficulty articulating their need for contraception, and when they did, many were unable to confront doctors, even obstetricians and gynecologists, who dismissed them and ignored their demands. In fact, the researchers who conducted interviews with women's health specialists in public hospitals in 1988 concluded that "it seems like the birth control issue is not on the agenda that the physician should be addressing, discussing, and resolving, whatever the condition of the patient, as is routine with other preventative practices."[51]

This reaffirmed the argument of the AAPF that family planning was more than dispensing contraception to patients; it was teaching women, men, and health care professionals that it was a human right with numerous benefits to society, the family, and the individual. A year after decree 2,274, Olivares complained that the press was fixated on promoting it as the liberalization of contraceptive commercialization, especially the birth control pill. Olivares argued that fair media coverage should disseminate the definition of family planning as a human right and educate audiences about the social and personal advantages of contraception as well as the many options available according to the age, health, and lifestyle of women and couples. Olivares believed that this information could empower citizens to demand that union leaders and local authorities open family clinics in their hospitals and to petition insurance companies to cover contraceptives. With the support of the law, patients could now protest, legally dispute, and reaffirm their right to have medical advice and access to contraception if a doctor or a medical facility refused to provide them.[52] An underaged patient could now confront doctors such as the head of the Department of Gynecology of the Hospital Durand, who refused contraception to minors based on his Catholic beliefs. Yet experts affirmed that in the case of teenagers, responding to their needs was more complex than securing access to contraception. It first required understanding their sexuality in the new postauthoritarian context and effectively addressing the urgent need for sex education in the midst of the destape.

## SEX AND THE YOUNG

Specialists on sexuality agreed that patterns of sexual conduct had been transformed profoundly since the 1960s, when premarital sex gained social acceptance, changing a tradition in which men had their first sexual experience at a younger age than women, with an older woman, while most women remained virgins until marriage.[53] During the dictatorship, the bulletin of the Ministry of Social Welfare condemned premarital sex while warning young men about the *"amiga promiscua"* ("the promiscuous girlfriend"), who had replaced the prostitute as the main transmitter of venereal diseases.[54] Furthermore, the regime promoted abstinence in moral and civic education textbooks for high school students, asserting that "a clean marriage is the fruit of a clean courtship. This means that the courtship must be virtuous, with all the purity and respect owed to a loved one."[55] Despite warnings and indoctrination, by the 1980s, experts noticed that young men delayed their sexual initiation and young women anticipated it like never before. As a consequence, young men and women were having their first sexual experience at a similar age. Women had their first sexual experience between fifteen and seventeen years of age, but a woman who was fifty years old in the 1980s had had her first sexual encounter at twenty. Moreover, a poll from the mid-1980s showed that only 17 percent of women were virgins at the time of marriage. This number reveals the exponential growth of premarital sex since the late 1960s, when surveys indicated that only around 20 percent of women had sexual intercourse before marriage. It also demonstrates the limited impact that the messages of the dictatorship had in promoting sexual abstinence among the young.[56]

To explain the 1980s polls, many experts drew attention to the unexpected consequences of the dictatorial period for youth sexuality. Although the military emphasized the role of the young in the construction of a new nation, youth was synonymous with danger and subversion. Thus, the regime campaigned extensively—such as in the television commercial that asked "¿Usted sabe dónde está su hijo ahora?" ("Do you know where you son is right now?") or the open letter "Carta a los padres argentinos" ("Letter to the Argentine parents") published in *Gente* magazine—to make parents responsible, remorseful, and apologetic for their children's behavior while postulating the family and the home as spaces of containment, discipline, and safety. As Judith Filc has argued, the dictatorship conceived the nation as an aggregate of isolated families, both private and passive.[57] This resulted in the "privatization of everyday life," the strengthening of family over other social relations, and the prevalence of intergenerational cooperation over conflict.[58] In this context, influenced by the official discourse and afraid of the repressive regime and its control over streets, public activities, and spaces of socialization, the parents of teenagers, especially among the middle classes, became extremely permissive toward their children's sexuality. This operated as a sort of "trade-off," where parents allowed or at least did not object to their children's sex life as compensation for the lack of freedom and the oppressive climate these teenagers and young adults experienced in different spheres of their lives. In fact, in many cases, these parents, who had been raised under strict parental control of their own sexuality and had been educated with a very disapproving view of premarital sex, ignored situations that would have been unthinkable just a few years earlier, such as knowing their children were having sex in their homes. And, in so doing, parents were unintentionally challenging the mission that the dictatorship had assigned to the family as the natural school of moral education.[59]

The unprecedented permissiveness with which parents compensated their children for the lack of freedom and personal expression imposed by the military regime was not complemented with dialogue and guidance. Experts argued that even among the middle classes, where parents and children communicated more effectively than previous generations had, sex talk was nonexistent. Parents came from and lived in a very repressive sexual culture, unprepared, worried, and unwilling to offer sex information to their children. Without parental guidance or sex education at school, the young were having sex younger but were profoundly uninformed about both reproduction and pleasure, and were severely ill-equipped to deal with unwanted consequences such as frustration, dissatisfaction, uncertainty, and, even more significantly, pregnancy. Sociologist Julio Mafud concluded that "in modern-day Argentine society, the sexual experience occurs long before sexual maturity."[60]

During the dictatorship, moreover, parental tolerance and scant advice were combined with a culture that silenced sexuality and condemned non-reproductive sex and sex outside marriage, leaving teenagers confused and uninformed. Furthermore, there was no public discussion of teen sexuality and no recognition of teenagers as sexual beings. A clear example is the censorship of the popular play *¿Cómo te explico?* (Chiqui Gonzales), which opened in Rosario in 1980. Created especially for teenage audiences by a group of young artists, the play was promptly banned for minors under eighteen by local authorities because a mute male character used signs to explain to a female friend how sexual intercourse happened. Even though the director agreed to cut the scene to keep the play rated for all ages, government officials continued to attend the show. However, the troupe changed to the original, uncut version when they knew censors were not present.[61] Another interesting illustration of the silence on youth sexuality was the extremely popular column "Laura de hoy," published in the Sunday supplement for teenagers of the newspaper *La Nación*. Authored by journalist Dionisia Fontán, the column, which began in 1980 and continued until 1991, was a fictional first-person diary entry by Laura, a thirteen-year-old girl from a middle-class family of Buenos Aires who grew with the column until her farewell, when the character was in her early twenties. Given its success, Fontán compiled many of these columns into three best-selling books, published in 1984, 1986, and 1991.[62]

Each week, Laura wrote about her everyday experiences, such as meeting new friends, dealing with a disease, adopting a puppy, and celebrating Christmas, and reflected about themes such as friendship, being an adolescent, family life, and falling in love. Two of the most striking characteristics of "Laura de hoy" is the complete absence of references to sexuality and the body, and the chaste, nonphysical relationship of Laura and her boyfriend. While young women between thirteen and twenty-one years of age experienced a fascinating and frustrating period of physical change and sexual experimentation and learning, and while statistics showed that real Argentine young women were indeed sexually active, Laura expresses no experience of these issues and remains mum about virginity, menstruation, sexual initiation, sexual fears, and body transformation. Themes connected to these topics are treated in a veiled, oblique, and infantilized manner. For example, Laura's pediatrician recommends she start seeing a female doctor who specializes in teenagers, and Laura is taken aback when she finds out her mother had dated a man before getting married to her father. Similarly, the mother offers a very naive account of Laura's birth when Laura asks her about labor.[63] In an interview, Fontán maintained that given the conservative character of *La Nación* and the cultural and social context of the military dictatorship, she never thought of including sexuality in Laura's story. Moreover, readers in tune with the current circumstances—parents and teenagers who wrote frequent and copious letters to the character more than to the author—never complained or inquired about the absence of this theme in the column. In fact, Fontán believed that this chastity was what made the character popular among adults, such as the principals who invited her to give talks in their schools.[64]

In 1984, by the time Laura turned seventeen, the stringent censorship of the previous years had disappeared, but the media offered no content on sexuality for the young population. As a case in point, after 1983, "Laura de hoy" remained disconnected from the increasing public debate about sex education and from the media coverage of adolescent sexuality. Even though by the late 1980s Laura was transitioning into her twenties and real young people of her generation were sexually active—and were becoming so at a younger age than their parents had—her stories continued to be as chaste and asexual as in the previous years.[65]

In contrast, with the destape at its peak, its effects on the young became a heated topic of debate and concerns, and anxieties abounded. Experts recognized that the destape was not a proper pedagogical tool but conceded that its contents were sources of information. Particularly after years in which sex for pleasure had been censured, erotic media content was "the only way to see how it is done" while detaching sex from reproduction. In 1984, sexologist León Roberto Gindin affirmed that "until a short time ago, kids in Buenos Aires did not have the chance to see what male or female genitalia look like. The books did not show them, nor did the magazines, and the schoolbooks showed a drawing that conveyed almost nothing. In any case, pornography allows them to see what an erect penis looks like, what it is all about . . . and do away with myths and fears."[66]

For others, in contrast, the destape was far from offering solutions to teenagers but raised a different set of problems as young people "are trapped in the magical world of sex in the media."[67] The destape did not equal sex education, and, indeed, for these social commentators it deepened the confusion and misunderstandings of an immature audience whose parents were unqualified to help them make sense of the erotic landslide. A naked body shown in a magazine or a sex scene in a movie were different from those addressed in a sex education class. The new cultural and social backdrop presented, in fact, a glaring contradiction. While children and especially teenagers were bombarded with the new sexual content in the media that, though targeting adults, still reached them profusely, they had no effective guidance or accurate, proper information with which to understand this content. Equally important, they lacked tools to comprehend their own sexual awakening and bodily transformation.[68]

A poll conducted in 1988 by sexologists of the Instituto Kinsey in a public high school in Villa Constitución, a small city in the Santa Fe province, reveals the views on sexuality of 376 high school students—223 girls and 153 boys—between fifteen and eighteen years of age. Thirty-four percent of the teenagers were sexually active, 96 percent wanted to have sex education at school, and only half of them had received some sort of sex information in the past. Before planning several talks for the students, the sexologists wanted to evaluate what they knew about sexuality by testing how they reacted to common sexual myths. Thus, the students—87 percent of whom declared themselves Catholics—were given a list of twenty-three statements and were asked to respond if they were true or false. The researchers were pleasantly surprised by some answers. For example, 60 percent of the students did not agree with the idea that women could only be fulfilled by motherhood, and only 20 percent believed that the main goal of sex was procreation.

However, the survey also showed profound misunderstandings and dangerous ignorance. Half of the students believed women had fewer sexual needs than men and that women did not need to masturbate, 65 percent thought that masturbation was a debilitating practice for both men and women, 70 percent affirmed that methods of contraception were harmful, and 66 percent believed that coitus interruptus was totally effective. Researchers concluded that the results confirmed the urgent need to incorporate sex education in schools to help younger generations to live a better, more gratifying life. Quoting renowned pediatrician and sex educator Florencio Escardó, the sexologists argued that in the face of these results, sex education was the only tool that would allow teenagers to turn sex into "a source of happiness and vital fulfillment instead of a cause for suffering and degradation."[69]

## SEX EDUCATION IN THE 1970S

According to Luis María Aller Atucha, AAPF director of communication and information and the editor of *Contribuciones*, it was the collaboration with pastor Luis Parrilla, the founder of COVIFAC, that moved the AAPF toward a more active role both in promoting sex education beyond hospitals, clinicians, and patients and into schools, and in the training of sex educators. An active member of the AAPF and its vice president in the early 1980s, Parrilla was a committed sex educator and author of sex education manuals for parents and teachers. Early on, Parrilla included sex education in the curricula of the Laura and Henry Fishbach primary school he headed in Buenos Aires. By the mid-1970s, under Parrilla's guidance, Aller Atucha, a communication expert, and sociologist Jorge Pailles transformed the AAPF communication strategy and began to develop manuals, films, and brochures. These educational materials became extremely popular among specialists all over the country, when, after the return to democracy, public discussion about and interest in sex education thrived and the training of sex educators boomed.[70]

Parrilla's inclusion of sex education in the Laura and Henry Fishbach kindergarten, preschool, and primary levels in the 1970s was a unique experience in a context in which sex education classes were absent from both public and private schools. During the dictatorship, Minister of Education Juan Llerena Amadeo called sex education in schools "unnecessary" and "artificial," regarded sex information for children and teenagers as the "natural" responsibility of the parents, and further recommended a "division of labor" in which fathers would talk with sons and mothers with daughters.[71] Even in the Fishbach school, the climate of fear and censorship during the military dictatorship seriously impacted the way in which instructors taught the class. A teacher working at the school in those years remembered that students were required to have separate notebooks for sex education because when the school district superintendent visited the institution, the notebooks were hidden—and the children knew exactly why. Teachers not only instructed students in being silent about this class but also explained to them the political and social context of oppression that required this measure.[72]

The other pioneering experience in sex education in the 1970s was the ARESS in Rosario, headed by gynecologist Ana María Zeno, whose house was, in the beginning, a safe space to discuss sexology materials, plan educational strategies, and design instructional documents. Formally created in 1978, ARESS counted among its founding members ob-gyn Walter Barbato, who was affiliated with the AAPF, and psychologist Mirta Granero, who would establish and direct the Instituto Kinsey with the return to democracy and would become ARESS president in 1988.[73] After its official foundation and the establishment of its bylaws, ARESS began offering its services to schools in Rosario and the whole Santa Fe province, and slowly started receiving requests from principals to schedule talks and other educational activities with students. Both Granero and Barbato argued that ARESS remained active and visible during the dictatorship, but its members were cautious, meetings were quiet, and activities in schools were kept discreet. Granero affirmed that ARESS associates knew the importance of maintaining a low profile while dealing with a sensitive subject in such a repressive context since many, including Barbato and herself, were fired from their university teaching positions after the military coup. Furthermore, Granero, her partner, and others were detained and imprisoned for a few months, and Zeno's daughter was disappeared.[74]

ARESS had among its members some of the best-trained sex educators in the country. These educators were part of a minority of Argentine professionals interested in sex education who, in the 1970s, became part of international and regional networks specializing in the discipline and received first-class training abroad. Essential to this development was the

Swedish International Development Agency (SIDA), which was in charge of Sweden's plan of assistance to developing countries. In the early 1970s, SIDA ran a program to train sex educators in Stockholm and provided generous fellowships to numerous professionals from all over Latin America so they could enter the program with all costs covered. The AAPF's Luis María Aller Atucha completed the program in 1972, but the systematic training of Argentine specialists began in 1976, when, led by a group of Colombian sex educators, the first cohorts of Latin Americans educated in Sweden founded the Comité Regional de Educación Sexual para América Latina y el Caribe (CRESALC; Regional Committee of Sex Education in Latin America and the Caribbean) with headquarters in Bogotá, Colombia, the only country in Latin America where, by the 1980s, sexology was part of the university curricula.[75]

Funded by SIDA and the IPPF, CRESALC became a regional center for the conceptualization of and advocacy for sex education, the development of instructional and promotional materials and research projects, and the training of educators. In fact, SIDA moved its program for Latin Americans from Stockholm to Bogotá. Fellows stayed there for over a month, during which they met for intensive training from Monday to Saturday, both mornings and afternoons. Jorge Pailles of the AAPF—who would become part of CRESALC's board of directors—and Mirta Granero and Ana María Zeno of ARESS were among the several members of both organizations who received fellowships and completed the program in Bogotá in the late 1970s and early 1980s.[76] CRESALC promoted the idea that sex education was vital for social and individual development and recognized that given cultural, historical, and social idiosyncrasies, Latin Americans had to think and theorize about sex education in their particular terms while still considering national variations within the region. Between 1976 and 1980, CRESALC trained 164 sex educators from all over Latin America and celebrated the multiplying effects these specialists produced in their own countries, in many cases leading a variety of projects directly sponsored by CRESALC. In fact, 77 percent of these sex educators engaged in community work devoted to expanding sex education, 62 percent participated in school activities, and 83 percent trained new sex educators.[77]

By the return to democracy, Argentine professionals had been organizing, thinking, discussing, and training in sex education inconspicuously for a few years, and all conditions were set for the public discussion of school-based sex education for the very first time in the history of the country. Freedom, the destape, the boom of sexology, and the rise of family planning further encouraged the social debate and the search for public support to develop and consolidate the field. ARESS and the AAPF became leading institutions in the promotion of sex education, the search for government support, and the training of sex educators. For both organizations, educating patients and health care professionals was fundamental, but beyond the world of adults, sex education in schools was key to helping younger generations—particularly children and teenagers from low-income sectors, "the forgotten of the forgotten"—enjoy a healthy and fulfilling sexuality now and later in life.[78]

## SEX EDUCATION AFTER THE RETURN TO DEMOCRACY

After 1983, advocates particularly promoted school-based sex education as a means to prevent teen pregnancy, supported by statistics that showed earlier sexual initiation and growing numbers of teen mothers who were increasingly younger. Indeed, hospitals in Buenos Aires and Rosario were treating pregnant patients of twelve and thirteen years of age. A study conducted among low-income pregnant adolescents in three hospitals in the city of Buenos Aires between 1982 and 1983 revealed that most patients were younger than sixteen years of age, and only 30 percent had some knowledge of contraceptive methods, which had nevertheless been ineffective in preventing pregnancy. Arguments about premature sexual initiation and teen pregnancy also helped sex educators refute the idea that sex education encouraged youngsters to become sexually active. Sex among teenagers was a reality independent from sex education, and sex education was, in turn, the most effective tool to control sexual behavior and channel it positively.[79]

In an article about the urgent need for including sex education in schools, journalist Luis Frontera argued that "educating today means allowing students to question a society that has been unfair and that wants to improve itself with democracy. Authoritarianism at high school is not just a problem with the system: instead, for many years, it was one of its basic objectives."[80] For this reason, Jorge Pailles argued, citizens and the government had to work together for "an education for democracy," that is, integral instruction that would embrace all aspects related to personal and social life, including sexuality. School-based sex education allowed students to develop successfully as sexual beings, subjects, and citizens—to become free and conscientious individuals and well-adjusted adults. Pailles explained that "sex education creates the conditions necessary for personal health and well-being, indispensable requirements for people to grow up free and to accept and exercise a democratic lifestyle."[81] Advocates explicitly linked sex education and a language of rights—a vital component of the democratic project—affirming that the right to education guaranteed by the constitution implicitly included sex education. The state had the social responsibility to ensure all citizens could exercise that right regardless of social and marital status, sexual orientation, and age.[82]

Furthermore, and similar to arguments in favor of family planning, advocates redefined sex education to make it more relevant to national development, personal and social well-being, and the liberation of the individual after years of obscurantism. In the new democratic context, sex education was promoted not only as a tool for public health but also as an asset for a better life. Echoing the message of the destape in the media aimed at adults—yet excluding the erotic content—the central idea behind sex education was that sexuality was positive and enriching. The discursive emphasis was less on the avoidance of negative and harmful experiences—unwanted pregnancy, early sexual initiation, and abortion—and more on the creation of an affirmative and confident attitude toward sex and the body in particular, and toward life and others in general.[83] Far from conventional, outdated propositions centered on anatomy, innovative sex education in democracy conceived sexuality as more than biology by including anthropological, psychological, sociological, philosophical, and historical viewpoints. This type of education required training creativity, allowing students to freely explore their capabilities and express their needs and curiosity without censorship, incorporating social reality into the classroom, and encouraging the open debate of different ideas and positions. It also called upon teaching individuals responsibility, autonomy, and respect for themselves and others.[84]

The same experts who emphasized the decisive contribution of sex education to personal growth believed that parents were unprepared, fearful, and unwilling to successfully educate their children about sexuality. As an example, experts commonly mentioned the fact that parents typically scolded small children for touching and exploring their genitals and employed made-up names to refer to them, sending the negative and repressive message that they were shameful, were dirty, and should be hidden and remained unknown. This was particularly the case for girls, who, sexologists argued, struggled greatly with sexual pleasure as adult women because of these inhibitions and ignorance promoted by their parents in childhood. Probably because of the same reason, a poll among women showed that 47 percent believed sex education in schools was a necessity and 13 percent approved of it in high school.[85]

However, older women disapproved. A survey reported that while women fifty years and older acknowledged that their lack of sexual information had been a source of frustration and distress throughout their lives, posing a serious challenge to keeping a happy marriage, they still rejected sex education. These older women tended to naturalize the lack of communication with children about sexual matters and to disregard the consequences. A fifty-six-year-old woman, for example, affirmed that when she was a young mother, "I never discussed the topic of sex with the girls and they never brought it up with me, either. I suppose they worked it out for themselves, just the way I once did."[86] Sex education was more broadly accepted among younger women and mothers who understood the importance of avoiding the mistakes of their parents. In a survey conducted by sexologist María Luisa Lerer, 72 percent of women revealed that sexuality was a topic of conversation their parents had repressed completely, addressed only reluctantly and shamefully, or associated with something prohibited or offensive.[87] Similarly, in a poll conducted by *La Mujer*, the women's supplement of newspaper *Tiempo Argentino*, a woman in her late thirties reflected that "our generation was ill-prepared for healthy sexual behavior. Our mothers did not have it so they had no way of teaching us. We made it on our own and today we are still learning."[88]

Despite the approval of younger parents in comparison to older generations, the enthusiastic advocacy of the media, and the unparalleled public visibility of experts who began educating audiences on the content and goals of sex education, active support among parents did not occur overnight. Between 1986 and 1987, for example, sex educators Liliana Pauluzzi and María del Carmen Marini and a small group of collaborators visited twenty-one primary schools in Rosario, where they screened *La aventura de crecer* to an audience of seven hundred parents. The twenty-five-minute

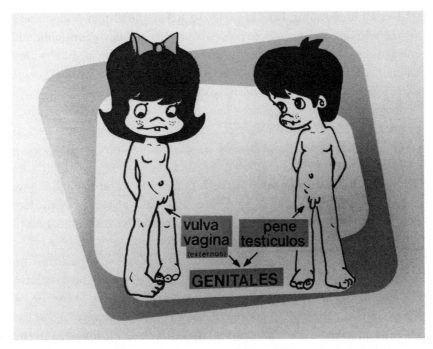

Figure 4.2. In *La aventura de crecer*, sex educator Liliana Pauluzzi challenged parents to abandon euphemisms. Courtesy Mabel Bianco.

cartoon for children explained topics such as sexual intercourse, desire,
pregnancy, and labor based on the premise that sex education was "the
path to mental health that our society needs to keep sexuality from con-
tinuing as an area where conflicts arise."[89] The screening was followed by a
debate that Pauluzzi and her team used to evaluate the parents' responses
to the film as a pedagogical tool to be employed with their children.

Reactions to the film revealed deep anxieties, repression, and conservatism about sex education in particular and about sexuality more generally.
For parents, the effects of the destape were to be strictly confined to the
world of adults. Most parents rejected the discussion about sexual pleasure
and gratification, disapproved of showing a couple in bed, and feared that
this type of information could encourage sexual exploration among the
children, particularly among girls. Fathers disapproved of the film more
than mothers and expressed more fears and discomfort about their roles as
sex educators at home. Given this reaction, only six out of the twenty-one

schools allowed Pauluzzi and her team to screen the film to students and organized a talk to discuss it. In those six schools, though—five public and one private—the event was enthusiastically welcomed by eight hundred students of the fifth, sixth, and seventh grades (between ten and twelve years of age), who asked the specialists more than 550 questions.[90]

In other cases, however, sex educators received strong support from parents. This happened, for example, when in 1988 the Liga por la Decencia and a radio show in Rosario, alerted by a small group of parents, began a bitter campaign to denounce a survey conducted by sexologists with the Instituto Kinsey in a high school in Villa Constitución and demanded government intervention. The Liga was fundamentally disturbed by the fact that the questionnaire asked students about sexual pleasure and orgasm. When the Santa Fe minister of education summoned the school and the Instituto Kinsey authorities to discuss the survey, a group of parents, who had given written consent to allow their children to answer the questions, traveled to the meeting to offer their support. According to sexologist Mirta Granero, director of Instituto Kinsey, the minister approved of the survey and neither the school authorities nor the staff involved in the organization were sanctioned. Still, Granero remained concerned for the Instituto Kinsey and the ARESS, thinking that, in light of the bomb at the AAPF offices five years earlier, the episode at the school would provide a test to see if times had indeed changed. Despite her apprehension, activities continued as usual and support grew. Granero affirmed that after the scandal, the most influential union leader of the metalworkers in Villa Constitución—whose most important employer was the metallurgical plant ACINDAR—became an open supporter and interceded in several schools so the sexologists could expand the range of the survey to a broader student population. For his part, the principal of the school where the survey had been originally conducted, and the site of the scandal with the Liga, began his training in sex education with the Instituto Kinsey a year later.[91]

Despite tensions and criticisms, experts rarely dismissed the role of parents as sex educators. On the contrary, they regarded it as the first form of sex education and as a parent's right. Parents had to provide and adapt sex education as their children grew, and these children would become, in turn, sex educators themselves. Specialists argued that sex education was permanent, that is, a learning process for life in which individuals were compelled to experience and understand transformations in their own sexuality as they aged and family and personal relations changed. As a consequence, experts such as Luis Parrilla and Domingo Olivares argued that sex education, essential for children and teenagers, should also target adults, and in particular parents.[92]

Based on this premise, workshops, talks, and sex education books for parents boomed. Moreover, advocates recruited the state, the school, the hospital, and different social and cultural institutions such as unions, churches, and neighborhood centers for the common mission of educating or sponsoring sex education for grown-ups. Without losing momentum, the press ran numerous articles on how to talk to children and teens about sexuality, printed supplements, published sex education manuals for parents, and even organized and sponsored conferences with specialists. Experts affirmed that becoming a good sex educator and, as a result, a better parent entailed removing fear and shame, eradicating euphemisms, and cherishing and celebrating the body and its changes. It also involved allowing children to express themselves freely while understanding sexual development as a natural process that required guidance and dialogue.[93]

Sex education for parents was not a new idea but had emerged as part of a new child-rearing paradigm popularized by psychologist Eva Giberti and pediatrician Florencio Escardó in the 1960s. In the late 1950s, Giberti launched her Escuela para Padres (School for Parents), where she met with mothers to discuss the problems they faced in raising their children—sexuality included. Those early meetings were followed with popular weekly columns Giberti wrote in newspapers La Razón and El Mundo and that she later compiled in Escuela para padres (1961) and Adolescencia y educación sexual (1968), which sold a combined total of 250,000 copies. Edited four times in nine years, Escardó's Sexología de la familia (1961) achieved comparable success. Giberti's and Escardó's work favored a psychoanalytic explanation of child sexuality, with scarce attention paid to social and cultural aspects, and disregarded contraception as a fundamental aspect of sex education for teenagers. Both focused on targeting middle-class parents rather than aiming at audiences of all classes and expanding sex education beyond the realm of the home. Furthermore, they never explicitly addressed sexuality. As historian Mariano Plotkin has suggested, Giberti provided a model for parents to explain where babies come from but said nothing about how they actually get into the womb in the first place. Despite the fact that

Giberti and Escardó never crossed the threshold of traditional morality, the rise of repression in the 1970s severely silenced them both. In 1973, Giberti was prohibited in the media, and in 1976, after the military coup, her offices of the Escuela para Padres were raided and most of her archives destroyed.[94]

The sex education that rose in the 1980s had significant differences from this antecedent. Sex educators working after the return to democracy believed that sex education was a social, collective project requiring classes to be taught at school that could effectively benefit all social sectors. Specialists in the field argued that sex information reached children spontaneously, whether adults approved it or not. The silence or the vague explanations of parents, the messages from peers or the media, and the behaviors that children and teenagers observed in others were sources of sex information, though generally incomplete and incorrect. Curricular sex education was the opposite of spontaneous sex information because it was precise, appropriate, and purposeful, and thus the best antidote against erroneous ideas. In addition, sex educators argued that humans were sexual beings since birth, and for this reason, sex education in school had to start as soon as possible, adapting to the different developmental stages of childhood and adolescence.[95]

In an interview with newspaper *La Capital*, members of ARESS explained that given the oversexualization of culture in the return to democracy, the "corrective role" of school-based sex education was even more imperative. They argued that "given all the hullabaloo surrounding the destape and sexuality, it is fundamental to give it the place it deserves to avoid misunderstandings."[96] Indeed, while the press was the motor of the destape, it supported school-based sex education by arguing that children needed guidance to make sense of the avalanche of sexual images and discourses that suddenly surrounded them.[97] In quite a fatalistic fashion, for example, an article on sex education published in the magazine *Para Ti* asserted: "Nowadays sex education is not a mission or a luxury: it is a need. In the face of the sexual wave, everyone runs risks but those most vulnerable to grave dangers—dangers that can alter or ruin their lives forever—are precisely those who deserve the most protection: children, adolescents, youth."[98]

School-based sex education required securing the support of the state, imposing a legal framework, and solving the logistics of developing a cur-

Figure 4.3. The magazine *Sex Humor* both supported and parodied school-based sex education. *Sex Humor*, March 1986.

ricula and training instructors. While some believed that schools should employ professional educators devoted exclusively to the discipline, most experts agreed that sex education could be taught by regular teachers properly trained and that the subject should be incorporated into fields such as history, biology, and civic education so students could understand sexuality through different lenses. Advocates knew that teacher proficiency was vital to get parents to fully support sex education in the classroom, but they also agreed that teachers would feel deeply challenged, as becoming a sex educator involved more than knowledge of content and pedagogical tools to transmit it. Being an effective sex educator demanded a deep sense of personal and social responsibility, openness, and maturity. It further required a profound exercise of introspection where individuals would be faced with evaluating their own values and sexual conduct, fighting taboos and prejudices, and understanding and respecting the beliefs and behaviors of others.[99]

Casting teachers in this role opened a new set of logistic complications, as some felt uncomfortable with assuming this position or overwhelmed by adding new responsibilities to their teaching schedules and by training after work to get a certification in sex education. Others, aware of the importance of the subject and in tune with the demands and needs of students, responded enthusiastically and took the lead. This is evident in the high numbers of schools that invited the AAPF and ARESS not only to give talks to their students but also to conduct workshops with their faculty. It also shows in the increasing numbers of teachers who, out of pocket, trained to become certified sex educators.[100]

Teachers also took the initiative to meet and organize workshops to share ideas and openly discuss their experiences in the classroom. In Rosario, for example, Pauluzzi's animated film *La aventura de crecer* triggered workshops of teachers interested in the subject. The meetings started in 1986, sponsored by the Casa de la Mujer, a feminist organization, and continued until the end of the decade, sometimes under the coordination of Pauluzzi herself. The teachers read extensively on sexology and the pedagogy of sex education, recognizing that in order to become sex educators, they had to defeat their own "sexual illiteracy."[101] This required them to be able to differentiate reproduction from pleasure and pleasure from genitality, to recognize children as sexual beings, and to problematize sexual stereotypes. They also designed strategies to answer common and challenging questions from students; agreed on the best language to address certain topics; reflected on the relationship of sexuality to politics, culture, and the economy; and elaborated plans of action to propose the incorporation of sex education in their schools. Furthermore, this group of educators organized workshops for parents and students, formalized a course of sex education for teachers—particularly popular among those who worked in poor neighborhoods where teen pregnancy, abortion, and sexual violence were common—and promoted the screening of *La aventura de crecer* in schools.[102] However, the most important revelation came "by looking inside themselves" and discovering that, as sex education experts warned, the most important impediments to effectively fulfilling their roles as sex educators were their own repression and prejudices. Analyzing their experiences in the workshops, the teachers affirmed that "our biases, both conscious and unconscious, were establishing the guidelines for us to follow, interfering with our activities. That was quite painful and difficult. We suppose that one of the reasons why the group suffered attrition was related to the fact that we began dealing with issues connected to our personal experiences and problems, with all things personal, because considering sex conflictive is the result of one's own suffering."[103]

For their part, many municipal governments organized and sponsored training for teachers. The pioneering example was set by the city of Buenos Aires, which, with a municipal ordinance passed in 1984, established a quarter-long sex education course for primary school teachers, organized by the Escuela Superior de Capacitación Docente (School of Advanced Studies in Education), in different neighborhoods across the city. During the first quarter, the course, which was optional, trained 250 teachers, and in the second, 350. Since applicants rapidly exceeded the number of available spots for the course, the Escuela Superior de Capacitación Docente established a lottery system to fairly distribute seats among teachers.[104] Another early example is the experience of Avellaneda, Buenos Aires, where the city offered a six-month course for local preschool and primary school teachers, taught by the AAPF.[105]

Although experts celebrated these initiatives, they knew that the effective and comprehensive incorporation of sex education in schools required a national law and its implementation all over the country. While Alfonsín's decree 2,274—which lacked concrete implementation—recognized the role of the state in providing citizens assistance with and information about family planning, there was no legal equivalent for sex education. The Alfonsín administration had no concrete plans to introduce sex education in schools.[106] Only in the 1990s, a handful of provinces passed laws of sex education with different levels of application and reach, with Santa Fe pioneering the trend in 1992. Argentines had to wait twenty years for the approval, in 2006, of the first national law recognizing the right of citizens to receive sex education in both private and public schools and at all levels. However, since education is a sphere fundamentally controlled by the provincial states, concrete national application of law 26,150 was uneven and incomplete. This was the case even within the provinces themselves since some schools and school districts refused to incorporate the mandated contents into the curricula and to train their teachers, and provincial authorities were unable or unwilling to intervene and force application.[107]

## THE CONTENT OF DEMOCRATIC SEX EDUCATION

Sex education experts positioned family planning as the fundamental component of sex education by underlining its definition as a human right. Similarly important, advocates pointed to the increasing population of teen mothers and the high rates of abortion among teenagers and addressed the fact that with or without social and parental approval, and despite an emphasis on sexual abstinence, teenagers were sexually active while lacking the necessary information to prevent pregnancy.[108] In most pedagogical and promotional materials, sex educators resignified family planning as a strategy to have children under the best conditions rather than as contraception to avoid pregnancy—despite the fact that one was intrinsically dependent on the other. The emphasis was on positive achievement—having the number of desired children when it was appropriate to have them—rather than on avoidance, refusal, or evasion. When educating teenagers and children, more so than adults, family planning was connected to social, economic, and cultural factors first and to contraceptive methods later. Thus, family planning promoted a discussion about the health of the mother—underlining the health complications of mothers who were too young—the support of a partner, the importance of a healthy relationship, the desire to have a baby, the magnitude of parental responsibilities, and the economic resources to provide for a child. Teaching about family planning in schools was, therefore, preparing students for life and educating them about personal and social responsibility.[109]

When making a case for the social significance of sex education and the urgent need for its incorporation into the classroom, advocates neglected its role in the prevention of sexually transmitted diseases. This continued even in the late 1980s, when public discussions about HIV escalated and sex education could have been more powerfully brought to the forefront as an effective tool against the disease, an argument that became common in the 1990s.[110] However, teenagers demanded information and advice even when teachers and coordinators had not initially included sexually transmitted diseases in the course outline. The importance of filling the gap between the theory and the practice of sex education became sadly evident to a sex educator when she found out that one of her students—a teenager from a poor and marginal neighborhood—had contracted syphilis after a yearlong sex education workshop in which venereal diseases had not been discussed.[111]

Alongside sexually transmitted diseases, the other two controversial topics within sex education were pleasure and sexual diversity. Remarkably, in the context of the destape and the boom of sexology, Argentine experts avoided addressing pleasure in sex education—a characteristic they shared with most of their colleagues in Europe and the United States.[112] The centrality of nonreproductive sex for sex education was clear in its emphasis on family planning, yet teaching contraception methods and educating about responsible parenthood did not directly imply addressing sexual pleasure and sexual desire and their contributions to personal well-being. Sex educators knew that this was an uphill battle with parents—as evident in their reactions to the bed images in *La aventura de crecer* and the incident in Villa Constitución—that could compromise the whole endeavor.

In contrast, clinical sexologists—who fully supported sex education— slightly criticized sex educators for their silence on sexual pleasure. Sexologists argued that for the young and teenagers, sexuality was and should be about pleasure since they were ready to enjoy sex but unprepared for parenthood. Sex education should be tailored to this reality by providing family planning information as well as advice for a gratifying sex life. Sexologist León Roberto Gindin maintained that sex education typically ignored the "how" of pleasant sex based on the incorrect belief that individuals would "naturally discover" it. Yet the rising numbers of adult patients in sexology clinics proved this theory wrong. Sexologists argued that enjoyable sex could and should be taught early on; thus, CETIS offered a sex education workshop for teenagers especially designed by sexologists to address their needs.[113]

The discussion on pleasure mostly permeated into publications such as *Contribuciones* when the AAPF journal published sex educators from other Latin American countries. For example, in a piece printed in the late 1980s by pioneering Colombian sexologist and sex educator Octavio Giraldo Neira—president of the Federación Latinoamericana de Sociedades de Sexología y Educación Sexual (FLASESS; Latin American Federation of Sexology and Sex Education Societies) in the 1980s—the author openly addressed the importance of teaching teenagers to appreciate and enjoy eroticism without reducing sexuality to genitality and sexual intercourse. Giraldo Neira argued that "the sex education of an adolescent should be based on the premise that one of its main goals is to develop the sensory capacities for pleasure as a source of personal well-being and of a uniting bond with a potential mate."[114] The fact that the AAPF did not include these types of discussions more explicitly does not mean Argentine sex educators did not address the topic. In fact, an active and pioneering group of women sex educators in Rosario, led by psychologists Liliana Pauluzzi and Liliana Szot, were particularly interested in studying and opening a debate on children's experiences of pleasure. However, they did recognize, based on their extensive experience training teachers and educating parents, how reluctant adults were to address this subject.[115]

Like in the case of pleasure, Giraldo Neira also addressed without euphemisms the need to develop sex education that included sexual minorities, warning that these groups were too often forgotten by sex educators. To do this, educators had to develop empathy and compassion for teenagers who were experiencing pain, frustration, and confusion because they were stigmatized, marginalized, and deprived of their rights. Giraldo Neira promoted sex education that could teach sexual minorities self-acceptance and help them foster a sense of personal dignity while instilling in heterosexuals feelings of respect and appreciation for those who were different. The AAPF claimed to share Giraldo Neira's conceptualization, but there are no direct references to sexual minorities in its documents. Discussion of sexual and gender identities was extremely rare, and in those exceptional occasions that happened, the language supported inclusion and tolerance but remained extremely vague.[116]

A good example is an article about adolescent sexuality in which Luis María Aller Atucha argues that sex education proposes a profound and continuous dialogue about who we are and how we relate to others, denoting the complexity of identity. Aller Atucha maintains that there is no "universally established" sexual behavior and "what is sexually acceptable varies from person to person but in any case, one should be sensitive to the needs of others and avoid the exploitation of another human being."[117] This is the closest an Argentine sex education expert writing in *Contribuciones*, the leading journal in the field, came to posing the issue of sexual diversity and sexual identity in the 1980s. This absence is disappointing yet historically attuned with the silence about sexual minorities evident in the media destape and sexology alike. Yet, once again, the reality of sexual minorities slipped into sex education classes (and into *Contribuciones* itself), even though sex education theory disregarded it. In an article by a social worker trained as a sex educator in which she discusses the challenges of leading a yearlong weekly sex education workshop with low-income teenagers, the author reflects on her fears and pedagogical inability when a student brought to class a newspaper clipping about the police detention of gay men and asked for clarification and discussion about homosexuality and its repression.[118]

Even though these most heated issues were largely absent from the proposals of sex educators, the Argentine Catholic Church disapproved of sex education in schools. The church did not oppose sex education when it was confined within the home, but it vehemently rejected the notion of experts teaching in schools and topics such as nonreproductive sex. Catholics were concerned about a law that could impose school-based sex education, so while they demanded state intervention against the destape in the name of children and the preservation of morality, they also believed the state should refrain from legislating on sex education. In rejecting the circulation of sexual knowledge in the classroom, the Catholic Church attempted, like in its campaign against the destape, to regulate sexual morality by controlling sexual speech. Catholic organizations defended the right of parents to decide what type of sex education they wanted for their children, against the homogenizing effects of a state-imposed curriculum that they viewed as a government intrusion into the privacy of the family and the faith.[119]

The official position of the church was stated in 1981 when Pope John

Paul II wrote *Familiaris Consortio*, a postsynodal apostolic exhortation that affirmed that sex education was a right and a duty of parents and that the school should always accommodate its teachings, "entering into the same spirit that animates the parents." The school, then, could not contradict or refute the family's messages. Furthermore, sex education should be an education for chastity that fostered the "nuptial meaning" of the body since virginity was "the supreme form of self-giving that constitutes the very meaning of human sexuality." Dissociated from this principle, sex education would be reduced to "an introduction to the experience of pleasure" while "opening the way to vice."[120] For ultra-Catholic organizations such as the Liga por la Decencia, family planning in the school equaled the corruption of the youth, the desecration of the body, and the destruction of the family. Furthermore, for the Liga, it offered confirmation of conspiracy theories of "massive sterilization" being promoted by organizations such as the AAPF.[121]

Catholics supported an "education for love" or an "affective-sexual education." Inspired by the faith, this education was attentive to feelings and emotions and promoted maturity, morality, and modesty. Interestingly, for the church, sex education experts, sexologists, and clinicians had little to no role in the conceptualization of the Catholic version of sex education. In 1983, for example, the Sacred Congregation for Catholic Education published its outlines for sex education and only listed the contributions of specialists in moral and pastoral theology, catechists, and Catholic psychologists in creating sex education materials for students. In addition, the outlines denounced pedagogical textbooks, films, and images that, given "their naturalist character," crudely presented sexual realities. As a result, these educational materials harmed children and teenagers, creating "traumatic impressions" and raising "an unhealthy curiosity which leads to evil."[122]

Along these lines, the Mendoza chapter of the Liga de Madres de Familia equated sex education textbooks and films with "pornography" because they naturalized masturbation and provided information on contraception. The women claimed that some schools were actually replicating the contents of the destape and, like the media, were "encouraging" sexual behavior in children and teenagers, with terrible moral consequences.[123] Similarly, the Catholic Sociedad Argentina de Ética y Moral Médica y Biológica (SAEMB; Argentine Society of Medical and Biologic Ethics and Morality) warned parents against the proposals of sex education experts because they "are nothing more than attempts to teach adolescents to copulate without it weighing on their conscience, without the risk of disease, and without getting pregnant." The SAEMB rejected sex education plans that used "scientific terminology" to emphasize messages about "recreational sex," "hedonism," and "ethical relativism" while completely disregarding issues of decorum and virtuousness.[124]

With the return to democracy, experts transformed advocacy for family planning, which had traditionally been linked to the reduction of abortion rates and maternal mortality, by embracing and disseminating its definition as a human right, inalienable and universal, that society should assert and enjoy and the state should acknowledge and protect. Furthermore, specialists enriched this definition by turning the abstraction of legal entitlement into a more concrete promise for tangible bliss. As the destape media and sexology celebrated sexual pleasure for its contributions to individual happiness, experts successfully linked family planning to the achievement of personal well-being and fulfillment, drawing attention to the many difficulties and problems caused by unintended parenthood: the dissatisfaction and frustration of reluctant parents overwhelmed by responsibilities, the conflicts that arose in couples, the constraints for personal and professional growth imposed on women, the struggle and distress of teenage parents, and the suffering of unwanted children. The discourse of family planners was pervaded by the idea of responsible parenthood, but the emphasis was on self-realization. Personal achievement was, in turn, a crucial factor in social well-being and ultimately in the preservation of democracy. Because of family planning's contribution to health, happiness, and individual and family harmony, advocates celebrated it as the best defense against authoritarianism. Alongside education, full employment, housing, and food security, experts proposed family planning as an antidote to poverty and underdevelopment, and thus as a pillar of democracy. Family planning was not a threat to the nation like conservatives, ultra-Catholics, the military, and the Left had affirmed but, on the contrary, a factor for social progress.

Like family planning, sex education became central for the building of a new democracy. Advocates argued that school-based sex education was a right; a source of individual, family, and social prosperity; and thus the basis of a fair and advanced society whose citizens conceived of and approached sexuality with responsibility, confidence, and joy. Although, for the most part, sex education ignored the issue of pleasure, and most experts considered it a corrective to the information and the images of the destape, sex education shared with the destape several characteristics. Sex education proposed to break censorship and silence, aimed at resetting the balance between the public and the private as appropriate arenas to talk about sex, and advanced a positive view of sexuality that was considered central for personal growth as well as for identity formation. In so doing, sex education was the ultimate example of a true "democratic education." Yet, similar to the destape, sex education in the 1980s focused on heterosexuality and disregarded the voices and needs of sexual minorities, omitting a lesson in acceptance and solidarity, and therefore failing to train citizens for an inclusive democracy. For their part, conservative and ultra-Catholic sectors saw in school-based sex education a threat to the family, the social order, and parental authority, and opposed its emphasis on family planning, which they considered as a challenge to morality and love.

Despite how advocates emphasized the many benefits of family planning and sex education for the consolidation of the democratic system and the multiple links they shared with the social agenda of the Alfonsín administration, the government did little to advance either cause. Anti-family planning laws were abolished, and local authorities made efforts to expand sex education in schools, but experts' demands for active and wide-ranging state intervention and support remained unfulfilled. However, family planning and sex education continued to spread and develop. The cultural and social influences of the destape, a society eager to openly discuss sexuality, and the boom of sexology all contributed to the visibility of both fields, to advocacy, and to a rich public debate.

# 5

## THE OTHER *DESTAPE*

Feminists, Gay and Lesbian Activists, and
the Fight for Sexual Rights

**Argentine feminism and gay activism** in the 1970s were short-lived
experiences, both born and eclipsed in the first half of the decade. Pioneering organizations such as the Unión Feminista Argentina (UFA; Argentine Feminist Union), created in 1970; the Movimiento de Liberación
Feminista (MLF; Feminist Liberation Movement), founded in 1973; and
the Frente de Liberación Homosexual (FLH; Homosexual Liberation
Front), established in 1971, emerged as original attempts to challenge
gender conventions and the sexual status quo but were unable to survive
the increasingly repressive climate. Sexuality was an important topic of
debate and source of activism among feminists and gay advocates in this
period, and issues that resurfaced after the return to democracy, such
as access to contraception, sexual freedom, and abortion, were central
in writings, publications, meetings, and consciousness-raising groups.
Around twenty members of the UFA, the MLF, and the FLH established
the Grupo de Política Sexual (GPS; Sexual Politics Group), which met to
discuss readings, write, and organize small public events guided by the
idea that a true sexual revolution was contingent upon social liberation.
Among other activities aimed at questioning heteronormativity and patriarchy, the members of the GPS attended psychoanalytic and medical

conferences to challenge the characterizations of same-sex desire and the clitoral orgasm as pathologies that were common in both fields. Though focused on sexuality, the GPS remained silent about lesbianism, and like in other feminist and gay organizations from the 1970s, lesbian members were "invisible."[1]

Incipient and small—the UFA, for example, had around seventy members at its peak—feminist and gay groups struggled to prevail after President Isabel Perón took power; her administration was dominated by right-wing Peronists who called to "eliminate homosexuals" and referred to contraception as "sterilization."[2] Furthermore, feminist organizations saw an exodus of members and sympathizers who, in a context of growing political radicalization, decided to prioritize action in parties and leftist organizations. As historian Karina Felitti has argued, for some women, feminism turned into a "distraction" from the social revolution. Gay people, for their part, did not escape the homophobia of the Left, which prevented them from being active in both gay and leftist organizations. Revolutionary groups stigmatized homosexuality as a product of capitalist and bourgeois decadence and as a source of physical and moral weakness, forcing their members to hide their sexual identities to avoid disciplining and expulsion.[3]

Already debilitated by internal tensions and external threats, feminist and gay groups dissolved after the 1976 military coup, when repression reached new heights. Some members went into exile, most laid low, and public events stopped. Feminists continued reading, meeting, and debating quietly, but open activism vanished. Reinsertion in public life began slowly in the last years of the dictatorship; in 1979, several feminists publicly denounced discrimination and campaigned in support of a public servant in Mendoza who had been fired based on "moral reasons" when her supervisors discovered she was a single mother. In 1982, with the dictatorship weakened, feminists organized a congress that featured three hundred presentations and attracted close to eight hundred attendees, but sexuality, a topic considered too problematic for the context, was absent.[4]

With the return to democracy, feminist and gay activism reemerged powerfully, attaining unparalleled levels of visibility and organization all over the country. Furthermore, lesbian advocacy and associations surfaced for the first time in the late 1980s, ending a long history of silence. Militants created numerous organizations and membership swelled; protests and demonstrations became recurring, popular, and well-publicized events; publications and congresses multiplied; and advocates, besides being regularly interviewed in the press, were frequent guests on television and radio shows. Activists voiced many claims, but sexual rights were a central component of their programs for change. Sociologist Diane Richardson has argued that sexual rights are discursively framed in relation to practices, identities, and relationships. Following Richardson's model, this chapter shows that Argentine feminists and gay and lesbian activists redefined the meanings of sexual citizenship in democracy by asserting claims to the right to pleasure and the right to sexual and reproductive self-determination (sexual practices), the right to self-definition and the right to self-expression (identities), and the right to consent to sex, the right to freely select sexual partners, and the right to social legitimacy for romantic and sexual encounters (relationships).[5] This chapter argues that feminists and gay and lesbian advocates articulated their demands, employing a language of sexual rights that epitomized a different type of destape, one that exposed and denounced citizenship as the institutionalization of heterosexuality and male privilege. In addition to criticizing the commercial male-created destape and offering alternative narratives and imagery, feminists and gay and lesbian militants placed the sexual citizen—a citizen defined by his or her sexual subjectivity—at the epicenter of an inclusive definition of democracy and made sexual rights central to their fight. In so doing, activists embodied a destape: they revealed themselves to society and took the lid off the suffering of women and sexual minorities.[6]

## FEMINISTS AND THE DESTAPE

While journalists, intellectuals, artists, sexologists, and politicians oscillated between enthusiastically celebrating and silently tolerating the destape, feminists considered most of its manifestations the triumph of a hypermasculine culture in which "men are not asked to put their body on the line."[7] In response to discourses that connected the commercial destape with freedom, modernity, and adulthood, feminism posed probing questions: How could objectified women be symbols of a culturally and socially advanced society? How could real women be free if popular culture reduced them to sexualized props for male consumers, viewers, and readers? For feminism, "a naked and willing woman," the iconic image of the destape, was the most evident example of the misogyny that had historically pervaded Argentine society and culture but now openly colonized mass culture as well.[8] Feminists recognized that the new context of freedom of expression enabled the production, circulation, and consumption of those representations but pointed to long-lasting machismo and the enduring power of patriarchy rather than to democracy, which they defended fervently, as the main cause of these hypersexualized images and narratives.[9]

The significance of cultural representations of women was evident at the Quinto Encuentro Feminista Latinoamericano y del Caribe (Fifth Latin American and Caribbean Feminist Meeting) held in 1990 in San Bernardo, Buenos Aires, where participants designated September 14 the Latin American Day of Women's Image in the Media. The declaration identified education and advocacy as the means to fight against damaging portrayals of women.[10] Feminists denounced that the photographs featured in magazines such as *Destape*, *Viva*, or *Shock* did not show women as subjects but merely and exclusively as "robotic," "perfect," commodified sexual bodies. The ultimate objectification of the female body was evident in the obsession with hypersexualized breasts and backsides. Feminists argued that this fixation further refuted women's subjectivity by turning them into a human puzzle where some body parts, the objects of desire that were chosen by men and for men, were unmistakably more important than others.[11]

To illustrate this point, a reporter writing for *Alternativa Feminista* told readers that when she asked a male friend how a common acquaintance was doing, he responded that the man was "dating one of the Jordache asses." Jordache was a brand of jeans that became extremely popular during the return of democracy for a legendary, provocative television commercial that showed a beautiful woman changing into tight jeans in an elevator with the camera frequently zooming in on her buttocks both before and after squeezing into the jeans. The reporter's anecdote shows the role of advertising and market culture in commodifying the female body and objectifying women as well as the rapid naturalization and social appropriation of these ideas by men. The reporter explained that, for her male friend, the girlfriend was not a woman but merely an oversexualized body part popularized in advertising. The result, both in the television commercial and in the anecdote, was what feminist activist and sexologist Sara Torres called *la mujer des-trozada*, a fragmented person whose subjectivity was challenged and whose body was dismembered.[12]

In contrast to conservatives and the Catholic Church, feminists did not oppose the media destape in the name of decency, morality, religion, culture, or children but in the name of women. They underlined that their stance against the sexualization of the press and popular culture was completely different from those who blamed it on democracy, mistrusted the freedom of expression, and served as "spokespeople for a sanctimonious prohibitionism that portends a descent into debauchery."[13] Feminists rejected the destape for popularizing the image of a woman as a voiceless and passive "doll" who offered herself willingly to men, fulfilled their fantasies, and lacked desires of her own. They affirmed that through these images, "a free body is subjugated. Pure pleasure, repressed. Movement, halted. Exploration, prohibited. Sexuality, pruned, crushed, impoverished."[14] Feminism warned that the "ideal woman" produced by the male-dominated mass culture reinforced women's subordination, an argument that photographer Alicia D'Amico summarized best by concluding that the imagery of the commercial destape "is a way of keeping us with our heads down."[15]

By adopting beauty models created by men, women submitted to extraneous feminine ideals as if they were their own. Feminists affirmed that at the peak of the destape, women saw and valued themselves through the eyes and by the standards of men. Furthermore, feminists noticed that unlike in the anecdote, most women did not have the perfect buttocks of the young model in the Jordache commercial. This was, they argued, another form of oppression, as the media imposed unattainable models of beauty that made real women feel ugly, inferior, old, and unhappy. Women were unable to see that media images were not only sources of dissatisfaction but also distractions—"a smokescreen" that diverted energy and money away from more important goals. Feminists denounced that male-created destape images alienated and isolated women, generating fictitious needs that immersed them in a world of frivolity and banality while depriving them of self-confidence.[16]

Feminists defended and celebrated the female sexual body and recognized the value of fashion, diets, beauty routines, and exercise. However, they argued that women should set their own principles and promote a model of sexuality and beauty attuned to their own wants and fantasies rather than to male demands. An article in feminist magazine *Muchacha*, whose motto was "For women's liberation. No longer objects in the hands of men or society," condensed this argument by maintaining that "we are not against looking good or against the beauty and harmony women freely seek but we are against these virtues being used to enslave women."[17] Women were expected to reclaim their bodies but embrace a holistic subjectivity in which the body would not colonize their identities, diminishing other aspects of the self. Beauty and sexual desire should be liberating—governed by choice rather than obligation—promote individual expression, and respect personal idiosyncrasies.

Feminists agreed that achieving these aims was a monumental task for women. Even reflective women were disinclined to "radically break with that image of what we are not, an image that does not have anything to do with our bodies, tastes, imagination."[18] Critical voices denounced that while women celebrated the return of freedom and democracy, they were unable to recognize that hypersexualized body ideals proposed by the destape were expressions of a form of male authoritarianism that made women victims of "body fascism." In an article in *alfonsina*, for example, journalist María Moreno illustrated the insidious nature of the man-run media and its power over female readers and viewers. Moreno affirmed that even conscientious women who marched for the divorce law and enrolled in the "guerilla warfare of the orgasm" were quick to forget that taking complete control over their bodies and experiencing pleasure also required destroying oppressive female representations and male-created paradigms of sexiness and beauty.[19]

Although the work on pornography by feminist American scholars Catharine MacKinnon and Andrea Dworkin circulated in Argentina's feminist press, study groups, and conferences, local activists did not openly equate the destape with pornography, avoided causal links between pornography (and the destape) and sexual violence against women, and rejected any media controls and restrictions. Argentine feminists agreed with their American counterparts that most commercial media depictions represented a form of discrimination against women but rejected the use of legal methods, censorship, and state intervention against the destape. Sexologist María Luisa Lerer expressed this when she argued that "in no way am I against pornography, an expression of freedom under democracy.

As feminists, we fight for freedom, peace, and life. We cannot prohibit, no matter what the circumstances."[20] Instead, Argentine feminists emphasized the role of public pressure and the use of the feminist and women's press to change public perceptions and to create and inspire alternative discourses and imagery with empowering effects for women.[21]

Feminists saw their press as the best antidote to the male-dominated commercial media responsible for the destape. With the exception of *alfonsina*, feminist publications—mostly short bulletins and newsletters—had a limited circulation, but they effectively contested the destape by giving voice to critical women who felt oppressed by the new standards of beauty and sexualized female stereotypes.[22] Furthermore, feminists recognized that beyond their own press, some commercial women's publications offered a version of the destape by women and for women that also challenged the imagery and ideas of the male-conceived destape. For example, the magazine *Mujer 10*—published by Perfil, the same publishing house responsible for *Libre* and *Hombre*, icons of the destape press—frequently printed articles denouncing the commodification of the female body and the damaging effects of unrealistic beauty standards. Writing for feminist publication *alfonsina*, journalist María Moreno praised *Mujer 10* for effectively defending female sexual pleasure without guilt and for underlining its significance to a satisfying and productive life for women of all social classes. Moreno argued that those who believed that the defense of female orgasm in *Mujer 10* sometimes sounded too "epic" should remember that the bedroom was a space of power. Denouncing women's obstacles to pleasure and sexual dissatisfaction thus became a radical offensive against female passivity and subservience with equalizing effects well beyond the sheets.[23] Similarly, *La Mujer*—the supplement of the newspaper *Tiempo Argentino*—published contributions by local feminists and espoused a radical stance against the objectification of women in the current media culture. Television shows such as *Veinte Mujeres*, sexology books such as María Luisa Lerer's *Sexualidad femenina* (1986) and Laura Caldiz's *Viviendo nuestra sexualidad* (1986), and the new erotic literature by female writers are also examples of a women's destape that celebrated female sexual expression and desires.[24]

On television, the only space for criticism from an openly feminist perspective was *La Cigarra* (Channel 11), a one-hour show that aired every night at 8 p.m. starting in January 1984 and covered news, entertainment, and general interest topics from a woman's perspective. Among the seven hostesses of *La Cigarra* were poet, writer, and composer María Elena Walsh and singer Susana Rinaldi—both outspoken about their feminist views— and journalists Moira Soto and Dionisia Fontán (the author of *Laura de hoy*)—both with vast experience writing about women's issues. Fontán explained that the goal of the show was to "vindicate female qualities that had been only secondary until now."[25] Indeed, *La Cigarra* proposed a thoughtful, informed, and vocal type of woman as an alternative to the objectified sex symbols who, silent and half naked, populated television. With its topics and its hostesses, *La Cigarra* demonstrated that women were more than looks, youth, and body, and that the approving, desirous, and sexualizing male gaze was irrelevant. Yet the experience, original and important, was short-lived, as the show was cancelled after less than a year on the air.[26]

Art also provided women with significant opportunities for the production and dissemination of alternatives to the male-created destape images circulating in the media. An interesting example is *Mitominas 1*, a collective art show of a heterogeneous group of women artists in Buenos Aires in 1986 that included theater, sculpture, poetry, dance, and painting. Through a female voice and vision, the exhibit, which lasted almost a month, questioned the myths of womanhood and femininity that served to perpetuate patriarchal power: "Why is Eve guilty of original sin and not (like Prometheus) the curious, strong, disobedient heroine who acquires the light of knowledge for the female and male race?"[27] In 1988, *Mitominas 2: Los mitos de la sangre* opened in Buenos Aires with the same goal of contesting stereotypical female images, but this time with a particular emphasis on AIDS and violence against women.[28]

Film served as another space for reflection about femininity and sexuality for women creators after the return to democracy. In 1988, a group that included photographer Sara Facio, actress Marta Bianchi, and director María Luisa Bemberg, and was led by director Susana Lopez Merino, organized the inaugural film festival "La mujer y el cine" ("Women and Film") in Mar de Plata, the site of one of Latin America's most traditional and important film festivals since the 1950s. In a historical context in which women film directors represented only 7 percent of all filmmakers worldwide, "La mujer y el cine" screened a selection of international films by and about women. The festival was conceived as a celebration of "a feminine perspective that protects, chooses, organizes, and puts into movement a world of her own."[29]

María Luisa Bemberg came to epitomize this female perspective. In the 1980s, she was one of the four women filmmakers in the history of Argentina, the most popular and successful in the country and abroad, and the only one who was openly feminist. In the early 1970s, Bemberg founded the Organización Feminista Argentina (OFA; Argentine Feminist Organization) and, after the return to democracy, was founder, member, and collaborator of several new feminist organizations, including Lugar de Mujer. She was also an important feminist voice in the media, one whose opinion journalists sought and respected due to the success of her films, especially *Camila* (1984), her biggest box-office hit.[30]

Born into a traditional, wealthy family, Bemberg—a divorced mother of four—did not start her career in film until her late forties, first as a screenwriter and later as a director.[31] Her first works as director were the documentaries *El lugar de la mujer* (1972), about a home and beauty expo targeting women, and *Juguetes* (1978), on an exhibit for children. Both short films revealed the traditional expectations for women and the construction of gender roles fundamentally through a look at consumption and material culture, the world of domestic appliances, cosmetics, food, fashion, and toys. In the feature films that followed, Bemberg intensified her criticism of the social mechanisms condemning women to subordinate and unproductive roles and focused on the figures of the father, the husband, the brother, the Catholic Church, the state, and the mother as culprits behind women's constricted lives. Bemberg's attention to the family responded to her idea that "fascism begins at home. It begins in the family, where the father believes himself to be the supreme power and authority and where the woman is relegated to the status of supplicant." Bemberg further affirmed that "the urge to denounce this authority is a constant in all my films."[32]

*Momentos* (1980), a film about a married woman who starts an affair with a younger man, and *Señora de nadie* (1982), about a devoted housewife who leaves her husband and children after discovering he has a lover, are powerful denunciations of marriage as a confining, paralyzing, and restricting institution in a country in which divorce was still illegal. Controversial as they were for the censors, these films were screened because the dictatorship was debilitated and entering its final phase. In fact, when

Bemberg first submitted the screenplay for approval to the government, *Señora de nadie* was rejected based on "moral reasons"—it had an openly gay character and "was a very bad example for Argentine mothers."[33]

In 1984, *Camila* became the highest-grossing film of the year and the second Argentine film to be nominated for the Academy Award for Best Foreign Language Film. Based on a true story, the movie recounts the forbidden relation between Camila O'Gorman, the daughter of a wealthy and despotic landowner, and Jesuit priest Ladislao Gutiérrez under the authoritarian rule of Juan Manuel de Rosas in mid-nineteenth-century Buenos Aires. The couple flees Buenos Aires to start a new life and Camila gets pregnant, but they are caught shortly after, brought back to Buenos Aires, and executed. Bemberg's next film was *Miss Mary* (1986). Set in the late 1930s and 1940s, the film centers on a conservative English governess employed by a rich Argentine landowning family to supervise the children, especially the two young daughters. *Miss Mary* portrays, once again, the confinement and repression of women within the domestic sphere and their unfulfilled, isolated, and unhappy existence as wives, daughters, and mothers. *Yo, la peor de todas* (1990)—Bemberg's last film of the decade—is a biopic of Sor Juana Inés de la Cruz, a scholar, poet, and nun in seventeenth-century New Spain and one of the greatest contributors to the Spanish Golden Age.[34]

Bemberg believed that female film characters were traditionally a "function of male ambition" and the "object of a distorting, grotesque misogyny." Thus, women "are never really presented as beings with ideas."[35] In contrast, she denounced women's objectification and the annihilating effects of patriarchy by proposing unusual alternative images. For example, in several scenes of *Yo, la peor de todas*, Sor Juana Inés de la Cruz magnetically captures the attention of male scholars and clergymen with her ideas, poems, and conversation. In a context in which education and free expression were forbidden for women, Sor Juana is not a woman men looked at but one they listened to.

For Bemberg, women's subordinate social position included the bedroom. In 1983, she asserted that "until today, women have been like perpetual minors, always told what to do, how to think, and even what to feel and how to enjoy themselves in the bedroom. Everything has been externally imposed."[36] Although much has been written about Bemberg's work, scholars have generally overlooked the role of sexuality in her films. This silence is puzzling because female sexuality was crucial in her storytelling and because Bemberg's vision offered a compelling alternative to the prudish and contrived images supported by the dictatorship and the banal and objectified representations popularized by the commercial destape. In all her films, Bemberg shows women who resist the traditional models of ideal femininity by actively pursuing their love and sexual interests, rejecting the social value placed on virginity, refusing marriage, and questioning motherhood.[37]

Bemberg reveals how patriarchal ideology represses female sexuality through compulsory, unequal, and loveless marriages; the sexual double standard; the lack of sex education; the secrecy and shame around the female body and its functions; and the connection between virginity, family honor, and women's value. However, when Bemberg's female characters seize control of their sexuality, sex appears as an invigorating, creative, and almost healing sphere where they experiment, rebel, and express themselves. When women become autonomous sexual agents, sex is pleasure or the promise of pleasure. Thus, unrestricted female sexuality is a powerful metaphor for the exercise of freedom and personal choice and the search for individual satisfaction. The frustrated and unhappy woman who takes a younger lover and abandons her husband in *Momentos*; the cheated wife who engages in occasional relations in *Señora de nadie*; the strict governess who has sex with the young son of the family, as well as the young daughter who loses her virginity before marriage in *Miss Mary*; and Sor Juan Inés de la Cruz, who chooses celibacy to pursue her academic interests and challenges motherhood as women's ultimate source of fulfillment, are all sexually assertive women who defy sexual conventions and are unafraid of the consequences, which range from loss of employment and social condemnation to death.

*Camila* encapsulates all these aspects perfectly. Political repression is tantamount to sexual repression in this film, which tells the story of a young woman's defiance to both. In this regard, Bemberg does not divorce Camila's sexual assertiveness from her intellectual competence. Camila is portrayed as a curious reader who is informed about politics, reads prohibited books, and is outspoken and confident enough to voice her views against violence and political authoritarianism. Consequently, rather than depicting her as a passive, innocent girl who is seduced and kidnapped by her lover, Bemberg choses to make her "the daring one."[38]

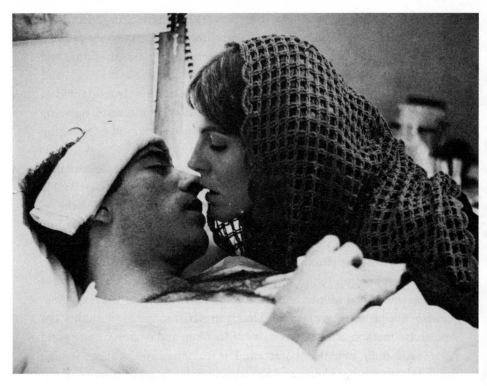

Figure 5.1. Director María Luisa Bemberg made Camila (Susú Pecoraro)
"the daring one." Lobby card from author's personal collection.

Determined to obtain erotic and sentimental fulfillment, Camila is the one
who takes the initiative, pursues Ladislao sexually, and later is stronger
and more composed when they are imprisoned and about to be executed.
The Catholic Church condemned *Camila* as an example of the "sick age of
the destape" and its "constant erotic-sexual fixation" while describing the
bedroom scenes as "the 'mating' of two human beings, compounded by
a dose of sensuality and lust that animals do not have." Ultra-Catholics
further criticized the sex scenes as a *"porno gancho"* ("porno hook") to
attract more spectators.[39]

   Beyond the press, art, and film, feminist activists, organizations, and
forums took action on the ground, inspiring women to challenge the
male-produced, nudity-focused, and buttocks-obsessed female imagery
with their own alternatives. An interesting example is "Autorretrato"

("Self-portrait"), a photography workshop led by Alicia D'Amico with the help of feminist psychologist and sexologist Graciela Sikos under the sponsorship of the feminist organization Lugar de Mujer. D'Amico explained that "there is a woman's eye in photography that is capable of creating a new aesthetic, redefining the traditional concept of beauty, looking at things in a different way, judging and creating in a different way. Women can transform the image of women."[40] The workshop—held at Lugar de Mujer, as well as at several women's conferences and congresses—invited women participants to select the makeup, clothing, and props for their individual photo shoots, rehearse expressions and movements in front of a mirror, and pose for D'Amico however they wanted. Participants were asked to guide the camera so the photos would reflect how they wished to be portrayed. After the individual photo sessions, participants reconvened to discuss the images with Sikos and D'Amico individually and as a group.

"Autorretrato" encouraged participants to forget demands that constantly afflicted women, such as "everyone is watching" or "this is how they like me," to focus on just one premise: "I look at myself."[41] Examining her photo, in which she looks at the camera reflectively, almost sad, with a line she had drawn in the middle of her face dividing it in two, a workshop participant in her forties affirmed that the image expressed the dichotomy she shared with most women: "One part I learned through education and from the media; this has to do with the woman as an object. The other, which I formed through the choices I made over the course of my life, has nothing to do with the models. It is exposed, with no disguises, no makeup. It is the part that thinks and reflects. Both live inside of me!"[42] Employing photography as a tool for self-discovery, the workshop gave women control over their self-representations, freeing them to embody their identities and thus to respond, on their own terms, to the images of the destape. This message of empowerment pervaded all the components of the feminist agenda in the return to democracy, including sexuality right at its core.

## FEMINISTS AND SEXUALITY

Sexuality was a central concern in feminist writings and the feminist press, in publications such as *Mujeres, Brujas, Unidas, Cuaderno de Existencia Lesbiana, Persona, Prensa de Mujeres, Alternativa Feminista,* and *La*

*Chancleta*, just to name a few. It was also an omnipresent and crucial component of feminist conferences, congresses, forums, and conventions, one that always attracted some of the largest and most enthusiastic groups of participants and the public.[43] This was the case, for example, of the biggest and most important annual event of the women's movement, the Encuentro Nacional de Mujeres (ENM; National Women's Meeting), in which both feminists and members of different types of women's organizations—from labor unions to associations of neighborhood women, housewives, and female professionals—convened for discussion and reflection. The first ENM, held in 1986 in Buenos Aires, brought together one thousand women from all over the country. They gathered in workshops on different topics organized by the ENM planning committee and in *talleres autoconvocados*, workshops not included in the program that were proposed and arranged by the participants on site and run parallel to the formal workshops.[44]

In 1986, three out of the twenty-one formal workshops focused on sexuality (sexuality, the female body, and teenage sexuality and pregnancy), while in five others (women's health, the family, the media, women and education, and women and the law) measures were debated and proposed on sex topics such as sex education, sexual stereotypes in the media, and abortion. This was an important triumph for feminists over some women's organizations that had initially resisted the inclusion of sexuality in the program. The increasing importance of sexuality in the ENM over the course of the decade became evident in the organization of a growing number of *talleres autoconvocados* such as the *taller* on lesbianism in Córdoba in 1987, on abortion in Mendoza in 1988, and on pornography in Rosario a year later. In fact, in Rosario, the "most feminist ENM" of the 1980s—according to feminist activist Magui Bellotti—the workshop on sexuality devoted to themes such as the right to pleasure, the double moral standard, and bisexuality was the "star" of the meeting. Bellotti characterized it as "an explosion" that attracted three hundred of the three thousand women in attendance, and the most popular of thirty-three workshops.[45]

The significance of sexuality at the ENM reflected its centrality in the institutional life of feminist organizations that offered a variety of activities focused on women and sex.[46] For example, the Casa de la Mujer in Rosario, funded in 1986, had free psychological counseling and discussion groups for victims of sexual abuse, besides sponsoring sex education workshops and seminars with leading sex educator Liliana Pauluzzi.

Lugar de Mujer, which opened in Buenos Aires in 1983, organized sexual enrichment groups frequently overseen by sexologist María Luisa Lerer, one of its founders. Similarly, the Centro de Estudios de la Mujer (CEM), created in 1979 in Buenos Aires and headed by psychologist Gloria Bonder, began coordinating therapeutic support groups and seminars devoted to alternative sex therapies for women in the mid-1980s. In addition, all of these organizations offered regular consciousness-raising groups, talks, workshops, book discussions, and film screenings.

Feminist study and research groups like the CEM, which flourished all over the country during these years, also provided a space to read, research, write about, and debate female sexuality. Likewise, feminist publications and organizations edited and distributed a variety of educational and informational materials on diverse sex topics. For instance, the Instituto de Estudios Jurídicos Sociales de la Mujer (INDESO Mujer; Women's Institute of Legal and Social Studies), funded in Rosario in 1984, not only published the monthly *La Chancleta* but also *Cuaderno de Divulgación*, addressing topics such as sex violence and eroticism and power. Lugar de Mujer and CEM—which regularly published its bulletin *Voces de Mujeres*—also printed and distributed short publications on subjects such as marriage, sexuality, body, and contraception. Furthermore, organizations like CEM and INDESO Mujer built up libraries that specialized on women subjects and were open to the general public.[47]

Feminist activists shared numerous definitions, concerns, and goals with sexologists, family planning specialists, and supporters of sex education, the leading groups engaged in the public discussion of sexuality that represented a true alternative to the sex narratives of the commercial destape. These commonalities were reinforced by the presence of feminist practitioners in all three fields. Like sexologists, feminists defined sexuality and sexual health as rights, reclaimed women's right to pleasure, masturbation, and the clitoral orgasm, and promoted the importance of battling "sexual illiteracy" and women's need to know and understand their bodies and desires. Similar to the way sexologists questioned standards of "normality," feminists encouraged women to search, without inhibitions, for their personal satisfaction. At the same time, they criticized both the "Victorian prudishness" and "the alienating sexual revolution that makes women feel like we are repressed and frigid if we do not make love with impunity, without anxiety, under any condition, and with absolutely anyone."[48]

Figure 5.2: "Every child should be a wanted child." INDESO Mujer actively promoted contraception in its journal *La Chancleta*, June–September 1989. Courtesy of INDESO Mujer, Rosario.

Feminists also joined family planning experts in the fight, first, for the abolition of decrees 659 and 3,938, which prohibited all activities directly and indirectly related to family planning, and later, for the democratization of women's access to contraception. Like the AAPF or ARESS, feminists defined family planning as a human right and sponsored educational activities to inform women about birth control methods and reproductive health.[49] Finally, feminist organizations promoted the importance of sex education for all and at school. Sex education was an important component of the ENM since the first congress in 1986. Feminists denounced the irreparable psychological and social consequences of the lack of sex information among children and teenagers, parents' inadequacy to address sexual issues at home, and the resulting need to contest taboos and prejudices in younger generations through formal school-based sex education.[50]

Overlapping agendas notwithstanding, feminists distinguished themselves from sexologists, family planning specialists, and sex educators by their focus on women. While all sectors debated and proposed changes to the same problems and agreed on important aspects, feminists were the only ones who did so from a total female perspective, one exclusively motivated by women's needs and committed to the defense of women's rights. Because the denunciation of men's power over women and the reversal of the conditions of inequality that oppressed them lay at the core of this fight, the feminist voice was the most combative and unapologetic. It was also conceptually more complex: sexuality was a social relation and a political institution.[51] As a result, feminists linked changes in public perceptions and cultural representations, the legal framework, and public policy with the urgent need to eliminate patriarchy and machismo. This was a destape in its fullest meaning: the revelation that transforming female sexuality depended on ending patriarchal oppression.[52]

An article in *Unidas* expressed this argument clearly by affirming that female preorgasmia and lack of sexual desire were not divorced from what women experienced outside the bedroom every day and that "this machista culture means we are always second-class and there is no reason to expect that feelings of inferiority and impotence will disappear between the sheets."[53] Power, a concept that generally eluded the discourses of sexologists, sex educators, and family planning specialists, was central to the feminist conceptualization of sex. Thus, for feminists, understanding the roots of women's subordination and repression was as relevant as the proposals to overcome them. Sexologists used data on preorgasmia to vindicate sex treatment and sexual health, and family planning and sex education specialists employed statistics of teen pregnancy and abortion to validate their programs. Feminists, however, avoided a language of justifications to frame their demands and argued that the rights of women were absolute and unconditional.[54]

While sexologists, family planning experts, and sex education advocates tended to defend the right to pleasure, reproductive rights, and the right to sex education independently from one another, feminists successfully brought them together in a single platform as the sexual rights of women. Feminists understood female sexuality as a whole that could only work effectively if all its interconnected parts—eroticism, procreation, and education—were equally healthy, functioning, and valued. Argentine feminists shared this view with their Latin American counterparts and embraced the definition of women's sexual rights that Colombian sexologist María Ladi Londoño presented at the Primer Encuentro Feminista Latinoamericano y del Caribe (First Latin American and Caribbean Feminist Meeting) in Bogotá, Colombia, in 1981. The inalienable sexual rights of women were the right to sexuality independent from reproduction and marital status, the right to know and love one's body, the right to orgasm, the right to affection and an enjoyable sex life, the right to express one's sexuality freely, the right to family planning through the control of both the male and the female body, the right to not be treated as a sexual object, the right to sexual pleasure independent from sexual penetration, and the right to refrain from being sexual.[55] To reinforce this language of rights, local feminists drew on the United Nations Convention on the Elimination of All Forms of Discrimination against Women adopted by the United Nations General Assembly in 1979, often considered the international bill of rights for women. Although the Argentine state did not ratify the convention until 1985, feminists employed it actively to denounce different forms of discrimination against women, from lack of access to birth control to mass media objectification.[56]

Although female pleasure, contraception, and sex education were important demands for feminists, their most original contribution to the 1980s discussion on sexuality was the debate on three crucial topics that no other sectors addressed, at least publicly, and the destape media avoided: a critique of motherhood connected to pleasure, sexual violence, and the right to abortion. Feminists denounced the burdens of mother-hood and challenged definitions that made it women's natural and most important role. Activists mobilized to make motherhood a choice rather than an obligation—thus the emphasis on contraception and, among some groups, abortion—and to protect mothers and children. On March 8, 1984, when feminists and different women's organizations came together to celebrate International Women's Day for the first time under democracy, the list of common demands included the law of *patria potestad compartida* (parenting rights), a divorce law, legal equality for children born out of wedlock, and social security for housewives. But that was not all. The most unorthodox position came from what contemporaries called "radical feminists" who defied all conventions by turning the discussion about motherhood into one about sex.[57]

The iconic figure of this radical feminism was María Elena Oddone, the founder of the MLF in the 1970s. Oddone had been threatened by the Peronist far-Right death squad known as the Argentine Anticommu-nist Alliance (or "Triple A") during Isabel Perón's government and had cautiously remained silent—as most feminists did—during the military dictatorship. Yet she powerfully resurfaced with the return to democracy.[58] Oddone founded the OFA and reestablished the feminist bulletin *Persona* that she had introduced in the 1970s, though it had lasted only briefly at that time. Outspoken, visible in the media, and contentious, Oddone incarnated an uncompromising, fearless feminism, critical of "accommo-dating" feminists. In an interview in 1984, for example, Oddone declared that "Argentine feminism is underdeveloped, afraid of not being liked, of not pleasing and above all, of being alone. That is why feminists forge alli-ances with political parties. Feminism is lost and diluted in such alliances. The strength of feminism lies not in the numbers but in the courage to raise one's voice in the desert and say things that may be frightening but that deep down, ring true to every woman."[59]

Sexual violence, abortion, and the demands of motherhood, Oddone asserted, were the most important "truths" that feminists had to uncover. Following American radical feminist writer Adrianne Rich, the OFA ar-gued that the current model of patriarchal motherhood constrained and dominated women while degrading female potentialities. In current-day society, mothers were required to repress their selfhood and lived by rules they had not created. Thus, it was essential for women to search for feminist forms of mothering, devising alternatives to the patriarchal model or rejecting motherhood altogether.[60] Oddone emphasized that motherhood was a social and historical construct and affirmed that the maternal instinct was a myth and a mechanism for the domination of women, that is, a "successful way of keeping women subjugated and of blaming them if they do not love their children." In fact, Oddone equated children to the links of a chain that went from the hand of the male master to the neck of the female slave.[61]

Oddone and the OFA made their criticism of motherhood explicit in the 1984 celebration of International Women's Day, when Oddone proudly displayed a combative banner that read "No to motherhood, yes to pleasure." The OFA rejected motherhood as an oppressive institution and contrasted it with sexual pleasure, which was considered a sphere of liberation. The sign also highlighted a dichotomy between two types of womanhood, maternal and sexual, reinforcing a common stereotype of asexual motherhood. The arguments were further strengthened by other OFA banners in the same march with belligerent messages such as "Enough of phallocracy, let's vindicate the clitoris together."[62]

With her picture and those of the incendiary banners in the hands of other OFA members all over the press, Oddone became an overnight sensation. By zooming in on her and the OFA out of thousands of activists, dozens of organizations, and hundreds of placards with numerous demands, the media reduced feminism to its most provocative expression, stereotyped it as a misfit, and then condemned it. The reaction of the popular magazine *Gente* is a case in point. The photos of the OFA members are published under the title "¿Mujeres?" ("Women?"), suggesting that women who challenged motherhood and exalted sex might not be "real" women.[63] Most importantly, in her "Carta abierta de mujer a mujer" ("Open letter from one woman to another"), journalist Renée Salas condemned the OFA banners by asking: "Why so much animosity? Why no shame? I felt like they [the banners] were a low blow (sorry for the double entendre). Like they were excessive and irresponsible, something we did not deserve." Salas argued that the OFA demand was not "serious" and that claims for an unrepressed and satisfying sexuality did not belong in the public sphere: "Why this vindication for such a private, intimate, personal sphere where people can impose and manage their own rules without depending on the laws passed by Congress?" Salas affirmed that she felt embarrassed by the

Figure 5.3. María Elena Oddone was featured in *Gente* holding a photograph of herself with the controversial "No to motherhood, yes to pleasure" sign. *Gente*, March 15, 1985.

signs and questioned if a Plaza de Mayo mother, a housewife, a saleswoman, or a businesswoman would carry the banners displayed by the OFA activists. With this argument, Salas suggested that OFA members were not mothers, professional and middle-class women, or women devoted to their homes. Furthermore, she implied that these types of women were not interested in sex or in debates about sex or were, like her, ashamed by those messages. Moreover, Salas felt appalled at the thought of how a mother would respond if asked by a child about the meanings of words included on the banners, such as "clitoris." To conclude, Salas called the OFA members "failed" and "reckless" and condemned them for being "defiant" rather than "conciliatory."[64]

In this central article, *Gente* revealed a profound prejudice and incomprehension of feminism and contributed to its misrepresentation and the disparagement of its claims. Equally significant, *Gente* exemplified the hypocrisy of some media outlets that propelled and celebrated the destape and the hypersexualization of culture while severely disapproving of the word "clitoris" on a banner. Yet the problem was not the sexual terms, which sexologists, writers, and journalists were using in public and discussing on those very same pages but who employed the terms and why. In the wake of the destape, the "real scandal" was not the vindication of sexual pleasure, which authoritative experts could demand for women, but the image of proud women demanding it themselves, voicing it in public, and, in so doing, contesting patriarchy, motherhood, and machismo. In her response to the article in *Gente*, feminist journalist María Moreno argued that Salas was unable to see that all "serious" demands articulated by feminists, such as a divorce law, were intrinsically connected to the sexual demands she criticized and belittled. As a consequence, all claims should be displayed on banners. Moreno also ridiculed Salas for her incompetence and discomfort if faced with a child's question about the meaning of clitoris, warning that this "Victorian prudishness" contributed to raising "another generation of men brought up on tango, breadwinners of penetration (*asalariados de la penetración*), and ignorant of how a woman experiences pleasure."[65]

Some activists disagreed with Oddone's arguments about motherhood, while others who shared them thought they were detrimental to public support for feminism. Many condemned her participation in the March 8 demonstration as a "provocation" and resented the "bad press" it had caused. Years later, Oddone saw in these criticisms a sign of class privilege. These middle- and upper-class feminists, she asserted, could not relate to the majority of economically and culturally disadvantaged women for whom the separation between sexual pleasure and procreation was still unattainable. Oddone explained that these lower-class women "spend their lives encumbered by children, without ever discovering sexual pleasure, the pleasure of doing what they like, or the pleasure of not doing anything, which is off limits for the mothers of many children." Oddone lashed out against her critics for their lack of solidarity by arguing that "the ones who were offended were educated hypocrites who have no more than two children and who want poor women—those who do not know how to avoid having many children, and cannot avoid it—to continue upholding the cult of motherhood."[66]

While Oddone's views on motherhood were contentious, her denunciation of violence against women was massively shared by feminist organizations. Feminists fundamentally mobilized against domestic and sexual violence as part of their condemnation of patriarchy and male control over the female body. By exposing sexual violence, feminist organizations challenged the sexy, festive tone of the destape and problematized the media that turned women into objects eager to please along with the discourses that emphasized male pleasure. Sexual violence reintroduced a discussion of sex as a sphere of pain, fear, power, and inequality. This was a timely wake-up call to a reality that was more complicated, less glamorous, and extremely more poignant than the media fantasy world of sensual enjoyment in which domination over women was almost perfectly disguised and sexual abuse ignored or minimized.

Violence against women had been traditionally taboo, historically neglected by the state, and disregarded by the media. This was even more evident during the military dictatorship as the regime raped, tortured, and killed women in clandestine detention centers. The silence of the press and the state's indifference to sexual violence changed little after the return to democracy. Yet, now, feminists, who were empowered by freedom and excited about reuniting and reorganizing after years of dismemberment and concealment, made the fight to stop violence against women a banner they carried alone but with fervor and urgency. Indeed, organizations such as INDESO Mujer in Rosario, the Asociación de Trabajo y Estudio de la Mujer 25 de Noviembre (ATEM; November 25th Women's Association for

Work and Research)—created in Buenos Aires in 1982 and named after the International Day for the Elimination of Violence against Women— and the Grupo Feminista de Denuncia (Feminist Denunciation Group), founded in Buenos Aires in 1986, materialized with the explicit goal to fight violence against women.[67]

Feminists organized conferences to debate the topic, offered support groups and legal counsel for victims, produced and circulated materials to instruct women on how to proceed after a rape or beating, and created awareness about psychological violence and verbal abuse. They also spoke out against groping and indecent exposure in public and denounced the police for mistreating and ignoring women who wanted to file a report for these types of crimes. Oddone, for example, frequently accompanied victims to the police station to support them and make sure the police complied with procedures. Feminists also educated women about sexual abuse in the context of marriage and dating. They urged women to under- stand that being forced to have sex by a husband or a boyfriend, giving in to sexual demands due to threats or accusations of infidelity or "frigidity," and being coerced into sex practices that were physically and emotionally harmful were forms of violence and should not be tolerated. Although feminists at the time did not denounce the torture and rape of women prisoners during the military dictatorship, feminists did remind citizens that violence against women under democracy was "also" a violation of human rights.[68]

To this effect, feminists rallied around infamous, shocking cases that, unlike most instances of sexual abuse and domestic violence suffered by ordinary women in silence and isolation, the media could not ignore. In 1983, ATEM joined forces with the OFA and Reunión de Mujeres (Women's Meeting) to create the Tribunal de Violencia contra la Mujer (Violence Against Women Tribunal), a forum for mobilization and denunciation of the case of Mabel Montoya, an eighteen-year-old door-to-door saleswom- an who jumped to her death from a fourth-floor apartment to avoid being raped by a client. The Tribunal de Violencia contra la Mujer coordinated marches and demonstrations to demand justice for Montoya and for the countless women who were victims of sexual assault. The tribunal argued that "sexual violence is only the most attention-grabbing aspect of a vi- olence that is continuously repeated, in all forms. . . . Violence against women is a political issue. It is a conscious process of sexual terrorism

Figure 5.4. Feminist organizations such as Lugar de Mujer used education-al materials such as simple drawings to ignite discussion and encourage the participation of women victims of violence in their support groups. Courtesy of INDESO Mujer, Rosario.

that accompanies the exercise of patriarchal power."[69] Feminists recon-ceptualized rape by arguing that it was not only a horrific crime but also a mechanism for control that conditioned how women behaved—how they traveled, dressed, spoke—limiting their freedom, inhibiting the expres-sion of their identities, and amplifying feelings of guilt.[70]

Similarly, the Grupo Feminista de Denuncia had a very active role in publicly discussing and condemning the death of Alicia Muñiz in February 1988. Muñiz was murdered by her famous husband, world middleweight boxing champion Carlos Monzón, who strangled her and then pushed her off a balcony while the two were vacationing in the resort town of Mar del Plata. Feminists reproved Monzón fans who encouraged and justified the boxer's actions and denounced media outlets that echoed these sympathies and, for years, had minimized his well-known philandering and violent behavior toward women. ATEM defined Muñiz as a "victim of patriarchal power" and warned women about the tragic end of those who put up with men's abuse. Yet feminists also argued that this was more than a cautionary tale for women. They affirmed that when a week after the murder, an unapologetic Monzón declared to the press that he had beaten all his partners, he was actually exposing a society where violence against women was shockingly natural and unimportant, the female body was unremorsefully violated, and women's lives had no value.[71]

In her column in *El Informador Público*, Oddone argued that this situation was sadly evident in the abandonment of victims and the lack of social support. She denounced the complicity of family members, neighbors, doctors, and friends who looked away and of judges, police, and congressmen who remained indifferent and even hostile toward abused women. Indeed, four months before being murdered, Muñiz had filed a police report because Monzón had attacked her, but the judge dismissed the demand. This was a common occurrence that Oddone characterized as a "chronicle of a death foretold" while denouncing that "when a woman is beaten to death in our country, there is not a single perpetrator but many. We accuse judges who endorse the abuse of women by letting the abusers walk away scot-free."[72] ATEM, for its part, demanded the opening of police departments with an all-female staff for cases of rape and violence against women, as well as special sections in hospitals and safe houses to treat and support these victims.[73]

While violence against women was a unifying topic, widely embraced by feminists and supported by women's organizations of different kinds, abortion was divisive. Due to ideological, religious, and strategic reasons, the heterogeneous women's movement oscillated between silence and unacceptance. For their part, feminists, who recognized abortion as a key component of a serious debate about women's rights, hesitated to place it at the forefront of the agenda. Although feminists were decidedly pro-choice, many feminist organizations made legal abortion a secondary goal and an inconspicuous matter of discussion, present but discreet. In some cases, feminists prioritized the fight for public access to contraception. This was fundamentally the case early in the decade when they realized that the Alfonsín administration, which took three years to repeal decree 659, prohibiting family planning, did not share their sense of urgency on

Figure 5.5. Feminist organizations employed pamphlets to denounce violence against women. Courtesy CEDINCI, Buenos Aires.

the matter. In other cases, feminists understood that the right to abortion was vital but too controversial at a time in which they had to attract more members for their organizations. Thus, they focused on other demands, relegated abortion to intramural conversations and reflection groups, and generally kept it separate from public campaigning.[74]

Yet the fight for abortion did not disappear, and numerous feminist organizations provided safe spaces for enthusiastic debate and dedicated activism. Indeed, as early as November 1982, in the conference organized by the ATEM and the Centro de Estudios de la Mujer Argentina (CESMA; Center for the Study of Argentine Women) on women and the family, the committee on family and sexuality concluded that "abortion should be legalized because it is currently widespread, unsafe, and economically discriminatory."[75] This demand also transcended meetings and internal documents and was taken to the streets shortly after the return to democracy. On March 8, 1984, during the International Women's Day demonstration in Buenos Aires, feminists openly displayed banners demanding legal abortion—"My body is my own, no more deaths from abortion" and "Freedom to abort: We give birth, we decide"—and fervently sung songs that denounced the death of women due to back-alley procedures.[76]

Abortion had been considered a crime without exception since its inclusion in the first penal code promulgated in 1886. In 1921, the provisions on abortion were amended and punishment was lifted when the life or health of the pregnant woman was in danger, pregnancy was the result of rape, or the pregnant woman was mentally disabled. In 1968, during the dictatorship of Juan Carlos Onganía, decree 17,567 introduced further restrictions on abortion, requiring "grave" danger to the life and health of the pregnant woman, the initiation of criminal proceedings in the case of rape, and the consent of a legal representative in the case of a mentally disabled woman or a minor. In 1973, these modifications were revoked but were once again reinstalled by the military dictatorship in 1976. In 1984, the new democratically elected government returned to the 1921 wording, reinstating the exceptions—though it established no regulations to grant actual access to an abortion in these cases—but with a difference. The exception to preserve the life or health of the pregnant woman remained, but the placement of a comma in the wording of the second exception suggested that abortion was only available with the consent of a legal representative when the pregnancy had resulted from the rape of a mentally disabled woman. The phrasing left open to interpretation whether legal abortion was available to rape victims who did not suffer from mental disability. The law mandated prison terms for women who had an abortion—between one to four years—and for abortion practitioners and, in the case of doctors, nurses, and pharmacists, the suspension of their professional licenses.[77]

While sexologists—many of whom supported legal abortion privately—were unconcerned with reproductive rights, and family planning experts and sex educators used abortion to emphasize the urgency of contraception and sex education as antidotes, feminists fought in solitude to decriminalize abortion. In 1985, Alternativa Feminista, CEM, the Tribunal de Violencia contra la Mujer, Libera, Prima, and Lugar de Mujer convened in Movimiento Feminista (Feminist Movement), an umbrella organization that, with ATEM, was one of the first to publicly include the decriminalization of abortion among its demands. Movimiento Feminista underlined that motherhood was an option, defined an unwanted pregnancy as a form of slavery, and denounced the inhumane, unsafe, and unsanitary conditions of illegal practices that harmed and killed women. Although there were no official statistics, Movimiento Feminista estimated that 350,000 illegal abortions took place annually. Feminists drew attention to the fact that poor women who lacked economic and cultural resources suffered the most but highlighted that the fear, shame, and oppression associated with an illegal abortion affected all women regardless of social class or age.[78]

In 1987, a group of feminists who had come together in the fifth conference on women organized by ATEM debated whether to establish a group exclusively focused on the fight for legal abortion. The idea came to fruition a year later when a group of activists, female doctors, and lawyer Dora Coledesky—who would become a leading public figure for the right to abortion—established the Comisión por el Derecho al Aborto (CDA; Abortion Rights Committee) under the motto "Contraception to avoid abortion, legal abortion to avoid death." Unlike family planning experts who proposed access to contraception to end abortion, the CDA viewed both as part of women's same right to make decisions related to their bodies. The committee focused on legalizing abortion, and, in so doing, they went further than earlier calls for decriminalization, demanding that legal abortion be available at no cost in public hospitals. The CDA also insisted on extending sex education and access to contraception and promoted research to document the reality of unsafe abortions.[79]

Also in 1987, a group of Catholic women founded Católicas por el Derecho a Decidir (CDD; Catholics for the Right to Decide). The group emerged as a consequence of contacts with the American Catholics for Choice and with Catholic women from other Latin American countries at the Quinto Encuentro Internacional de Mujer y Salud (Fifth International Meeting on Women and Health) in Costa Rica that same year.[80] Safina Newbery, a former nun and feminist anthropologist, became a prominent figure in the CDD and an active member of the CDA. The Catholic Church, which opposed feminism as a "servile" and "imported" ideology that disregarded the "reality" of Argentine women, rejected the CDD vehemently. For the church, the CDD was a group of "wolves in sheep's clothing," and abortion was the "worst" crime against humanity—a definition that, after the church's silence about human rights violations during the military dictatorship, showed a historically convenient and highly selective use of the language of human rights.[81]

The ENM in Mendoza in 1988 further confirmed the increasing focus on abortion within both the feminist and the women's movements. In Mendoza, a *taller autoconvocado* on abortion defined it as an absolute right for all women and openly rejected the patriarchal, state, and medical powers that curtailed the exercise of that right. In their conclusions, the women at the ENM demanded "the right to public, free abortion, with no limits on age or nationality, free from the intrusion of judges, doctors, social workers, parents or husbands, in national or municipal hospitals, without the need to state the reasons."[82]

By the end of the decade, feminist mobilization for the right to abortion had gained momentum, but it peaked in the 1990s when public discussion—fueled by the attempt of President Carlos Menem to include "the defense of human life from conception" in the Constitution—intensified without precedent. In 1989, the CDA participated for the first time in the International Women's Day demonstration and began editing a publication, *Nuevos aportes sobre aborto*. A year later, it organized its first symposium. Also in 1989, feminist organizations published a full-page newspaper ad in support of a woman who had been raped and had gone to court to demand access to an abortion in a public hospital. In 1990, the CDA, Lugar de Mujer, ATEM, INDESO Mujer, and CDD, among other feminist organizations, signed a public petition in favor of a bill set before Congress to modify the penal code and make abortion legal for victims of rape. In 1992, the CDA submitted its first draft of an abortion law and later collaborated with different congressmen in the elaboration of similar bills.[83]

## LESBIAN SEXUALITY: COMING INTO EXISTENCE

The problems, rights, and needs of lesbians were notably absent on the feminist agenda after the return to democracy, reproducing the same invisible status they had in the feminist and gay organizations of the early 1970s.[84] Both heterosexual and gay feminists embraced a sort of "strategic silence" about lesbianism to increase social approval and protect the credibility and respectability of feminist organizations. Despite reaching the highest levels of public visibility to that date, feminism continued to be ridiculed, condemned, and stigmatized in the media with stereotypes of feminists as masculine, zealous, aggressive, unattractive, and asexual.[85] In fact, during the 1989 ENM in Rosario, many women who attended the workshop on feminism shared that they were reluctant to publicly identify themselves as feminists due to social prejudices and discrimination.[86]

Feminists believed that, in this context, associations between feminism and lesbianism would further complicate the attempts of their organizations to grow and prosper because same-sex desire was generally synonymous with aberration and pathology.[87] Although the American Psychiatric Association had removed homosexuality from the *Diagnostic and Statistical Manual of Mental Disorders* in 1973, it was not until 1990 that the World Health Organization (WHO) eliminated homosexuality from the *International Statistical Classification of Diseases and Related Health Problems*.[88] In Argentina, authoritative voices disseminated these ideas of abnormality. In 1984, for example, Minister of the Interior Antonio Tróccoli declared that homosexuality was a disease and justified arrests of gay people and police raids on gay clubs. That same year, internationally renowned cardiologist René Favaloro stated on television that homosexuality was a deviation of nature, a "tragedy," and condemned gay organizations for "staging a defense" of what he termed a "plague."[89] These ideas permeated society as a whole. In 1984, readers accused *Mujer 10* of "immorality" for publishing a piece on lesbianism, and, similarly, members of the audience disapproved when in 1991, famous television host Mirtha Legrand decided to discuss gay and lesbian sexualities on her famous midday show. Guests on Legrand's show included a sexologist, a physician, the president of the CHA Rafael Freda, and Ilse Fuskova, who would rise as a leading voice among lesbian activists. Some viewers, whose phone messages Legrand read on the air, slammed the show, one calling it "disgusting."[90]

Thus, many feminists who were devoted to the growth and consolidation of their organizations believed that, given the prevalent lesbophobia, engaging in a public discussion of lesbianism would be a costly mistake. And, quite the reverse, they highlighted the difference between feminism and lesbianism to fight media representations that considered them one and the same. In so doing, they walked a thin line between arguing that not all feminists were lesbians and more or less deliberately erasing lesbians from their organizations and stigmatizing lesbianism. Hesitations and silences in public reflected those taking place behind closed doors. While female heterosexuality was a central, omnipresent topic in feminist publications, lesbian sexuality was conspicuously absent. When *alfonsina* exceptionally printed a translation of an interview with two gay women titled "Amar a otra mujer"—which had originally appeared as "Loving Another Woman" in *Notes from the Third Year: Women's Liberation* (1971), a publication by radical American feminists based in New York—the magazine received angry letters from feminists who complained that the article "endangers the face of the movement." Interestingly, *alfonsina* had a broad circulation and probably reached readers outside feminism, but the most staunchly feminist publications had a small print run and were still blatantly silent about lesbianism.[91] Similarly, although lesbian sexuality was addressed in the ENM sexuality workshops and *talleres autoconvocados* on the topic appeared as early as in the second ENM in Córdoba in 1987, a workshop on lesbianism was only included in the formal program of the annual women's meetings in 1992.[92]

In 1984, in a paper presented at the ATEM annual meeting, writer Hilda Rais, one of the founders of Lugar de Mujer, introduced the discussion on lesbianism at a feminist conference for the first time. In her paper, Rais proposed to consider lesbianism "as a sexual behavior and as a lifestyle with political meaning, situating it in a system—the patriarchal system—and in our country—a dependent, authoritarian, capitalist country at the mercy of the Catholic Church."[93] Yet, despite this presentation, Rais remembered that there was only "a cursory acknowledgment" of lesbianism. Feminists never openly declared "lesbians bother me" or "make me nervous," but feminist organizations engaged in no real dialogue about same-sex sexuality as part of a broader discussion on the experience of womanhood. Attempts at debating lesbianism in regular workshops organized by heterosexual women failed, and when a group of lesbians began meeting in their own

Grupo de Reflexión de Lesbianas (Lesbians' Reflection Group), Lugar de Mujer decided not to make it public or advertise the meetings in its bulletin. When in 1988, the group members identified themselves as lesbian women in the demonstration on International Women's Day, Lugar de Mujer disapproved. A year later, the clique, which became the Grupo Autogestivo de Lesbianas (Self-Managed Lesbians' Group), split with Lugar de Mujer.[94]

In gay men's organizations, lesbians were also silent and concealed. Only a handful of gay women participated sporadically in the CHA, which was founded in 1984, and throughout the 1980s, they still occupied a secondary, marginal position. Carlos Jáuregui, the first president of the CHA, suggested that lesbians privileged militancy in feminist organizations over the CHA because they saw it as a more "legitimate" form of activism. He also affirmed that lesbians felt safer as feminist activists because they were not required to disclose their sexual orientation. Jáuregui argued that, as a consequence, while lesbians were called "feminists," gay men advocates were called "fucking fags."[95] Official publications declared that "the CHA wants women," and the organization urged lesbians to become active and engaged members, valued their contribution, and opposed their "self-marginalization."[96] However, in 1989—with a woman, Teresa de Ritó, as vice president of the organization and promoter of *Vamos a andar mujer*, the first CHA publication for women—internal CHA documents still lamented the lack of women's involvement. In a spirit of self-criticism, the CHA asserted that "sadly, for the past five years, women have come and gone, without finding a place to stay, a place where they can join in efforts that address their issues."[97]

Even in intimate, all-female, feminist settings, lesbians found it difficult to express themselves freely and find support. Rais makes this frustration clear in *Diario Colectivo*, a coauthored volume that compiled the journal entries, discussions, and interactions of Rais, María Inés Aldaburu, Inés Cano, and Nené Reynoso, who met weekly to discuss different topics and then reflected on them in writing. Rais complained to the group that she was made to feel "different" and that "they act like they accept it [lesbianism], but I cannot talk freely or act on things having to do with this, I cannot be totally me, so I get depressed or absolutely furious." Rais's friends reacted to her declaration with a range of emotions, from denial, shock, and irritation to acknowledging that "I find lesbianism confusing, upsetting, frightening."[98]

Amid incomprehension and disapproval, gay women suffered from problems with self-acceptance that were even more challenging for those who, unlike Rais, were young, not feminist, and without a support network, and thus felt even more disempowered. Research presented in Lugar de Mujer and conducted among more than one hundred lesbians between the ages of eighteen and twenty-six revealed that they not only concealed their sexual orientation but also experienced low self-esteem and feelings of self-rejection because they saw themselves as "sick" and "deviant."[99] Consequently, these women struggled to find their voice and mobilize, which further contributed to their sweeping public invisibility. In this respect, Rais affirmed that "in our country, lesbians do not exist socially because they do not say they are lesbians."[100]

For some lesbian feminists, their loyalty to feminist organizations, even when these organizations silenced them, was stronger. Although Rais was an early acknowledged figure among gay women, she herself never identified as lesbian first nor considered activism for the rights of gay people a priority. She openly rejected lesbian separatism—which American proponents such as Charlotte Bunch understood not only as separation from men but also from women who benefited from heterosexuality—and equated it to a process of "ghettoization" with damaging consequences for the fight of feminists. Rais affirmed that "my identity was not about being lesbian back then, nor is it now. My identity was always about being a woman and a feminist. So my intention and my desire, back in '84 and '85, was that lesbian groups were not necessary. I hoped that all women could be part of feminism, that feminism would include us all."[101]

Rais did not believe in lesbian organizations because she did not distinguish the particular forms of repression suffered by gay women. She argued that lesbians were oppressed because of their gender without openly recognizing the specific discrimination that affected lesbians because of their sexual orientation. Yet Rais acknowledged that her prominent position among fellow feminists and outside the feminist circle—for example, among sexologists who often asked her to participate in their graduate seminars and conferences—was related to her "acceptable" image. Rais believed that she was welcomed because of her professional prestige, social status, and the fact that she was feminine, middle-class, educated, and childless but wondered if the same individuals would be as accepting of a lesbian mother or a "masculine lesbian."[102]

While Rais can be credited with starting the discussion about lesbianism in feminist circles right after the return to democracy, it was Ilse Fuskova who became the leading lesbian activist by the end of the 1980s. Fuskova fueled a process of increasing lesbian social visibility and independent organization that peaked in the following decade—the first gay pride march took place in 1992. Fuskova contributed greatly to this process with her presence, in 1991, on prime-time television to discuss her sexual identity and with the publication, in 1994, of *Amor de mujeres: El lesbianismo en la Argentina hoy*, coauthored with her partner, Claudina Marek.[103] Fuskova is paradigmatic of an extensive group of women who by the late 1980s had publicly recognized, for the first time, the specificity of their rights and needs and thus, of their fight, a breaking point with the previous quiet and unassuming position of lesbians within feminism and gay organizations. In the 1988 ATEM congress, for example, the Grupo Autogestivo de Lesbianas—former members of Lugar de Mujer—voiced this specificity by affirming that "we see the need to fight for the construction of an egalitarian system, one in which sexual roles are not imposed and there is no oppression. As women and as lesbians, we are part of this struggle and this search, but we also have specific problems that stem from our sexual choices."[104] This was, in fact, a process that Argentina shared with the rest of the region, as evident in the 1987 organization of the Primer Encuentro de Lesbianas de Latinoamérica y el Caribe (First Meeting of Latin American and Caribbean Lesbians), which took place in Cuernavaca, Mexico, and congregated 250 participants, including women from Argentina.[105]

A writer and artist, Fuskova was one of the founders of important feminist groups such as Libera and the Grupo Feminista de Denuncia before focusing on the organization of gay women. According to her own accounts, Fuskova discovered herself as a lesbian in 1985, when she was fifty-six years old and participating in the Tercer Encuentro Feminista Latinoamericano y del Caribe (Third Latin American and Caribbean Feminist Meeting) in Bertioga, Brazil. Here, she met the influential Spanish lesbian activist Empar Pineda, an inspirational model for her and many others. Pineda introduced Fuskova to Adrianne Rich's 1980 essay "Compulsory Heterosexuality and Lesbian Existence" when she visited Buenos Aires after leaving Brazil. Fuskova later recognized the profound impact of Rich's text, which allowed her to understand that heterosexuality was a source of male power and women's subjugation and lesbianism was a form of resistance. Fuskova argued that, with Rich, she understood that true women's liberation required contesting lesbian invisibility. Fuskova affirmed that "all other alienations we suffer are based on the alienation of our sexuality."[106] Inspired by these arguments, Fuskova maintained that releasing lesbians from oppression and marginalization had far-reaching, socially redeeming effects, a process that she equated to the liberation of Argentine society after the fall of the 1970s military dictatorship.[107]

Fuskova maintained that lesbians' most important goal was to live a free and dignified life. This required them to fight for their right to be, thus gaining both social and self-acceptance. Fuskova argued that leading an open life as a gay woman without fear of discrimination or rejection was a therapeutic and political act that unified the self and destroyed the dichotomy between forbidden and permitted aspects of one's identity. It was the recognition of "This is me. All of me."[108] This process exceeded sexuality. Following Rich, Fuskova believed in a lesbian continuum, that is, a broad spectrum of intimate relations between women, from those involving sex to friendships and ties of political solidarity that were women's most powerful tool to overthrow the patriarchy. Lesbianism threatened the patriarchal prohibition of positive, profound relations among women and challenged the "sexual tyranny" that rejected nonnormative types of desire and forms of attraction and constrained sexuality to reproduction. Thus, lesbianism was a liberating utopia for all women, whether they had sex with other women or not.[109]

In 1986, Fuskova and Adriana Carrasco began the first lesbian reflection workshops, an independent space of interaction that offered gay women an arena of debate, readings, and sharing to help them come into being. Ana Rubiolo, one of the first members, argued that communication had been very difficult for lesbians in joint reflection groups because heterosexual women were reluctant to admit that compulsory heterosexuality, which imposed a sole acceptable model of sexual and romantic relationships, denied people's sexual self-determination. Rubiolo maintained that, consequently, heterosexual women in discussion groups were devoted to identifying and understanding the sources of patriarchal oppression without questioning heterosexuality. In contrast, gay women challenged the compulsory nature of heterosexuality as the first step to recognizing they existed, that is, to acknowledge an identity that society denied and rejected. It was a process of self-discovery and legitimation that hetero-sexual women found "obvious" or took for granted. Rubiolo also affirmed that, unlike heterosexual women, gay women had to question labels of perversion and disease to see themselves clearly and embrace who they were. A reflection group exclusively for lesbians allowed them to "acknowl-edge how positive it is to build a 'resistant me,' the product of an internal and external fight to maintain our place and our desires. We are in the middle of that tug-of-war; a struggle to get to know ourselves, to recognize one another, sometimes after a lengthy period of isolation."[110] Only then could lesbians leave behind a defensive and reactive position to engage in creative and productive actions, and achieve true social change.[111]

In 1988, during the March 8 demonstration for International Women's Day, lesbian feminists participated as an identifiable independent group for the first time since the first celebration under democracy in 1984. A few years later, Fuskova remembered the excitement and the pride they had felt in the march and how they had experienced it as a true destape, even though social prejudice erased them from the newspapers the fol-lowing day: "We were excited, euphoric, we dared to show our faces, we wore flowers on our blouses and purple ribbons that said 'Passionately Lesbian' around our foreheads. We were the most photographed group that afternoon. The journalists could not believe what they were seeing. . . . Despite how great we looked beneath our pink sign, the press did not publish a single one of those pictures."[112]

Fuskova explained that by choosing to ignore the happy and proud gay women in the demonstration, the media continued its common practice of obliterating positive images of lesbians. Still, lesbian militants succeeded on other fronts during the march. In addition to reaffirming their identity, claiming a place within the women's movement, and neutralizing fear and shame, Fuskova and her group circulated *Cuaderno de Existencia Lesbiana*, the first lesbian publication in the country that they had started a year earlier.[113] *Cuaderno* communicated the energetic, hopeful, curious, open, and welcoming spirit of the incipient lesbian activism of the late 1980s and became a fundamental outlet for the circulation of foundational texts and authors such as Audre Lorde, Adrienne Rich, Charlotte Bunch, Monique Witting, and Kate Millet—which in many cases were translated by Fuskova and her friends. *Cuaderno* also published local activists and disseminated local and international news. The goal was to challenge "the terrible rock-solid prohibition against getting to know each other, loving each other, and helping each other live a better life."[114] Therefore, *Cuaderno* printed anonymous personal testimonies and questionnaires that were collected in workshops or that readers mailed in. This allowed for the socialization of common experiences such as fears of marginalization and discrimination after coming out, feelings of guilt, and falling in love. By sharing this information, *Cuaderno* contributed to the creation of a community and a network that exceeded face-to-face encounters and encouraged and empowered gay women. At a smaller scale, *Cuaderno* offered a platform for democratic participation and the socialization of sex knowledge and experience that commercial destape publications provided to heterosexual readers.[115]

## GAY ACTIVISM AND THE *DERECHO DE SER PERSONA*

Born right after the return to democracy in 1984, the CHA—an umbrella organization for small gay groups—redefined sex culture and politics by giving gay sexuality an unprecedented visibility.[116] The CHA spoke a language that dignified gay people; contested the equation of homosexuality with abnormality, immorality, and perversion; and took an openly combative position against the views of the Catholic Church.[117] In its first half-page ad published in 1984—its public letter of introduction—the CHA "humanized" and made gays socially and historically relevant by claiming that Argentine gays "work, study, feel, love, worry about our national reality and lived through the tough years of the dictatorship just as you did." Gays, the document highlighted, were no different from heterosexuals, and not separate from or outside culture. In fact, they shared the pain of the country's recent violent past with the rest of Argentine society.[118] Similarly, in one of his first interviews after the publication of the half-page ad, CHA president Carlos Jáuregui distinguished between sex and morality to highlight a common ground between gay and heterosexual people. He affirmed that "morality is about indecency and indecency is not a thing of the bedroom; hunger, misery, discrimination, the exploitation of men by other men, these are bad words. We are human beings like all the rest. No better, no worse. Simply different. Looking up towards the sun."[119]

The CHA recognized that in order to make society aware of gay sexuality, it had to strengthen the institution but also make gay people visible. In turn, this would contribute to the CHA's conspicuousness. The CHA considered that numbers were important for legitimacy, as evident in its first half-page ad that began by affirming that Argentina was home to 1.5 million gay citizens. Numbers were also important for detractors; the ultra-Catholic Liga por la Decencia argued that there was no evidence for such claims and that the CHA was merely using those figures to show "something abnormal as something normal."[120]

The social visibility of the gay community depended on the individual decision of coming out, a choice with crucial social and personal consequences that was even more difficult in the repressive and homophobic culture of 1980s Argentina. The CHA, which acknowledged the extreme difficulties of disclosure, oscillated between empathy and criticism of those who silenced their identities. In 1985, for example, an article in the CHA bulletin emphatically claimed that the organization was not the "Salvation Army"—it lacked the necessary power and numbers to become a defense force of the gay community, and its main goal was not to act as a militia to rescue others.[121] For this reason, all gay people, the article claimed, should mobilize for their rights; relying on the sacrifice of others was both unjust and ultimately futile. Yet CHA calls for activism were generally considerate and accepting rather than pushy, with an emphasis on personal rewards and the freedom of being. When, in an interview with *Libre*, Jáuregui was asked if he had any regrets about the past, he lamented having lived in fear and in silence for so many years, and having placed too much importance on others' opinions. Becoming a gay activist, in contrast, was the best decision he had ever made. Jáuregui declared that militancy and openness about his sexuality were not only liberating but also the only way to have a fulfilling life that was worth living.[122]

The CHA argued that in order to enjoy living in a true democratic society, gay people had to fight to bring down the legal and political obstacles that prevented the exercise of their rights. While lesbian organizations favored internal discussion and introspection to embrace a gay identity proudly, the CHA—which also organized reflection groups—privileged a course of action that was louder, public, legal, in the press, and on the streets, and that required extensive commitment and participation. In 1987, Alejandro Salazar, the president of the CHA, reflected on the importance of militancy by arguing that it is a fantasy to think that this democracy guarantees total freedom without us having to do anything; and it is selfish to think that something that happens to the other guy is his problem and his alone. These falsehoods arise from fear. How can we combat this? We were repressed for so many years that it is not easy to stand up and demand respect! But the repressors' most powerful weapon is ignorance, the ignorance that afflicts many of those unaware of their rights as citizens. He who vindicates his rights starts to overcome his own fear and starts to beat repression.[123]

In this campaign for social visibility and increasing militancy, the CHA introduced, more or less intentionally, a model of gay man strongly linked to respectability and embodied in an educated, middle-class, virile, young professional such as Jáuregui, as well as the most visible members of the organization. According to Marcelo Ferreyra, an early member of the CHA, Jáuregui was also pleasant, handsome, well-traveled, and good at conversation. He had the courage and idealism to defy marginalization and stigmatization through a vocal and proud form of gay activism that was more inspiring than provoking. This model that Jáuregui represented was of vital importance because issues of relatability and unthreatening militancy were central for the CHA's legitimacy. In a 1984 interview, Jáuregui categorically rejected the idea of "gay power" while highlighting that the goal of the CHA was the social integration of gay people, and that with this goal achieved, the organization would disappear. Activists reevaluated this early conciliatory, reassuring position of the CHA later. In the 1990s, for example, new gay organizations—some of which included former CHA members—criticized the pioneering institution for rejecting the concept of gay pride, which they fully embraced, and for adopting gay dignity as a more pleasant, less combative, and less "arrogant" alternative.[124]

The CHA's early position is especially clear in an article in *Vamos a andar*, in which Hugo Espósito rejected *mariconería*, defined as a parody of femininity, as a method for gay rebellion while arguing that, instead, masculine models of gay activism should prevail. Espósito was implicitly distinguishing the CHA from the 1970s FLH, which had, before its dissolution following the 1976 military coup, recuperated and celebrated the figure of the *marica* as the ideal activist and one of the most important challenges to patriarchy and machismo.[125] In contrast, Espósito warned those who proposed "a flamboyant militancy" that "sissy," "effeminate" stereotypes seriously damaged the social acceptability and prospects of growth for gay activism. He affirmed that in order to promote collaboration toward a common cause, discrimination within the gay movement should be avoided, but at the end of the day, the CHA should put on a "respectable" face in public. Consequently, the organization avoided public mention of other sexual minorities and queer identities. In line with this politics of respectability and social integration, when in 1987 a news agency referred to CHA members as *travestis*, the organization denounced that given that travestis provoked profound rejection in society, the language employed was a deliberately damaging strategy "to lessen the worth of our protest and strip our demands of dignity." Furthermore, the CHA denied any association between the organization and travestis.[126]

Although the CHA offered a uniform and united public front, some voices within the gay community expressed concern about the homogenizing and "normalizing" effects of the CHA discourses and questioned the limited representation of alternative identities that did not conform to the CHA's model of middle-class, masculine, and professional gays. This perspective could result in an unwanted ghettoization of the gay community, isolated from both other nonnormative sexual identities and heterosexuals. Equally important, some lamented the abandonment of a more radical and comprehensive diagnosis and program that proposed sexual liberation as a broader enterprise connected with the downfall of patriarchy. These ideas were particularly shared by former members of the FLH, such as Néstor Perlongher, who was living abroad, or Zelmar Acevedo, a visible face of the CHA, and of organizations such as the Grupo de Acción Gay (Gay Action Group), which was part of the CHA. Yet their positions did not translate into open criticism of the CHA or into alternative organizations until the early 1990s.[127]

In addition to making the gay community and its problems visible and combating degrading and pathological views of gay sexuality, the most important contribution of the CHA to the other destape was the equation of sexual freedom with human rights. From its inception, the CHA placed itself solidly among the new social movements that championed the defense of fundamental, inalienable rights that only a few years earlier had suffered terrible infringements. In so doing, it established important channels of collaboration and dialogue with human rights organizations, was visibly present at marches and demonstrations, and adopted a discourse that, focused on the defense of human dignity, legitimized the fight.[128] This discourse on rights, democracy, and the social acceptance of difference represented a major departure from the leftist FLN, which, imbued with the political spirit of the 1960s, had embraced an anti-capitalist, anti-imperialist, anti-patriarchal, and national liberation stance. For the FLH, sexual oppression was intrinsically related to social oppression and thus a social revolution was the only path to a true sexual revolution.[129] In contrast, for the CHA, devoid of the more radical language of liberation and uncomfortable with the dichotomy between a "revolutionary homosexuality" and a "reactionary heterosexuality," the goal was to reform rather than overthrow the system, broadening the legal, political, and cultural limits of social inclusion within the current institutions.[130]

In this sense, the CHA was a child of its time, championing sexual rights with the prevalent language of the democratic transition. However, the CHA fought for sexual rights without openly discussing sex and thus remained untouched by the sexually explicit tone set by the destape. In a traditionally homophobic culture where the persecution of queer sexualities continued, silencing eroticism was a strategy that the CHA adopted to make its demands more palatable and relatable. This approach was different from the FLH, which had not suppressed sex to denounce sexual repression, even in the far more oppressive context of the early 1970s. The FLH discourse was noticeably more sexual, more explicit about homoeroticism and desire.[131] The FLH had no media presence comparable to the CHA, and the open hostility and threats from the Peronist Right pushed it to increasing secrecy and concealment. This situation could have unexpectedly prompted the FLH to favor a more provocative and direct, as well as theoretically driven, discussion and language. A flyer, for example, illustrated with the drawing of a naked man, genitals prominently exposed, argued: "I want to make love to a boy without getting arrested. Am I asking too much? Total freedom for homosexual pleasure in streets, bars, nightclubs, and everywhere."[132]

Ten years later, the CHA pursued the same goal but carefully worded it without mentions of sensuality or desire. Furthermore, in his book, Jáuregui explained that even though sexuality underwent its "darkest moment" during the dictatorship, living their sexuality uninhibitedly was a problem that all Argentines, regardless of sexual orientation, experienced both before and after the military regime. The activist explained that, indeed, not even the destape changed the fact that Argentina was a country "that rejects pleasure, refuses to acknowledge the possibility of sexual gratification, ignores the body and its functions, and has not been taught about love."[133] Partly based on this diagnosis, and partly as a strategy for social acceptance, the mission of the CHA was not formulated as a fight against "the heterosexual dictatorship." This position may explain the independent organization of lesbian activists who, led by Fuskova, were interested in denouncing the relations of power and the privileges embedded in heterosexuality.[134]

Instead, the CHA stressed that the current democracy imposed constraints and posed dangers to heterosexual and gay people alike. The CHA argued that repression was particularly severe for gays but that its platform and discourse were broad and inclusive enough to underline commonalities with heterosexuals and encourage identification. The CHA's second half-page ad, published in 1985, for example, denounced police repression, illegal detentions, and raids but described them in general terms, without making any arguments about how they particularly affected gay people or individuals "profiled" as gays. Readers were left to make this connection themselves by associating the content of the half-page ad with the CHA as the signing entity and, with its motto, the only two instances in which the word "homosexual" appeared in the text.[135]

The CHA warned Argentines that human rights should not be considered a gift handed down from above or the automatic result of the return to democracy. Gay activists publicly denounced police harassment to alert the heterosexual majority of something gay people knew all too well: that the current democracy was imperfect and that to make it complete, all citizens should be equal before the law and unconstitutional practices should be eliminated. The CHA also emphasized that the fight for human rights should exceed the search for justice for the desaparecidos to include the demands of marginalized and wronged social sectors in democracy. Although in the first issue of its bulletin, the CHA claimed that "during the eight tragic years of the dictatorship, homosexuals across the country became one of the main victims of repression," what drove the organization was not denunciation and reparation for the past but social inclusion in the postdictatorial context.[136]

The CHA emphasized that, after the return to democracy, gays were citizens whose liberties were severely curtailed, and, from its inception until the late 1980s, when AIDS forced a redefinition of priorities, the organization concentrated its efforts on two fronts.[137] First based on the decision by the WHO to eliminate homosexuality from its list of diseases, the CHA fought to end sexual discrimination. Gay people lied about and denied their identities to protect their jobs, families, status, and physical well-being, a process that annulled their selfhood and obliterated their self-esteem. Their sexual orientation even interfered, in theory, with the exercise of their political rights. Although virtually unenforceable, an electoral law in Buenos Aires dating from the mid-1940s prohibited gay individuals from voting. For the CHA, ending discrimination was tantamount to demanding the most fundamental right of all for gay people: *el derecho de ser persona* (the right to be a person). Thus, it lobbied and mobilized to add sexual orientation to an antidiscrimination bill debated in Congress for the first time in 1985. However, when passed three years later, the law included race, religion, sex, nationality, ideology, physical characteristics, and private actions but omitted sexual orientation.[138]

The CHA's second goal was to end police repression and harassment as well as the legal tools—common since the 1930s and reinforced under both authoritarian and democratic governments—that prompted and allowed them.[139] Here, even more so than when debating discrimination, gay activists in the 1980s warned Argentines, exultant in the new climate of freedom, that as long as a whole sector of society was persecuted based on sexual identity, democracy was not complete. The CHA offered a chilling reminder that dismantling the repressive apparatus of the dictatorship demanded more than purging the armed forces because both the courts and the police continued to operate as authoritarian mechanisms.[140] The two legal tools that validated police persecution in democracy were the 333/58 decree, the *ley de averiguación de antecedentes* that enabled the police to detain people for twenty-four hours with the sole purpose of conducting background checks and, in Buenos Aires, the infamous *2do H*, a subsection in a municipal edict that mandated the detention of a person of any sex "who publicly incited or offered sexual acts" and that was also commonly employed to arrest sex workers.[141]

Just like they had done during the dictatorship, the police—and its feared División de Moralidad (Morality Squad), which was frequently behind the raids—used both laws to relentlessly seize men "suspected of being gay" on the streets and to raid gay gathering places, which ended

Figure 5.6. Carlos Jáuregui, president of the CHA. Courtesy CEDINCI, Buenos Aires.

with massive arrests. Once in the police station, the detainees were forced to sign self-incriminatory documents while the police officers threatened to call—or sometimes did call—families and employers. In the documents and calls, the police revealed the motives of detention and thus exposed these men's sexual orientation. For the CHA, these procedures were the clearest example of the continuities between dictatorship and democracy; the only difference was that after 1983, the police did not beat or torture gay detainees.[142] Thus, the CHA responded by mobilizing energetically against these practices. The organization circulated instructions on how to proceed if arrested, organized a legal department that assisted and counseled detainees, and urged individuals to resist police raids and arrests. It also kept an archive of detentions for legal and research purposes, encouraged all victims to go to the CHA to file a report, and promoted appeals and led legal actions and reports of abuse against the police and judges. In their fight to end police repression along with legal and sexual discrimination, the CHA reminded Argentines of the limits of full citizenship for sexual minorities.[143]

During the transition from military dictatorship, the discourse of citizenship was central in public life and social mobilization. Democratization was intrinsically related to the human rights movement that made the right to life and physical integrity the foundations of democratic citizenship. By initiating a public debate on a different set of critical issues such as sexual discrimination, sexual identities, abortion, and sexual violence, feminists and gay and lesbian activists recentered the discussion about freedom and democracy on intimate citizenship. Sociologist Ken Plummer has defined intimate citizenship as decisions over the control (or not) over one's body, feelings, and relationships; the access (or not) to representations, relationships, and public spaces; and socially grounded choices (or not) about identities, gender, and erotic experiences.[144] In their fight for egalitarian control, access, and choices related to sexuality in all these areas, feminist, gay, and lesbian organizations reformulated citizenship as a gendered and sexualized concept and made a unique contribution not only to the public debate about the meanings of democracy but also to democracy as a lived experience. Their mobilization expanded the public sphere and the grounds for political and social participation, exposed and strengthened the bridge between the personal and the political, and extended the definition of citizenship beyond formal politics and electoral practices. In so doing, these activists propelled a different, more contentious and consequential form of destape that uncovered sexual minorities, revealed the significance of sexual rights in a true democracy, and drew attention to the inequalities and injustices suffered by women, gays, and lesbians who, democratic discourses notwithstanding, remained second-class citizens.

# EPILOGUE

## Sexual Culture in Argentina Today

**Sociologist Jeffrey Weeks has argued** that a common trap for scholars of sexuality is "to believe that despite all huffing and puffing nothing has really changed."[1] Exemplifying arguments of this view are that rape is now better recognized and denounced as a crime but that sexual violence against women is still widespread, that women are able to express their sexual desires but are still largely objectified for the male gaze, and that queer sexualities have gained more social recognition and legal protection, but in Argentina, for example, the life expectancy of trans people is between thirty-five and forty years of age.[2] And although these arguments are painfully true, the trap makes us forget the power of agency, the past and present fights, and the possibility that, even when out of sight, all unfinished revolutions can be finished. In other words, the trap causes us to ignore that "we make our own sexual histories, even if not always in circumstances of our own choosing."[3] Surely, in a book that opened with a claim about historical transformation, these final reflections about the present in light of the destape are not intended as an argument about genealogy or an overemphasis on historical continuities. Instead, the following considerations and brief overview are meant to avoid the trap that Weeks has warned against and therefore are focused on the transformation of sexual culture and politics today but without overlooking some of its 1980s historical roots and certain legacies of the destape. It is in light of those roots and legacies that the historical significance of present-day sexual culture can be more clearly appreciated.

If we look at current Argentine sexual culture through the lens of the destape, we can see that the most problematic examples of the hypersexualized media culture of the 1980s have metamorphosed, gaining unparalleled prominence and power. Since the 1990s, media scholars such as Brian McNair have drawn attention to the rise of "porno-chic" or the "pornographication of the mainstream," the appropriation and transfer of the conventions of pornography into all forms of cultural production. Argentina could be a poster child of the new "pornified culture."[4] In the past two decades, Argentine television has reached extreme levels of sexual explicitness, with vulgar and sexual language used at all hours; quite graphic depictions of sexual intercourse in fiction and soap operas (even those targeting young audiences); and high levels of nudity and sexual overtones. Argentina's most popular television show—a local version of *Dancing with the Stars*—has included pole dancing and striptease as two of the routines for its participants in which fully charged erotic choreographies culminate with the female dancers topless and in a thong. Similarly, the show host has infamously employed scissors to dispose of the skimpy miniskirts wore by the dancers for some of their performances.[5]

Yet the fixation with body image, the hypersexualization of the female body, and sexual and body exhibitionism extends beyond television. As active participants of the "global pornosphere," all Argentines, but fundamentally women, and from all social classes, are eagerly consuming the *Fifty Shades of Grey* books and films; making *cumbia villera*, with its sexist and obscene lyrics, one of the most popular dance genres in Buenos Aires and thus a huge commercial success; paying for pole dancing classes, sexy photo sessions, and sex coaches to improve their sexual performance and learn sexual techniques; going to strip clubs and visiting sex shops; considering vaginal beautification as a common surgical procedure; and giving teenage daughters or wives breast augmentation as a gift.[6] Many of these practices and types of consumption make evident that Argentine sexual culture is now as much a product of a globalized world as of local conditions. In many ways, the 1980s destape pioneered this trend. The destape was homegrown and the offshoot of cultural and historical conditions that made it quite unique but at the same time was pervaded by international influences and inspirations, foreign actors, and transnational debates. The Spanish destape, foreign films, magazines, writers, sex experts, and porn stars; the Institute for Advanced Study of Human Sexuality in San Francisco, which became a center for the education of Argentine sexologists; the Swedish International Development Agency, which trained Argentine sex educators; the 1980s anti-pornography discussions in the United States; the international meetings of lesbian and feminist activists; and the international professional organizations of sexologists and sex educators where Argentines participated actively are some of the most relevant examples.

Like in the destape, women are at the center of the new hypersexual media culture, but it now appears harder to differentiate between sexual objectification and sexual subjectification. Feminist writer Ariel Levy named the present-day porno-culture "raunch culture," drawing attention to the fact that now hypersexual, objectifying female representations are greatly encouraged and embraced by women. Critics agree that in raunch culture, women are still sexual objects mainly for male consumption but that this objectification, this "lusty, busty exhibitionism," is repackaged as a form of empowerment.[7] A good local example is one of the 2017 hit songs in Argentina, "QLO" ("Ass") by singer Jimena Barón, which combines lyrics about embracing "body exhibitionism" on social media as a means of personal expression and as a message of agency and independence with a music video—showed with restrictions and warnings on YouTube because of its content—plagued by close-ups of exposed and sexualized butts, including Barón's. The song celebrates positive body image and personal freedom, and offers a critique of social media as a sphere where individuals, and particularly women, are bullied. Yet this message is marketed through the hypersexualization of the female body—especially the fit, young, conventionally attractive, white female body.[8]

The current raunch culture is historically unique because female sexual objectification—in which women are, however, depicted as knowing and active—and body commodification are framed as women's choice and agency, emphasizing subjective feelings of empowerment based on performing a confident oversexual heterosexiness. Critics such as Rosalind Gill have argued that by becoming an object of desire, women are being offered merely a promise of power, rather than "real power." In other words, to what extent does current media culture truly challenge the fact that, traditionally, women have been hypersexualized while their sexuality has been restrained, subordinated, and disciplined? Despite their claims, how effective are the attempts of present-day commercial culture at subverting older tropes of female sexual passivity on women's own terms?[9] As film studies scholar Mari Ruti has suggested, is this about women's recovering the right to sexual pleasure and over their own bodies—crucial to women's empowerment—or are these "entirely secondary to looking hot"?[10]

Levy has argued that despite individual feelings of empowerment, women should not expect sexual freedom from mimicking the commodified versions of sexy proposed by the media and mass culture. Nor are these spheres—as they should not be—the only ones where women must assert their power over sexuality. Many Argentine women know this too well. As I am writing these last pages, the country is experiencing a public debate and social mobilization of utmost historical significance. Women have taken to the streets in large numbers, raised their voices, clenched their fists, and donned green handkerchiefs—the flag of the fight for legal abortion emblazoned with the motto "Sexual education to decide, contraception to avoid abortion, legal abortion to avoid death." On June 14, 2018, the House of Representatives approved the draft bill to legalize abortion in the country. Yet, two months later, the Senate rejected the bill, preventing Argentines from joining the very small group of Latin American countries—Uruguay, Guyana, Cuba, and Puerto Rico—in which abortion without restrictions is legal.[11]

Among the numerous contributions to the debate about abortion in the press in the months before the vote, sex educator Eva Giberti retold two anecdotes to show how different the climate of the 1980s was from the present moment. Giberti remembered that right after Raúl Alfonsín took power, writer María Elena Walsh—who a few years earlier had protested the censorship during the dictatorship, calling for the military to let Argentine citizens "grow up"—was summoned to advise the new government and personally underlined the importance of legislating abortion in a talk with the president. According to Giberti, Alfonsín's refusal to even discuss the topic was so adamant that Walsh, profoundly disheartened, never returned to the government house. Giberti also recounted that in those years, she had published an article about abortion rights in the journal of the Asamblea Permanente por los Derechos Humanos (Permanent

Assembly for Human Rights) and was later reprimanded by some of its authorities, given the complaints of many members.[12]

Giberti is right to point out the difference between the two historical moments. The current campaign for making abortion legal, safe, and free is massive, public, open, energetic, and visible, and has taken the media by storm. Women who had demonstrated all over the country traveled to Buenos Aires to march and participate in the vigil the day of the vote; teenagers proudly wear their green handkerchiefs everywhere; and students have taken over their schools to support the law, with male students staying in the institutions to allow female students to go to the marches and vigils. Famous actresses, singers, and celebrities have publicly supported the cause, mobilized, signed a collective petition, and spoken out; thinkers and academics have voiced their reasons for supporting legalization; and social media has become a privileged site for debate and militancy. Some call feminists *feminazis*, but now, more than ever, women, especially young women, happily declare themselves feminists and exhibit this identity with pride to explain why they support a law for legal abortion. In the context of discourses that underline empathy and sorority among women across social classes, women of all ages and walks of life tell, for the first time, their stories of abortion. This is quite a different setting from the campaign for abortion in the 1980s, when women were reluctant to publicly identify themselves as feminists because feminism was "a bad word" and some feminists abstained from campaigning for the right to abortion out of fear this would weaken popular support for feminism.[13]

Yet despite the differences and its idiosyncrasy, the present moment is deeply rooted in the recent past. It is difficult to deny that the paths forged and tools created in the feminist destape of the 1980s have brought us to the present-day, explosive, new destape. First, there is the organizational, institutional, and historical power and experience of the Argentine women's movement, the feminist groups, and the militants, all of which have fought for decades in solitude and marginalized, before their minority crusade evolved into the massive social movement it is today. Second, there is the indelible rallying cry, "Sexual education to decide, contraception to avoid abortion, legal abortion to avoid death," which synthetizes, now and then, a feminist understanding of female sexuality where pleasure, reproduction, and education are interrelated parts that must operate in harmony. The discourses inscribed in this rallying cry reflect a broader language of sexual rights, sex without guilt, power over one's body, and motherhood by choice. These are ideas that eighty-year-old grandmothers and sixteen-year-old young women now shout in demonstrations and debate on Facebook but that emerged inconspicuously in small discussion groups more than thirty years ago. Finally, there is the green handkerchief that, adopted by the activists behind the Campaña Nacional por el Derecho al Aborto Legal, Seguro y Gratuito (National Campaign for Legal, Safe, and Free Abortion) in 2003, brings to mind the white kerchief worn by the Mothers and Grandmothers of Plaza de Mayo, an icon of the defense of human rights that rose in the transition to democracy.[14]

The same historical roots can be traced to the massive Argentine mobilization against femicides—the intentional killings of women or girls because they are females, that is, on account of their gender—known as Ni una menos (Not one woman less). In 2015, there were 235 victims of femicide, and in 2016 the number ascended to 254. Between 2008 and 2015, 1,808 women were brutally murdered in Argentina.[15] Since 2015, Ni una menos has brought to the forefront violence, domestic violence, and sexual violence against women while also voicing claims about the gender pay gap, sexual objectification, abortion, and the rights of trans people. The collective emerged with a massive protest organized by women journalists, artists, and feminist activists in June 2015 that gathered more than 200,000 people in Buenos Aires to protest the murder of a fourteen-year-old pregnant teenager, beaten to death and buried by her boyfriend in the backyard of his home. Ni una menos spread like wildfire over a region plagued by the rape, sexual assault, murder, kidnapping, and torture of women, prompting mobilizations in Uruguay, Mexico, Chile, and El Salvador, among other Latin American countries.[16] Ni una menos fervently denounces the machista culture, condemns patriarchy and aggressive hypermasculinity, and is belligerent and visible, with unprecedented levels of organization. The media—probably as a result of a broader social mind-set, its short-term memory, and incredulity—has seized on the hype to reach two incorrect conclusions: that violence in general and sexual violence in particular against women are new social ills, and the women's mobilization against it is, consequently, a novel social phenomenon.[17]

On the contrary, the historical roots of current women's organization and mobilization against femicides can again be traced back to the battle feminists fought in the 1980s—activists accompanying rape victims to the police station, feminist organizations educating women about violence in consensual relations, marches for murdered women, protests against boxer Carlos Monzón for the assassination of his wife, and the denunciation of negligent judges—and to the destape of a topic that had been traditionally taboo. However, thirty years ago the "womanhood" of a small group of feminists who took to the streets to demand recognition of their sexual and reproductive rights could be put into question. Today, womanhood is, on the contrary, defined in marches and the mobilization for those rights, and women of all classes, ages, and cultural backgrounds are part of the protests. In fact, women's resistance has become a central component in the construction of femininity, while a woman does not need to identify as a feminist to fight back.

Like femininity, queer identities have also been objects of a profound redefinition in the past decade as a result of a dramatic transformation in laws, society, and culture. Mass media today has little in common with the years of the destape, in which gay culture was enveloped in silence, press coverage was reluctant or prejudiced, and portrayals, negative or ridiculing. In the 1990s, television saw a rise in the number of gay characters but continued the tradition that Huguito Araña had introduced in the early 1980s with affected, over-the-top, effeminate, "harassing" characters, most famously in the comedy *La familia Benvenuto* (1991–95), and dark and corrupt gay roles—associating homosexuality with danger and marginality—such as in the drama *Zona de riesgo* (1992–93), which depicted the first gay kiss on national television. In the early 2000s, the comedy *Los Roldán* had the first trans character of Argentine television played by a trans actress, Florencia de la V, who in 2012 would be the first trans television host, of the show *La Pelu* (2012–13). This is, in fact, the cultural context for *Farsantes* (2013)—dubbed "Argentina's first gay soap opera" by the press—the first television series that, rather than using gay characters for dramatic effect, focused the main storyline on a gay love story. Only later, lesbian characters, which have been on television since the early 2000s, gained similar preeminence in storylines, with more balanced and honest portrayals that challenged sexist stereotypes. In 2017, the comedy *Las estrellas* and the drama *El maestro* had main lesbian characters and made lesbian love stories central to their narratives.[18]

Alongside the transformation in popular culture, crucial legal changes in the past decade represent the completion of the project against discrimination and for social integration that the CHA began during the transition to democracy. In 2002, based on a draft proposed by the CHA, the city of Buenos Aires passed a municipal law for same-sex legal unions that allowed gay and lesbian couples many of the rights of heterosexual couples, such as joint loan applications, health and life insurance, or the right to assume the responsibilities of the primary caregiver in the case of illness. Yet the legalization of civil unions outside of Buenos Aires proved unsuccessful, and many of the rights granted to married heterosexual couples—with regard, for example, to adoption and property—were denied to members of same-sex civil unions. In 2006, this lack of equality prompted the rise of the Federación Argentina LGBT (Argentine LGBT Federation), which was instrumental to the passage of the same-sex marriage law in 2010. Argentina thus became the first Latin American country to grant married gays and lesbians the same rights and responsibilities as married heterosexuals. One of these was the right to adoption, which was, according to the press, "the most sensitive aspect" of the debate. Two years later, Argentina passed the first gender identity law, allowing transgender people to modify their name and gender on state-issued documents and identification cards without any further requirements or authorizations and to have sex reassignment surgeries and treatments covered by insurance and free of charge in public hospitals.[19]

Though transcendental, legal changes do not automatically transform cultural representations and social attitudes. The lives of transgender people in Argentina are a case in point as brutal transphobic violence, unemployment, and homelessness continue to deeply afflict and marginalize this community.[20] And as was the case during the destape, sexuality continues to be a focus of division. As Weeks has correctly suggested, "the body and its pleasures and pains is, to an extraordinary degree, at the heart of many of today's conflicts, both national and global."[21] Resonating with their views and positions in the transition to democracy, the most conservative social sectors and the Catholic Church have, in the last decade, vehemently opposed the legal and social changes that represent an improvement in the lives and dignity of women and sexual minorities. During the 2010 debate for same-sex marriage, Cardinal Jorge Bergoglio—who would become Pope Francis in 2013—appealed to the congregation to actively mobilize against the law, arguing that "this is not just a political struggle; it is an attempt to destroy God's plan." In 2018, the pope strongly criticized the decision of the House of Representatives to approve the draft for legal abortion while calling abortion "child homicide" and comparing it with the Nazi genocide.[22]

In the light of the present, the destape as both a mass media phenomenon and lived experience appears an interesting historical prelude to the ways in which Argentines represent, think about, and deal with questions of pleasure, freedom, desire, and choice today. Current developments might not be linear, conscious, or direct effects of the 1980s sexual culture, but the first sparks and the beginnings of many paths can be traced to this period. A deep look at the destape is also useful for the present because it offers a lesson against easily falling into the trap of the history of sexuality as a history of permanencies while still understanding that sexuality does not represent a consistent and inevitable historical transformation from sexual darkness and oppression to complete, widespread sexual liberation. Yet, promisingly, many fight, create, and advocate to achieve that transformation.

# NOTES

## INTRODUCTION: A POEM AND THE *DESTAPE*

1. On the contributions of Josep Vicent Marqués, see J. Fernández de Quero, "Josep Vicent Marqués (in Memoriam)," *Revista Sexpol*, July–August 2008, 3, and Joan Romero, "Josep Vicent Marqués, sociólogo," *El País*, June 5, 2008, https://elpais.com/diario/2008/06/05/necrologicas/1212616802_850215.html.

2. Josep Vicent Marqués, "Sexualidad, represión, deformación y liberación," *El Viejo Topo*, February 1977, 28.

3. Feona Attwood, "Sexed Up: Theorizing the Sexualization of Culture," *Sexualities* 9, no. 1 (2006): 78.

4. For representative political approaches to democratization in other parts of the world, see, for example, Larry Jay Diamond and Marc Plattner, eds., *Democratization and Authoritarianism in the Arab World* (Baltimore: Johns Hopkins University Press, 2014); Harald Wydra, *Communism and the Emergence of Democracy* (New York: Cambridge University Press, 2007); and Timothy Frye, *Building States and Markets after Communism: The Perils of Polarized Democracy* (New York: Cambridge University Press, 2010).

5. See, for example, Gregory Carleton, *Sexual Revolution in Bolshevik Russia* (Pittsburgh: University of Pittsburgh Press, 2005); Darmar Herzog, *Sex after Fascism: Memory and Morality in Twentieth-Century Germany* (Princeton, NJ: Princeton University Press, 2005); Josie McLlelan, *Love in the Time of Communism: Intimacy and Sexuality in the GDR* (New York: Cambridge University Press, 2011); and Laurie Marhoefer, *Sex and the Weimar Republic: German Homosexual Emancipation and the Rise of the Nazis* (Toronto: University of Toronto Press, 2015).

6. On Reich, see Myron Sharaf, *The Fury on Earth: A Biography of Wilhelm Reich* (New York: St. Martin's Press, 1983), and Robert Corrington, *Wilhelm Reich: Psychoanalyst and Radical Naturalist* (New York: Farrar, Straus, and Giroux, 2003).

7. Gayle Rubin, "Thinking Sex: Notes for a Radical Theory of the Politics of Sexuality," in *The Lesbian and Gay Studies Reader*, ed. Henry Abelove, Michele Barale, and David Halperin (New York: Routledge, 1993), 4.

8. Linda Williams, *Screening Sex* (Durham, NC: Duke University Press, 2008), 7, and Linda Williams, *Hard Core: Power, Pleasure, and the "Frenzy of the Visible"* (Durham, NC: Duke University Press, 1999), 282.

9. Williams, *Screening Sex*, 6.

10. Brian McNair, *Striptease Culture: Sex, Media and the Democratisation of Desire* (New York: Routledge, 2009), 111–12. See also Eric Schaefer, ed., *Sex Scene: Media and*

*the Sexual Revolution* (Durham, NC: Duke University Press, 2014), and Elana Levine, *Wallowing in Sex: The New Sexual Culture of 1970s Television* (Durham, NC: Duke University Press, 2007).

11. Williams problematizes the relation between sexual speech and sexual repression and freedom in *Hard Core*, 15, 283.

12. For a history of the dictatorship, see Hugo Quiroga, *El tiempo del Proceso: Conflictos y coincidencias entre civiles y militares (1976–1983)* (Rosario: Editorial Fundación Ross, 1994), and Marcos Novaro and Vicente Palermo, *La dictadura militar, 1976/1983: Del golpe de estado a la restauración democrática* (Buenos Aires: Paidós, 2003).

13. For one of the latest reassessments of Alfonsín's government, see Roberto Gargarella, María Victoria Murillo, and Mario Pecheny, eds., *Discutir Alfonsín* (Buenos Aires: Siglo Veintiuno, 2010).

14. For a general historical account of the transition to democracy and Alfonsín's government, see Luis Alberto Romero, *A History of Argentina in the Twentieth Century* (University Park: Pennsylvania State University Press, 2006), 215–84, and Juan Suriano, ed., *Nueva Historia Argentina: Dictadura y democracia (1976–2001)* (Buenos Aires: Sudamericana, 2005).

15. A thorough account of the massive historiographical production on the dictatorship is unfeasible. Representative examples of the prevalent scholarship on political violence are Pilar Calveiro, *Poder y desaparición: Los campos de concentración en Argentina* (Buenos Aires: Colihue, 1998); Pablo Pozzi, *Por las sendas argentinas: El PRT-ERP, la guerrilla marxista* (Buenos Aires: Eudeba, 2001); Hugo Vezzetti, *Pasado y presente: Guerra, dictadura y sociedad en la Argentina* (Buenos Aires: Siglo Veintiuno, 2002); Antonius C. G. M. Robben, *Political Violence and Trauma in Argentina* (Philadelphia: University of Pennsylvania Press, 2005); Lucas Lanusse, *Montoneros: El mito de sus 12 fundadores* (Buenos Aires: Vergara, 2005); Gabriela Águila, *Dictadura, represión y sociedad en Rosario, 1976–1983: Un estudio sobre la represión y los comportamientos y actitudes sociales en dictadura* (Buenos Aires: Prometeo, 2008); and Vera Carnovale, *Los combatientes: Historia del PRT-ERP* (Buenos Aires: Siglo Veintiuno, 2011). For a comprehensive and up-to-date historiographical assessment, see Marina Franco and Daniel Lvovich, "Historia reciente: Apuntes sobre un campo de investigación en expansión," *Boletín del Instituto de Historia Argentina y Americana Dr. Emilio Ravignani*, no. 47 (2017): 190–217.

16. See, for example, Elizabeth Jelin, *Los trabajos de la memoria* (Buenos Aires: Siglo Veintiuno, 2002); Emilio Crenzel, *La historia política del Nunca Más: La memoria de las desapariciones en la Argentina* (Buenos Aires: Siglo Veintiuno, 2008); Barbara Sutton, *Surviving State Terror: Women's Testimonies of Repression and Resistance in Argentina* (New York: New York University Press, 2018); David Sheinin, *Consent of the Damned: Ordinary Argentinians in the Dirty War* (Gainesville: University Press of Florida, 2012); Sebastián Carassai, *The Argentine Silent Majority: Middle Classes, Politics, Violence, and Memory in the Seventies* (Durham, NC: Duke University Press, 2014); James Brennan, *Argentina's Missing Bones: Revisiting the History of the Dirty War* (Los Angeles: University of California Press, 2018); and Antonius C. G. M. Robben, *Ar-*

*gentina Betrayed: Memory, Mourning, and Accountability* (Philadelphia: University of Pennsylvania Press, 2018).

17. For example, Flavio Rapisardi and Alejandro Modarelli, *Fiestas, baños y exilios: Los gays porteños en la última dictadura* (Buenos Aires: Sudamericana, 2001); Paola Martínez, *Género, política y revolución en los años setenta: Las mujeres del PRT-ERP* (Buenos Aires: Imago Mundi, 2009); Débora D'Antonio, ed., *Deseo y represión: Sexualidad, género y estado en la historia argentina reciente* (Buenos Aires: Imago Mundi, 2015); Alejandra Oberti, *Las revolucionarias: Militancia, vida cotidiana y afectividad en los setenta* (Buenos Aires: Edhasa, 2015). Two exceptional works that incorporate sexuality are Frank Graziano, *Divine Violence: Spectacle, Psychosexuality and Radical Christianity in the Argentine "Dirty War"* (Boulder, CO: Westview Press, 1992), and Diana Taylor, *Disappearing Acts: Spectacles of Gender and Nationalism in Argentina's Dirty War* (Durham, NC: Duke University Press, 1997).

18. See, for example, Marina Franco, *Un enemigo para la nación: Orden interno, violencia y "subversión," 1973–1976* (Buenos Aires: Fondo de Cultura Económica, 2012); Claudia Feld and Marina Franco, eds., *Democracia, Hora Cero: Actores, políticas y debates en los inicios de la posdictadura* (Buenos Aires: Fondo de Cultura Económica, 2015); Paula Canelo, *La política secreta de la última dictadura argentina (1976–1983): A 40 años del golpe* (Buenos Aires: Edhasa, 2016).

19. Franco and Lvovich, "Historia reciente," 205.

20. Rubin, "Thinking Sex," 11.

21. Isabella Cosse, *Pareja, sexualidad y familia en los años sesenta* (Buenos Aires: Siglo Veintiuno, 2010). For studies on the sexual culture in 1960s Argentina that also question the nature of the "sexual revolution" and explore the conservative sexual culture of the period, see Isabella Cosse, Karina Felitti, and Valeria Manzano, eds., *Los 60s de otra manera: Vida cotidiana, género y sexualidades en la Argentina* (Buenos Aires: Prometeo, 2010); Karina Felitti, *La revolución de la píldora: Sexualidad y política en los sesenta* (Buenos Aires: Edhasa, 2012); Valeria Manzano, *The Age of Youth in Argentina: Culture, Politics, and Sexuality from Perón to Videla* (Chapel Hill: University of North Carolina Press, 2014).

22. For a representative example of this scholarship, see Gert Hekma and Alain Giami, eds., *Sexual Revolutions* (New York: Palgrave Macmillan, 2014).

23. For a thorough reconstruction of the history of the studies of transition to democracy, see Cecilia Lesgart, *Usos de la transición a la democracia: Ensayo, ciencia y política en la década del 80* (Rosario: Homo Sapiens, 2003).

24. Emblematic examples of this scholarship are Oscar Oszlak, ed., *"Proceso," crisis y transición democrática* (Buenos Aires: CEAL, 1984); Guillermo O'Donnell, Philippe Schmitter, and Laurence Whitehead, eds., *Transitions from Authoritarian Rule: Prospects for Democracy* (Baltimore: Johns Hopkins University Press, 1986); José Nun and Juan Carlos Portantiero, eds., *Ensayos sobre la transición a la democracia en Argentina* (Buenos Aires: Puntosur, 1987); and Joseph Tulchin, ed., *The Consolidation of Democracy in Latin America* (Boulder, CO: Lynne Rienner Publishers, 1995).

25. See, for example, Edgardo Catterbeg, *Los argentinos frente a la política: Cul-*

*tura política y opinión pública en la transición Argentina* (Buenos Aires: Sudamericana, 1989); Alison Brysk, *The Politics of Human Rights in Argentina: Protest, Change, and Democratization* (Stanford, CA: Stanford University Press, 1994); Elizabeth Jelin and Eric Hershberg, eds., *Constructing Democracy: Human Rights, Citizenship, and Society in Latin America* (Boulder, CO: Westview Press, 1996); Gerardo Aboy Carlés, *Las dos fronteras de la democracia argentina: La reformulación de las identidades políticas de Alfonsín a Menem* (Rosario: Homo Sapiens, 2001); Sergio Emiliozzi, Mario Pecheny, and Martín Unzué, eds., *La dinámica de la democracia: Representación, instituciones y ciudadanía en Argentina* (Buenos Aires: Prometeo, 2007); Ricardo Lorenzetti and Alfredo Kraut, *Derechos Humanos: Justicia y reparación* (Buenos Aires: Sudamericana, 2011); Leslie E. Anderson, *Democratization by Institutions: Argentina's Transition Years in Comparative Perspective* (Ann Arbor: University of Michigan Press, 2016); Rosario Figari Layús, *The Reparative Effects of Human Rights Trials: Lessons from Argentina* (New York: Routledge, 2017). An important exception is Mala Htun, *Sex and the State: Abortion, Divorce, and Family under Latin American Dictatorships and Democracy* (New York: Cambridge University Press, 2003), about the passing of laws connected to reproductive health in Argentina, Chile, and Brazil.

26. See, for example, Alfredo Raúl Pucciarelli, ed., *Los años de Alfonsín: ¿El poder de la democracia o la democracia al del poder?* (Buenos Aires: Siglo Veintiuno, 2006), and Marcela Ferrari and Mónica Gordillo, eds., *La reconstrucción democrática en clave provincial* (Rosario: Prohistoria, 2015).

27. Guillermo O'Donnell, *Counterpoints: Selected Essays on Authoritarianism and Democratization* (Notre Dame, IN: University of Notre Dame Press, 1999), 58.

28. On reproductive rights with an emphasis on the tensions and negotiations among women, physicians, and the state, see, for example, Eileen Suárez-Findley, *Imposing Decency: The Politics of Sexuality and Race in Puerto Rico, 1870–1920* (Durham, NC: Duke University Press, 1999); Laura Briggs, *Reproducing Empire: Race, Sex, Science, and U.S. Imperialism in Puerto Rico* (Los Angeles: University of California Press, 2002); Jadwiga Pieper Mooney, *The Politics of Motherhood: Maternity and Women's Rights in Twentieth-Century Chile* (Pittsburgh, PA: University of Pittsburgh Press, 2009); Okezi Otovo, *Progressive Mothers, Better Babies: Race, Public Health, and the State in Brazil, 1850–1945* (Austin: University of Texas Press, 2016); Nora Jaffary, *Reproduction and Its Discontents in Mexico: Childbirth and Contraception, 1750–1905* (Chapel Hill: University of North Carolina Press, 2016). On sex work, the state, and public health, see, for example, Donna Guy, *Sex and Danger in Buenos Aires: Prostitution, Family, and Nation in Argentina* (Lincoln: University of Nebraska Press, 1991); Katherine Bliss, *Compromised Positions: Prostitution, Public Health, and the State in Revolutionary Mexico* (University Park: University of Pennsylvania Press, 2001); and Tiffany Sippial, *Prostitution, Modernity, and the Making of the Cuban Republic, 1840–1920* (Chapel Hill: University of North Carolina Press, 2013). On gay men and masculinities, see, for example, James Green, *Beyond Carnival: Male Homosexuality in Twentieth-Century Brazil* (Chicago: University of Chicago Press, 1999); Robert McKee Irwin, Edward J. McCaughan, Michelle Rocio Nasser, eds., *The Famous 41: Sexuality and Social Control*

*in Mexico, 1901* (New York: Palgrave Macmillan, 2003); Víctor Macías-Gonzalez and Anne Rubenstein, eds., *Masculinity and Sexuality in Modern Mexico* (Albuquerque: University of New Mexico Press, 2012). Other representative works on studies of sexuality in Latin America from an interdisciplinary perspective are Daniel Balderston and Donna Guy, eds., *Sex and Sexuality in Latin America* (New York: New York University Press, 1999), and Javier Corrales and Mario Pecheny, eds., *The Politics of Sexuality in Latin America: A Reader on Lesbian, Gay, Bisexual, and Transgender Rights* (Pittsburgh, PA: University of Pittsburgh Press, 2010).

29. For studies on youth cultures and countercultures that have paid attention to sexuality, see Manzano, *The Age of Youth*; Christopher Dunn, *Contracultura: Alternative Arts and Social Transformation in Authoritarian Brazil* (Chapel Hill: University of North Carolina Press, 2016); and Patrick Barr-Melej, *Psychedelic Chile: Youth, Counterculture, and Politics on the Road to Socialism and Dictatorship* (Chapel Hill: University of North Carolina Press, 2017). On the intersection between politics, political change, and sexual cultures, see Jocelyn Olcott, Mary Kay Vaughan, and Gabriela Cano, eds., *Sex in Revolution: Gender, Politics, and Power in Modern Mexico* (Durham, NC: Duke University Press, 2006); Carrie Hamilton, *Sexual Revolutions in Cuba* (Chapel Hill: University of North Carolina Press, 2012); Cymene Howe, *Intimate Activism: The Struggle for Sexual Rights in Postrevolutionary Nicaragua* (Durham, NC: Duke University Press, 2013); and Benjamin Cowan, *Securing Sex: Morality and Repression in the Making of Cold War Brazil* (Chapel Hill: University of North Carolina Press, 2016). On sexual politics and the revolutionary Left in Argentina, see Martínez, *Género, política y revolución en los años setenta*; Oberti, *Las revolucionarias*; and Andrea Andújar, Débora D'Antonio, Fernanda Gil Lozano, Karin Grammático, and María Laura Rosa, eds., *De minifaldas, militancias y revoluciones: Exploraciones sobre los 70 en la Argentina* (Buenos Aires: Luxemburg, 2009).

30. Guillermo O'Donnell and Philippe Schmitter, "Resurrecting Civil Society," in O'Donnell, Schmitter, and Whitehead, *Transitions from Authoritarian Rule*, 48–56.

## 1. THE RETURN TO DEMOCRACY AND THE SEXUALIZATION OF MEDIA CULTURE

1. "Comenzó el destape," *Salimos*, August 27, 1982, 8.

2. For a general history of censorship in Argentina in the twentieth century, see Fernando Ferreira, *Una historia de la censura: Violencia y proscripción en la Argentina del siglo XX* (Buenos Aires: Norma, 2000). For analyses of censorship in cinema before the 1970s dictatorship, see Fernando Ramírez Llorens, "Noches de sano esparcimiento: La censura cinematográfica en Argentina, 1955–1973," *Nuevo Mundo, Mundos Nuevos* (December 2015), https://journals.openedition.org/nuevomundo/68565?lang=en, and César Maranghello, "El discurso represivo: La censura entre 1961 y 1966," in *Cine argentino: Modernidad y vanguardias, 1957/1983*, ed. Claudio España (Buenos Aires: Fondo Nacional de las Artes, 2005), 268–83. For an analysis of censorship of literature before and during the 1970s dictatorship, see Patricia Funes, "Los que queman libros: Censores en Argentina (1956–1983)," in *Problemas de historia reciente del Cono*

*Sur*, vol. 1, ed. Ernesto Bohoslavsky, Marina Franco, Mariana Iglesias, and Daniel Lvovich (Buenos Aires: Prometeo, 2010), 303–25.

3. Andrés Avellaneda, *Censura, autoritarismo y cultura: Argentina, 1960–1983*, vol. 1 (Buenos Aires: Centro Editor de América Latina, 1986), 14. For a study of censorship of sex content in magazines in the 1960s, see Ariel Eidelman, "Moral católica y censura municipal de las revistas eróticas en la ciudad de Buenos Aires durante la década del sesenta," in D'Antonio, *Deseo y represión*, 1–20.

4. Calveiro, *Poder y desaparición*, 27.

5. Herzog, *Sex after Fascism*, 261.

6. Emilio Massera, *El camino a la democracia* (Buenos Aires: El Cid Editor, 1979), 88–89.

7. Valeria Manzano makes this argument for the 1960s; see her *The Age of Youth in Argentina*, 113. For this argument in the case of the military dictatorship in Brazil, see Cowan, *Securing Sex*, 110.

8. Robben, *Political Violence and Trauma in Argentina*, 170–73, 232.

9. Quoted in Judith Filc, *Entre el parentesco y la política: Familia y dictadura, 1976–1983* (Buenos Aires: Biblos, 1997), 36, 47–48. Avellaneda, *Censura, autoritarismo y cultura*, 1:19–25.

10. I borrow the concept of moral technocrats from Benjamin Cowan's *Securing Sex*, 13.

11. Laura Schenquer, "Agencias e 'inmoralidades': La circulación de directivas político-culturales entre la Secretaría de Información Pública, el Ministerio del Interior y la Dirección General de Informaciones de la provincia de Santa Fe durante la última dictadura militar argentina (1976–1983)," *Nuevo Mundo, Mundos Nuevos* (February 2018), https://journals.openedition.org/nuevomundo/?lang=es.

12. Novaro and Palermo, *La dictadura militar 1976–1983*, 139.

13. On the relation between the Catholic Church and the dictatorship, see Martín Obregón, *Entre la cruz y la espada: La Iglesia católica durante los primeros años del Proceso* (Buenos Aires: UNQUI, 2005).

14. Quoted in Avellaneda, *Censura, autoritarismo y cultura*, 1:143. On the *ligas*, see Lilia Vázquez Lorda, "Intervenciones e iniciativas católicas en el ámbito familiar: Las Ligas de Madres y Padres de Familia (Argentina, 1950–1970)," MA thesis, Buenos Aires, Universidad de San Andrés, 2012.

15. Avellaneda, *Censura, autoritarismo y cultura*, 1:32–35; Judith Gociol and Hernán Invernizzi, *Cine y dictadura: La censura al desnudo* (Buenos Aires: Capital Intelectual, 2006), 48–50.

16. For an analysis of the censorship of erotic magazines in Buenos Aires during Juan Carlos Onganía's dictatorship (1966–70), see Eidelman, "Moral católica y censura municipal de revistas eróticas en la ciudad de Buenos Aires durante la década del sesenta," 1–20.

17. Indeed, censorship in Argentina was more effectual than in other Latin American countries, including Brazil, where despite a clear moralistic agenda, implementation remained problematic. See, for example, Cowan, *Securing Sex*, 211–24.

18. Quoted in Avellaneda, *Censura, autoritarismo y cultura*, 2:213. See also 1:18–31.

19. According to the Comisión Nacional sobre la Desaparición de Personas (CONADEP; National Commission on the Disappearance of Persons), eighty-four reporters disappeared during the dictatorship, a number that grew to 172 in 2016 based on new research. On disappeared journalists, see Comisión Nacional sobre la Desaparición de Personas, *Nunca Más* (Buenos Aires: Eudeba, 1996), 372–74; Asociación de Periodistas de Buenos Aires, *Periodistas desaparecidos: Con vida los queremos* (Buenos Aires: Unión de Trabajadores de Prensa de Buenos Aires, 1987); "Amplían la lista de periodistas desaparecidos en la dictadura," *Tiempo Argentino*, December 3, 2016, https://www.tiempoar.com.ar/articulo/view/62818/ampla-an-la-lista-de-periodistas-desaparecidos-en-la-dictadura.

20. The role of the press in supporting the regime, misrepresenting reality, and silencing the opposition has been the cause of both mea culpa and a heated debate. See Eduardo Blaustein and Martín Zubieta, *Decíamos ayer: La prensa argentina bajo el Proceso* (Buenos Aires: Colihue, 1998), 49, 98. On the relation between the print press and the dictatorship, see also Jorge Saborido and Marcelo Borrelli, eds., *Voces y silencios: La prensa argentina y la dictadura militar (1976–1983)* (Buenos Aires: Eudeba, 2011).

21. "El mejor afrodisíaco sigue siendo el amor," *La Semana*, August 29, 1985, 26–27.

22. Quoted in Carlos Ulanovsky, *Paren las rotativas: Una historia de grandes diarios, revistas y periodistas argentinos* (Buenos Aires: Espasa, 1997), 251.

23. Author interview with Alcira Bas via Skype, July 29, 2016.

24. Quoted in Mara Burkart, "La revista Humor, espacio crítico bajo la dictadura militar argentina," *Revista Afuera: Estudios de crítica cultural* 7, no. 13 (September 2013), http://www.revistaafuera.com/articulo.php?id=284&nro=13. For a history and analysis of *Humor*, see Andrés Cascioli, *La revista Humor y la dictadura* (Buenos Aires: Musimundo, 2005); Abelardo Castillo, *Los irresponsables: La revista Humor como medio opositor a la dictadura* (Buenos Aires: Del Tratado, 2009); Mara Burkart, *De Satiricón a Humor: Risa, cultura y política en los años setenta* (Buenos Aires: Miño y Dávila, 2017).

25. Quoted in Blaustein and Zubieta, *Decíamos ayer*, 184. Ulanovsky, *Paren las rotativas*, 266.

26. Burkart, *De Satiricón a Humor*, 41–69.

27. Avellaneda, *Censura, autoritarismo y cultura*, 2:206.

28. Ulanovsky, *Paren las rotativas*, 282.

29. The article was titled "Moda y pudor: ¿Hasta dónde se destaparán las argentinas?" Avellaneda, *Censura, autoritarismo y cultura*, 2:194.

30. Cited in Robben, *Political Violence and Trauma in Argentina*, 395.

31. Gociol and Invernizzi, *Cine y dictadura*, 31.

32. Quoted in Gociol and Invernizzi, *Cine y dictadura*, 43.

33. Gociol and Invernizzi, *Cine y dictadura*, 54.

34. Gociol and Invernizzi, *Cine y dictadura*, 35–37.

35. A few films were released after extensive cuts of scenes considered problem-

atic by the board and reclassified as "forbidden for minors." Gociol and Invernizzi, *Cine y dictadura*, 41.

36. Gociol and Invernizzi, *Cine y dictadura*, 45. María Elena de las Carreras, "Contemporary Politics in Argentine Cinema, 1981–1991" (PhD diss., University of California, Los Angeles, 1995), 103.

37. In 1978, the ECC members gathered to watch 468 movies, and in 1981, they reached a record of 528. Gociol and Invernizzi, *Cine y dictadura*, 58.

38. "Estos son los films permitidos," *Destape*, April 10, 1984, 2–3; de las Carreras, "Contemporary Politics in Argentine Cinema, 1981–1991," 133, 158.

39. Quoted in César Maranghello, "La censura afloja sus cuerdas: Octavio Getino libera films prohibidos y se respira libertad cultural," in *Cine Argentino: Modernidad y vanguardias, 1957/1983*, ed. Claudio España (Buenos Aires: Fondo Nacional de las Artes, 2005), 652–61, 658; Gociol and Invernizzi, *Cine y dictadura*, 35–56; Fernando Varea, *El cine argentino durante la dictadura militar, 1976/1983* (Rosario: Editorial Municipal de Rosario, 2008), 51–56, 81–88.

40. The other subjects prohibited in films by law 18,019 were the vindication of crimes and criminals, a man's refusal of his duty to defend the country and rejection of authorities' right to require it (at the time, Argentina had mandatory military service for eighteen-year-old men, who were chosen for the service through a lottery system), and undermining national security and relations with allies or harming the interests of state institutions. Avellaneda, *Censura, autoritarismo y cultura*, 2:100–101.

41. Bó obtained a theatrical release permit for *El último amor en Tierra del Fuego* (1979), which featured very little nudity. Yet, after the release of his comedy *Una viuda descocada* (1980), censored by the ECC, the government denied him payment of *fondos de recuperación industrial*, a percentage the state paid producers based on box office numbers. After prohibition, censorship, and cheating, Bó promised he would only film in Argentina again after the fall of the dictatorship, but he died in 1981. On *Insaciable*, see Eliana Braslavsky, Tamara Drajner Barredo, and Bárbara Pereyra, "Insaciable (Armando Bó, 1984), entre la liberación sexual y el castigo moralizante," *Imagofagia* 8 (2013), http://www.asaeca.org/imagofagia/index.php/imagofagia/article/view/415/363. On Armando Bó's and Isabel Sarli's filmography, see Rodolfo Kuhn, *Armando Bo, el cine, la pornografía ingenua y otras reflexiones* (Buenos Aires: Corregidor, 1984), and Elena Goity, "Las batallas calientes: Armando Bó edifica a Isabel Sarli," in *Cine argentino: Modernidad y vanguardias, 1957/1983*, ed. Claudio España (Buenos Aires: Fondo Nacional de las Artes, 2005), 364–75. On Sarli, see Victoria Ruétalo, "Tempations: Isabel Sarli Exposed," in *Latsploitation, Exploitation Cinemas, and Latin America*, ed. Victoria Ruétalo and Dolores Tiernes (New York: Routledge, 2009), 201–14.

42. Alfredo Landa's films (*landismo*) became very popular during the last years of Francisco Franco's dictatorship in Spain and later during the destape. Landa's films combined women wearing skimpy clothing with light erotic humor and satirized Spanish *machismo*. José M. Ponce, *El destape nacional* (Barcelona: Glénat, 2004), 22–23; Tatjana Pavlovic, *Despotic Bodies and Transgressive Bodies: Spanish Culture from*

*Francisco Franco to Jesús Franco* (New York: State University of New York Press, 2002), 71–89. In Brazil, the pornochanchadas, inspired by Italian sex comedies, flourished during the dictatorship and relied more on suggestion than sexual explicitness. Stephanie Dennison and Lisa Shaw, *Popular Cinema in Brazil* (New York: Manchester University Press, 2004), 157–79; Emma Camarero, "From the Banal to the Indispensable: *Pornochanchada* and *Cinema Novo* during the Brazilian Dictatorship (1964–1985)," *L'Atalante: Revista de Estudios Cinematográficos* 23 (January–June 2017): 95–108.

43. For example, *Encuentros muy cercanos con señoras de cualquier tipo* (Hugo Moser, 1978), *Fotógrafo de señoras* (Hugo Moser, 1978), *Custodio de señoras* (Hugo Sofovich, 1979), and *A los cirujanos se les va la mano* (Hugo Sofovich, 1980).

44. Quoted in León Roberto Gindin, Cynthia Gindin, Silvina Ramos, Juan José Llovet, Alcira Camilucci, Adrián Helién, Laura Pietrasanta, Mario Kaplan, Mario Huguet, and Luis Frontera, *1ra Encuesta sobre sexualidad y pareja* (Buenos Aires: La Urraca, 1987), 105.

45. Out of 192 Argentine movies filmed during the dictatorship, 32 were comedias picarescas. On the comedias picarescas, see Varea, *El cine argentino durante la dictadura militar, 1976/1983*, 51–56. For an analysis of the genre that underlines the contradiction between the films and the official discourse of the dictatorship, see Débora D'Antonio, "Paradojas del género y la sexualidad en la filmografía durante la última dictadura militar argentina," *Estudos Feministas* 23, no. 3 (September–December 2015): 913–37.

46. For example, *Mirame la palomita* (Enrique Carreras, 1985), *El manosanta está cargado* (Hugo Sofovich, 1987), *Susana quiere, el negro también* (Julio De Grazia, 1987), and *Atracción peculiar* (Enrique Carreras, 1988).

47. The army controlled Channel 9 and 7 (ATC), the navy Channel 13, and the air force Channel 11, the four national state TV stations—all of which, with the exception of Channel 7, had been expropriated between 1973 and 1975 and later purchased by the state under military control in 1978. The military also intervened in state TV stations in the provinces, including Channel 7 of Mendoza, Channel 8 of Mar del Plata, Channel 11 of Formosa, and Channel 6 of San Rafael, Mendoza. On the military control over the media, see Glenn Postolski and Santiago Martino, "Relaciones peligrosas: Los medios y la dictadura entre el control, la censura y los negocios," in *Mucho ruido y pocas leyes: Economía y políticas de la comunicación en la Argentina (1920–2004)*, ed. Guillermo Mastrini (Buenos Aires: La Crujía, 2009), 155–84.

48. Quoted in Ferreira, *Una historia de la censura*, 252–53.

49. Mirta Varela, "Silencio, mordaza y optimismo," *Todo es Historia*, no. 104 (March 2001): 58.

50. Quoted in Avellaneda, *Censura, autoritarismo y cultura*, 2:177.

51. "Las prohibiciones del Proceso," *El Porteño*, November 1983, 44–46.

52. For a thorough examination of book censorship during the dictatorship, see Hernán Invernizzi and Judith Gociol, *Un golpe a los libros: Represión cultural durante la última dictadura militar* (Buenos Aires: Eudeba, 2002).

53. Oscar Landi, "Cultura y política en la transición democrática," in *Proceso, crisis y transición democrática*, vol. 1, ed. Oscar Oszlack (Buenos Aires: CEAL, 1984), 111.

54. Comisión Provincial de la Memoria, *Biblioteca de libros prohibidos* (Córdoba: Ediciones del Pasaje, 2012).

55. "El destape llegó a la televisión," *TV Semanal*, November 9, 1982, 21.

56. "La publicidad al desnudo," *La Semana*, September 12, 1985, 29. Author interview with Alcira Bas via Skype, July 29, 2016.

57. "Desnudos, provocadores y perseguidos," *Clarín*, November 24, 2011, https://www.clarin.com/espectaculos/desnudos-provocadores-perseguidos_0_HJumwE7x-RKe.html.

58. Theater was the epicenter of defiant cultural movements during the last years of the dictatorship, with Teatro Abierto, a group of artists who staged plays of quite controversial political and social content, and experimental and underground work led by figures such as Batato Barea, who would found the art and theater center Parakultural after the return of democracy. For a history of Teatro Abierto, see Miguel Ángel Giella, *Teatro Abierto 1981: Teatro argentino bajo vigilancia*, vol. 1 (Buenos Aires: Corregidor, 1992).

59. "Buenos Aires ya tiene su propio destape," *TV Semanal*, July 8, 1980, 28–29; "¿Llegó el destape a la Argentina?" *Siete Días*, August 27, 1980, 22–28. Authored by Santiago Moncada, *Violines y trompetas* was first launched in the Spanish destape.

60. Avellaneda, *Censura, autoritarismo y cultura*, 2:229. Varea, *El cine argentino en dictadura militar, 1976/1983*, 112; "Alfonsín culpa a la ultraderecha de la ola de bombas en la 'calle de los cines' de Buenos Aires," *El País* (Edición América), March 31, 1988, https://elpais.com/diario/1988/03/31/internacional/575762407_850215.html. For a history of theater during the dictatorship, see Jean Graham-Jones, *Exorcising History: Argentine Theater under Dictatorship* (Cranbury, NJ: Associated University Press, 2000).

61. "Informe Especial: Destape," *Esquiú*, November 22, 1981, 8–11.

62. "Informe Especial: Destape," *Esquiú*, November 22, 1981, 11.

63. Romero, *A History of Argentina in the Twentieth Century*, 247–54.

64. I borrow these concepts from "Sex as Spectator Sport," *Time*, July 11, 1969, 69, and "Morals: The Second Sexual Revolution," *Time*, January 24, 1964, 54.

65. "Señores, llegó el destape," *TV Semanal*, February 11, 1983, 48–49.

66. "Se mira y no se toca," *La Semana*, September 12, 1985, 30; "El desnudo más total del país," *Satiricón*, November 1983, 119.

67. "Eroticón se hace contra la pacatería argentina," *Eroticón*, October 1984, 3.

68. "La vida sexual de los bañeros," *Libre*, March 6, 1984, 18–23; "Una ciega cuenta como siente y hace el amor," *Libre*, March 6, 1984, 35–37; "Descubrimos en Rosario un viejo cementerio de prostitutas," *Libre*, March 6, 1984, 62–67; "El carnicero Marinaro cuenta como convence a sus clientas para cambiar carne por sexo," *Libre*, April 10, 1984, 94–98; "Para adelgazar siga el régimen del sexo," *Destape*, January 10, 1984, 30; "Historia de la represión sexual en Argentina," *El Porteño*, April 1984, 62–65; "Doña Petrona pasó muy bien toda su vida porque tiene una receta para que los hombres se

pongan fogosos," *Libre*, September 11, 1984, 54–57. On Gandulfo, see Rebekah Pite, *Creating a Common Table in Twentieth-Century Argentina: Doña Petrona, Women, and Food* (Chapel Hill: University of North Carolina Press, 2013).

69. See, for example, "Un año pobre y de expectativas frustradas," *Anuario Esquiú 85/86*, 123–26.

70. "Era una señora potra la Señorita Jacinta," *Libre*, January 1, 1985, 90–91.

71. "¿Revolución sexual? No exageremos, por favor," *La Semana*, September 5, 1985, 28.

72. Marcelo Raimon interview with Norberto Chab, Buenos Aires, September 29, 2005. Editorial Perfil ad, *Libre*, May 15, 1984, n/p.

73. "El negocio del destape," *Somos*, July 27, 1984, 57–61, see esp. 57. There are no official statistics on periodical publications for the 1980s.

74. *Playboy* began publication in Argentina in 1985.

75. "Prohibido, prohibir," *Dar la cara en entrevista*, April 1985, 25.

76. Blaustein and Zubieta, *Decíamos ayer*, 548.

77. Gustavo Aprea, *Cine y políticas en Argentina: Continuidades y discontinuidades en 25 años de democracia* (Buenos Aires: Biblioteca Nacional / Universidad Nacional de General Sarmiento, 2008), 14–16.

78. Quoted in Claudio España, "Introducción: Diez años de cine en democracia," in *Cine argentino en democracia, 1983/1993* (Buenos Aires: Fondo Nacional de las Artes, 1994), 16.

79. Eric Schaefer, *"Bold! Daring! Shocking! True!" A History of Exploitation Films, 1919–1959* (Durham, NC: Duke University Press, 1999), 337–39.

80. Quoted in De las Carreras, "Contemporary Politics in Argentine Cinema, 1981–1991," 204.

81. De las Carreras, "Contemporary Politics in Argentine Cinema, 1981–1991," 435–36.

82. *Last Tango in Paris* had been released in Argentina in 1973 but was prohibited after thirteen days in theaters. "Bailate un tango, Marlon," *Somos*, September 28, 1984, 62–63; "El destape cinematográfico," *La Semana*, January 10, 1985, 11–12.

83. "Cine el libertad condicionada," *El Periodista*, June 10–16, 1988, 54–56; "A la caza del pornógrafo," *El Periodista*, June 7–13, 1985, 47.

84. "Un negocio al desnudo," *Somos*, June 1, 1987, 45; Aída Quintar and José Borello, "Evolución histórica de la exhibición y consumo de cine en Buenos Aires," *H-industri@* 8, no. 14 (2014): 103.

85. "Sexo en TV," *Humor*, June 25, 1988, 23.

86. "Adriana Brodsky y el aviso de las colas," *La Semana*, December 22, 1983, 102–5.

87. "Vea, compre y goce," *La Semana*, September 19, 1985, 48.

88. On erotic literature in Argentina before and after the return to democracy, see Graciela Gliemmo, "El erotismo en la narrativa de las escritoras argentinas (1970–1990): Apropiación, ampliación y reformulación de un canon," in *Poéticas argentinas del siglo XX (Literatura y teatro)*, ed. Jorge Dubatti (Buenos Aires: Editorial de

Belgrano, 1998), 137–59, and Mónica Ojeda Franco, "Pornoerótica latinoamericana: Subversión en la narrativa de mujeres en el exilio," *Anales de Literatura Hispanoamericana* 43 (2014): 57–69.

89. Brochures and listings by publishing houses from sexologist and feminist activist Sara Torres's personal archive.

90. Interview with Jorge Fontevecchia, August 30, 2016.

91. "¿Revolución sexual? No exageremos, por favor," *La Semana*, September 5, 1985, 28.

92. On the Spanish transition to democracy, see José-Carlos Mainer Santos Juliá, *El aprendizaje de la libertad, 1973–1976: La cultura de la transición* (Madrid: Alianza Editorial, 2000). On the Spanish destape, see Ponce, *El destape nacional*. On Argentine exiles in Spain, see Guillermo Mira-Delli Zotti, "Explorando algunas dimensiones del exilio argentino en España," in *Memorias de la violencia en Uruguay y Argentina: Golpes, dictaduras, exilios (1973–2006)*, ed. Eduardo Rey Tristán (Santiago de Compostela: Universidad de Santiago de Compostela, 2007), 163–78.

93. "¿Qué opina del destape?" *Tal Cual*, November 25, 1983, 5.

94. "¿Qué es la obscenidad?" *Libre*, April 3, 1984, 3.

95. For an examination of *Eroticón* with an emphasis on its portrayal of masculinities, see Fermín Acosta and Lucas Morgan Disalvo, "La masculinidad en la punta de sus manos: *Eroticón* y la configuración de los imaginarios sexuales en la década de los ochenta," in *Cuerpos minados: Masculinidades en Argentina*, ed. José Maristany and Jorge Peralta (La Plata: EDULP, 2017), 195–219.

96. "Como Rabelais, Eroticón no se toma el sexo en serio," *Eroticón*, September 1984, 3; "Estos chistes son un aborto," *Eroticón*, September 1984, 94–95; "Las páginas pistolares," *Sex Humor*, July 1986, 11; Fierro ad in *Sex Humor*, November 1984, 37.

97. "¿Qué es y no es obsceno?" *Somos*, June 1, 1984, 60; "Las argentinas y la pornografía," *La Mujer*, December 17, 1983, 4–5.

98. "Erotismo, pornografía y libertad de prensa," *La Semana*, November 24, 1983, 80. On current research about the complexity of defining pornography and the influence of changing factors such as gender, race, religious background, and marital status in individual understandings of pornography, see Brian Willoughby and Dean Busby, "In the Eye of the Beholder: Exploring Variations in the Perceptions of Pornography," *Journal of Sex Research* 53, no. 6 (2016): 678–88.

99. "¿Qué es lo obsceno? ¿Quién puede medirlo? ¿Se puede limitar el ejercicio de la sexualidad?" *Hombre*, April 1984, 5–10; "La tensión del destape," *Salimos*, August 27, 1982, 13.

100. "¿Quién dijo que la virginidad es una virtud?" *La Semana*, September 19, 1985, 46–47.

101. "Esta es la encuesta completa," *La Semana*, December 8, 1983, 79.

102. "¿Destape sí o no? ¿Pornografía sí o no?" *La Semana*, November 24, 1983, 84.

103. "Política de cultura," *La Semana*, November 10, 1983, 34–35.

104. "El destape," *Revista de La Nación*, June 15, 1986, 10–11.

105. Piero Gleijeses, "Afterword: The Culture of Fear," in *Secret History: The CIA's*

*Classified Account of Its Operations in Guatemala, 1952–1954*, ed. Nick Cullather (Stanford, CA: Stanford University Press, 1999), xxiii–xxxvi. For an examination of the culture of fear in other Latin American contexts, see Maria Helena Moreira Alves, *State and Opposition in Military Brazil* (Austin: University of Texas Press, 1985), and Noam Chomsky, "The Culture of Fear," in *Colombia: The Genocidal Democracy*, ed. Javier Giraldo (New York: Common Courage Press, 1996), 7–16.

106. "¿Qué es lo obsceno? ¿Quién puede medirlo? ¿Se puede limitar el ejercicio de la sexualidad?" *Hombre*, April 1984, 5–10; June 1984, 134–35; July 1984, 140–41.

107. María Elena Walsh, *Desventuras en el país jardín de infantes* (Buenos Aires: Sudamericana, 1994), 13–18; Guillermo O'Donnell, "Democracy in Argentina: Macro and Micro," in *Counterpoints*, 51–62, 53.

108. "De sexo, ni hablar . . . ," *Adultos*, May 1984, 3.

109. "La tensión del destape," *Salimos*, August 27, 1982, 13.

110. "¿Destape sí o no? ¿Pornografía sí o no?" *La Semana*, November 24, 1983, 80; "Destape, pornografía y democracia," *El Observador*, December 2, 1983; "Erotismo, pornografía y libertad de prensa," *La Semana*, November 24, 1983, 80.

111. "¿Destape sí o no? ¿Pornografía sí o no?" *La Semana*, November 24, 1983, 80.

112. During death flights, prisoners were thrown out of military planes into the ocean. See Horacio Verbitsky, *The Flight: Confessions of an Argentine Dirty Warrior* (New York: New Press, 1996).

113. "Periodiscidio: ¿Quién se beneficia con el tráfico de cadáveres?" *El Porteño*, February 26, 1984, 22–25. On the "horror show," see Claudia Feld, "La prensa de la transición ante el problema de los desaparecidos: El discurso del 'show del horror,'" in Feld and Franco, *Democracia, Hora Cero*, 269–316.

114. "La tortura como pornografía," *alfonsina*, January 26, 1984, 3.

115. "Sólo cinco revistas semanales venden más de 100,000 ejemplares," *Libre*, May 15, 1984, 77.

116. *Humor*, February 1984, 9, quoted in Feld, "La prensa de la transición ante el problema de los desaparecidos," 303.

117. "La tortura como pornografía," *alfonsina*, January 26, 1984, 3.

118. "¿Quién dijo que la virginidad es una virtud?" *La Semana*, September 19, 1985, 46–47. Similarly, psychiatrist and sexologist Juan Carlos Kusnetzoff argued that during the dictatorship, Argentines had experienced "percepticide," or the death of perception, a process of deliberate blinding that entailed seeing violence and repression without admitting it. Juan Carlos Kusnetzoff, "Renegación, desmentida, desaparición y perceptididio como técnicas psicopáticas de la salvación de la patria (Una visión psicoanalítica del informe de la Conadep)," in *Argentina. Psicoanálisis: Represión política*, ed. Comisión de Investigación Psicoanalítica sobre las Consecuencias de la Represión Política (Buenos Aires: Kargieman, 1986), 95–114.

119. Quoted in Gliemmo, "El erotismo en la narrativa de las escritoras argentinas (1970–1990)," 144.

120. Georges Bataille, *Death and Sensuality: A Study of Eroticism and the Taboo* (New York: Ayer, 1984), 11.

121. Graziano, *Divine Violence*, 154–55; Taylor, *Disappearing Acts*, 6.

122. *Mundo Erótico* ad, *Adultos*, August 28–September 16, 1984, back cover.

123. "El destape de la ultraderecha en Rosario," *El Periodista*, March 1–7, 1985, 52.

124. "Una grata celebración de la Liga de la Decencia," *La Capital*, July 25, 1976, 7.

125. "El pudor, defensa de la intimidad humana," *Boletín Informativo de la Agencia Informativa Católica Argentina (AICA)*, no. 1462, December 27, 1984, 7–8.

126. "49ª Asamblea Plenaria de la Conferencia Episcopal Argentina," *Documento No. 147, Suplemento del Boletín Informativo AICA*, no. 1456, November 15, 1984, 65.

127. "La Liga por la Decencia de Rosario," *Sex Humor*, May 1987, 21–23.

128. "Pareja," *Boletín de la Liga por la Decencia*, no. 146, June 1989, 2.

129. "Primero el cine, ahora la TV," *Boletín de la Liga por la Decencia*, no. 91, June 1984, 1.

130. "Pronunciamiento sobre la televisión," *Boletín de la Liga por la Decencia*, no. 94, September 1984, 3; "Ley Moral," *Boletín de la Liga por la Decencia*, no. 95, October 1984, 3.

131. "Ante la oficialización de la pornografía," *Boletín de la Liga por la Decencia*, no. 89, April 1984, 3; "Sorprendentes declaraciones," *Boletín de la Liga por la Decencia*, no. 96, November 1984, 3; "Especuladores de debilidades humanas," *Boletín de la Liga por la Decencia*, no. 107, November 1985, 2.

132. This is how Juan Carlos Pugliese, the president of the House of Representatives, described Julio Triviño. "Sorprendentes declaraciones," *Boletín de la Liga por la Decencia*, no. 96, November 1984, 3.

133. "¿Quién dijo que la virginidad es una virtud?" *La Semana*, September 19, 1985, 46.

134. "Soy enemigo de la pornografía, dice Mario O'Donnell," *Boletín Informativo AICA*, no. 1443, August 16, 1984, 18–20.

135. "Moral y medios de comunicación," *Criterio*, March 10, 1983, 61–62; "Temas de actualidad en una conversación con Mons. Storni," *Boletín Informativo AICA*, no. 1518, January 23, 1986, 6–7.

136. *AICA Doc. 150: El pudor, defensa de la intimidad humana. Suplemento del Boletín Informativo AICA*, no. 1462, December 27, 1984, 9; "La moral en humoradas" and "Monseñor Di Stéfano: No sostener más el mercado del diablo," *Boletín Informativo AICA*, no. 1426, April 19, 1984, 9–12, 15.

137. "Por la libertad, contra la pornografía," *Boletín Informativo AICA*, no. 1506, October 31, 1985, 14.

138. "Opinan los obispos sobre temas de actualidad," *Boletín de la Liga por la Decencia*, no. 100, April 1985, 1; "La iglesia y el rumbo del país," *Boletín de la Liga por la Decencia*, no. 126, August 1987, 3; "La cultura en libertad," *Criterio*, July 26, 1984, 365.

139. "Destape," *Esquiú*, November 22, 1981, 11.

140. "Agresión de la pornografía en los medios de comunicación," *Boletín Informativo AICA*, no. 1430, May 17, 1984, 4–5; "Moral y medios de comunicación," *Criterio*, March 10, 1983, 61–62.

141. "Ataques a la religión," *Boletín de la Liga por la Decencia*, no. 107, November 1985, 1.

142. "Decadencia moral," *Boletín de la Liga por la Decencia*, no. 110, March 1986, 1;

"Denuncian los obispos el avance de la pornografía," *Boletín de la Liga por la Decencia*, no. 97, December 1984, 1.

143. "¿Estamos sufriendo el castigo?" *Boletín de la Liga por la Decencia*, no. 101, May 1985, 1.

144. "Se proyecta pasar por TV películas inaceptables," *Boletín Informativo de la AICA*, no. 1448–9, September 27, 1984, 14.

145. "Reflexión pastoral: Ante el auspicio oficial de la pornografía," *Boletín de la Liga por la Decencia*, no. 88, March 1984, 2; "El triunfo de la pornografía," *Boletín de la Liga por la Decencia*, no. 89, April 1984, 1. Predictably, when controversial film censor Miguel Paulino Tato passed away in 1986, the Liga por la Decencia celebrated him as a "courageous soldier," concluding that "as time passes, his legend grows greater." "Nos deja un valiente," *Boletín de la Liga por la Decencia*, no. 112, May 1986, 2. For an analysis of the relationship between Alfonsín's government and the church, see Mariano Fabris, *Iglesia y democracia: Avatares de la jerarquía católica en la Argentina post autoritaria (1983–1989)* (Rosario: Prohistoria Ediciones, 2001), and Juan Cruz Esquivel, *Detrás de los muros: La Iglesia católica en los tiempos de Alfonsín y Menem (1983–1989)* (Buenos Aires: UNQUI, 2004).

146. "Censura," *Boletín de la Liga por la Decencia*, no. 95, October 1984, 3.

147. "La pornografía conduce a la desintegración social," *Boletín Informativo AICA*, no. 1411, January 5, 1984, 8.

148. "La provincia de San Juan en lucha contra la pornografía," *AICA Doc. 146, Suplemento del Boletín Informativo AICA*, no. 1455, November 8, 1984.

149. "Pornoshow," *Boletín de la Liga por la Decencia*, no. 96, November 1984, 2; "Chevalier," *Boletín de la Liga por la Decencia*, no. 130, December 1987, 2; "Fotos obscenas," *Boletín de la Liga por la Decencia*, no. 141, December 1988, 1.

150. "Denuncian un film brasilero," *Boletín Informativo AICA*, no. 1451–52, October 18, 1984, 23.

151. "El placer de poder hacer esta revista," *Sex Humor*, February 1985, 5.

152. "Prisión para pornógrafos," *Boletín de la AICA*, no. 1428, May 3, 1984, 17–18.

153. *Esquiú Color*, July 13–19, 1986, 7, quoted in Fabris, *Iglesia y democracia*, 145.

154. "Contra la pornografía," *Boletín de la Liga por la Decencia*, no. 94, September 1984, 4; "Rosario contra la pornografía, ante la Catedral metropolitana," *Boletín de la Liga por la Decencia*, no. 100; April 1985, 2–3; "Por una vida más humana," *Boletín de la Liga por la Decencia*, no. 105, September 1985, 1.

155. On the conflicts between the state and the church in the return to democracy, see Htun, *Sex and the State*.

156. Guillermo O'Donnell, "On the Fruitful Convergences of Hirschman's *Exit, Voice, and Loyalty* and *Shifting Involvements*: Reflections from the Recent Argentine Experience," in *Counterpoints*, 63–79; Carassai, *The Argentine Silent Majority*.

157. "Se produjo la primera reacción contra el destape," *La Razón*, December 29, 1983, 5.

158. Sex ad, *Adultos*, October 30–November 19, 1984, 75; "El negocio de todos," *Adultos*, August 20–September 9, 1985, 3.

159. "Acerca del último tango," *Boletín de la Liga por la Decencia*, no. 97, December 1984, 3; "Dos importantes ordenanzas," *Boletín de la Liga por la Decencia*, no. 108, December 1985, 1; "Prisión preventiva para un exhibidor cinematográfico," *Boletín de la Liga por la Decencia*, no. 111, April 1986, 2.

160. "Eroticón," *Boletín de la Liga por la Decencia*, no. 101, May 1985, 5; "Secuestro de revistas pornográficas," *Boletín Informativo AICA*, no. 1426, April 19, 1984, 13.

161. "La censura ha muerto pero goza de buena salud," *Sex Humor*, December 1984, 5; "Por la libertad contra la pornografía," *Boletín de la Liga por la Decencia*, no. 107, November 1985, 3.

162. "Informe especial: Destape," *Esquiú*, November 22, 1981, 11.

163. "Y el destape llegó a la pantalla," *La Semana*, September 5, 1985, 32.

164. "Corporación de Abogados Católicos: Juicio a la pornografía," *Boletín de la AICA*, no. 1423–424, April 5, 1984, 5–6; "El pudor al poder y la anormalidad de los normales," *Sex Humor*, January 1985, 5.

165. "Esa moral no es nada moral y esa libertad no es nada libre," *Eroticón*, September 1984, 50–53; "El sexo en Argentina," *El Porteño*, November 1983, 8–13.

## CHAPTER 2. A REAL CHALLENGE TO TRADITIONAL SEXUAL CULTURE?

1. Laura Mulvey, "Visual Pleasure and Narrative Cinema," in *Feminism and Film*, ed. E. Ann Kaplan (New York: Oxford University Press, 2000), 40.

2. For a history of women's magazines in twentieth-century Argentina, see Paula Bontempo, "Para Ti: Una revista moderna para una mujer moderna, 1922–1935," *Estudios Sociales* 41 (2001): 127–56; Isabella Cosse, "*Claudia*: La revista de la mujer moderna en la Argentina de los años sesenta (1957–1973)," *Mora* 17, no. 1 (July 2011), http://www.scielo.org.ar/scielo.php?script=sci_arttext&pid=S1853-001X2011000100007.

3. Rosalind Gill, "From Sexual Objectification to Sexual Subjectification: The Resexualization of Women's Bodies in the Media," *Feminist Media Studies* 3, no. 1 (2003): 100–105.

4. Ken Plummer, *Telling Sexual Stories: Power, Change, and Social Worlds* (London: Routledge, 1995), 3.

5. Taylor, *Disappearing Acts*, 89.

6. Manzano, *The Age of Youth in Argentina*, 193–220.

7. On the Madres the Plaza de Mayo and their public visibility see, Diana Taylor, "Making a Spectacle: The Mothers of Plaza de Mayo," *Journal of the Association for Research on Mothering* 3, no. 2 (2001): 97–109. For a general history and testimonies, see Matilde Mellibovsky, *Circle of Love over Death: Testimonies of the Mothers of Plaza de Mayo* (Willimantic, CT: Curbstone Press, 1997).

8. For an analysis of beauty as a historical and cultural construct, see Naomi Wolf, *The Beauty Myth: How Images of Beauty Are Used against Women* (New York: Harper Perennial, 2002).

9. "El negocio del destape," *Somos*, July 27, 1984, 57–61.

10. "Adriana Brodsky y el aviso de las colas," *La Semana*, December 22, 1983, 102–5; "Publicidad al desnudo," *La Semana*, September 12, 1985, 29.

11. "Cola-less: ¿cara o ceca?," *Somos*, December 21, 1984, 31; "Dejemos en paz las colas," *Mujer 10*, February 2, 1984, 65.

12. "Las colas, ¿son un invento argentino?," *La Mujer*, August 6, 1983, 6.

13. "¡Señores, la mujer no es una cosa!" *La Mujer*, June 4, 1983, 5; "Teleteatros: Hipocresías a la hora de la siesta," *El Periodista*, March 1–7, 1985, 48–49; "¿Quién dijo que la virginidad es una virtud?," *La Semana*, September 19, 1985, 47.

14. "¡Señores, la mujer no es una cosa!" *La Mujer*, June 5, 1983, 5.

15. "El sexo en la publicidad," *Sex Humor*, October 1986, 51–56; "El erotismo en la publicidad," *Sex Humor*, November 1986, 51–57.

16. Mulvey, "Visual Pleasure and Narrative Cinema," 39.

17. "El cola-less," *Shock*, February 6–12, 1985, 3.

18. "Consecuencias del destape," *Contribuciones*, December 1983, 14.

19. "No me daba cuenta que era una mercancía," *Clarín*, May 13, 2018, https://www.clarin.com/espectaculos/teatro/silvia-perez-daba-cuenta-mercancia_0_HJCocjQAG.html.

20. On Jáuregui, see Mabel Bellucci, *Orgullo: Carlos Jáuregui, una biografía política* (Buenos Aires: Emecé, 2010).

21. See, for example, "Cazadores de homosexuales en Buenos Aires: Misterio," *Shock*, June 27–July 4, 1983, 12; "Terror: Quieren exterminar a los homosexuales," *Tal Cual*, August 20, 1982, 17; "Los gays: ¿Otra vez los corren de atrás?," *Destape*, April 10, 1984, 4–5. Santiago Joaquín Insausti argues that reporting on gay murders and gays as victims in the late 1970s and early 1980s reversed an earlier sensationalist tradition of reporting on gays as amoral murderers. Santiago Joaquín Insausti, "De maricas, travestis y gays: Derivas identitarias en Buenos Aires (1966–1989)," PhD diss., School of Social Sciences, Universidad de Buenos Aires, 2016, 183.

22. See, for example, "Así es el submundo gay," *Shock*, March 28–April 4, 1984, 3–6; "Los homosexuales alteran el orden social y eso es un grave delito," *Destape*, July 3, 1984, 4–5; "Mi hijo es homosexual ¿Y qué?," *Libre*, January 10, 1984, 59–81; "Nadie puede estar contra los gays," *Libre*, June 19, 1984, 67–74. Carlos Jáuregui, *La homosexualidad en la Argentina* (Buenos Aires: Tarso, 1987), 121–26. Reporting on transvestites, for example, was quite infrequent, yet this is the only nonheteronormative identity beyond gays that had a minimal presence in the media.

23. See, for example, "Ser gay en la Argentina," *El Periodista*, June 17, 1988, 15–20; "Identidad y conducta sexual," *El Porteño*, March 1985, 82.

24. "El riesgo de ser homosexual en la Argentina," *Siete Días*, May 23–29, 1984, 42–53.

25. "Los homosexuales de la Argentina," *Ahora*, February 21, 1985, 20–21.

26. "Editorial," *Boletín de la CHA* 8, September 1985, 1.

27. "SIDA: En la Argentina hay 21 víctimas fatales," *Semanario*, August 14, 1985, 2–3; "El Sida en la Argentina," *Clarín*, August 16, 1985, 34–35; "La peste rosa en la Argentina," *La Semana*, April 11, 1985, 3–7; "Mal uso de los medios," *Boletín de la CHA* 7, August 1985, 16.

28. Quoted in Osvaldo Bazán, *Historia de la homosexualidad en Argentina: De la Conquista de América al siglo XXI* (Buenos Aires: Marea, 2004), 234.

29. "Sobre ciertas libertades," *Boletín de la CHA* 11, January–April 1986, 10–11, quotation on 10. See also "Otra nota, otro error," *Boletín de la CHA* 12, May 1986, 16–17; "Eroticón o la revolución," *Vamos a andar* 2, October 1986, 3.

30. "Los medios y nosotros," *Boletín de la CHA* 8, September 1985, 14–15.

31. "Editorial," *Mujer 10*, January 31, 1984, 3.

32. "Mujer contra mujer," *La Prensa*, December 1, 1989, 17. See also "Contra natura," *La Opinión* (Pergamino), November 19, 1989, 8. Mihanovich's songs "Puerto Pollensa" (1982), written by singer and composer Marilina Ross, and "Soy lo que soy" (1984), a version of "I Am What I Am," a song originally introduced in the Broadway musical *La Cage aux Folles*, became hymns of the Argentine gay movement.

33. For a general analysis of lesbian characters in destape films, see Gustavo Blázquez, "El amor de l@s rar@s: Cine y homosexualidad durante la década de 1980 en Argentina," *Fotocinema* 15 (2017), http://www.revistas.uma.es/index.php/fotocinema/article/view/3500/3208.

34. For a general analysis of both films, see Ricardo Rodríguez Pereyra, "Adiós Roberto y Otra historia de amor: Gays en democracia," in *Otras historias de amor: Gays, lesbianas y travestis en el cine argentino*, ed. Adrián Melo (Buenos Aires: Ediciones Lea, 2008), 253–79, and Blázquez, "El amor de l@s rar@s."

35. Quoted in Raúl Manrupe and María Alejandra Portela, *Un diccionario de films argentinos* (Buenos Aires: Corregidor, 1995), 435; "Otra historia de amor: Una historia de libertad y dignidad," *Diferentes*, June 4, 1986, 14–15.

36. "Un director presenta sus quejas," *Página/12*, February 26, 1988, 27.

37. Pablo Sirvén argues that *Amo y señor*, the classic telenovela of the destape and one of the first shows to introduce sexual content, originally had a gay character, but pressures from the Comité Federal de Radiodifusión forced the creator to rapidly turn him into a womanizer. Pablo Sirvén, *Quién te ha visto y quién TV: Historia informal de la televisión argentina* (Buenos Aires: Ediciones de la Flor, 1998), 256.

38. "Antes nos negaban, ahora nos ridiculizan," *Boletín de la CHA* 7, August 1985, 4–5, quotation on 4.

39. *Groncho* is Argentine slang for a bum, a low-class, tacky individual.

40. "En mis elencos siempre incluyo homosexuales por la simple razón que ellos también componen la sociedad," *Libre*, June 19, 1984, 78–80.

41. "¿Argentinas siglo 19 o siglo 21?," *La Semana*, June 23, 1983, 75.

42. "¿Argentinas siglo 19 o siglo 21?"

43. *Milanesas* are breaded meat fillets.

44. For a historical overview of these subjects, see Marisa Miranda, *Controlar lo incontrolable: Una historia de la sexualidad en la Argentina* (Buenos Aires: Biblos, 2011), and Dora Barrancos, Donna Guy, and Adriana Valobra, eds., *Moralidades y comportamientos sexuales: Argentina, 1880–2011* (Buenos Aires: Biblos, 2011).

45. On the dictatorship's vision of women as mothers, see, for example, Massera, *El camino de la democracia*, 55, and Claudia Laudano, *Las mujeres en los discursos militares: Un análisis semiótico (1976–1983)* (La Plata: Editorial de la Universidad Nacional de La Plata, 1995). See also *Vivir en pareja*, September 1981.

46. Julio Mafud, *La conducta sexual de la mujer argentina* (Buenos Aires: Distal, 1991), 61.

47. *Vivir en pareja*, September 1981.

48. "El sexo es higiene," *La Semana*, September 5, 1985, 28.

49. Author interview with Alcira Bas via Skype, July 29, 2016.

50. "¿Esto que sentí es gozar o hay algo más?," *Mujer 10*, July 3, 1984, 79–81.

51. "Punto G. La zona del placer total," *Shock*, March 19–April 4, 1984, 33–35.

52. "El clítoris," *Mujer 10*, April 10, 1984, 6–9; "Para Vos," *Sex Humor*, December 1985; "Orgasmar es un nuevo verbo," *Sex Humor*, November 1986, 68–69.

53. Thomas Maier, *Masters of Sex: The Life and Times of William Masters and Virginia Johnson, the Couple Who Taught America How to Love* (New York: Basic Books, 2013), 175.

54. See, for example, "El clítoris" and "Estoy embarazada y tengo una espléndida vida sexual," *Mujer 10*, April 10, 1984, 6–9, 48–49; "El orgasmo total," *Mujer 10*, November 15, 1983, 56–57; and "En el punto G está el secreto del orgasmo," *Mujer 10*, August 23, 1983, 56–57.

55. Unsurprisingly, the Ente de Calificación Cinematográfica (ECC, Board of Film Ratings) vetoed the script in the early 1980s and requested sixty changes for approval. Jorge Asís, who had cowritten the script with director Héctor Olivera, decided to abandon the project until the end of the dictatorship, when it came to fruition in collaboration with director Antonio Ottone. Manrupe and Portela, *Un diccionario de films argentinos II, 1996–2002*, 271.

56. "¿Es usted democrática consigo mismo?," *Mujer 10*, March 27, 1984, 56.

57. "Sí a la maternidad, sí al placer," *Mujer 10*, May 15, 1984, 7. See also "Mujer," *Mujer 10*, July 15, 1983, 2.

58. "¿Por qué él se asusta cuando me libero en la cama?," *Mujer 10*, August 7, 1984, 78–81.

59. See, for example, *Mujer 10* ads in *Libre*, February 28, 1984, 37, and March 6, 1984, 75.

60. "Revistas femeninas: El enemigo de las mujeres," *alfonsina*, January 12, 1984, 7. For a similar assessment on *Mujer 10*, see also "Revistas femeninas: Fiestas de disfraces," *El Porteño*, June 1987, 66–68.

61. "Sí a la maternidad, sí al placer," *Mujer 10*, May 15, 1984, 6–9.

62. "Deporte y farándula: Una maratón de amor y sexo," *Libre*, February 28, 1984, 18–25. See also "Las costumbres sexuales de los famosos," *Libre*, November 13, 1984, 94–98; "Soy gordito, pecoso y retacón pero miren con quien duermo todas las noches," *Libre*, February 12, 1985, 46–49.

63. "La vida sexual de los bañeros," *Libre*, March 6, 1984, 18–24; "El carnicero Marinaro cuenta como convence a sus clientas para cambiar carne por sexo," *Libre*, April 10, 1984, 94–98; "Las adolescentes no dejan nada sin probar," *Libre*, February 28, 1984, 78–82.

64. See, for example, in *Sex Humor*, "Las depredadoras de hombres," November 1984, 53–54; "Breve manual de táctica y estrategia del levante femenino," January 1985, 16–17; "Mujeres peligrosas," November 1986, 16–17; and "Todo ha cambiado," September 1987, 52–53.

65. Ana María Shua, *Los amores de Laurita* (Buenos Aires: Sudamericana, 1995) [1984]. For a literary analysis of Shua's novel, see Laura Beard, "Celebrating Female Sexuality from Adolescence to Maternity in Ana María Shua's *Los amores de Laurita*," in *El río de los sueños: Aproximaciones críticas a las obra de Ana María Shua*, ed. Rhonda Dahl Buhanan (Washington, DC: OEA, 2001), 35–47, and Graciela Gliemmo, "Erotismo y narración en *Los amores de Laurita*," in Buhanan, *El río de los sueños*, 49–61.

66. "Cada mujer tiene su propia sexualidad," *Adultos*, October 9–30, 1984, 94–97.

67. "¿Esto que sentí es gozar o hay algo más?," *Mujer 10*, July 3, 1984, 79–81. See also "El manual de la esposa perfecta es machista," *Mujer 10*, April 10, 1984, 17; "Tener relaciones no es hacer el amor," *Mujer 10*, February 2, 1984, 74; and "¿Se puede hacer el amor sin amor?," *Mujer 10*, September 20, 1983, 68–69.

68. "El sexo en Argentina," *El Porteño*, November 1983, 8–14, quotation on 9.

69. See, for example, "La fiera," *Sex Humor*, April 1987, 50; June 1987, 71; September 1987, 50; August 1988, 50.

70. Other important comic artists from this period were Patricia Breccia and María Alcobre. Maitena became extremely popular for her "Mujeres Alteradas," a comic strip she began creating for *Para Ti* in the early 1990s about the female world— the body, sisterhood, motherhood, love, family—and turned her into a best-selling author when she compiled her work in several volumes. Interestingly, in these works, women's sexual fulfillment and lust are virtually impossible, and sex is frequently a burden. For an analysis of Maitena's works from the 1990s and early 2000s, see Cynthia Tompkins, "Las *Mujeres alteradas* y *Superadas* de Maitena Burundarena: Feminismo 'Made in Argentina,'" *Studies in Latin American Popular Culture* 22 (2003): 35–60, and Melisa Fitch, *Side Dishes: Latin American Women, Sex, and Cultural Production* (New Brunswick, NJ: Rutgers University Press, 2009), 52–57.

71. Interview with Maitena, Buenos Aires, August 22, 2016.

72. Maitena, *Lo peor de Maitena* (Buenos Aires: Sudamericana, 2015).

73. Interview with Maitena, Buenos Aires, August 22, 2016.

74. "Publicidad al desnudo," *La Semana*, September 12, 1985, 29; "Dame otra piña," *El Periodista*, November 15–21, 1985, 25.

75. "TV Crítica," *Somos*, May 18, 1984, 80–81.

76. Carole Sheffield, "Sexual Terrorism," in *Women: A Feminist Perspective*, ed. Jo Freeman (Palo Alto, CA: Sage, 1989), 3–19.

77. For classic analyses of horror movie heroines, femmes fatales, and feminism, see Carol Clover, *Men, Women, and Chainsaws: Gender in the Modern Horror Film* (Princeton, NJ: Princeton University Press, 1992), and Mary Ann Doane, *Femmes Fatales: Feminism, Film Theory, Psychoanalysis* (London: Routledge, 1991), 2–3. For recent studies on the relation between women and violence in films, see Jacinta Reed, *The New Avengers: Feminism, Femininity, and the Rape-Revenge Cycle* (Manchester: Manchester University Press, 2000), and Hilary Neroni, *The Violent Woman: Femininity, Narrative, and Violence in Contemporary American Cinema* (Albany: State University of New York Press, 2005).

78. On the relation between womanhood and violence, see Belinda Morrisey, *When Women Kill: Questions of Agency and Subjectivity* (New York: Routledge, 2003).

79. The lack of records about the intentions of directors, producers, and screenwriters, and the impossibility of interviewing them as the majority have passed away, leaves the issue of the intended meanings and purposes of the films' creators, unfortunately, unanswered.

80. Taylor, *Disappearing Acts*, 137–82; Graziano, *Divine Violence*, 147–90.

81. For testimonies and analyses about sexual violence during the dictatorship, see Miriam Lewin and Olga Wornat, *Putas y guerrilleras* (Buenos Aires: Planeta, 2014); Analía Aucía, Florencia Barrera, Celina Berterame, Susana Chiarotti, Alejandra Paolini, and Cristina Zurutuza, *Grietas en el silencio: Una investigación sobre la violencia sexual en el marco del terrorismo de Estado* (Rosario: CLADEM, 2011); and Claudia Bacci, María Capurro Robles, Alejandra Oberti, and Susana Skura, *"Y nadie quería saber": Relatos sobre violencia contra las mujeres en el terrorismo de Estado en Argentina* (Buenos Aires: Memoria Abierta, 2012).

82. The first prison sentence for rape that was considered a particular crime against humanity during the dictatorship, that is, separate and different from torture, was handed down in Mar del Plata in 2010. On the relation between sexual violence during the dictatorship, the law, and human rights violations, see María Sonderéguer and Violeta Correa, "Género y violencias en el terrorismo de Estado en Argentina," in *Género y poder: Violencias de género en contextos de represión política y conflictos armados*, ed. María Sonderéguer (Buenos Aires: Universidad Nacional de Quilmes Editorial, 2012), 289–302; María Sondereguer and Violeta Correa, eds., *Cuaderno de Trabajo: Análisis de la relación entre violencia sexual, tortura y violación de los derechos humanos* (Buenos Aires: Universidad Nacional de Quilmes, 2008); Elizabeth Jelin, "Sexual Abuse as a Crime against Humanity and the Right to Privacy," *Journal of Latin American Cultural Studies* 21, no. 2 (June 2012): 343–50; and Cecilia Macón, *Sexual Violence in the Argentinean Crimes against Humanity Trials* (Lanham, MD: Lexington Books, 2016).

83. Eric Schaefer, "Dirty Little Secrets: Scholars, Archivists, and Dirty Movies," *The Moving Image* 5, no. 2 (Fall 2005): 79–105, quotation on 91.

84. For an analysis of the representations and narratives about the detention centers in the 1980s cinema, see Lior Zylberman, "Estrategias narrativas de un cine post dictatorial," *Revista Afuera: Estudios de crítica cultural* 13, September 2013, http://www.revistaafuera.com/articulo.php?id=280&nro=13.

85. For a general analysis of the *policial post-proceso*, see Elena Goity and David Oubiña, "El policial argentino," in *Cine argentino en democracia, 1983/1993*, ed. Claudio España (Buenos Aires: Fondo Nacional de las Artes, 1994), 208–29.

86. Tina Rosenberg, "Foreword," in Munú Actis, Cristina Aldini, Liliana Gardella, Miriam Lewin, and Elisa Tokar, *That Inferno: Conversations of Five Women Survivors of an Argentine Torture Camp* (Nashville, TN: Vanderbilt University Press, 2006), xi.

87. Actis, Aldini, Gardella, Lewin, and Tokar, *That Inferno*, 152–209.

88. Laura Kipnis, *Bound and Gagged: Pornography and the Politics of Fantasy in America* (Durham, NC: Duke University Press, 1999), 164.

89. "La tensión del destape," *Salimos*, August 27, 1982, 13.

90. Although sections like erotic fiction and photos from readers may have include published stories by professional columnists and writers, as well as pictures of models instead of ordinary people, testimonies from journalists and editors confirm the veracity of readers' contributions.

91. "Una cosa seria . . ." *Adultos*, August 28–September 16, 1984, 3.

92. See, for example, "Sí, el machismo existe y es internacional," *La Mujer*, October 1, 1983, 6–7; "El sexo en la familia, ¿un contrasentido?," *La Mujer*, September 17, 1983, 2.

93. McNair, *Striptease Culture*, 88–108; Michel Foucault, *The History of Sexuality*, vol. 1 (New York: Vintage Books, 1990), 63.

94. In contrast to the horizontal voice that flourished in democracy, O'Donnell argued that the dictatorship, which silenced most voices, privileged a vertical voice that allowed a minority to communicate with the authorities, mainly as supplicants. O'Donnell, "On the Fruitful Convergences of Hirschman's *Exit, Voice, and Loyalty* and *Shifting Involvements*," in *Counterpoints*, 63–80.

95. Isabella Cosse, "Cultura y sexualidad en la Argentina de los sesenta: Usos y resignificaciones de la experiencia transnacional," *Estudios Interdisciplinarios de América Latina y el Caribe* 17, no. 1 (2006): 39–60.

96. Gindin, Gindin, Ramos, Llovet, Camilucci, Helién, Pietrasanta, Kaplan, Huguet, and Frontera, *1ra Encuesta sobre Sexualidad y Pareja*, 39.

97. Gindin, Gindin, Ramos, Llovet, Camilucci, Helién, Pietrasanta, Kaplan, Huguet, and Frontera, *1ra Encuesta sobre Sexualidad y Pareja*, 40.

98. See, for example, "Te quiero pero no tanto," *Somos*, October 26, 1984, 101–2; "Encuesta: La Mujer hoy," *Mujer 10*, November 1, 1983, 70–73; "Las argentinas y la pornografía," *La Mujer: Suplemento de Tiempo Argentino*, December 17, 1983, 4; "Encuesta: La gente es cada vez menos careta," *El Porteño*, September 1984, 16–19; and "Resultados de la primera encuesta sobre sexualidad femenina," *Sex Humor*, September 1986, 36–38.

99. Gindin, Gindin, Ramos, Llovet, Camilucci, Helién, Pietrasanta, Kaplan, Huguet, and Frontera, *1ra Encuesta sobre Sexualidad y Pareja*. Phone interview with Luis Frontera, September 9, 2016. Frontera was the coordinator of "Investigación Especial" as well as many of the surveys published in *Sex Humor*.

100. "Encuesta sobre sexualidad," *Sex Humor*, April 1986, 14.

101. "Primera encuesta de sexualidad juvenil," *Sex Humor*, August 1990, 8; "Encuesta sexualidad y pareja," *Sex Humor*, December 1986, 95–98; "El placer en la ciudad de hoy," *La Mujer: Suplemento de Tiempo Argentino*, December 15, 1984, 5.

102. See, for example, "Las argentinas y el sexo," *La Mujer*, April 30, 1983, 5, and "Las argentinas y la pornografía," *La Mujer*, December 17, 1983, 4.

103. "Qué le pasa a las mujeres argentinas con su sexo," *Sex Humor*, March 1986, 13; "Qué les pasa a las argentinas con su sexo," *Sex Humor*, June 1986, 14.

104. "La mujer, hoy," *Mujer 10*, November 1, 1983, 70–73, and November 8, 1983, 32–33.

105. "Destape convoca," *Destape*, January 10, 1984, 36.

106. See, for example, "Y fueron protagonistas," *Pareja*, July 1984, 8–10; September 1984, 7–10.

107. The section worked under the assumption that pictures had been willingly submitted by the models or with their consent. There is no archival information to determine if these "common women" could have been professional models.

108. "Sea usted protagonista," *Dar la cara en entrevista*, April 1984, 32.

109. Interview with Norberto Chab, conducted by Marcelo Raimon, Buenos Aires, September 29, 2005.

110. "Olga agradece a Entrevista," *Pareja*, July 1984, 3. Interview with Norberto Chab, conducted by Marcelo Raimon, Buenos Aires, September 29, 2005.

111. "Sres. Editores," *Dar la cara en entrevista*, July 1984, 66.

112. This is an argument based on the examination of personal ads published in *Destape* and *Pareja* during 1984–85 and 1984, respectively. In the return to democracy, *Diferentes*, which published a personal ads section, advertised itself as the "first and only gay magazine."

113. McNair, *Striptease Culture*, 11–12.

## CHAPTER 3. SEX IN DEMOCRACY

1. "El sexo en Argentina," *El Porteño*, November 1983, 8–15; "El mejor afrodisíaco sigue siendo el amor," *La Semana*, August 29, 1985, 26–27. On the dictatorship's meanings of family and their relation to morality, see Filc, *Entre el parentesco y la política*, 33–60.

2. Manzano, *The Age of Youth in Argentina*, and "Sex, Gender and the Making of the 'Enemy Within' in Cold Ward Argentina," *Journal of Latin American Studies* 47, no. 1 (2014): 1–29; María Florencia Osuna, "Políticas de la última dictadura argentina frente a la 'brecha generacional,'" *Revista Latinoamericana de Ciencias Sociales, Niñez y Juventud* 15, no. 2 (2017): 1097–1110. For Brazil, see Cowan, *Securing Sex*. For Mexico, see Jaime Pensado, *Rebel Mexico: Student Unrest and Authoritarian Political Culture during the Long Sixties* (Stanford: Stanford University Press, 2013), and Elaine Carey, *Plaza of Sacrifices: Gender, Power, and Terror in 1968 Mexico* (Albuquerque: University of New Mexico Press, 2005). For the United States, see David Johnson, *The Lavender Scare: Cold Ward Persecution of Gays and Lesbians in the Federal Government* (Chicago: University of Chicago Press, 2004), and Elaine Tyler May, *Homeward Bound: American Families in the Cold War Era* (New York: Basic Books, 2017).

3. Manzano, *The Age of Youth in Argentina*, 205–6, 216; Oberti, *Las revolucionarias*, 33–55; Isabella Cosse, "Infidelities: Morality, Revolution, and Sexuality in Left-Wing Guerrilla Organizations in 1960s and 1970s Argentina," *Journal of the History of Sexuality* 23, no. 3 (September 2014): 415–50; Karina Felitti, "Poner el cuerpo: Género y sexualidad en la política revolucionaria de Argentina en las décadas de los sesenta y setenta," in *Political and Social Movements during the Sixties and Seventies in the Americas and Europe*, ed. Avital Bloch (Colima, Mexico: Universidad de Colima, 2010), 69–93; Carnovale, *Los combatientes*, 250–60.

4. Marta Diana, *Mujeres guerrilleras: Sus testimonios en la militancia de los setenta* (Buenos Aires: Booket, 2006); Martínez, *Género, política y revolución en los años setenta*, 91–105.

5. Cosse, *Pareja, sexualidad y familia en los años sesenta*, 103–4.

6. Rubin, "Thinking Sex," 11.

7. "Doña María y el destape," *Mujer 10*, December 20, 1983, 38.

8. "El mejor afrodisíaco sigue siendo el amor," *La Semana*, August 29, 1985, 26–27.

9. "¿Esto que sentí es gozar o hay algo más?" *Mujer 10*, July 3, 1974, 79–78.

10. "El erotismo es un estimulante sano y útil," *La Semana*, September 5, 1985, 26–27; "Destape, pornografía y democracia," *El Observador*, December 2, 1983, 62.

11. Ken Plummer, "Representing Sexualities in the Media," *Sexualities* 6, nos. 3–4 (2003): 275.

12. "Resultados de la primera encuesta de sexualidad femenina," *Sex Humor*, September 1986, 36–38.

13. "Las argentinas y el sexo," *La Semana*, September 5, 1985, 23; "La mujer, hoy," *Mujer 10*, November 1, 1983, 70–73, see esp. 72.

14. "El erotismo es un estimulante sano y útil," *La Semana*, September 5, 1985, 26–27, quotation on 27.

15. "¿Revolución sexual? No exageremos, por favor," *La Semana*, September 5, 1985, 28; "El destape es más verbal que real," *La Semana*, September 12, 1985; "La sexualidad femenina," *Adultos*, July 30–August 19, 1985, 32–41.

16. "¿Quién dijo que la virginidad es una virtud?" *La Semana*, September 19, 1985, 47.

17. "El destape es más verbal que real," *La Semana*, September 12, 1985, 26–27.

18. "Investigación Especial: El orgasmo," *Sex Humor*, April 1986, 46–53, quotation on 50.

19. "Las argentinas y el sexo," *La Semana*, September 5, 1985, 23; "La mujer, hoy," *Mujer 10*, November 1, 1983, 70–73, see esp. 72.

20. "El destape ahuyenta la libido," *Sex Humor*, August 1985, 58–59, quotation on 59.

21. Haydée Jofre Barroso, *Las argentinas y el amor* (Buenos Aires: Galerna, 1985), 51–54.

22. "Las argentinas y el sexo," *La Mujer*, April 30, 1983, 5.

23. "Las argentinas y el sexo: Tercera Parte," *La Mujer*, May 14, 1983, 6; "¿Somos buenos amantes los argentinos?," *Hombre*, February 1984, 52–62, see esp. 53.

24. "La mujer, hoy," *Mujer 10*, November 8, 1983, 70–73; Mafud, *La conducta sexual de la mujer argentina*, 203; *Vivir en Pareja*, September 1981.

25. Mafud, *La conducta sexual de la mujer argentina*, 19–20.

26. "El sexo se ha transformado en un objeto de consumo," *Página/12*, January 25, 1988, 17; Gindin, Gindin, Ramos, Llovet, Camilucci, Helién, Pietrasanta, Kaplan, Huguet, and Frontera, *1ra Encuesta sobre sexualidad y pareja*, 42–43; Julio Mafud, *La conducta sexual de los argentinos* (Buenos Aires: Distal, 1988), 35, 38.

27. "¿Somos buenos amantes los argentinos?," *Hombre*, February 1984, 52–62.

28. "La democracia trae cambios en las parejas," *Mujer 10*, September 6, 1983, 12–13.

29. "La democracia trae cambios en las parejas."

30. "A las parejas argentinas: ¿Qué les pasó en los 'últimos años'?," *La Mujer*, February 18, 1984, 7.

31. Diana Maffia, "Normalidad y alteración sexual en los 50: El primer departamento sexológico," in Barrancos, Guy, and Valobra, *Moralidades y comportamientos sexuales, Argentina, 1880–2011*, 217–31. On the medical study of "deviant sexualities," see also Jorge Salessi, *Médicos, maleantes y maricas: Higiene, criminología y homosexualidad en la construcción de la nación argentina (Buenos Aires, 1871–1914)* (Rosario: Beatriz Viterbo, 1995), and Patricio Simonetto, "Del consultorio a la cama: Discurso, cultura visual, erótica y sexología en la Argentina," *Sexualidad, salud y sociedad*, no. 22 (April 2016): 103–28.

32. Giberti and Escardó did not exclusively focus on sexuality and the sexual education of children in the family, but these were key factors in the new style of parenting they championed and that advocated the psychologization of childcare. On Giberti and Escardó, see Cosse, "Cultura y sexualidad en la Argentina de los sesenta," 39–60, and "Argentine Mothers and Fathers and the New Psychological Paradigm of Child-Rearing (1958–1973)," *Journal of Family History* 35, no. 2 (2010): 180–202; Mariano Plotkin, *Freud in the Pampas: The Emergence and Development of a Psychoanalytic Culture in Argentina* (Stanford, CA: Stanford University Press, 2001), 108–14.

33. Mónica Gogna, Daniel Jones, and Inés Ibarlucía, *Sexualidad, Ciencia y Profesión en América Latina: El campo de la sexología en la Argentina* (Rio de Janeiro: CEPESC, 2011), 35; Catalina Trebisacce, "Una batalla sexual en los setenta: Las feministas y los militantes homosexuales apostando a otra economía de placeres," in Débora D'Antonio, *Deseo y represión*, 43–61; author phone interview with Isabel Boschi, July 23, 2016.

34. IV Congreso Argentino de Sexología (Brochure), CEDINCI Archive, Fondo Sara Torre FA-96, Box 47.

35. On psychoanalysis and sexuality in Argentina, see Plotkin, *Freud in the Pampas*, 117–18.

36. Author interviews with Adrián Sapetti, July 17, 2016 (Skype); Mirta Granero, August 17, 2016 (Rosario); and León Roberto Gindin, August 29, 2016 (Buenos Aires).

37. "Investigación Especial: El sexo nacional," *Sex Humor*, March 1986, 43–47, quotation on 47.

38. "¿Para qué sirve la sexología?" *La Mujer*, September 15, 1984, 4–5.

39. World Health Organization, *Education and Treatment in Human Sexuality: The Training of Health Professionals: Report of a WHO Meeting* (Geneva: World Health Organization, 1975), 6.

40. Laura Caldiz and León Roberto Gindin, "Ética y salud sexual," *Revista Latinoamericana de Sexología* 2, no. 1 (1987): 81–88.

41. "El erotismo es un estimulante sano y útil," *La Semana*, September 5, 1985, 26–27; "El destape de la privacidad," *Somos*, May 18, 1984, 79.

42. Quoted in Hilda Rais, "Homosexualidad," paper presented at the Second Multidisciplinary Symposium on Human Sexuality, Buenos Aires, August 1987, 5, CEDINCI Archive, Lugar de Mujer Collection, Box 12.

43. For an analysis of Argentine exiles during the dictatorship, see, for example, Silvina Jensen, *Los exiliados: La lucha por los derechos humanos durante la dictadura*

*militar* (Buenos Aires: Sudamericana, 2010), and Marina Franco, *El exilio: Argentinos en Francia durante la dictadura* (Buenos Aires: Siglo Veintiuno, 2008).

44. Author interviews with Laura Caldiz, July 6, 2016 (Skype), and August 25, 2016 (Buenos Aires).

45. Janice Irvine, *Disorders of Desire: Sexuality and Gender in Modern American Sexology* (Philadelphia: Temple University Press, 2005), 75–96.

46. Gindin traveled to the United States to continue his education a couple years later.

47. Author interviews with Laura Caldiz, July 6, 2016 (Skype), and August 25, 2016 (Buenos Aires); León Roberto Gindin, July 28, 2016 (Skype), and August 29, 2016 (Buenos Aires); and Sara Torres, May 7, 2015 (Buenos Aires).

48. Author interviews with Laura Caldiz, August 25, 2016 (Buenos Aires); León Roberto Gindin, July 28, 2016 (Skype); and Mirta Granero, August 17, 2016 (Rosario). For a detailed history of Sexarama, see Irvine, *Disorders of Desire*, 93–96.

49. Gogna, Jones, and Ibarlucía, *Sexualidad, Ciencia y Profesión en América Latina*, 111. Author interviews with Laura Caldiz, August 25, 2016 (Buenos Aires), and León Roberto Gindin, July 28, 2016 (Skype). On cognitive behavior therapy, see Judith Beck, *Cognitive Behavior Therapy: Basics and Beyond* (New York: Guilford Press, 2012).

50. On the rise and importance of psychoanalytical culture in Argentina, see Plotkin, *Freud in the Pampas*, and *Argentina on the Couch: Psychiatry, State, and Society, 1880 to the Present* (Albuquerque: University of New Mexico Press, 2003).

51. Additionally, Kaplan reformulated the sexual response cycle conceived by Masters and Johnson in four stages (excitement, plateau, orgasmic, and resolution phases) by including desire to better understand and treat disorders of sexual desire. Irvine, *Disorders of Desire*, 152–57.

52. Author interviews with Laura Caldiz, July 6, 2016 (Skype), and Mirta Granero, August 17, 2016 (Rosario). Gogna, Jones, and Ibarlucía, *Sexualidad, Ciencia y Profesión en América Latina*. "Terapia sexual: Curso de posgrado," personal archive of Mirta Granero.

53. Andrés Flores Colombino, "Historia y evolución de la sexología clínica en Latinoamérica," Sociedad Uruguaya de Sexología, n.d., http://www.susuruguay.org/index.php/articulos/91-historia-y-evolucion-de-la-sexologia-clinica-en-latinoamerica-i.

54. Andrés Flores Colombino, "La enseñanza de la sexología en Latinoamérica," *Revista Latinoamericana de Sexología* 1, no. 1 (1986): 113–32.

55. Author interview with Walter Barbato, August 16, 2016 (Rosario). See also "La sexualidad femenina," *Adultos*, July 30–August 19, 1985, 32–41, see esp. 37.

56. "Nuestros padres, los ginecólogos," *El Porteño*, November 1985, 50–53, quotation on 52.

57. Author interview with Walter Barbato, August 16, 2016 (Rosario). "Investigación Especial: La Sexología," *Sex Humor*, January 1987, 40–44.

58. AASH, Curso introductorio a la sexualidad humana: Temario (Seminar Program), CEDINCI Archive, Fondo Sara Torre FA-96, Box 47.

59. "Investigación Especial: El negocio de la sexología," *Sex Humor*, March 1986; "La sexualidad femenina," *Adultos*, July 30–August 19, 1985, 32–41, see esp. 35.

60. "¿Qué hacen los argentinos en la cama?," *Somos*, May 18, 1988, 26–28, see esp. 28.

61. "Desde candorosas propuestas de amor hasta cochinadas indecentes, de todo se escribe en las paredes de Buenos Aires," *Libre*, September 15, 1987, 26.

62. "Cuando la sexualidad se cuela en las calles de Buenos Aires, *Página/12*, October 18, 1988, 17.

63. "El sexo en Argentina," *El Porteño*, November 1983, 8–13, quotation on 8.

64. Author interviews with sexologists Mirta Granero, August 17, 2016 (Rosario), and Laura Caldiz, July 6, 2016 (Skype), and August 25, 2016 (Buenos Aires). "Derechos sexuales son derechos humanos," *Prensa de Mujeres*, December 1983, 13–14. See also Trebisacce, "Una batalla sexual en los setenta," 43–61.

65. Instrucciones para Grupo de enriquecimiento sexual personal femenino, Mirta Granero Personal Archive.

66. TRIS, Taller de reflexión e información en sexualidad (Syllabus), CEDINCI Archive, Fondo Sara Torre FA-96, Box 47.

67. Diana Kordon and Lucila Edelman, "Psychological Effects of Political Repression," in *Psychological Effects of Political Repression*, ed. Diana Kordon, D. M. Lagos, E. Nicoletti, and R. C. Bozzolo (Buenos Aires: Sudamericana Planeta, 1988), 33–40.

68. Author interviews with sexologists Mirta Granero, August 17, 2016 (Rosario); Laura Caldiz, July 6, 2016 (Skype), and August 25, 2016 (Buenos Aires); and María Laura Lerer, August 30, 2016 (Buenos Aires). "Las argentinas y el sexo," *La Mujer*, April 30, 1983, 5.

69. Author interviews with León Roberto Gindin, July 28, 2016 (Skype); Adrián Sapetti, July 17, 2016 (Skype); and María Luisa Lerer, July 19, 2016 (Skype), and August 30, 2016 (Buenos Aires). "Investigación Especial: La Sexología," *Sex Humor*, January 1987, 50–58; "Investigación Especial: El negocio de la sexología," *Sex Humor*, March 1986, 45–54.

70. "El negocio del destape," *Somos*, July 27, 1984, 57–61, quotation on 59.

71. Author interview with Laura Caldiz, July 6, 2016 (Skype).

72. "La nueva cara de la sexualidad," *Tiempo Argentino*, 2da Sección, January 27, 1984, 1–2.

73. In fact, in a survey published in 1985, 97 percent of all women respondents affirmed they just heard of the G-spot in the press for the very first time in the past year. "Las argentinas y el sexo (Tercera parte)," *La Semana*, September 12, 1985, 27. Author interview with Laura Caldiz, July 6, 2016 (Skype). Author interview with sexologist Mirta Granero, Rosario, August 17, 2016.

74. "¿Esto que sentí es gozar o hay algo más?" *Mujer 10*, July 3, 1984, 79–81; "¿Qué hacen los argentinos en la cama?," *Somos*, May 18, 1988, 26–28.

75. Author interview with Adrián Sapetti, July 17, 2016 (Skype).

76. María Seoane, *Amor a la argentina: Sexo, moral y política en el siglo XX* (Buenos Aires: Planeta, 2007), 329. Laura Caldiz, *Viviendo nuestra sexualidad* (Buenos Aires: Estaciones, 1986); María Luisa Lerer, *Sexualidad femenina: Mitos, realidades y el sentido de ser mujer* (Buenos Aires: Sudamericana/Planeta, 1986), and *La dulce espera de la pareja: Mitos, sexo y maternidad* (Buenos Aires: Sudamericana/Planeta, 1987); León Roberto Gindin, *La nueva sexualidad del varón* (Buenos Aires: Paidós, 1987); Adrián

Sapetti and Mario Kaplan, *La sexualidad masculina* (Buenos Aires: Galerna, 1986); Adrián Sapetti and Roberto Rosenzvaig, *Sexualidad en la pareja: Todas las preguntas, todas las respuestas* (Buenos Aires: Galerna, 1987).

77. Author interview with Mirta Granero, August 17, 2016 (Rosario).

78. "La señora best-sexo," *Para Ti*, June 26, 1986, 49–51.

79. Author interview with María Luisa Lerer, July 19, 2016 (Skype), and August 30, 2016 (Buenos Aires); Carlos Ulanovsky, Silvia Itkin, and Pablo Sirvén, *Estamos en el aire: Una historia de la televisión en la Argentina* (Buenos Aires: Planeta, 1999), 449.

80. Ulanovsky, *Estamos en el aire*, 448.

81. "La amenaza del placer," *El Periodista*, March 15–21, 1985, 48; "Comunicado," *Contribuciones* 6, no. 23 (December 1983): 6–7.

82. Author interview with Laura Caldiz, July 6, 2016 (Skype).

83. "La mujer, hoy," *Mujer* 10, November 1, 1983, 70–73, see esp. 71.

84. Author interviews with María Luisa Lerer, July 19, 2016 (Skype), and August 30, 2016 (Buenos Aires). Interestingly, while Caldiz and Gindin refrained from publicly supporting feminism, CETIS advertised its clinical services in feminist publications just like CEAS, directed by Lerer, did. See, for example, *Alternativa Feminista* 1, no. 1 (1985). CETIS's ad announced: "A satisfying female sexuality is one of our most important achievements. Let's defend it!"

85. Lerer, *Sexualidad femenina*, 31.

86. Lerer, *Sexualidad femenina*, 31.

87. Lerer, *Sexualidad femenina*, 217.

88. Lerer, *Sexualidad femenina*, 207–14.

89. Lerer, *Sexualidad femenina*, 215–17.

90. See, for example, "El sexo en la familia: ¿Un contrasentido?," *La Mujer*, September 17, 1983, 2.

91. "La señora best-sexo," *Para Ti*, June 26, 1986, 49–51.

92. Clip from *La Noticia Rebelde*, María Luisa Lerer personal archive.

93. Lerer, *Sexualidad femenina*, 35.

94. Lerer, *Sexualidad femenina*, 35.

95. "¿Para qué sirve la sexología?" *La Mujer*, September 15, 1984, 4–5; "Las mujeres debemos aceptarnos como somos," *Clarín Revista*, January 15, 1985, 3.

96. "La señora best-sexo."

97. Moreira Alves, *State and Opposition in Military Brazil*, 125–28; O'Donnell, "On the Fruitful Convergences of Hirschman's *Exit, Voice, and Loyalty* and *Shifting Involvements*: Reflections of the Recent Argentine Experience," 71–73.

## CHAPTER 4. FAMILY PLANNING, SEX EDUCATION, AND THE REBUILDING OF DEMOCRACY

1. Jorge Balán and Silvina Ramos, *La medicalización del comportamiento reproductivo: Un estudio exploratorio sobre la demanda de anticonceptivos en los sectores populares*, Documentos CEDES/29 (Buenos Aires: CEDES, 1989), 8.

2. The institution started as ARES but became ARESS in 1978 by adding "sexology" to its name. "Historia de ARESS" (unpublished précis), Mirta Granero Archive.

3. Author interviews with Walter Barbato, August 16, 2016 (Rosario), and Luis María Aller Atucha, July 13, 2016 (phone). See also "Inauguración de la sede central," *Contribuciones*, October 1982, 8–9.

4. Felitti, *La revolución de la píldora*, 123–52.

5. Felitti, *La revolución de la píldora*, 74–77. For an example of how the Peronist Right characterized and opposed family planning, see "El decálogo de la castración argentina," *Las Bases*, March 12, 1974, 24–29. For an example of the Peronist Left, see "La píldora o la bomba," *Noticias*, November 25, 1973, 7.

6. Felitti, *La revolución de la píldora*, 108–9.

7. Felitti, *La revolución de la píldora*, 131–39; "Quienes somos, que hacemos," *Contribuciones*, October 1982, 1.

8. "Inauguración de la sede central," *Contribuciones*, October 1982, 8–9.

9. República Argentina, *Boletín Oficial*, March 3, 1974, 2.

10. República Argentina, *Boletín Oficial*, February 8, 1978, 187.

11. Balán and Ramos, *La medicalización del comportamiento reproductivo*, 18.

12. Juan José Llovet and Silvina Ramos, "La planificación familiar en Argentina: Salud pública y derechos humanos," *Cuadernos Médico Sociales*, no. 38 (1986): 25–39, see esp. 25; Felitti, *La revolución de la píldora*, 148–49.

13. "Comunicado," *Contribuciones*, December 1983, 6–7; "Bienvenida democracia," *Contribuciones*, December 1983, 30; "Investigación Especial: Planificación Familiar, el momento de actuar," *Sex Humor*, April 1987, 31–36.

14. Author interview with Walter Barbato, August 16, 2016 (Rosario); Felitti, *La revolución de la píldora*, 145–50; Balán and Ramos, *La medicalización del comportamiento reproductivo*, 7–9. Quoted in Carolina Kaufmann, "Memoria de las urbanidades: Los manuales de formación moral y cívica en la dictadura," in *Historiografía y memoria colectiva: Tiempos y territorios*, ed. Cristina Godoy (Buenos Aires: Miño y Dávila, 2002), 232.

15. "Anticoncepción y pobreza," *El Periodista*, September 27–October 3, 1985, 22.

16. República Argentina, *Boletín Oficial*, March 27, 1987, 14; "Planificación familiar y educación sexual," *Contribuciones*, December 1989, 2–5. On the revocation of decree 3,938, see Susana Novick, "La posición argentina en las tres conferencias mundiales de población," *Papeles de Población* 5, no. 20 (April–June 1999): 25–67.

17. United Nations Human Rights Office of the High Commissioner, *Reproductive Rights Are Human Rights: A Handbook for National Human Rights Institutions* (New York: United Nations, 2014), 24.

18. Comisión Nacional de Políticas Familiares y de Población, "Planificación familiar y educación sexual," *Contribuciones*, December 1989, 2–5; "Editorial," *Contribuciones*, June 1987, 1.

19. "El sexo en la familia, ¿un contrasentido?," *La Mujer*, September 17, 1983, 2; Julia Debernadi, "La educación sexual en el documental institucional de los años 70 y 80," paper presented at the 10th Conference in Sociology organized by the Facultad de Ciencias Sociales, Universidad de Buenos Aires, Buenos Aires, 2013.

20. "Los embarazos no queridos y la ley de la cureta," *Sex Humor*, March 1986, 36–38.

21. Julia Pomies, "Cuando las frutillas se ponen amargas," *Contribuciones*, December 1984, 6–7; "Los ambiguos sentimientos de las frutillas con crema," *Contribuciones*, December 1984, 8–9; "El niño no deseado," *Contribuciones*, December 1984, 10–14.

22. "El grito silencioso," *Boletín de la AICA*, August 1, 1985, 7.

23. "El grito mentiroso," *El Periodista*, November 15–21, 1985, 24; "Los embarazos no queridos y la ley de la cureta," *Sex Humor*, March 1986, 36–38; Ana María Zeno, "El grito silencioso y la educación sexual," *Documentos del Centro de Estudios Sociales Rafael Barret*, no. 9 (1986): 2–3.

24. On the feminist fight for the democratization of birth control methods and the conceptualization of family planning as a human right, see *Prensa de Mujeres*, September 1983, and *La Chancleta*, June–September 1989.

25. "Creación del Comité de Mujeres Voluntarias de la AAPF," *Contribuciones*, March 1983, 14. Lack of documentation and information on the committee prevents an assessment of its actions and success.

26. Debernadi, "La educación sexual en el documental institucional de los años 70 y 80."

27. "Carta abierta a los parlamentarios argentinos," *Contribuciones*, December 1984, 3.

28. "Carta abierta a los parlamentarios argentinos."

29. "Planificación familiar en Argentina: Sus fundamentos," *Contribuciones*, December 1984, 4–5.

30. Mónica Gogna and Silvina Ramos, "El acceso a la anticoncepción: Una cuestión de derechos humanos y salud pública," *Perspectivas Bioéticas en las Américas* 1, no. 2 (1996): 134–40. Law 25,673, known as *ley de salud sexual y procreación responsable* (law of sexual health and responsible procreation), required provinces to partner with the federal government for implementation, which made the real application of the law quite unequal, as it depended in part on varying local politics and resources.

31. "Carta abierta a los parlamentarios argentinos."

32. Felitti, *La revolución de la píldora*, 153–88.

33. Asociación Argentina de Protección Familiar, *Guía de métodos argentinos* (Buenos Aires: AAPF, n.d.); Asociación Argentina de Protección Familiar, *El mejor momento para tener hijos* (Buenos Aires, n.d.); "La Iglesia Católica promueve la planificación familiar," *Contribuciones*, December 1983, 1, 10; "Perfil de la población asistida en la Clínica Central de la Asociación Argentina de Protección Familiar," *Contribuciones*, February–April 1988, 16–19.

34. "1987–1988," *Boletín Liga por la Decencia*, no. 130, December 1987, 1.

35. "Liberan la venta de anticonceptivos," *Boletín Liga por la Decencia*, no. 120, January–February 1987, 1.

36. "Anticonceptivos, control de la natalidad, métodos naturales," *Boletín Liga por la Decencia*, no. 122, April 1987, 1; "Educación sexual y planificación familiar estatal," *Boletín Liga por la Decencia*, no. 128, October 1987, 1.

37. This information was published in the section "Noticias" (News) in *Contribuciones*, which described the different activities and events of the AAPF.

38. Mujeres Metalúrgicas para la Salud, *Cuadernillo No. 2: La sexualidad y la anti-concepción* (Quilmes: c. 1985).

39. "Nuevos servicios de la AAPF," *Contribuciones*, May 1989, 38–39.

40. "Distribución de los métodos anticonceptivos," *Contribuciones*, December 1989, 31–36.

41. Gindin, Gindin, Ramos, Llovet, Camilucci, Helién, Pietrasanta, Kaplan, Huguet, and Frontera, *1ra Encuesta sobre sexualidad y pareja*, 32.

42. "Perfil de la población asistida en la Clínica Central de la Asociación Argentina de Protección Familiar."

43. Balán and Ramos, *La medicalización del comportamiento reproductivo*, 18, 21.

44. "Perfil de la población asistida en la Clínica Central de la Asociación Argentina de Protección Familiar."

45. "Perfil de las pacientes atendidas en los primeros seis meses del consultorio de planificación familiar," *Contribuciones*, December 1989, 37–38.

46. Balán and Ramos, *La medicalización del comportamiento reproductivo*, 8.

47. "Nuestros padres, los ginecólogos," *El Porteño*, November 1985, 50–53, quotation on 52.

48. "Una profesional opina sobre educación sexual y anticoncepción," *Boletín de la AICA*, March 6, 1986, 13–14.

49. "Investigación Especial: Planificación Familiar, el momento de actuar," see esp. 35.

50. Balán and Ramos, *La medicalización del comportamiento reproductivo*, 26–30.

51. Balán and Ramos, *La medicalización del comportamiento reproductivo*, 36.

52. "Investigación Especial: Planificación Familiar, el momento de actuar."

53. For sexuality in the 1960s, see Cosse, *Pareja, sexualidad y familia en los años sesenta*, and Manzano, *The Age of Youth in Argentina*, 97–122.

54. Osuna, "Políticas de la última dictadura argentina frente a la 'brecha generacional,'" 1103.

55. Quoted in Kaufmann, "Memoria de las urbanidades," 231.

56. "La moral media," *El Porteño*, September 1984, 14–19, see esp. 17; "La nueva cara de la sexualidad," *Tiempo Argentino*, 2da Sección, January 27, 1984, 1–2; Manzano, *The Age of Youth in Argentina*, 119.

57. Filc, *Entre el parentesco y la política*, 43. On youth culture during the dictatorship, see Laura Luciani, *Juventud en dictadura: Representaciones, políticas y experiencias juveniles en Rosario (1976–1983)* (La Plata: Universidad Nacional de La Plata, 2017). On youth sociability and the control of the family during the dictatorship, see O'Donnell, "On the Fruitful Convergences of Hirschman's *Exit, Voice, and Loyalty* and *Shifting Involvements*," 68–69.

58. Cecilia Braslavsky, *La juventud argentina: Informe de situación* (Buenos Aires: CEAL, 1986), 31.

59. "El destape es más verbal que real," *La Semana*, September 12, 1985, 26–27.

60. Mafud, *La conducta sexual de los argentinos*, 43.

61. Luciani, *Juventud en dictadura*, 233–35.

62. In 1996, *Laura de hoy: Una adolescente argentina*, the first book of the series, was in its ninth edition.

63. Dionisia Fontán, *Laura de hoy: Una adolescente argentina* (Buenos Aires: Galerna, 1984); Dionisia Fontán, *Laura de hoy crece* (Buenos Aires: Galerna, 1986); Dionisia Fontán, *Laura de hoy, Laura de siempre* (Buenos Aires: Galerna, 1991).

64. Author interview with Dionisia Fontán, January 13, 2017 (phone).

65. Fontán explained that she did not feel prepared or comfortable addressing sexual themes even when the social, cultural, and media context promoted them, and that she doubted the editor would have accepted it. Fontán maintained that by the late 1980s, she had gotten tired of the character and the story and was thinking about ending it, but that the event that precipitated her decision was the negative response of the editor when she told him she wanted Laura to discuss the death of María Soledad Morales, a seventeen-year-old student who was raped, tortured, and murdered in Catamarca in 1990 by a group of wealthy men, a crime that caused a media and social frenzy. Fontán discussed the editor's refusal as an example of how *La Nación* wanted to keep Laura's world as ideal and rosy as possible and how, as a consequence, sexuality, if incorporated within the narrative, would have threatened this image. Author interview with Dionisia Fontán, January 13, 2017 (phone).

66. "La nueva cara de la sexualidad," *Tiempo Argentino*, 2da Sección, January 27, 1984, 1–2.

67. Mafud, *La conducta sexual de los argentinos*, 44.

68. "La sexualidad femenina," *Adultos*, July 30–August 19, 1985, 32–41, see esp. 41.

69. Silvana Musso, Irma Recoaro de Kruger, Mónica de Sanctis, and Gloria Partemio, "Mitos sexuales en los adolescentes," paper presented at the Second Conference on Sexology of the Instituto Kinsey, Rosario, December 1988, INDESO Archive, Box Sexualidad.

70. Author interview with Luis María Aller Atucha, July 13, 2016 (phone).

71. Laudano, *Las mujeres en los discursos militares*, 26–27.

72. Felitti, *La revolución de la píldora*, 141.

73. "Historia de ARESS" (unpublished précis), Mirta Granero Archive.

74. Author interviews with Walter Barbato, August 16, 2016 (Rosario), and Mirta Granero, August 17, 2016 (Rosario).

75. Luis María Aller Atucha, "Educación sexual en Argentina: La historia que yo viví," www.educacionsexual.com.ar. Author interview with Luis María Aller Atucha, July 13, 2016 (phone). Flores Colombino, "La enseñanza de la sexología en Latinoamérica."

76. Author interview with Mirta Granero, August 17, 2016 (Rosario).

77. CRESALC, *CRESALC* (Bogotá, n.d.).

78. "Adolescencia: Un desafío para el educador," *Contribuciones*, May 1984, 1.

79. Hilda Bonaparte, "Embarazo precoz y educación sexual," *Contribuciones*, October 1982, 4–7; "Una investigación," *Contribuciones*, June 1987, 32–33.

80. "Investigación Especial: Educación y sexualidad: La escuela secundaria," *Sex Humor*, June 1987, 75–79.

81. Jorge Pailles, "Educación para la democracia," *Contribuciones*, April 1984, 8.

82. Octavio Giraldo Neira, "Educación sexual," *Contribuciones*, May 1989, 19–22, see esp. 20.

83. "Sexualidad y educación permanente," *Contribuciones*, March 1983, 1.

84. "El sexo en la familia, ¿un contrasentido?" *La Mujer*, September 17, 1983, 2.

85. Alcira Camillucci, "El placer femenino," in Gindin, Gindin, Ramos, Llovet, Camilucci, Helién, Pietrasanta, Kaplan, Huguet, and Frontera, *1ra Encuesta sobre sexualidad y pareja*, 59–62; "Encuesta: Las argentinas y el sexo: Tercera parte," *La Semana*, September 12, 1985, 27.

86. "Las argentinas y el sexo," *La Mujer*, May 14, 1983, 6.

87. "Resultados de la primera encuesta sobre sexualidad femenina," *Sex Humor*, September 1986, 36–38.

88. "La frigidez es nada más que un mito," *La Mujer*, July 9, 1983, 4.

89. Pauluzzi, a psychologist, created the film when the principal of her children's school invited her to give a talk on sex education for the students. Liliana Pauluzzi and María del Carmen Marini, "Implicancias de la educación sexual en la escuela primaria," paper presented at the Asociación Médica de Rosario 1987 Symposium on Human Sexuality, Rosario, December 1987, 7, INDESO Archive, Box Sexualidad.

90. Pauluzzi and Marini, "Implicancias de la educación sexual en la escuela primaria."

91. "Educación sexual," *Boletín de la Liga por la Decencia*, no. 140, November 1988, 2. Author interview with Mirta Granero, August 17, 2016 (Rosario). The leader of the metalworkers was Alberto Piccinini.

92. See, for example, Luis Parrilla, *¡No sé que decirle! Elementos para una educación sexual: Conversaciones con padres* (Buenos Aires: Ediciones La Aurora, 1986); Julia Pomiés and Alicia Antel, *Educación sexual (0 a 18 años)* (Buenos Aires: Ediciones Vivir, 1985).

93. Domingo Olivares, "Planificación familiar y sexualidad," *Contribuciones*, December 1984, 8–9; Luis Parrilla, "Carta abierta a los padres," *Contribuciones*, July 1980, 4–5, 8–10. On sex education in the press, see, for example, "Como hablar de sexo con un hijo pre-adolescente," *Mujer 10*, April 8, 1986, 44–45; "Como explicarles a los chicos como se hacen los chicos," *Mujer 10*, July 7, 1984, n.p. (magazine supplement); "Investigación Especial: La sexualidad adolescente," *Sex Humor*, February 1985, 41–48.

94. Plotkin, *Freud in the Pampas*, 111. On Escardó and Giberti, see also Cosse, "Argentine Mothers and Fathers and the New Psychological Paradigm of Child-Rearing (1958–1973)"; Karina Felitti, "Difundir y controlar: Iniciativas de educación sexual en los años sesenta," *Revista Argentina de Estudios de Juventud*, no. 1 (2009), http://perio.unlp.edu.ar/ojs/index.php/revistadejuventud/.

95. AAPF, *Cuaderno de Educación 5: Adolescencia* (Buenos Aires: AAPF, n.d.); Luis Parrilla, "Educación sexual del escolar: Los niños se abren al mundo," in *Sexualidad humana y relaciones personales*, ed. René Jaimes (New York: IIPF, 1978), 145–60.

96. "Anuncian un curso sobre la educación para la sexualidad," *La Capital*, May 10, 1985.

97. "Qué hacer frente al destape," *Semanario*, February 22, 1984, 21–23.

98. "La educación sexual en la familia," *Para Ti*, May 30, 1988, 70–76.

99. Juan Carlos Romi, "Consideraciones básicas sobre educación sexual," *Revista Latinoamericana de Sexología* 1, no. 2 (1986): 225–41; Luis María Aller Atucha, "Dialogando sobre sexualidad con adolescentes," *Contribuciones*, October 1982, 12–13; "La educación sexual, un tema para pensar," *La Mujer*, March 17, 1984, 3. For a specific example of teacher training, see Luis Parrilla, *Educación sexual: Manual para docentes* (Buenos Aires: Ediciones La Aurora, 1986).

100. Cecilia Alicia González, "Al que le corresponda que se calce el sayo . . . ," *Contribuciones*, December 1989, 21–24; Irma Kruger, Silvana Musso, and Nélida Nicastro, "Una experiencia en educación sexual personalizante," paper presented at the Third Conference on Sexology of the Instituto Kinsey, Rosario, December 7, 1989, INDESO Archive, Box Sexualidad.

101. Laura Airaldi, Estela Clozman, Carlos de la Torre, Patricia Gascard, Marcela Kalil, Maricel Kalil, María del Carmen Marini, and Liliana Pauluzzi, *Taller de educación sexual para educadores, Rosario, 1987*, unpublished mimeograph, INDESO Archive, Box Sexualidad.

102. Liliana Pauluzzi, ¿Qué preguntan los chicos sobre sexo? Educación sexual para padres y docentes (Rosario: Homo Sapiens, 1993), 14–18.

103. Airaldi, Clozman, de la Torre, Gascard, Kalil, Kalil, Marini, and Pauluzzi, *Taller de educación sexual para educadores, Rosario, 1987*.

104. "Enseñar a enseñar," *El Porteño*, October 1985, 67–69.

105. "Actividades," *Contribuciones*, December 1989, 14; "Epistolares," *Contribuciones*, June 1987, 52.

106. Preserving a healthy relation with the Catholic Church played no role in the decision of the government to avoid introducing sex education in schools since tensions with the church were already prevalent due to the divorce law and the government's plans to secularize the educational system. On the tensions between the Alfonsín administration and the Catholic Church regarding education, see Fabris, *Iglesia y democracia*, 179–220; Michael Burdick, *For God and Fatherland: Religion and Politics in Argentina* (Albany: State University of New York Press, 1995), 216–53. On the conflicts surrounding the divorce law, see Htun, *Sex and the State*, 78–112.

107. For a brief description of the sex education provincial laws from the 1990s and the 2000s as well as the national law 26,150, see Mario Pecheny and Mónica Petracci, *Derechos humanos y sexualidad* (Buenos Aires: CEDES, 2007), 114–25.

108. Although family planning was fully endorsed by sex educators in the 1980s, the issue had divided Latin American experts until the mid-1970s, when CRESALC fully endorsed it. Luis María Aller Atucha, Fernando José Bianco Colmenares, and Dora Magalí Rada Cadenas, "Perspectiva histórica de la educación sexual y la sexología clínica en América Latina," paper presented at the VII Latin American Conference on Sexology and Sex Education organized by FLASSES, November 1994, Havana, Cuba. Comisión Nacional de Políticas Familiares y de Población. See also "Planificación familiar y educación sexual," *Contribuciones*, December 1989, 2–5.

109. AAPF, *El mejor momento para tener hijos.*

110. Comisión Nacional de Políticas Familiares y de Población, "Planificación familiar y educación sexual," *Contribuciones*, December 1989, 2–5.

111. Adriana Clemente, "Adolescencia, un desafío para el educador: Relato de una vivencia profesional," *Contribuciones*, May 1984, 10–13; Kruger, Musso, and Nicastro, "Una experiencia en educación sexual personalizante."

112. On the relation between sex education and pleasure, see Lutz D. H. Sauerteig and Roger Davidson, "Shaping the Sexual Knowledge of the Young," in *Shaping Sexual Knowledge: A Cultural History of Sex Education in Twentieth Century Europe* (New York: Routledge, 2009), 1–15; Nancy Kendall, *The Sex Education Debates* (Chicago: University of Chicago Press, 2013); Michelle Fine, "Sexuality, Schooling, and Adolescent Females: The Missing Discourse of Desire," *Harvard Educational Review* 58, no. 1 (April 1988): 29–54.

113. "La nueva cara de la sexualidad," *Tiempo Argentino*, January 27, 1984, 1–2; "Taller de sexualidad para adolescentes," *Mujer* 10, September 27, 1983, 45.

114. Giraldo Neira, "Educación sexual," quotation on 20.

115. Liliana Szot, *Educación Sexual* (Rosario, n.p., 1989); Pauluzzi and Marini, "Implicancias de la educación sexual en la escuela primaria."

116. Giraldo Neira, "Educación sexual," 21.

117. Luis María Aller Atucha, "Dialogando sobre sexualidad con adolescentes," *Contribuciones*, October 1982, 12–13.

118. Clemente, "Adolescencia, un desafío para el educador."

119. "¿Qué es la educación sexual," *Anuario Esquiú 87/88*, 161.

120. John Paul II, *Familiaris Consortio: Apostolic Exhortation on the Role of the Christian Family in the Modern World*, November 22, 1981, http://w2.vatican.va/content/john-paul-ii/en/apost_exhortations/documents/hf_jp-ii_exh_19811122_familiaris-consortio.html.

121. "Educación sexual: Manipulaciones populacionales," *Boletín de la Liga por la Decencia*, no. 128, October 1987, 1.

122. Sacred Congregation for Catholic Education, *Educational Guidance on Human Love: Outlines for Sex Education*, November 1, 1983, http://www.vatican.va/roman_curia/congregations/ccatheduc/documents/rc_con_ccatheduc_doc_19831101_sexual-education_en.html. See also Enrique Fabbri, "Persona, sexo y fe, hoy," *Criterio*, December 22, 1983, 689–94.

123. "Algo más sobre la educación sexual," *Boletín de la Liga por la Decencia*, no. 127, September 1987, 2.

124. "Una sociedad médica alerta contra los planes de educación sexual," *Boletín de la AICA*, February 27, 1986, 3–4.

## CHAPTER 5. THE OTHER *DESTAPE*

1. For a history of feminism in the 1970s, see Centro de Encuentros Cultura y Mujer, *Feminismo por Feministas: Fragmentos para una historia del feminismo argentino, 1970–1996* (Buenos Aires: Ediciones del Centro Cultura y Mujer, 1996), 9–26; Marcela Nari, "Abrir los ojos, abrir la cabeza: El feminismo en la Argentina de los

años '70," *Feminaria* 10, no. 18–19 (1996): 15–21; Catalina Trebisacce, "Modernización y experiencia feminista en los años setenta en Argentina," in *Hilvanando historias: Mujeres y política en el pasado reciente latinoamericano*, ed. Andrea Andújar, Débora D'Antonio, Karin Grammático, and María Laura Rosa (Buenos Aires: Luxemburg, 2010), 63–81; Karina Felitti, "Traduciendo prácticas, tejiendo redes, cruzando fronteras: Itinerarios del feminismo argentino de los '70s," *Cadernos Pagu* 44 (January–June 2015): 229–260. On the FLH, see Pablo Ben and Santiago Joaquín Insausti, "Dictatorial Rule and Sexual Politics in Argentina: The Case of the Frente de Liberación Homosexual, 1967–1976," *Hispanic American Historical Review* 97, no. 2 (May 2017): 297–325. On the role and status of gay women in feminist organizations in the 1970s, see Florencia Gemetro, "Lesbianas jóvenes en los 70: Sexualidades disidentes en años de autonominación del movimiento gay-lésbico," in *Jóvenes en cuestión: Configuraciones de género y sexualidad en la cultura*, ed. Silvia Elizalde (Buenos Aires: Biblos, 2011), 59–83, and Mónica Tarducci, "Hitos de la militancia lesbofeminista de Buenos Aires (1984–1995)," in *Feminismo, lesbianismo y maternidad en Buenos Aires*, ed. Mónica Tarducci (Buenos Aires: Librería de Mujeres Editoras, 2014), 37–59.

2. Ben and Insausti, "Dictatorial Rule and Sexual Politics in Argentina," 319; Felitti, *La revolución de la píldora*, 76.

3. Manzano, *The Age of Youth in Argentina*, 217–218; Cosse, "Infidelities," 429–430; Rapisardi and Modarelli, *Fiestas, baños y exilios*, 140–173. For an assessment of the homophobia of the revolutionary Left in other parts of Latin America, see Rafael de la Dehesa, *Queering the Public Sphere in Mexico and Brazil: Sexual Rights Movements in Emerging Democracies* (Durham, NC: Duke University Press, 2010), 63–66.

4. Karina Felitti, "Sexualidad y reproducción en la agenda feminista de la segunda ola en la Argentina (1970–1986), *Estudios Sociológicos* 28, no. 84 (September–December 2010): 791–812.

5. Diane Richardson, *Rethinking Sexuality* (London: Sage, 2000), 98–115.

6. For a theoretical discussion of sexual citizenship and sexual rights, see Plummer, *Telling Sexual Stories*, 144–166, and *Intimate Citizenship: Private Decisions and Public Dialogues* (Seattle: University of Washington Press, 2003); Jeffrey Weeks, "The Sexual Citizen," *Theory, Culture, and Society* 15, nos. 3–4 (1998): 35–52; Diane Richardson, "Rethinking Sexual Citizenship," *Sociology* 51, no. 2 (2017): 208–24; Roger Raup Rios, "Sexual Rights of Gays, Lesbians, and Transgender Persons in Latin America," in Corrales and Pecheny, *The Politics of Sexuality in Latin America*, 251–58.

7. Sonia Contardi, *La imagen de la mujer en los medios de comunicación masiva: Cuadernos de Divulgación INDESO Mujer No. 2* (Rosario: INDESO, ca. 1986), 21.

8. "La tortura como pornografía," *alfonsina*, January 26, 1984, 3.

9. "¡Es que me andan sexualizando todo!" *Alternativa Feminista* 1, no. 3, September 8, 1985, 8–9.

10. The date was chosen in homage to a radio show hosted by journalist Mara Régia, *Viva María*, which denounced the violation of women's rights in Brazil for almost

a decade beginning in 1981. Claudia Laudano, "Mujeres y medios de comunicación: Notas para un debate," *Travesías* 3, no. 4 (November 1995): 11–16, 13.

11. "Los magros traseros femeninos," *Brujas* 1, no. 3, 1982, 11–12.

12. "Mujeres des-trozadas," *Alternativa Feminista* 2, no. 5, October 8, 1986, 19–23.

13. "No destapes la olla que se nos mueve el piso," *alfonsina*, January 26, 1986, 16.

14. María Inés Aldaburu, Inés Cano, Hilda Rais, and Nené Reynoso, *Diario Colectivo* (Buenos Aires: La Campana, 1982), 180.

15. "Alicia D'Amico," *Mujeres* 1, no. 3, August 1982, 25–26.

16. "Jóvenes, lindas y delgadas," *Brujas* 1, no. 1, 1982, 12–15.

17. "La mujer objeto sexual," *Muchacha* 1, no. 2, 1982, 5–6.

18. Aldaburu, Cano, Rais, and Reynoso, *Diario Colectivo*, 133.

19. "El fascismo del cuerpo," *alfonsina*, December 29, 1983, 9.

20. "Pornografía y feminismo," *El Porteño*, January 1985, 68–70, quotation on 70.

21. "Mujeres des-trozadas," and "Estados Unidos: Entre la pornografía y la censura," *Alternativa Feminista* 2, no. 5, October 8, 1986, 19–23 and 23–24; "El destape argentino: ¿Toda la vida es sueño, y los sueños, de varón?" *alfonsina*, December 15, 1983, 6–7. Andrea MacKinnon and Catharine Dworkin proposed the anti-pornography civil rights ordinance, which would have made pornography a violation of women's civil rights and allowed women harmed by pornography to sue (e.g., movie producers and distributors) for damages. Andrea Dworkin, *Pornography: Men Possessing Women* (New York: Perigee Books, 1981); Andrea Dworkin and Catharine MacKinnon, *The Reasons Why: Essays on the New Civil Rights Law Recognizing Pornography as Sex Discrimination* (New York: Women against Pornography, 1985).

22. For an analysis of *alfonsina*, see Tania Diz, "Tensiones, genealogías y feminismos en los 80: Un acercamiento a alfonsina, primer periódico de mujeres," *Mora* 17, no. 2 (2011), http://www.scielo.org.ar/scielo.php?script=sci_abstract&pid=S1853-001 X2011000200004, and Paula Bertúa and Lucía De Leone, "Estéticas de la subjetividad: Identidades textuales y visuales en el periódico argentino alfonsina (1983–1984)," *Revista Afuera: Estudios de crítica cultural* (2010), http://www.revistaafuera .com/articulo.php?id=114&nro=9.

23. "Revistas femeninas: El enemigo de las mujeres," *alfonsina*, January 12, 1984, 7.

24. "Las mujeres y el nuevo orden informativo de comunicación," *Persona* 2, no. 7, May–June 1981, 7–13.

25. "Esta cigarra canta, es periodista y tiene ambiciones políticas," *Mujer*, January 24, 1984, 90–93.

26. Carlos Ulanovsky, Silvia Itkin, and Pablo Sirvén, *Estamos en el aire: Una historia de la televisión en la Argentina* (Buenos Aires: Planeta, 1999), 433–34.

27. *Mitominas 1: Un paseo a través de los mitos: Del 7 al 30 de noviembre* (Buenos Aires: Municipalidad de la Ciudad de Buenos Aires, 1986), 2.

28. *Mitominas 3: Cóleras de América* took place in 1992. For an analysis of *Mitominas*, see María Laura Rosa, *Legados de libertad: El arte feminista en la efervescencia democrática* (Buenos Aires: Biblos, 2014).

29. *La mujer y el cine: Segundo Festival Internacional de Cine realizado por Mujeres*, Mar del Plata, March 1989, 7.

30. "María Luisa Bemberg demostró que, al menos en el cine, las mujeres son mejores que los hombres," *Libre*, December 2, 1985, 94–98.

31. Bemberg wrote scripts for three films: *Crónica de una señora* (Raúl de la Torre, 1970), *Triángulo de cuatro* (Fernando Ayala, 1975), and *El impostor* (Alejandro Maci, 1997).

32. Zuzana Pick, "An Interview with María Luisa Bemberg," *Journal of Film and Video* 44, nos. 3–4 (Fall 1992–Winter 1993): 76–82, quotation on 79.

33. Bemberg filed *Señora de nadie* and moved forward with *Momentos*, but when this project was finished, she decided to film the rejected screenplay anyway. "Pride and Prejudice: María Luisa Bemberg. Interview with Sheyla Whitaker," in *The Garden of Forking Paths: Argentine Cinema*, ed. John King and Nissa Torrents (London: British Film Institute, 1988), 115–21, quotation on 116. Lila Stantic, "El cine que compartimos," in *María Luisa Bemberg*, ed. Grupo Némenis (Buenos Aires: Museo Roca, 2005), 21–23.

34. Bemberg's last film was *De eso no se habla* (1993). For an analysis of Bemberg's complete filmography, see Clara Fontana, *María Luisa Bemberg* (Buenos Aires: Centro Editor de América Latina, 1993); John King, Sheila Whitaker, and Rosa Bosch, eds., *An Argentine Passion: María Luisa Bemberg and Her Films* (London: Verso, 2000); and Catalina Trebisacce, "Historias feministas desde la lente de María Luisa Bemberg," *Revista Nomadías* 18 (November 2013): 19–41.

35. Pick, "An Interview with María Luisa Bemberg," 78.

36. "Tripas, corazón y cabeza," *Mujer 10*, September 20, 1983, 78–81, quotation on 80.

37. An interesting exception is David William Foster, *Contemporary Argentine Cinema* (Columbia: University of Missouri Press, 1992), 14–25.

38. Pick, "An Interview with María Luisa Bemberg," 77.

39. "Camila," *Boletín de AICA*, August 16, 1984, 14; "Carta de Lectores: Camila," *Boletín de la Liga por la Decencia*, July 1984, 3.

40. "Como somos," *alfonsina*, January 12, 1984, 8–9, quotation on 8.

41. "La mirada femenina puede volverse como un boomerang," *La Mujer*, August 13, 1983, 2.

42. "Como somos," 9.

43. For an examination of the feminist press in this period, see Marcela Nari, "En busca de un pasado: Revistas, feminismo y memoria: Una historia de las revistas feministas, 1982–1997," *Feminaria* 10, no. 20 (1997): 32–40.

44. "Fervor y espíritu de trabajo en el Encuentro Nacional de Mujeres," *La Mujer*, May 29, 1986, 2. For a history of the ENM, see Amanda Alma and Paula Lorenzo, *Mujeres que se encuentran: Una recuperación histórica de los Encuentros Nacionales de Mujeres en Argentina (1986–2005)* (Buenos Aires: Feminaria Editora, 2009).

45. *Encuentro Nacional de Mujeres, 23, 24, y 25 de mayo de 1986: Centro Cultural San Martín, Buenos Aires* (Buenos Aires, 1987); "Primer Encuentro Nacional de Mujeres," *Brujas*, November 1986, 30–41; Magui Bellotti, "¿Hacia un movimiento autónomo de mujeres?, *Brujas*, November 12, 1988, 26–33; Claudia Laudano and Silvana Fernández, "IV Encuentro Nacional de Mujeres," *Brujas*, November 11, 1989, 33–38; "Tercer

Encuentro Nacional de Mujeres. Mendoza, 10–12 de junio de 1988," *Ritmo Mujer*, September 1988, 5–7; Magui Bellotti, Feminismo y movimiento de mujeres: Prácticas y discursos sobre sexualidad y lesbianismo," *Brujas*, October 2004, 36–42, see esp. 37.

46. Laudano and Fernández, "IV Encuentro Nacional de Mujeres," 36.

47. This information about the numerous activities and publications on sexuality of feminist organizations was gathered by examining published and unpublished materials in the INDESO Mujer Archive in Rosario and the CEDINCI Archive in Buenos Aires. The latter has, in the Sara Torres Collection, archive materials of Lugar de Mujer (Box 12), the CEM (Box 13), and an extensive assortment of pamphlets, flyers, and brochures of events organized and sponsored by numerous feminist organizations (Colección Folletos/Volantes). Author interview (via Skype) with Gloria Bonder, August 3, 2016.

48. "Sexualidad de la mujer," *Brujas* 1, no. 2, 1983, 5. See also Sara Torres, "Reflexiones acerca de la sin nombre," *Alternativa Feminista* 1, no. 1, March 8, 1985, 21–24, and Leonor Calvera, *El género mujer* (Buenos Aires: Editorial de Belgrano, 1982), 137–45.

49. See, for example, *La Chancleta*, June–September 1989, and "¿Hacia un movimiento autónomo de mujeres?, *Brujas*, November 12, 1988, 26–33.

50. Centro de Estudios de la Mujer, *Propuestas para el mejoramiento de la situación de la mujer argentina* (Buenos Aires: Centro de Estudios de la Mujer, 1989); *Prensa de Mujeres*, October 1983; Laudano and Fernández, "IV Encuentro Nacional de Mujeres."

51. Magui Bellotti, "Feminismo y movimiento de mujeres: Prácticas y discursos sobre sexualidad y lesbianismo," *Brujas*, October 2004, 36–42, see esp. 41.

52. Marta Fontela, "Apuntes sobre política sexual," *Brujas*, November 12, 1988, 34–39.

53. "Sexualidad: La cultura que nos imponen," *Unidas* 2, no. 3, October 1983, 52.

54. "El cuerpo de la mujer," *Persona*, March–May 1983, 20–30.

55. "Los 10 derechos sexuales inalienables de la mujer," *Brujas* 1, no. 2, c. 1983, 6–7. For a brief analysis of the meeting, see Marysa Navarro, "El primer encuentro feminista de Latinoamérica y el Caribe," in *Sociedad, subordinación y feminismo*, ed. Magdalena León (Bogotá: ACEP, 1982), 261–67.

56. INDESO Mujer, *Cuadernos de Divulgación No. 1: Convención sobre la Eliminación de Todas las Formas de Discriminación contra la Mujer* (Rosario: INDESO Mujer, ca. 1986); "Mujeres des-trozadas," *Alternativa Feminista* 2, no. 5, October 8, 1986, 19–23.

57. The celebration was promoted by the Multisectorial de la Mujer (Women's Multisectoral Association), established in 1983 by the increasing number of women's and feminist organizations. "¿Mujeres?," *Gente*, March 15, 1984, 21–24.

58. Mabel Bellucci, *Historia de una desobediencia: Aborto y feminismo* (Buenos Aires: Capital Intelectual, 2014), 142–49.

59. "María Elena Oddone: Devenir feminista," *alfonsina*, January 26, 1984, 10–11, quotation on 11.

60. "La maternidad: Instrumento ideológico," *Persona*, October 1983, 7–12; "El matricentrismo y la veneración a la madre," *Persona*, July–August 1981, 2–8; Adrianne Rich, *Of Woman Born: Motherhood as Experience and Institution* (New York: Norton, 1976). For an interpretation of Rich's work, see Andrea O'Reilly, ed., *From*

*Motherhood to Mothering: The Legacy of Adrianne Rich's* Of Woman Born (New York: State University of New York Press, 2004).

61. María Elena Oddone, *La pasión por la libertad: Memorias de una feminista* (Asunción, Paraguay: Colihué-Mimbipá, 2001), 42, 48.

62. "¿Mujeres?" *Gente*, March 15, 1984, 21–24.

63. In contrast, "true" womanhood is reaffirmed in the articles "Mujeres (I)" and "Mujeres (II)," which are devoted to the first woman to become the orchestra director of the Colón Theater and the first to head the traffic department in the city of Buenos Aires. *Gente*, March 15, 1984, 17–20.

64. "Carta abierta de mujer a mujer," *Gente*, March 15, 1984, 28–29.

65. "Revista Gente: ¡Qué Gente!," *alfonsina*, April 5, 1985, 11.

66. Oddone, *La pasión por la libertad*, 177.

67. Magui Bellotti, *Cuadernos Feministas ATEM No. 34. 1984/1989: El feminismo y el movimiento de mujeres* (Buenos Aires: ATEM, 1989), 3–5.

68. *La Chancleta*, no. 3, November 1985; *La Chancleta*, no. 7, March 1987; *La Chancleta*, no. 18, November 1989; "Materiales de educación popular para la prevención de la violencia contra la mujer: Juego de tarjetas," unpublished materials produced by Lugar de Mujer for educational purposes and work with reflection groups, INDESO Mujer Archive, Box: Violencia; Lugar de Mujer, *Cartilla No. 1 para mujeres golpeadas* (Buenos Aires, 1988), unpublished document, CEDINCI Archive, Sara Torre Collection, Box 12: Lugar de Mujer; María Elena Oddone, *48 artículos seleccionados de la columna semanal de María Elena Oddone: Movimiento Feminista* (Buenos Aires: El Informador Público, 1990).

69. Quoted in Silvia Chejter, "Los ochenta," in *Feminismo por feministas*, 27–64, quotation on 34.

70. "Violencia sexual, renovada amenaza," *La Mujer*, November 5, 1983, 9; Inés Hercovich, "Erotismo, violencia y poder: la violación," paper presented at the Primer Simposio sobre Prevención de la Violencia Familiar, Buenos Aires, August 1985, INDESO Archive, Box Violencia Sexual.

71. "A todas les pegué y nunca pasó nada," *Página/12*, February 17, 1988, 10–11; Red Feminista de Derechos Humanos de América Latina y el Caribe, "¿Cuántas Alicias no están en el país de las maravillas?," Buenos Aires, February 17, 1988, unpublished document, CEDINCI Archive, Sara Torres Collection, Box 50: Muñiz.

72. Oddone, *48 artículos seleccionados de la columna semanal de María Elena Oddone*. The same judge that had dismissed Muñiz's demand initiated contempt proceedings against Oddone when she publicly denounced him and accused him of negligence. Indeed, Oddone was sued by judges and even defendants on several occasions when she denounced them in her column in *El Informador Público*. Oddone, *La pasión por la libertad*, 193.

73. "Alicia Muñiz: Víctima del poder patriarcal," *Brujas*, no. 12, March 3, 1988, 39–40.

74. Bellucci, *Historia de una desobediencia*, 271.

75. "Conclusiones de las Primeras Jornadas Nacionales sobre la mujer y la familia," *Brujas* 1, no. 3, 1982, 19–24, quotation on 21.

76. "¿Mujeres?," *Gente*, March 15, 1984, 21–24.

77. Marianne Mollmann, *Decisions Denied: Women's Access to Contraceptives and Abortion in Argentina* (New York: Human Rights Watch, 2005); Diana Maffia, "Aborto no punible: ¿Qué dice la ley?" in *Realidades y coyunturas del aborto: Entre el derecho y la necesidad*, ed. Susana Checa (Buenos Aires: Paidos, 2006), 149–57.

78. Movimiento Feminista, unpublished document, CEDINCI Archive, Sara Torre Collection, Colección Folletos/Volantes; "Aborto: Culpable, quién," *Unidas*, December 1982, 19–22; "En defensa de nuestro cuerpo," *Unidas*, May 1986, 3–8.

79. Comisión por el Derecho al Aborto, "Anticonceptivos para no abortar, aborto legal para no morir," Buenos Aires, June 1988, unpublished document, CEDINCI Archive, Sara Torre Collection, Colección Folletos/Volantes.

80. The regional office of Católicas por el Derecho a Decidir in Latin America was established in 1989 in Montevideo, Uruguay, and functioned under the direction of feminist doctor Cristina Grela. Bellucci, *Historia de una desobediencia*, 298–99.

81. "La cultura en libertad," *Criterio*, July 1984, 363–65, quotations on 363; "Divorcio, aborto, educación y moralidad pública: Temas de una carta pastoral," *Boletín de la AICA*, no. 149, March 1, 1984, 4–6, see esp. 5; "Católicos por el derecho a escoger: Una organización de lobos disfrazados de ovejas," *Boletín de la Liga por la Decencia*, no. 146, June 1989, 3.

82. Magui Bellotti, "¿Hacia un movimiento autónomo de mujeres?" *Brujas*, November 12, 1988, 26–33, quotation on 33.

83. Bellucci, *Historia de una desobediencia*, 312–23; Dora Coledesky, "Historia de la Comisión por el Derecho al Aborto," Campaña Nacional por el Derecho al Aborto Legal Seguro y Gratuito, January 27, 2008, http://www.abortolegal.com.ar/historia-de-la-comision-por-el-derecho-al-aborto/.

84. Mónica Tarducci mentions the group Safo, within the FLH created in 1971, as the first lesbian group but calls it "mythical" because there are no documents or other types of written evidence of its existence. Tarducci, "Hitos de la militancia lesbofeminista de Buenos Aires (1984–1985)." See also Gemetro, "Lesbianas jóvenes en los 70."

85. See, for example, "Las feministas," *Hombre*, June 1984, 141–46; "Ser feminista, ¿Es paquete?" *El Periodista de Buenos Aires*, July 19–25, 1985, 28.

86. Laudano and Fernández, "IV Encuentro Nacional de Mujeres," 37.

87. "La mujer, hoy," *Mujer*, November 1, 1983, 70–73, see esp. 71.

88. Yet the ICD still retained a list of sexual disorders, such as sexual maturation disorder and ego-dystonic sexual orientation, that selectively targeted individuals with gender nonconformity or a same-sex orientation.

89. Quoted in Jáuregui, *La homosexualidad en la Argentina*, 71–72.

90. "La homosexualidad femenina," *Mujer 10*, January 24, 1984, 84–88; "Editorial," *Mujer 10*, January 31, 1984, 3. For Fuskova's analysis of her participation on the television show, see Ilse Fuskova and Claudina Marek, *Amor de mujeres: El lesbianismo en la Argentina hoy* (Buenos Aires: Planeta, 1994), 61–62.

91. "Amar a otra mujer," *alfonsina*, January 12, 1984, 14–15; "Feminismo y lesbianismo," *alfonsina*, March 22, 1984, 5.

92. Alma and Lorenzo, *Mujeres que se encuentran*, 257–60.

93. Hilda Rais, "Lesbianismo: Apuntes para una discusión feminista," paper presented at the Encuentro de Mujeres sobre mujer y violencia organized by ATEM in Buenos Aires, November 1984, 1, CEDINCI Archive, Sara Torres Collection, Box 12: Lugar de Mujer. Interestingly, before Rais, the first formal presentation about homosexuality in ATEM was a paper by sexologist Mirta Granero titled "Heterosexualidad y homosexualidad femenina" and presented at the 1983 ATEM congress. Chejter, "Los ochenta," 39.

94. These are the testimonies of Hilda Rais and Ana Rubiolo on their experiences in Lugar de Mujer. The interviews are printed in Chejter, "Los ochenta," 55–57.

95. "Nadie puede estar en contra de los gays: Si hasta en la Iglesia, el ejército y la ultra-derecha hay notorios homosexuales," *Libre*, June 19, 1984, 67–74, quotation on 72.

96. "Las chicas gay juegan a las tapaditas," *Boletín de la CHA* 3, February 1985, 8; "Y nosotras, ¿para cuándo?" *Boletín de la CHA* 5, June 1985, 3; "No a la auto-marginación," *Boletín de la CHA* 6, July 1985, 11.

97. The first issue of *Vamos a andar mujer* appeared in March 1989. CHA, "Por qué la existencia de una comisión de la mujer," May 20, 1989, Mimeo, CEDINCI Archive, Fondo Marcelo Manuel Benitez, Box 1, Folder 2. According to Mabel Bellucci, the initial Grupo de Mujeres de la CHA—created in 1985—had only seven members and struggled greatly to increase membership and gain participation within the organization. Bellucci, *Orgullo*, 118–23. Norma Mogrovejo argues that in the 1990s, women represented 50 percent of the CHA membership. Norma Mogrovejo, *Un amor que se atrevió a decir su nombre: La lucha de las lesbianas y su relación con los movimientos homosexual y feminista en América Latina* (Mexico City: Plaza y Valdés, 2000), 288.

98. Albaduru, Cano, Rais, and Reynoso, *Diario Colectivo*, 206.

99. "134 tímidas lesbianas," *El Porteño*, May 1985, 78.

100. Hilda Rais, "Mujeres, lesbianas," paper presented at Lugar de Mujer, January 30, 1987, 5, CEDINCI Archive, Sara Torres Collection, Box 12: Lugar de Mujer, 7.

101. Quoted in Chejter, "Los ochenta," 55.

102. Rais, "Mujeres, lesbianas."

103. Fuskova had been on television and the radio a year earlier, but Legrand's show was one of the most popular in the country and was aired at noon. Ilse Fuskova and Claudina Marek, *Amor de mujeres: El lesbianismo en la Argentina hoy* (Buenos Aires: Planeta, 1994), 59–60. In a 1989 interview on television, the famous singer Celeste Carballo—who had been on the cover of *Mujer 10* in December 1983—told the show host she and singer Sandra Mihanovich were a couple.

104. "Anexo: Documento 4. Articulaciones entre política sexual y lesbianismo desde la perspectiva feminista. Ana Rubiolo. Grupo Autogestivo de Lesbianas," in Centro de Encuentros Cultura y Mujer, *Feminismo por feministas*, 142–44, quotation on 143.

105. "Comenzamos a tejer nuestra red de lesbianas en el continente," *Cuaderno de Existencia Lesbiana* 10, November 1990, 9.

106. "Editorial," *Cuaderno de Existencia Lesbiana* 11, March 1991, 1.

107. Ilse Fuskova, "Para la historia de Cuaderno de Existencia Lesbiana," *Brujas* 20, no. 28, August 2001, 65–68.

108. Fuskova and Marek, *Amor de mujeres*, 76.

109. Fuskova and Marek, *Amor de mujeres*, 84, 104.

110. "Anexo: Documento 4. Articulaciones entre política sexual y lesbianismo desde la perspectiva feminista. Ana Rubiolo. Grupo Autogestivo de Lesbianas," 144.

111. Ana Rubiolo, "Grupo de reflexión de existencia lesbiana o el otro lado de la luna," *Cuaderno de Existencia Lesbiana* 5, May 1988, 2–3.

112. Ilse Fuskova, "Un poco de historia reciente: Las lesbianas y las mujeres peronistas," *Cuaderno de Existencia Lesbiana* 15, November 1993, 5–6, quotation on 5.

113. Fuskova and Marek, *Amor de mujeres*, 59.

114. "Editorial," *Cuaderno de Existencia Lesbiana* 2, May 1987, 1.

115. For an analysis of *Cuaderno de Existencia Lesbiana* as an editorial experiment, see Paula Torricella, "Comentarios sobre la experiencia editorial de *Cuaderno de Existencia Lesbiana*," *Revista Interdisciplinaria de Estudios Sociales* no. 2 (July–December 2010): 85–107. The Grupo Autogestivo de Lesbianas, which was initially affiliated with Lugar de Mujer, also started its own publications: *Codo a codo* in 1988 and *Sin candado* in 1989. Chejter, "Los ochenta," 58.

116. Some of the participating organizations were San Telmo, Oscar Wilde, Pluralista, Grupo Federativo Gay, Dignidad, and Grupo de Acción Gay, just to name a few.

117. In 1986, the CHA fervently contested the Catholic Church's "Letter to the Bishops of the Catholic Church on the Pastoral Care of Homosexual Persons," which argued that homosexuality was not morally acceptable. In 1987, the CHA denounced the visit of Pope John Paul II to Argentina. See, for example, "¡No al Papa!" *Vamos a andar* 4, March 1987, 6–7.

118. "Algo de historia," *Boletín de la CHA* 7, August 1985, 12.

119. "Los homosexuales de la Argentina," *Ahora*, February 21, 1985, 20–21.

120. "Algo de historia," *Boletín de la CHA* 7, August 1985, 12; "Homosexuales del mundo, uníos," *Boletín de la Liga por la Decencia*, June 1984, 2.

121. In the mid-1980s, the CHA reached three hundred members, but the organization essentially consisted of around fifty core activists. Omar Encarnación, *Out in the Periphery: Latin America's Gay Rights Revolution* (New York: Oxford University Press, 2016), 99.

122. "Nadie puede estar en contra de los gays: Si hasta en la Iglesia, el ejército y la ultra-derecha hay notorios homosexuales," *Libre*, June 19, 1984, 74; "De prejuicios y miedos," *Boletín de la CHA* 8, September 1985, 3.

123. Alejandro Zalazar, "Hay que perder miedo al miedo," *Vamos a andar* 4, March 1987, 14.

124. Gays por los Derechos Civiles unpublished, undated document, CEDINCI Archive, Fondo Marcelo Manuel Benitez, Box 1, File 4. Bellucci, *Orgullo*, 188–89.

125. "Marica," usually a pejorative term, refers to a gay or effeminate man. On the FLH and the *marica*, see Insausti, "De maricas, travestis y gays," 329–41.

126. *Travestis* are transwomen. The first *travesti* organization, the Asociación de

Travestis Argentinas (ATA, Argentine *Travestis* Association) was founded in 1991. Hugo Espósito, "La cuestión no es ser gay sino saber serlo," *Vamos a andar* 3, November 1986, 21; Rafael Freda, "Prensa y prejuicios: A los gays se los usa de cortina de humo," *Vamos a andar* 9, October 1987, 22–24.

127. In 1991, for example, Jáuregui organized a new gay organization called Gays por los Derechos Civiles (Gays DC, Gays for Civil Rights). Néstor Perlongher, "El sexo de las locas," in *Prosa plebeya: Ensayos 1980–1982* (Buenos Aires: Colihue, 1997), 29–34. Insausti, "De maricas, travestis y gays," 371–86.

128. "Carta abierta a los legisladores," *Boletín de la CHA* 3, February 1985, 3.

129. Frente de Liberación Homosexual, "Sexo y revolución," unpublished manuscript, Buenos Aires, 1974, CEDINCI Archive. For a history of the FLH, see Insausti, "De maricas, travestis y gays," and Patricio Simonetto, *Entre la injuria y la revolución: El Frente de Liberación Homosexual: Argentina, 1967–1976* (Buenos Aires: Universidad Nacional de Quilmes, 2017).

130. Néstor Perlongher, "El sexo de las locas," in *Prosa plebeya: Ensayos 1980–1982* (Buenos Aires: Colihue, 1997), 32.

131. Perlongher, "El sexo de las locas," 30.

132. Undated FLH pamphlet, CEDINCI Archive, Fondo Marcelo Manuel Benitez, Box 1, File 1.

133. Jáuregui, *La homosexualidad en la Argentina*, 175.

134. The concept is used by Néstor Perlongher in "El sexo de las locas," 32.

135. "Solicitada," in Jáuregui, *La homosexualidad en la Argentina*, 227.

136. In his book, Jáuregui argues that despite the fact that there were no official statistics on the disappearance of gay people and that homosexuals were not included as a separate category in the CONADEP report *Nunca más*, one of the members of the commission revealed to the CHA that at least four hundred homosexuals were disappeared during the dictatorship and that they were victims of extremely sadistic mistreatment in the clandestine detention centers. Jáuregui, *La homosexualidad en la Argentina*, 171. "Editorial," *Vamos a andar* 5, May 1987, 3–6. For a critical assessment on the disappearance of gay people during the dictatorship, see Santiago Joaquín Insausti, "Los cuatrocientos homosexuales desaparecidos: Memorias de la represión estatal a las sexualidades disidentes en Argentina," in D'Antonio, *Deseo y represión*, 63–82. For a history of socialization and repression of gay people during the dictatorship, see Rapisardi and Modarelli, *Fiestas, baños y exilios*.

137. For an analysis of AIDS in Argentina from a public health perspective, see Fernando Lavadenz, Carla Pantanali, and Eliana Zeballos, *Thirty Years of the HIV/AIDS Epidemic in Argentina* (Washington, DC: World Bank Group, 2015). For an analysis of AIDS and human rights in Argentina, see Mario Pecheny, "Sexual Orientation, AIDS, and Human Rights in Argentina: The Paradox of Social Advance amid Health Crisis," in *Struggles for Social Rights in Latin America*, ed. Susan Evan Eckstein and Timothy Wickham-Crowley (New York: Routledge, 2003), 253–70.

138. "Ley sobre discriminación y propuestas," *Boletín de la CHA* 9, October 1985, 8–9; "Derecho al voto y derecho de minorías," *Vamos a andar* 7, July 1987, 3.

139. For a historical overview with a particular emphasis on Buenos Aires, see Patricio Simonetto, "La moral institucionalizada: Reflexiones sobre el Estado, las sexualidad y la violencia en la Argentina en el siglo XX," *e-l@tina: Revista electrónica de estudios latinoamericanos* 14, no. 55 (April–June 2016), https://www.researchgate. net/publication/304831687_La_moral_institucionalizadaReflexiones_sobre_el_Es-tado_las_sexualidades_y_la_violencia_en_la_Argentina_del_siglo_XX.

140. "Editorial," *Boletín de la CHA* 6, July 1985, 2.

141. "¿Fin del 2do H?" *Boletín de la CHA* 1, October 12–25, 1984, 1; "Derogación de la ley de averiguación de antecedentes," *Vamos a andar* 1, July 1986, 6.

142. "Editorial: Defender nuestros derechos es obligación de todos," and "Dere-chos humanos: Comunicado de prensa," *Boletín de la CHA* 3, February 1985, 1–2.

143. "Cartilla de seguridad," *Boletín de la CHA* 2, December 1984, 4; "Defiende tus derechos: ¿Qué haces si te detienen?" *Vamos a andar* 4, March 1987, 24; "Columna legal: No proceder como J.R.C," *Boletín de la CHA* 7, August 1985, 14–5.

144. Plummer, *Intimate Citizenship*, 14.

## EPILOGUE

1. Jeffrey Weeks, "Traps We Set Ourselves," *Sexualities* 2, nos. 1–2 (2008): 30.

2. "Asesinatos de personas trans, la violencia oculta en Argentina," *El País*, August 16, 2017, https://elpais.com/internacional/2017/08/15/argentina/1502750091_710967 .html; "En Argentina el promedio de vida de una trans es de 36 años," *Rosario Nuestro*, February 23, 2018, https://rosarionuestro.com/el-promedio-de-vida-de-una-trans -en-argentina-es-de-36-anos/.

3. Weeks, "Traps We Set Ourselves," 32.

4. McNair, *Striptease Culture*, 61–87.

5. "Los medios de comunicación en la Argentina y los estereotipos de mujer," *Revista Venceremos*, December 8, 2016, https://revistavenceremos.wordpress. com/2016/12/08/los-medios-de-comunicacion-en-la-argentina-y-los-estereoti-pos-de-mujer/; "Showmatch: El retorno de la cosificación," *Marcha*, April 28, 2014, http://www.marcha.org.ar/showmatch-el-retorno-de-la-cosificacion/; "Denuncia-rán a Showmatch por incumplir la ley contra la violencia de género," *parlamentario. com*, November 23, 2011, http://www.parlamentario.com/noticia-40965.html.

6. For an analysis of some of these practices, see Karina Felitti and Carolina Spataro, "Las 5 sombras y el mercado erótico argentino: Significaciones locales de un fenómeno transnacional," in *Perspectivas transculturais e transnacionais de gênero*, ed. Claudia Priori, Cleusa Gomes da Silva, and Georgiane Garabely Heil Vázquez (Porto Alegre: Editora Fi, 2018), 271–99, and Silvia Elizalde and Karina Felitti, "'Vení a sacar la perra que hay en vos': Pedagogía de la seducción, mercados y nuevos retos para los feminismos," *Revista Interdisciplinaria de Estudios de Género* 1, no. 2 (2015): 3–32. For a general analysis of sexual practices among the young, see Mario Margulis, ed., *Juventud, cultura, sexualidad: La dimensión cultural en la afectividad y la sexualidad de los jóvenes de Buenos Aires* (Buenos Aires: Biblos, 2003). For an analysis of *cumbia villera*, see Pablo Vila and Pablo Semán, *Troubling Gender: Youth and Cumbia in Argen-*

*tina's Music Scene* (Philadelphia: Temple University Press, 2011). See also "Cirugías estéticas, un regalo de moda," *La Nación*, September 4, 2010, https://www.lanacion. com.ar/1301238-cirugias-esteticas-un-regalo-de-moda, and "En silencio, una cirugía íntima se convirtió en la que más crece en el país," *Clarín*, June 23, 2018, https:// www.clarin.com/sociedad/silencio-cirugia-femenina-intima-convirtio-crece-pais_0 _Sy2fEZD1Q.html.

7. Ariel Levy, *Female Chauvinist Pigs: Women and the Rise of Raunch Culture* (New York: Free Press, 2006), 200.

8. "El nuevo tema de Jimena Barón fue censurado por YouTube," *Rosario Nuestro*, October 23, 2017, https://rosarionuestro.com/el-tema-de-jimena-baron-que-se-basa -en-los-comentarios-de-las-redes/.

9. Rosalind Gill, "Media, Empowerment, and the 'Sexualization of Culture' Debates," *Sex Roles* 66, nos. 11–12 (June 2012): 736–45. See also Claire Moran, "Re-positioning Female Heterosexuality within Postfeminist and Neoliberal Culture," *Sexualities* 20, nos. 1–2 (2017): 121–39; and Attwood, "Sexed Up."

10. Mari Ruti, *Feminist Film Theory and* Pretty Woman (New York: Bloomsbury, 2016), 93.

11. "Histórico: El proyecto de aborto legal recibió media sanción en Diputados," June 14, 2018, *El Cronista*, https://www.cronista.com/economiapolitica/Historico -el-proyecto-de-aborto-legal-consiguio-media-sancion-en-Diputados-20180613 -0068.html; "Argentine Senate Rejects Bill to Legalise Abortion," *Guardian*, August 9, 2018, https://www.theguardian.com/world/2018/aug/09/argentina-senate-rejects -bill-legalise-abortion.

12. "Aborto," *Página/12*, June 14, 2018, https://www.pagina12.com.ar/121411 -aborto.

13. "Nuestros derechos son nuestros," *Página/12*, June 15, 2018, https://www .pagina12.com.ar/121621-nuestros-deseos-son-nuestros-derechos; "Lo rupturista es hoy el aborto," *Página/12*, November 19, 2016, https://www.pagina12.com.ar/3972 -lo-rupturista-hoy-es-el-aborto; "La historia de Nelly Minyersky, la feminista de 88 años que celebró con las jóvenes de pañuelo verde," *La Nación*, June 19, 2018, https:// www.lanacion.com.ar/2145475-aborto-la-historia-de-nelly-minyersky-la-feminista- de-88-anos-que-celebro-con-las-jovenes-de-panuelo-verde; "Chicas de pañuelo y glitter verde, las nuevas protagonistas de la política argentina," *La Nación*, June 14, 2018.

14. "Aborto: ¿Qué simboliza el pañuelo verde?" *La Nación*, March 6, 2018, https:// www.lanacion.com.ar/2114538-aborto-que-simboliza-el-panuelo-verde; "El origen del pañuelo verde fue hace 15 años y en Rosario," *Rosario Plus*, June 17, 2016, https:// www.rosarioplus.com/enotrostemas/El-origen-del-panuelo-verde-fue-hace-15- anos-y-en-Rosario-20180616-0023.html.

15. This information is available in the statistics compiled by the Registo Nacional de Femicidios de la Justicia Argentina, https://www.csjn.gov.ar/om/femicidios. html. See also "En siete años asesinaron en la Argentina a 1.808 mujeres en situaciones de violencia de género," *Telam*, March 4, 2015, http://www.telam.com.ar/notas

/201503/96906-siete-anos-asesinaron-argentina-1808-mujeres-violencia-de-genero
.html.

16. "Marcela Ojeda: Detrás del grito 'vivas nos queremos,'" *La Nación*, December 23, 2016, https://www.lanacion.com.ar/1967044-detras-del-grito-vivas-nos-queremos -marcela-ojeda; "Ni una menos, vivas nos queremos," *Diagonal*, June 26, 2016, https:// www.diagonalperiodico.net/la-plaza/30760-ni-menos-vivas-nos-queremos-exito -marchas-contra-feminicidios-argentina.html; "Argentina's Women Joined across South America in Marches against Violence," *Guardian*, October 19, 2016, https:// www.theguardian.com/world/2016/oct/20/argentina-women-south-america -marches-violence-ni-una-menos.

17. "¿Aumentos de femicidios o mayor visibilidad? Qué pasó en Argentina después del 'Ni una menos,'" *Infobae*, October 16, 2016, https://www.infobae.com/ sociedad/2016/10/19/aumento-de-femicidios-o-mayor-visibilizacion-que-paso -en-argentina-despues-del-ni-una-menos/.

18. "La cuestión gay en la televisión argentina," *Los Andes*, July 1, 2013, https:// losandes.com.ar/article/cuestion-television-argentina-723905; "La primera telenov- ela gay," *Página/12*, August 23, 2013, https://www.pagina12.com.ar/diario/suplemen tos/espectaculos/8-29653-2013-08-23.html; "Lesbianas en prime time: Aptas para todo público," *Noticias*, October 20, 2017, http://noticias.perfil.com/2017/10/20/ lesbianas-en-prime-time-aptas-para-todo-publico/.

19. "La adopción por parte de parejas gays, el punto más sensible del debate," *La Nación*, April 29, 2010, https://www.lanacion.com.ar/1259096-la-adopcion-por -parte-de-parejas-gays-el-punto-mas-sensible-del-debate; "El derecho a la igualdad llegó al matrimonio," *Página/12*, July 15, 2010, https://www.pagina12.com.ar/diario/ elpais/1-149544-2010-07-15.html; "Elogio a la ley de identidad de género," *Página/12*, May 26, 2016, https://www.pagina12.com.ar/diario/sociedad/3-194931-2012-05-26. html. On same-sex marriage in Argentina, see Bruno Bimbi, *Matrimonio Igualitario: Intriga, tensiones y secretos en el camino hacia la ley* (Buenos Aires: Planeta, 2010), and Encarnación, *Out in the Periphery*, 134–48.

20. "Asesinatos de personas trans, la violencia oculta en Argentina"; "Transfobia express," *Página/12*, May 4, 2018, https://www.pagina12.com.ar/111999-transfobia -express; "Transgéneros: A pesar de la ley, aún son una población relegada," *La Nación*, October 15, 2015, https://www.lanacion.com.ar/1836527-transgeneros-a-pesar-de-la -ley-aun-son-una-poblacion-relegada.

21. Weeks, "Traps We Set Ourselves," 31.

22. "La Inquisición," *Página/12*, July 11, 2010, https://www.pagina12.com.ar/diario /elpais/1-149246-2010-07-11.html; "El Papa Francisco comparó el aborto con las prác- ticas nazis para conservar la pureza de la raza," *Clarín*, June 16, 2018, https://www .clarin.com/politica/papa-francisco-comparo-aborto-practicas-nazis-conservar -pureza-raza_0_Sy8p3kQZQ.html.

# BIBLIOGRAPHY

## INSTITUTIONAL ARCHIVES AND LIBRARIES

Archivo de Editorial Perfil, Buenos Aires

Archivo del Instituto de Estudios Jurídicos Sociales de la Mujer (INDESO Mujer), Rosario

Archivo del Museo del Cine Pablo Ducrós Hicken, Buenos Aires

Archivo General de la Nación, Departamento de Documentos Fotográficos, Buenos Aires

Biblioteca del Congreso Nacional, Buenos Aires

Biblioteca del Instituto Interdisciplinario de Género (IIEG), Facultad de Filosofía y Letras, Universidad de Buenos Aires

Biblioteca del Museo de la Memoria, Rosario

Biblioteca Nacional, Buenos Aires

Centro de Documentación e Investigación de la Cultura de las Izquierdas en la Argentina, Buenos Aires (CEDINCI)

Centro de Documentación sobre la Mujer, Buenos Aires

Hemeroteca del Congreso Nacional, Buenos Aires

Hemeroteca Nacional, Buenos Aires

M. D. Anderson Library, University of Houston

Nettie Lee Benson Latin American Collection, University of Texas, Austin

## PERSONAL ARCHIVES

Walter Barbato (physician, sex educator)

León Roberto Gindin (sexologist)

Mirta Granero (sexologist, sex educator)

María Luis Lerer (sexologist, sex educator)

Marcelo Raimon (journalist, filmmaker)

Sara Torres (feminist activist, sexologist)

## PERIODICALS

PLACE OF PUBLICATION IS BUENOS AIRES UNLESS NOTED.

*Adultos*

*Ahora*

*alfonsina*

*Alternativa Feminista*

*Anuario Esquiú*

*Aquí Nosotras*

*Boletín de la Comunidad Homosexual Argentina* (CHA)
*Boletín de la Liga por la Decencia*
*Boletín Informativo de la Agencia Informativa Católica Argentina* (AICA)
*Brujas*
*Cerdos y Peces*
*Clarín*
*Clarín Revista*
*Climax*
*Contribuciones*
*Criterio*
*Cuaderno de Existencia Lesbiana*
*Dar la cara en entrevista*
*Destape*
*Diferentes*
*El Expreso Imaginario*
*El Informador Público*
*El Observador*
*El Periodista de Buenos Aires*
*El Porteño*
*Eroticón*
*Esquiú*
*Fierro*
*Gente*
*Hombre*
*Humor*
*La Capital* (Rosario)
*La Chancleta* (Rosario)
*La Mujer* (*Tiempo Argentino* Supplement)
*La Nación*
*La Prensa*
*La Razón*
*La Semana*
*Libre*
*Muchacha*
*Mujer 10*
*Mujeres*
*Mundo Erótico*
*Noticias*
*Página/12*
*Para Ti*
*Pareja*
*Persona*
*Prensa de Mujeres*

*Revista Argentina de Sexualidad Humana*
*Revista de La Nación*
*Revista Latinoamericana de Sexología* (Cali, Colombia)
*Ritmo Mujer*
*Salimos*
*Satiricón*
*Semanario*
*Sex Humor*
*Sex Humor Ilustrado*
*Shock*
*Siete Días*
*Somos*
*Tal Cual*
*Tiempo Argentino*
*Todas*
*TV Semanal*
*Unidas*
*Vamos a andar*
*Vamos a andar mujer*
*Viva*
*Vivir*
*Vivir en pareja*

## PERSONAL INTERVIEWS

Luis María Aller Atucha (sex educator)
Alcira Bas (journalist)
Walter Barbato (physician, sex educator)
Mabel Bellucci (journalist, feminist activist, researcher)
Oscar Blando (lawyer)
Gloria Bonder (psychologist, feminist activist, researcher)
Isabel Boschi (sexologist)
Maitena Burundarena (writer, cartoon artist)
Laura Caldiz (sexologist)
Dionisia Fontán (journalist, writer)
Jorge Fontevecchia (journalist, Perfil CEO)
Luis Frontera (journalist)
León Roberto Gindin (sexologist)
Mirta Granero (sexologist, sex educator)
María Luisa Lerer (sexologist, sex educator)
Marcelo Raimon (journalist, filmmaker)
Sara Torres (sexologist, feminist activist)
Alicia Sanguinetti (photographer)
Adrián Sapetti (sexologist)

Graciela Sikos (sexologist)
Julia Pomies (journalist, writer)

## FILMOGRAPHY

*Adiós Roberto* (Enrique Dawi, 1985)
*A los cirujanos se les va la mano* (Hugo Sofovich, 1980)
*Atracción peculiar* (Enrique Carreras, 1988)
*Atrapadas* (Aníbal Di Salvo, 1984)
*Camarero nocturno en Mar del Plata* (Gerardo Sofovich, 1986)
*Camila* (María Luisa Bemberg, 1984)
*Correccional de mujeres* (Emilio Vieyra, 1986)
*Crónica de una señora* (Raúl de la Torre, 1970)
*Custodio de señoras* (Hugo Sofovich, 1979)
*De eso no se habla* (María Luisa Bemberg, 1993)
*El desquite* (Juan Carlos Desanzo, 1983)
*El manosanta está cargado* (Hugo Sofovich, 1987)
*El último amor en Tierra del Fuego* (Armando Bó, 1979)
*Encuentros muy cercanos con señoras de cualquier tipo* (Hugo Moser, 1978)
*En retirada* (Juan Carlos Desanzo, 1984)
*Flores robadas en los jardines de Quilmes* (Antonio Ottone, 1985)
*Fotógrafo de señoras* (Hugo Moser, 1978)
*Insaciable* (Armando Bó, 1976)
*La búsqueda* (Juan Carlos Desanzo, 1985)
*La historia oficial* (Luis Puenzo, 1985)
*La noche de los lápices* (Héctor Olivera, 1986)
*Las colegialas se divierten* (Fernando Siro, 1986)
*Las esclavas* (Carlos Borcosque, 1987)
*Las lobas* (Anibal Di Salvo, 1986)
*Los amores de Laurita* (Antonio Ottone, 1986)
*Los corruptores* (Teo Kofman, 1987)
*Los gatos (Prostitución de alto nivel)* (Carlos Borcosque, 1985)
*Luna caliente* (Roberto Denis, 1985)
*Mirame la palomita* (Enrique Carreras, 1985)
*Miss Mary* (María Luisa Bemberg, 1986)
*Momentos* (María Luisa Bemberg, 1980)
*Otra historia de amor* (Américo Ortiz de Zárate, 1986)
*Señora de nadie* (María Luisa Bemberg, 1982)
*Sucedió en el internado* (Emillio Vieyra, 1985)
*Susana quiere, el negro también* (Julio De Grazia, 1987)
*Tacos altos* (Sergio Renán, 1985)
*Una viuda descocada* (Armando Bó, 1980)
*Yo, la peor de todas* (María Luisa Bemberg, 1990)

## TELEVISION SHOWS

*Amo y señor* (1984)
*La noticia rebelde* (1986–89)
*Las gatitas y los ratones de Porcel* (1987–90)
*Matrimonios y algo más* (1982–89)
*Monumental Moria* (1986–89)
*No toca botón* (1981–87)
*Operación Ja-Já* (1981–84; 1987–91)
*Sexcitante* (1984–85)
*Rosa de lejos* (1980)
*Veinte mujeres* (1986)

## PRINT SOURCES

Aboy Carlés, Gerardo. *Las dos fronteras de la democracia argentina: La reformulación de las identidades políticas de Alfonsín a Menem.* Rosario: Homo Sapiens, 2001.

Acosta, Fermín, and Lucas Morgan Disalvo. "La masculinidad en la punta de sus manos: *Eroticón* y la configuración de los imaginarios sexuales en la década de los ochenta." In *Cuerpos minados: Masculinidades en Argentina*, edited by José Maristany and Jorge Peralta, 195–219. La Plata: EDULP, 2017.

Actis, Munú, Cristina Aldini, Liliana Gardella, Miriam Lewin, and Elisa Tokar. *That Inferno: Conversations of Five Women Survivors of an Argentine Torture Camp.* Nashville, TN: Vanderbilt University Press, 2006.

Águila, Gabriela. *Dictadura, represión y sociedad en Rosario, 1976–1983: Un estudio sobre la represión y los comportamientos y actitudes sociales en dictadura.* Buenos Aires: Prometeo, 2008.

Aldaburu, María Inés, Inés Cano, Hilda Rais, and Nené Reynoso. *Diario Colectivo.* Buenos Aires: La Campana, 1982.

Aller Atucha, Luis María. "Educación sexual en Argentina: La historia que yo viví." http://www.educacionsexual.com.ar/biblioteca-online/historia-del-movimiento-sexologico/historias-de-la-educacion-sexual.

Aller Atucha, Luis María, Fernando José Bianco Colmenares, and Dora Magalí Rada Cadenas. "Perspectiva histórica de la educación sexual y la sexología clínica en América Latina." Paper presented at the VII Latin American Conference on Sexology and Sex Education organized by FLASSES, November 1994, Havana, Cuba. Comisión Nacional de Políticas Familiares y de Población.

Alma, Amanda, and Paula Lorenzo. *Mujeres que se encuentran: Una recuperación histórica de los Encuentros Nacionales de Mujeres en Argentina (1986–2005).* Buenos Aires: Feminaria Editora, 2009.

Anderson, Leslie E. *Democratization by Institutions: Argentina's Transition Years in Comparative Perspective.* Ann Arbor: University of Michigan Press, 2016.

Andújar, Andrea, Débora D'Antonio, Fernanda Gil Lozano, Karin Grammático, and María Laura Rosa, eds. *De minifaldas, militancias y revoluciones: Exploraciones sobre los 70 en la Argentina.* Buenos Aires: Luxemburg, 2009.

Aprea, Gustavo. *Cine y políticas en Argentina: Continuidades y discontinuidades en 25 años de democracia.* Buenos Aires: Biblioteca Nacional / Universidad Nacional de General Sarmiento, 2008.

Asociación Argentina de Protección Familiar. *Adolescencia.* Buenos Aires: AAPF, n.d.

Asociación Argentina de Protección Familiar. *El mejor momento para tener hijos.* Buenos Aires: AAPF, n.d.

Asociación Argentina de Protección Familiar. *Guía de métodos argentinos.* Buenos Aires: AAPF, n.d.

Asociación de Periodistas de Buenos Aires. *Periodistas desaparecidos: Con vida los queremos.* Buenos Aires: Unión de Trabajadores de Prensa de Buenos Aires, 1987.

Attwood, Feona. "Sexed Up: Theorizing the Sexualization of Culture." *Sexualities* 9, no. 1 (2006): 77–94.

Aucía, Analía, Florencia Barrera, Celina Berterame, Susana Chiarotti, Alejandra Paolini, and Cristina Zurutuza. *Grietas en el silencio: Una investigación sobre la violencia sexual en el marco del terrorismo de Estado.* Rosario: CLADEM, 2011.

Avellaneda, Andrés. *Censura, autoritarismo y cultura: Argentina, 1960/1983,* 2 vols. Buenos Aires: Centro Editor de América Latina, 1986.

Bacci, Claudia, María Capurro Robles, Alejandra Oberti, and Susana Skura. *"Y nadie quería saber": Relatos sobre violencia contra las mujeres en el terrorismo de Estado en Argentina.* Buenos Aires: Memoria Abierta, 2012.

Balán, Jorge, and Silvina Ramos. *La medicalización del comportamiento reproductivo: Un estudio exploratorio sobre la demanda de anticonceptivos en los sectores populares,* Documentos CEDES/29. Buenos Aires: CEDES, 1989.

Balderston, Daniel, and Donna Guy, eds. *Sex and Sexuality in Latin America.* New York: New York University Press, 1999.

Barrancos, Dora, Donna Guy, and Adriana Valobra, eds. *Modalidades y comportamientos sexuales: Argentina, 1880–2011.* Buenos Aires: Biblos, 2011.

Barr-Melej, Patrick. *Psychedelic Chile: Youth, Counterculture, and Politics on the Road to Socialism and Dictatorship.* Chapel Hill: University of North Carolina Press, 2017.

Bataille, Georges. *Death and Sensuality: A Study of Eroticism and the Taboo.* New York: Ayer, 1984.

Bazán, Osvaldo. *Historia de la homosexualidad en Argentina: De la Conquista de América al siglo XXI.* Buenos Aires: Marea, 2004.

Beard, Laura. "Celebrating Female Sexuality from Adolescence to Maternity in Ana María Shua's *Los amores de Laurita.*" In *El río de los sueños: Aproximaciones críticas a las obra de Ana María Shua,* edited by Rhonda Dahl Buhanan, 35–47. Washington, DC: OEA, 2001.

Beck, Judith. *Cognitive Behavior Therapy: Basics and Beyond.* New York: Guilford Press, 2012.

Bellotti, Magui. *Cuadernos Feministas ATEM No. 34. 1984/1989: El feminismo y el movimiento de mujeres.* Buenos Aires: ATEM, 1989.

Bellotti, Magui. "Feminismo y movimiento de mujeres: Prácticas y discursos sobre sexualidad y lesbianismo." *Brujas,* October 2004, 36–42.

Bellucci, Mabel. *Historia de una desobediencia: Aborto y feminismo.* Buenos Aires: Capital Intelectual, 2014.

Bellucci, Mabel. *Orgullo: Carlos Jáuregui, una biografía política.* Buenos Aires: Emecé, 2010.

Ben, Pablo, and Santiago Joaquín Insausti. "Dictatorial Rule and Sexual Politics in Argentina: The Case of the Frente de Liberación Homosexual, 1967–1976." *Hispanic American Historical Review* 97, no. 2 (May 2017): 297–325.

Bertúa, Paula, and Lucía De Leone. "Estéticas de la subjetividad: Identidades textuales y visuales en el periódico argentino *alfonsina* (1983–1984)." *Revista Afuera: Estudios de crítica cultural* 5 (2010): 1–5.

Bimbi, Bruno. *Matrimonio Igualitario: Intriga, tensiones y secretos en el camino hacia la ley.* Buenos Aires: Planeta, 2010.

Blaustein, Eduardo, and Martín Zubieta. *Decíamos ayer: La prensa argentina bajo el Proceso.* Buenos Aires: Colihue, 1998.

Blázquez, Gustavo. "El amor de l@s rar@s: Cine y homosexualidad durante la década de 1980 en Argentina." *Fotocinema* 15 (2017), http://www.revistas.uma.es/index.php/fotocinema/article/view/3500/3208.

Bliss, Katherine. *Compromised Positions: Prostitution, Public Health, and the State in Revolutionary Mexico.* University Park: University of Pennsylvania Press, 2001.

Bontempo, Paula. "Para Ti: Una revista moderna para una mujer moderna, 1922–1935." *Estudios Sociales* 41 (2001): 127–56.

Braslavsky, Cecilia. *La juventud argentina: Informe de situación.* Buenos Aires: CEAL, 1986.

Braslavsky, Eliana, Tamara Drajner Barredo, and Bárbara Pereyra. "Insaciable (Armando Bó, 1984), entre la liberación sexual y el castigo moralizante." *Imagofagia* 8 (2013), http://www.asaeca.org/imagofagia/index.php/imagofagia/article/view/415/363.

Brennan, James. *Argentina's Missing Bones: Revisiting the History of the Dirty War.* Los Angeles: University of California Press, 2018.

Briggs, Laura. *Reproducing Empire: Race, Sex, Science, and U.S. Imperialism in Puerto Rico.* Los Angeles: University of California Press, 2002.

Brysk, Alison. *The Politics of Human Rights in Argentina: Protest, Change, and Democratization.* Stanford, CA: Stanford University Press, 1994.

Burdick, Michael. *For God and Fatherland: Religion and Politics in Argentina.* Albany: State University of New York Press, 1995.

Burkart, Mara. "La revista Humor, espacio crítico bajo la dictadura militar argentina." *Revista Afuera: Estudios de crítica cultural,* no. 13 (September 2013), http://www.revistaafuera.com/articulo.php?id=284&nro=13.

Burkart, Mara. *De Satiricón a Humor: Risa, cultura y política en los años setenta.* Buenos Aires: Miño y Dávila, 2017.

Caldiz, Laura. *Viviendo nuestra sexualidad.* Buenos Aires: Estaciones, 1986.

Caldiz, Laura, and León Roberto Gindin. "Ética y salud sexual." *Revista Latinoamericana de Sexología* 2, no. 1 (1987): 81–88.

Calveiro, Pilar. *Poder y desaparición: Los campos de concentración en Argentina*. Buenos Aires: Colihue, 1998.

Calvera, Leonor. *El género mujer*. Buenos Aires: Editorial de Belgrano, 1982.

Camarero, Emma. "From the Banal to the Indispensable: *Pornochanchada* and *Cinema Novo* during the Brazilian Dictatorship (1964–1985)." *L'Atalante: Revista de Estudios Cinematográficos* 23 (January–June 2017): 95–108.

Canelo, Paula. *La política secreta de la última dictadura argentina (1976–1983): A 40 años del golpe*. Buenos Aires: Edhasa, 2016.

Carassai, Sebastián. *The Argentine Silent Majority: Middle Classes, Politics, Violence, and Memory in the Seventies*. Durham, NC: Duke University Press, 2014.

Carey, Elaine. *Plaza of Sacrifices: Gender, Power, and Terror in 1968 Mexico*. Albuquerque: University of New Mexico Press, 2005.

Carleton, Gregory. *Sexual Revolution in Bolshevik Russia*. Pittsburgh: University of Pittsburgh Press, 2005.

Carnovale, Vera. *Los combatientes: Historia del PRT-ERP*. Buenos Aires: Siglo Veintiuno, 2011.

Cascioli, Andrés. *La revista Humor y la dictadura*. Buenos Aires: Musimundo, 2005.

Castillo, Abelardo. *Los irresponsables: La revista Humor como medio opositor a la dictadura*. Buenos Aires: Del Tratado, 2009.

Catterbeg, Edgardo. *Los argentinos frente a la política: Cultura política y opinión pública en la transición Argentina*. Buenos Aires: Sudamericana, 1989.

Centro de Encuentros Cultura y Mujer. *Feminismo por Feministas: Fragmentos para una historia del feminismo argentino, 1970–1996*. Buenos Aires: Ediciones del Centro Cultura y Mujer, 1996.

Centro de Estudios de la Mujer. *Propuestas para el mejoramiento de la situación de la mujer argentina*. Buenos Aires: Centro de Estudios de la Mujer, 1989.

Chejter, Silvia. "Los ochenta." In *Feminismo por feministas: Fragmentos para una historia del feminismo argentino, 1970–1996*, edited by Centro de Encuentros Cultura y Mujer, 27–62. Buenos Aires: Ediciones del Centro Cultura y Mujer, 1996.

Chomsky, Noam. "The Culture of Fear." In *Colombia: The Genocidal Democracy*, edited by Javier Giraldo, 7–16. New York: Common Courage Press, 1996.

Clover, Carol. *Men, Women, and Chainsaws: Gender in the Modern Horror Film*. Princeton, NJ: Princeton University Press, 1992.

Coledesky, Dora. "Historia de la Comisión por el Derecho al Aborto." Campaña Nacional por el Derecho al Aborto Legal Seguro y Gratuito, January 27, 2008, http://www.abortolegal.com.ar/historia-de-la-comision-por-el-derecho-al-aborto/.

Comisión Nacional sobre la Desaparición de Personas. *Nunca Más*. Buenos Aires: Eudeba, 1996.

Comisión Provincial de la Memoria. *Biblioteca de libros prohibidos*. Córdoba: Ediciones del Pasaje, 2012.

Contardi, Sonia. *La imagen de la mujer en los medios de comunicación masiva: Cuadernos de Divulgación INDESO Mujer no. 2*. Rosario: INDESO, ca. 1986.

Corrales, Javier, and Mario Pecheny, eds. *The Politics of Sexuality in Latin America: A*

*Reader on Lesbian, Gay, Bisexual, and Transgender Rights*. Pittsburgh, PA: University of Pittsburgh Press, 2010.

Corrington, Robert. *Wilhelm Reich: Psychoanalyst and Radical Naturalist*. New York: Farrar, Straus, and Giroux, 2003.

Cosse, Isabella. "Argentine Mothers and Fathers and the New Psychological Paradigm of Child-Rearing (1958–1973)." *Journal of Family History* 35, no. 2 (2010): 180–202.

Cosse, Isabella. "*Claudia*: La revista de la mujer moderna en la Argentina de los años sesenta (1957–1973)." *Mora* 17, no. 1 (July 2011), http://www.scielo.org.ar/scielo.php?script=sci_arttext&pid=S1853-001X2011000100007.

Cosse, Isabella. "Cultura y sexualidad en la Argentina de los sesenta: Usos y resignificaciones de la experiencia transnacional." *Estudios Interdisciplinarios de América Latina y el Caribe* 17, no. 1 (2006): 39–60.

Cosse, Isabella. "Infidelities: Morality, Revolution, and Sexuality in Left-Wing Guerrilla Organizations in 1960s and 1970s Argentina." *Journal of the History of Sexuality* 23, no. 3 (September 2014): 415–50.

Cosse, Isabella. *Pareja, sexualidad y familia en los años sesenta*. Buenos Aires: Siglo Veintiuno, 2010.

Cosse, Isabella, Karina Felitti, and Valeria Manzano, eds. *Los 60s de otra manera: Vida cotidiana, género y sexualidades en la Argentina*. Buenos Aires: Prometeo, 2010.

Cowan, Benjamin. *Securing Sex: Morality and Repression in the Making of Cold War Brazil*. Chapel Hill: University of North Carolina Press, 2016.

Crenzel, Emilio. *La historia política del Nunca Más: La memoria de las desapariciones en la Argentina*. Buenos Aires: Siglo Veintiuno, 2008.

D'Antonio, Débora, ed. *Deseo y represión: Sexualidad, género y estado en la historia argentina reciente*. Buenos Aires: Imago Mundi, 2015.

D'Antonio, Débora. "Paradojas del género y la sexualidad en la filmografía durante la última dictadura militar argentina." *Estudos Femenistas* 23, no. 3 (September–December 2015): 913–37.

De la Dehesa, Rafael. *Queering the Public Sphere in Mexico and Brazil: Sexual Rights Movements in Emerging Democracies*. Durham, NC: Duke University Press, 2010.

De las Carreras, María Elena. "Contemporary Politics in Argentine Cinema, 1981–1991." PhD diss., University of California, Los Angeles, 1995.

Debernadi, Julia. "La educación sexual en el documental institucional de los años 70 y 80." Paper presented at the Tenth Conference in Sociology organized by the Facultad de Ciencias Sociales, Universidad de Buenos Aires, Buenos Aires, 2013.

Dennison, Stephanie, and Lisa Shaw. *Popular Cinema in Brazil*. New York: Manchester University Press, 2004.

Diamond, Larry Jay, and Marc Plattner, eds. *Democratization and Authoritarianism in the Arab World*. Baltimore: Johns Hopkins University Press, 2014.

Diana, Marta. *Mujeres guerrilleras: Sus testimonios en la militancia de los setenta*. Buenos Aires: Booket, 2006.

Diz, Tania. "Tensiones, genealogías y feminismos en los 80: Un acercamiento a *alfon-*

*sina*, primer periódico de mujeres," *Mora* 17, no. 2 (2011), http://www.scielo.org.ar/scielo.php?script=sci_abstract&pid=S1853-001X2011000200004.

Doane, Mary Ann. *Femmes Fatales: Feminism, Film Theory, Psychoanalysis.* London: Routledge, 1991.

Dunn, Christopher. *Contracultura: Alternative Arts and Social Transformation in Authoritarian Brazil.* Chapel Hill: University of North Carolina Press, 2016.

Dworkin, Andrea. *Pornography: Men Possessing Women.* New York: Perigee Books, 1981.

Dworkin, Andrea, and Catharine MacKinnon. *The Reasons Why: Essays on the New Civil Rights Law Recognizing Pornography as Sex Discrimination.* New York: Women against Pornography, 1985.

Eidelman, Ariel. "Moral católica y censura municipal de las revistas eróticas en la ciudad de Buenos Aires durante la década del sesenta." In *Deseo y represión: Sexualidad, género y estado en la historia argentina reciente*, edited by Débora D'Antonio, 1–20. Buenos Aires: Imago Mundi, 2015.

Elizalde, Silvia, and Karina Felitti. "'Vení a sacar la perra que hay en vos': Pedagogía de la seducción, mercados y nuevos retos para los feminismos." *Revista Interdisciplinaria de Estudios de Género* 1, no. 2 (2015): 3–32.

Emiliozzi, Sergio, Mario Pecheny, and Martín Unzué, eds. *La dinámica de la democracia: Representación, instituciones y ciudadanía en Argentina.* Buenos Aires: Prometeo, 2007.

Encarnación, Omar. *Out in the Periphery: Latin America's Gay Rights Revolution.* New York: Oxford University Press, 2016.

*Encuentro Nacional de Mujeres, 23, 24, y 25 de mayo de 1986: Centro Cultural San Martín, Buenos Aires.* Buenos Aires, 1987.

España, Claudio. *Cine argentino: Modernidad y vanguardias, 1957/1983.* Buenos Aires: Fondo Nacional de las Artes, 2005.

España, Claudio. *Cine argentino en democracia, 1983–1993.* Buenos Aires: Fondo Nacional de las Artes, 1994.

Esquivel, Juan Cruz. *Detrás de los muros: La Iglesia católica en los tiempos de Alfonsín y Menem (1983–1989).* Buenos Aires: UNQUI, 2004.

Fabris, Mariano. *Iglesia y democracia: Avatares de la jerarquía católica en la Argentina post autoritaria (1983–1989).* Rosario: Prohistoria Ediciones, 2001.

Feld, Claudia, and Marina Franco, eds. *Democracia, Hora Cero: Actores, políticas y debates en los inicios de la posdictadura.* Buenos Aires: Fondo de Cultura Económica, 2015.

Felitti, Karina. "Difundir y controlar: Iniciativas de educación sexual en los años sesenta." *Revista Argentina de Estudios de Juventud*, no. 1 (2009): http://perio.unlp.edu.ar/ojs/index.php/revistadejuventud/.

Felitti, Karina. "Poner el cuerpo: Género y sexualidad en la política revolucionaria de Argentina en las décadas de los sesenta y setenta." In *Political and Social Movements during the Sixties and Seventies in the Americas and Europe*, edited by Avital Bloch, 69–93. Colima, Mexico: Universidad de Colima, 2010.

Felitti, Karina. *La revolución de la píldora: Sexualidad y política en los sesenta*. Buenos Aires: Edhasa, 2012.

Felitti, Karina. "Sexualidad y reproducción en la agenda feminista de la segunda ola en la Argentina (1970–1986). *Estudios Sociológicos* 28, no. 84 (September–December 2010): 791–812.

Felitti, Karina. "Traduciendo prácticas, tejiendo redes, cruzando fronteras: Itinerarios del feminismo argentino de los '70s." *Cadernos Pagu* 44 (January–June 2015): 229–260.

Felitti, Karina, and Carolina Spataro. "Las 5 sombras y el mercado erótico argentino: Significaciones locales de un fenómeno transnacional." In *Perspectivas transculturais e transnacionais de gênero*, edited by Claudia Priori, Cleusa Gomes da Silva, and Georgiane Garabely Heil Vázquez, 271–99. Porto Alegre: Editora Fi, 2018.

Ferrari, Marcela, and Mónica Gordillo, eds. *La reconstrucción democrática en clave provincial*. Rosario: Prohistoria, 2015.

Ferreira, Fernando. *Una historia de la censura: Violencia y proscripción en la Argentina del siglo XX*. Buenos Aires: Norma, 2000.

Figari Layús, Rosario. *The Reparative Effects of Human Rights Trials: Lessons from Argentina*. New York: Routledge, 2017.

Filc, Judith. *Entre el parentesco y la política: Familia y dictadura, 1976–1983*. Buenos Aires: Biblos, 1997.

Fine, Michelle. "Sexuality, Schooling, and Adolescent Females: The Missing Discourse of Desire." *Harvard Educational Review* 58, no. 1 (April 1988): 29–54.

Fitch, Melisa. *Side Dishes: Latin American Women, Sex, and Cultural Production*. New Brunswick, NJ: Rutgers University Press, 2009.

Flores Colombino, Andrés. "La enseñanza de la sexología en Latinoamérica." *Revista Latinoamericana de Sexología* 1, no. 1 (1986): 113–32.

Flores Colombino, Andrés. "Historia y evolución de la sexología clínica en Latinoamérica," Sociedad Uruguaya de Sexología, n.d., http://www.susuruguay.org/index.php/articulos/91-historia-y-evolucion-de-la-sexologia-clinica-en-latinoamerica-i.

Fontán, Dionisia. *Laura de hoy crece*. Buenos Aires: Galerna, 1986.

Fontán, Dionisia. *Laura de hoy, Laura de siempre*. Buenos Aires: Galerna, 1991.

Fontán, Dionisia. *Laura de hoy: Una adolescente argentina*. Buenos Aires: Galerna, 1984.

Fontana, Clara. *María Luisa Bemberg*. Buenos Aires: Centro Editor de América Latina, 1993.

Foster, David William. *Contemporary Argentine Cinema*. Columbia: University of Missouri Press, 1992.

Foucault, Michel. *The History of Sexuality*. Vol. 1. New York: Vintage Books, 1990.

Franco, Marina. *Un enemigo para la nación: Orden interno, violencia y "subversión," 1973–1976*. Buenos Aires: Fondo de Cultura Económica, 2012.

Franco, Marina. *El exilio: Argentinos en Francia durante la dictadura*. Buenos Aires: Siglo Veintiuno, 2008.

Franco, Marina, and Daniel Lvovich. "Historia reciente: Apuntes sobre un campo de investigación en expansión." *Boletín del Instituto de Historia Argentina y Americana Dr. Emilio Ravignani*, no. 47 (2017): 190–217.

Frye, Timothy. *Building States and Markets after Communism: The Perils of Polarized Democracy*. New York: Cambridge University Press, 2010.

Funes, Patricia. "Los que queman libros: Censores en Argentina (1956–1983)." In *Problemas de historia reciente del Cono Sur*, vol. 1, edited by Ernesto Bohoslavsky, Marina Franco, Mariana Iglesias, and Daniel Lvovich, 303–25. Buenos Aires: Prometeo, 2010.

Fuskova, Ilse, and Claudina Marek. *Amor de mujeres: El lesbianismo en la Argentina hoy*. Buenos Aires: Planeta, 1994.

Gambaro, Griselda. *Lo impenetrable*. Buenos Aires: Norma, 2000 [1984].

Gargarella, Roberto, María Victoria Murillo, and Mario Pecheny, eds. *Discutir Alfonsín*. Buenos Aires: Siglo Veintiuno, 2010.

Gemetro, Florencia. "Lesbianas jóvenes en los 70: Sexualidades disidentes en años de autonominación del movimiento gay-lésbico." In *Jóvenes en cuestión: Configuraciones de género y sexualidad en la cultura*, edited by Silvia Elizalde, 59–83. Buenos Aires: Biblos, 2011.

Giardinelli, Mempo. *Luna Caliente*. Buenos Aires: Edhasa, 2009 [1984].

Giella, Miguel Ángel. *Teatro Abierto 1981*. Vol. 1, *Teatro argentino bajo vigilancia*. Buenos Aires: Corregidor, 1992.

Gill, Rosalind. "From Sexual Objectification to Sexual Subjectification: The Resexualization of Women's Bodies in the Media." *Feminist Media Studies* 3, no. 1 (2003): 100–105.

Gill, Rosalind. "Media, Empowerment, and the 'Sexualization of Culture' Debates." *Sex Roles* 66, nos. 11–12 (June 2012): 736–45.

Gindin, León Roberto. *La nueva sexualidad del varón*. Buenos Aires: Paidós, 1987.

Gindin, León Roberto, Cynthia Gindin, Silvina Ramos, Juan José Llovet, Alcira Camilucci, Adrián Helién, Laura Pietrasanta, Mario Kaplan, Mario Huguet, and Luis Frontera. *1ra Encuesta sobre sexualidad y pareja*. Buenos Aires: La Urraca, 1987.

Gleijeses, Piero. "Afterword: The Culture of Fear." In *Secret History: The CIA's Classified Account of Its Operations in Guatemala, 1952–1954*, edited by Nick Cullather, xxiii–xxxvi. Stanford, CA: Stanford University Press, 1999.

Gliemmo, Graciela. "El erotismo en la narrativa de las escritoras argentinas (1970–1990): Apropiación, ampliación y reformulación de un canon." In *Poéticas argentinas del siglo XX (Literatura y teatro)*, edited by Jorge Dubatti, 137–59. Buenos Aires: Editorial de Belgrano, 1998.

Gliemmo, Graciela. "Erotismo y narración en *Los amores de Laurita*." In *El río de los sueños: Aproximaciones críticas a las obra de Ana María Shua*, edited by Rhonda Dahl Buhanan, 49–61. Washington, DC: OEA, 2001.

Gociol, Judith, and Hernán Invernizzi. *Cine y dictadura: La censura al desnudo*. Buenos Aires: Capital Intelectual, 2006.

Gociol, Judith, and Hernán Invernizzi. *Un golpe a los libros: Represión cultural durante la última dictadura militar*. Buenos Aires: Eudeba, 2002.

Gogna, Mónica, Daniel Jones, and Inés Ibarlucía. *Sexualidad, Ciencia y Profesión en América Latina: El campo de la sexología en la Argentina.* Rio de Janeiro: CEPESC, 2011.

Gogna, Mónica, and Silvina Ramos. "El acceso a la anticoncepción: Una cuestión de derechos humanos y salud pública." *Perspectivas Bioéticas en las Américas* 1, no. 2 (1996): 134–40.

Graham-Jones, Jean. *Exorcising History: Argentine Theater under Dictatorship.* Cranbury, NJ: Associated University Press, 2000.

Graziano, Frank. *Divine Violence: Spectacle, Psychosexuality and Radical Christianity in the Argentine "Dirty War."* Boulder, CO: Westview Press, 1992.

Green, James. *Beyond Carnival: Male Homosexuality in Twentieth-Century Brazil.* Chicago: University of Chicago Press, 1999.

Guy, Donna. *Sex and Danger in Buenos Aires: Prostitution, Family, and Nation in Argentina.* Lincoln: University of Nebraska Press, 1991.

Hamilton, Carrie. *Sexual Revolutions in Cuba.* Chapel Hill: University of North Carolina Press, 2012.

Heer, Liliana. *Bloyd.* Buenos Aires: Legasa, 1984.

Hekma, Gert, and Alain Giami, eds. *Sexual Revolutions.* New York: Palgrave Macmillan, 2014.

Herzog, Dagmar. *Sex after Fascism: Memory and Morality in Twentieth-Century Germany.* Princeton, NJ: Princeton University Press, 2005.

Howe, Cymene. *Intimate Activism: The Struggle for Sexual Rights in Postrevolutionary Nicaragua.* Durham, NC: Duke University Press, 2013.

Htun, Mala. *Sex and the State: Abortion, Divorce, and Family under Latin American Dictatorships and Democracy.* New York: Cambridge University Press, 2003.

Hunt, Lynn. *The Invention of Pornography: Obscenity and the Origins of Modernity, 1500–1800.* New York: Zone Books, 1993.

INDESO Mujer. *Cuadernos de Divulgación No. 1: Convención sobre la Eliminación de Todas las Formas de Discriminación contra la Mujer.* Rosario: INDESO Mujer, ca. 1986.

Insausti, Santiago Joaquín. "De maricas, travestis y gays: Derivas identitarias en Buenos Aires (1966–1989)." PhD diss., School of Social Sciences, Universidad de Buenos Aires, 2016.

Irvine, Janice. *Disorders of Desire: Sexuality and Gender in Modern American Sexology.* Philadelphia: Temple University Press, 2005.

Jaffary, Nora. *Reproduction and Its Discontents in Mexico: Childbirth and Contraception, 1750–1905.* Chapel Hill: University of North Carolina Press, 2016.

Jáuregui, Carlos. *La homosexualidad en la Argentina.* Buenos Aires: Tarso, 1987.

Jelin, Elizabeth. "Sexual Abuse as a Crime against Humanity and the Right to Privacy." *Journal of Latin American Cultural Studies* 21, no. 2 (June 2012): 343–50.

Jelin, Elizabeth. *Los trabajos de la memoria.* Buenos Aires: Siglo Veintiuno, 2002.

Jelin, Elizabeth, and Eric Hershberg, eds. *Constructing Democracy: Human Rights, Citizenship, and Society in Latin America.* Boulder, CO: Westview Press, 1996.

Jensen, Silvina. *Los exiliados: La lucha por los derechos humanos durante la dictadura militar.* Buenos Aires: Sudamericana, 2010.

Jofre Barroso, Haydée. *Las argentinas y el amor*. Buenos Aires: Galerna, 1985.

John Paul II. *Familiaris Consortio: Apostolic Exhortation on the Role of the Christian Family in the Modern World*, November 22, 1981, http://w2.vatican.va/content/john-paul-ii/en/apost_exhortations/documents/hf_jp-ii_exh_19811122_familiaris-consortio.html.

Johnson, David. *The Lavender Scare: Cold War Persecution of Gays and Lesbians in the Federal Government*. Chicago: University of Chicago Press, 2004.

Kaufmann, Carolina. "Memoria de las urbanidades: Los manuales de formación moral y cívica en la dictadura." In *Historiografía y memoria colectiva: Tiempos y territorios*, edited by Cristina Godoy, 227–41. Buenos Aires: Miño y Dávila, 2002.

Kendall, Nancy. *The Sex Education Debates*. Chicago: University of Chicago Press, 2013.

King, John, Sheila Whitaker, and Rosa Bosch, eds. *An Argentine Passion: María Luisa Bemberg and Her Films*. London: Verso, 2000.

Kipnis, Laura. *Bound and Gagged: Pornography and the Politics of Fantasy in America*. Durham, NC: Duke University Press, 1999.

Kordon, Diana, and Lucila Edelman. "Psychological Effects of Political Repression." In *Psychological Effects of Political Repression*, edited by Diana Kordon, D. M. Lagos, E. Nicoletti, and R. C. Bozzolo, 33–40. Buenos Aires: Sudamericana Planeta, 1988.

Kuhn, Rodolfo. *Armando Bó, el cine, la pornografía ingenua y otras reflexiones*. Buenos Aires: Corregidor, 1984.

Kusnetzoff, Juan Carlos. "Renegación, desmentida, desaparición y percepticidio como técnicas psicopáticas de la salvación de la patria (Una visión psicoanalítica del informe de la Conadep)." In *Argentina. Psicoanálisis. Represión política*, edited by Comisión de Investigación Psicoanalítica sobre las Consecuencias de la Represión Política, 95–114. Buenos Aires: Kargieman, 1986.

Landi, Oscar. "Cultura y política en la transición democrática." In *Proceso, crisis y transición democrática*, vol. 1, edited by Oscar Oszlack, 102–23. Buenos Aires: CEAL, 1984.

Lanusse, Lucas. *Montoneros: El mito de sus 12 fundadores*. Buenos Aires: Vergara, 2005.

Laudano, Claudia. *Las mujeres en los discursos militares: Un análisis semiótico (1976–1983)*. La Plata: Editorial de la Universidad Nacional de La Plata, 1995.

Laudano, Claudia. "Mujeres y medios de comunicación: Notas para un debate." *Travesías* 3, no. 4 (November 1995): 11–16.

Lavadenz, Fernando, Carla Pantanali, and Eliana Zeballos. *Thirty Years of the HIV/AIDS Epidemic in Argentina*. Washington, DC: World Bank Group, 2015.

Lerer, María Luisa. *La dulce espera de la pareja: Mitos, sexo y maternidad*. Buenos Aires: Sudamericana/Planeta, 1987.

Lerer, María Luisa. *Sexualidad femenina: Mitos, realidades y el sentido de ser mujer*. Buenos Aires: Sudamericana/Planeta, 1986.

Lesgart, Cecilia. *Usos de la transición a la democracia: Ensayo, ciencia y política en la década del 80*. Rosario: Homo Sapiens, 2003.

Levine, Elana. *Wallowing in Sex: The New Sexual Culture of 1970s Television.* Durham, NC: Duke University Press, 2007.

Levy, Ariel. *Female Chauvinist Pigs: Women and the Rise of Raunch Culture.* New York: Free Press, 2006.

Lewin, Miriam, and Olga Wornat. *Putas y guerrilleras.* Buenos Aires: Planeta, 2014.

Llovet, Juan José, and Silvina Ramos. "La planificación familiar en Argentina: Salud pública y derechos humanos." *Cuadernos Médico Sociales,* no. 38 (1986): 25–39.

Lorenzetti, Ricardo, and Alfredo Kraut. *Derechos Humanos: Justicia y reparación.* Buenos Aires: Sudamericana, 2011.

Luciani, Laura. *Juventud en dictadura: Representaciones, políticas y experiencias juveniles en Rosario (1976–1983).* La Plata: Universidad Nacional de La Plata, 2017.

Macías-Gonzalez, Víctor, and Anne Rubenstein, eds. *Masculinity and Sexuality in Modern Mexico.* Albuquerque: University of New Mexico Press, 2012.

Macón, Cecilia. *Sexual Violence in the Argentinean Crimes against Humanity Trials.* Lanham, MD: Lexington Books, 2016.

Maffia, Diana. "Aborto no punible: ¿Qué dice la ley?" In *Realidades y coyunturas del aborto: Entre el derecho y la necesidad,* edited by Susana Checa, 149–57. Buenos Aires: Paidos, 2006.

Maffia, Diana. "Normalidad y alteración sexual en los 50: El primer departamento sexológico." In *Moralidades y comportamientos sexuales, Argentina, 1880–2011,* edited by Dora Barrancos, Donna Guy, and Adriana Valobra, 217–31. Buenos Aires: Biblos, 2014.

Mafud, Julio. *La conducta sexual de la mujer argentina.* Buenos Aires: Distal, 1991.

Mafud, Julio. *La conducta sexual de los argentinos.* Buenos Aires: Distal, 1988.

Maier, Thomas. *Masters of Sex: The Life and Times of William Masters and Virginia Johnson, the Couple Who Taught America How to Love.* New York: Basic Books, 2013.

Mainer Santos Juliá, José-Carlos. *El aprendizaje de la libertad, 1973–1976: La cultura de la transición.* Madrid: Alianza Editorial, 2000.

Maitena. *Lo peor de Maitena.* Buenos Aires: Sudamericana, 2015.

Manrupe, Raúl, and María Alejandra Portela. *Un diccionario de films argentinos.* Buenos Aires: Corregidor, 1995.

Manzano, Valeria. *The Age of Youth in Argentina: Culture, Politics, and Sexuality from Perón to Videla.* Chapel Hill: University of North Carolina Press, 2014.

Manzano, Valeria. "Sex, Gender and the Making of the 'Enemy Within' in Cold War Argentina." *Journal of Latin American Studies* 47, no. 1 (2014): 1–29.

Margulis, Mario, ed. *Juventud, cultura, sexualidad: La dimensión cultural en la afectividad y la sexualidad de los jóvenes de Buenos Aires.* Buenos Aires: Biblos, 2003.

Marhoefer, Laurie. *Sex and the Weimar Republic: German Homosexual Emancipation and the Rise of the Nazis.* Toronto: University of Toronto Press, 2015.

Marqués, Josep Vicent. "Sexualidad, represión, deformación y liberación." *El Viejo Topo,* February 1977, 28–32.

Martínez, Paola. *Género, política y revolución en los años setenta: Las mujeres del PRT-ERP.* Buenos Aires: Imago Mundi, 2009.

Massera, Emilio. *El camino a la democracia*. Buenos Aires: El Cid Editor, 1979.

McKee Irwin, Robert, Edward J. McCaughan, and Michelle Rocio Nasser, eds. *The Famous 41: Sexuality and Social Control in Mexico, 1901*. New York: Palgrave Macmillan, 2003.

McLlelan, Josie. *Love in the Time of Communism: Intimacy and Sexuality in the GDR*. New York: Cambridge University Press, 2011.

McNair, Brian. *Striptease Culture: Sex, Media and the Democratisation of Desire*. New York: Routledge, 2009.

Medina, Enrique. *Perros de la noche*. Buenos Aires: Galerna, 1984 [1977].

Mellibovsky, Matilde. *Circle of Love over Death: Testimonies of the Mothers of Plaza de Mayo*. Willimantic, CT: Curbstone Press, 1997.

Mercado, Tununa. *Canon de Alcoba*. Buenos Aires: Seix Barral, 2010 [1988].

Mira-Delli Zotti, Guillermo. "Explorando algunas dimensiones del exilio argentino en España." In *Memorias de la violencia en Uruguay y Argentina: Golpes, dictaduras, exilios (1973–2006)*, edited by Eduardo Rey Tristán, 163–78. Santiago de Compostela: Universidad de Santiago de Compostela, 2007.

Miranda, Marisa. *Controlar lo incontrolable: Una historia de la sexualidad en la Argentina*. Buenos Aires: Biblos, 2011.

*Mitominas 1: Un paseo a través de los mitos: Del 7 al 30 de noviembre*. Buenos Aires: Municipalidad de la Ciudad de Buenos Aires, 1986.

Mogrovejo, Norma. *Un amor que se atrevió a decir su nombre: La lucha de las lesbianas y su relación con los movimientos homosexual y feminista en América Latina*. Mexico City: Plaza y Valdés, 2000.

Mollmann, Marianne. *Decisions Denied: Women's Access to Contraceptives and Abortion in Argentina*. New York: Human Rights Watch, 2005.

Moran, Claire. "Re-positioning Female Heterosexuality within Postfeminist and Neoliberal Culture." *Sexualities* 20, nos. 1–2 (2017): 121–39.

Moreira Alves, Maria Helena. *State and Opposition in Military Brazil*. Austin: University of Texas Press, 1985.

Morrisey, Belinda. *When Women Kill: Questions of Agency and Subjectivity*. New York: Routledge, 2003.

*La mujer y el cine: Segundo Festival Internacional de Cine realizado por Mujeres*. Mar del Plata, 1989.

Mulvey, Laura. "Visual Pleasure and Narrative Cinema." In *Feminism and Film*, edited by E. Ann Kaplan, 34–47. New York: Oxford University Press, 2000.

Nari, Marcela. "Abrir los ojos, abrir la cabeza: El feminismo en la Argentina de los años '70." *Feminaria* 9, nos. 18–19 (1996): 15–21.

Nari, Marcela. "En busca de un pasado: Revistas, feminismo y memoria: Una historia de las revistas feministas, 1982–1997." *Feminaria* 10, no. 20 (1997): 32–40.

Navarro, Marysa. "El primer encuentro feminista de Latinoamérica y el Caribe." In *Sociedad, subordinación y feminismo*, edited by Magdalena León, 261–67. Bogotá: ACEP, 1982.

Neroni, Hilary. *The Violent Woman: Femininity, Narrative, and Violence in Contemporary American Cinema*. Albany: State University of New York Press, 2005.

Novaro, Marcos, and Vicente Palermo. *La dictadura militar, 1976–1983: Del golpe de estado a la restauración democrática*. Buenos Aires: Paidós, 2003.

Novick, Susana. "La posición argentina en las tres conferencias mundiales de población." *Papeles de Población* 5, no. 20 (April–June 1999): 25–67.

Nun, José, and Juan Carlos Portantiero, eds. *Ensayos sobre la transición a la democracia en Argentina*. Buenos Aires: Puntosur, 1987.

O'Donnell, Guillermo. *Counterpoints: Selected Essays on Authoritarianism and Democratization*. Notre Dame, IN: University of Notre Dame Press, 1999.

O'Donnell, Guillermo, Philippe Schmitter, and Laurence Whitehead, eds. *Transitions from Authoritarian Rule: Prospects for Democracy*. Baltimore: Johns Hopkins University Press, 1986.

O'Reilly, Andrea, ed. *From Motherhood to Mothering: The Legacy of Adrianne Rich's Of Woman Born*. New York: State University of New York Press, 2004.

Oberti, Alejandra. *Las revolucionarias: Militancia, vida cotidiana y afectividad en los setenta*. Buenos Aires: Edhasa, 2015.

Obregón, Martín. *Entre la cruz y la espada: La Iglesia católica durante los primeros años del Proceso*. Buenos Aires: UNQUI, 2005.

Oddone, María Elena. *48 artículos seleccionados de la columna semanal de María Elena Oddone: Movimiento Feminista*. Buenos Aires: El Informador Público, 1990.

Oddone, María Elena. *La pasión por la libertad: Memorias de una feminista*. Asunción, Paraguay: Colihué-Mimbipá, 2001.

Ojeda Franco, Mónica. "Pornoerótica latinoamericana: Subversión en la narrativa de mujeres en el exilio." *Anales de Literatura Hispanoamericana* 43 (2014): 57–69.

Olcott, Jocelyn, Mary Kay Vaughan, and Gabriela Cano, eds. *Sex in Revolution: Gender, Politics, and Power in Modern Mexico*. Durham, NC: Duke University Press, 2006.

Osuna, María Florencia. "Políticas de la última dictadura argentina frente a la 'brecha generacional.'" *Revista Latinoamericana de Ciencias Sociales, Niñez y Juventud* 15, no. 2 (2017): 1097–1110.

Oszlak, Oscar, ed. *"Proceso," crisis y transición democrática*. Buenos Aires: CEAL, 1984.

Otovo, Okezi. *Progressive Mothers, Better Babies: Race, Public Health, and the State in Brazil, 1850–1945*. Austin: University of Texas Press, 2016.

Parrilla, Luis. *Educación sexual: Manual para docentes*. Buenos Aires: Ediciones La Aurora, 1986.

Parrilla, Luis. "Educación sexual del escolar: Los niños se abren al mundo." In *Sexualidad humana y relaciones personales*, edited by René Jaimes, 145–60. New York: IIPF, 1978.

Parrilla, Luis. *¡No sé qué decirle! Elementos para una educación sexual: Conversaciones con padres*. Buenos Aires: Ediciones La Aurora, 1986.

Pauluzzi, Liliana. *¿Qué preguntan los chicos sobre sexo? Educación sexual para padres y docentes*. Rosario: Homo Sapiens, 1993.

Pavlovic, Tatjana. *Despotic Bodies and Transgressive Bodies: Spanish Culture from Francisco Franco to Jesús Franco*. New York: State University of New York Press, 2002.

Pecheny, Mario. "Sexual Orientation, AIDS, and Human Rights in Argentina: The

Paradox of Social Advance amid Health Crisis." In *Struggles for Social Rights in Latin America*, edited by Susan Evan Eckstein and Timothy Wickham-Crowley, 253–70. New York: Routledge, 2003.

Pecheny, Mario, and Mónica Petracci. *Derechos humanos y sexualidad*. Buenos Aires: CEDES, 2007.

Pensado, Jaime. *Rebel Mexico: Student Unrest and Authoritarian Political Culture during the Long Sixties*. Stanford: Stanford University Press, 2013.

Peri Rossi, Cristina. *La nave de los locos*. Barcelona: Seix Barral, 1984.

Perlongher, Néstor. "El sexo de las locas." In *Prosa plebeya: Ensayos 1980–1982*, 29–34. Buenos Aires: Colihue, 1997.

Pick, Zuzana. "An Interview with María Luisa Bemberg." *Journal of Film and Video* 44, nos. 3–4 (Fall 1992–Winter 1993): 76–82.

Pieper Mooney, Jadwiga. *The Politics of Motherhood: Maternity and Women's Rights in Twentieth-Century Chile*. Pittsburgh, PA: University of Pittsburgh Press, 2009.

Pite, Rebekah. *Creating a Common Table in Twentieth-Century Argentina: Doña Petrona, Women, and Food*. Chapel Hill: University of North Carolina Press, 2013.

Plotkin, Mariano. *Argentina on the Couch: Psychiatry, State, and Society, 1880 to the Present*. Albuquerque: University of New Mexico Press, 2003.

Plotkin, Mariano. *Freud in the Pampas: The Emergence and Development of a Psychoanalytic Culture in Argentina*. Stanford, CA: Stanford University Press, 2001.

Plummer, Ken. *Intimate Citizenship: Private Decisions and Public Dialogues*. Seattle: University of Washington Press, 2003.

Plummer, Ken. "Representing Sexualities in the Media." *Sexualities* 6, nos. 3–4 (2003): 275–76.

Plummer, Ken. *Telling Sexual Stories: Power, Change, and Social Worlds*. London: Routledge, 1995.

Pomiés, Julia, and Alicia Antel. *Educación sexual (0 a 18 años)*. Buenos Aires: Ediciones Vivir, 1985.

Ponce, José M. *El destape nacional*. Barcelona: Glénat, 2004.

Postolski, Glenn, and Santiago Martino. "Relaciones peligrosas: Los medios y la dictadura entre el control, la censura y los negocios." In *Mucho ruido y pocas leyes: Economía y políticas de la comunicación en la Argentina (1920–2004)*, edited by Guillermo Mastrini, 155–84. Buenos Aires: La Crujía, 2009.

Pozzi, Pablo. *Por las sendas argentinas: El PRT-ERP, la guerrilla marxista*. Buenos Aires: Eudeba, 2001.

Pucciarelli, Alfredo Raúl, ed. *Los años de Alfonsín: ¿El poder de la democracia o la democracia del poder?* Buenos Aires: Siglo Veintiuno, 2006.

Pujol, Sergio. *La década rebelde: Los años 60 en la Argentina*. Buenos Aires: Emecé, 2002.

Quintar, Aída, and José Borello. "Evolución histórica de la exhibición y consumo de cine en Buenos Aires." *H-industri@* 8, no. 14 (2014): 81–120.

Quiroga, Hugo. *El tiempo del Proceso: Conflictos y coincidencias entre civiles y militares (1976–1983)*. Rosario: Editorial Fundación Ross, 1994.

Ramírez Llorens, Fernando. "Noches de sano esparcimiento: La censura cine-matográfica en Argentina, 1955–1973." *Nuevo Mundo, Mundos Nuevos* (December 2015), https://journals.openedition.org/nuevomundo/68565?lang=en.

Rapisardi, Flavio, and Alejandro Modarelli. *Fiestas, baños y exilios: Los gays porteños en la última dictadura*. Buenos Aires: Sudamericana, 2001.

Raup Rios, Roger. "Sexual Rights of Gays, Lesbians, and Transgender Persons in Latin America." In *The Politics of Sexuality in Latin America: A Reader on Lesbian, Gay, Bisexual, and Transgender Rights*, edited by Javier Corrales and Mario Pecheny, 251–58. Pittsburgh, PA: University of Pittsburgh Press, 2014.

Reed, Jacinta. *The New Avengers: Feminism, Femininity, and the Rape-Revenge Cycle*. Manchester: Manchester University Press, 2000.

Rich, Adrianne. *Of Woman Born: Motherhood as Experience and Institution*. New York: Norton, 1976.

Richardson, Diane. "Rethinking Sexual Citizenship." *Sociology* 51, no. 2 (2017): 208–24.

Richardson, Diane. *Rethinking Sexuality*. London: Sage, 2000.

Robben, Antonius C. G. M. *Argentina Betrayed: Memory, Mourning, and Accountability*. Philadelphia: University of Pennsylvania Press, 2018.

Robben, Antonius C. G. M. *Political Violence and Trauma in Argentina*. Philadelphia: University of Pennsylvania Press, 2005.

Rodríguez Pereyra, Ricardo. "Adiós Roberto y Otra historia de amor: Gays en democracia." In *Otras historias de amor: Gays, lesbianas y travestis en el cine argentino*, edited by Adrián Melo, 253–79. Buenos Aires: Ediciones Lea, 2008.

Roffé, Reina. *Monte de Venus*. Buenos Aires: Astier, 2013 [1976].

Romero, Luis Alberto. *A History of Argentina in the Twentieth Century*. University Park: Pennsylvania State University Press, 2006.

Romi, Juan Carlos. "Consideraciones básicas sobre educación sexual." *Revista Latinoamericana de Sexología* 1, no. 2 (1986): 225–41.

Rosa, María Laura. *Legados de libertad: El arte feminista en la efervescencia democrática*. Buenos Aires: Biblos, 2014.

Rubin, Gayle. "Thinking Sex: Notes for a Radical Theory of the Politics of Sexuality." In *The Lesbian and Gay Studies Reader*, edited by Henry Abelove, Michele Barale, and David Halperin, 3–44. New York: Routledge, 1993.

Ruétalo, Victoria. "Tempations: Isabel Sarli Exposed." In *Latsploitation, Exploitation Cinemas, and Latin America*, edited by Victoria Ruétalo and Dolores Tiernes, 201–14. New York: Routledge, 2009.

Ruti, Mari. *Feminist Film Theory and Pretty Woman*. New York: Bloomsbury, 2016.

Saborido, Jorge, and Marcelo Borrelli, eds. *Voces y silencios: La prensa argentina y la dictadura militar (1976–1983)*. Buenos Aires: Eudeba, 2011.

Sacred Congregation for Catholic Education. *Educational Guidance on Human Love: Outlines for Sex Education*, November 1, 1983, http://www.vatican.va/roman_curia/congregations/ccatheduc/documents/rc_con_ccatheduc_doc_19831101_sexual-education_en.html.

Salessi, Jorge. *Médicos, maleantes y maricas: Higiene, criminología y homosexualidad en la construcción de la nación argentina (Buenos Aires, 1871–1914)*. Rosario: Beatriz Viterbo, 1995.

Sapetti, Adrián, and Mario Kaplan. *La sexualidad masculina*. Buenos Aires: Galerna, 1986.

Sapetti, Adrián, and Roberto Rosenzvaig. *Sexualidad en la pareja: Todas las preguntas, todas las respuestas*. Buenos Aires: Galerna, 1987.

Sauerteig, Lutz D. H., and Roger Davidson. "Shaping the Sexual Knowledge of the Young." In *Shaping Sexual Knowledge: A Cultural History of Sex Education in Twentieth Century Europe*, 1–15. New York: Routledge, 2009.

Schaefer, Eric. *"Bold! Daring! Shocking! True!" A History of Exploitation Films, 1919–1959*. Durham, NC: Duke University Press, 1999.

Schaefer, Eric. "Dirty Little Secrets: Scholars, Archivists, and Dirty Movies." *The Moving Image* 5, no. 2 (Fall 2005): 79–105.

Schaefer, Eric, ed. *Sex Scene: Media and the Sexual Revolution*. Durham, NC: Duke University Press, 2014.

Schenquer, Laura. "Agencias e 'inmoralidades': La circulación de directivas político-culturales entre la Secretaría de Información Pública, el Ministerio del Interior y la Dirección General de Informaciones de la provincia de Santa Fe durante la última dictadura militar argentina (1976–1983)." *Nuevo Mundo, Mundos Nuevos* (February 2018), https://journals.openedition.org/nuevomundo/?lang=es.

Seoane, María. *Amor a la argentina: Sexo, moral y política en el siglo XX*. Buenos Aires: Planeta, 2007.

Sharaf, Myron. *The Fury on Earth: A Biography of Wilhelm Reich*. New York: St. Martin's Press, 1983.

Sheffield, Carole. "Sexual Terrorism." In *Women: A Feminist Perspective*, edited by Jo Freeman, 3–19. Palo Alto, CA: Sage, 1989.

Sheinin, David. *Consent of the Damned: Ordinary Argentinians in the Dirty War*. Gainesville: University Press of Florida, 2012.

Shua, Ana María. *Los amores de Laurita*. Buenos Aires: Sudamericana, 1995 [1984].

Simonetto, Patricio. "Del consultorio a la cama: Discurso, cultura visual, erótica y sexología en la Argentina." *Sexualidad, salud y sociedad*, no. 22 (April 2016): 103–28.

Simonetto, Patricio. *Entre la injuria y la revolución: El Frente de Liberación Homosexual: Argentina, 1967–1976*. Buenos Aires: Universidad Nacional de Quilmes, 2017.

Simonetto, Patricio. "La moral institucionalizada: Reflexiones sobre el Estado, las sexualidad y la violencia en la Argentina en el siglo XX." *e-l@tina: Revista electrónica de estudios latinoamericanos* 14, no. 55 (April–June 2016), https://www.researchgate.net/publication/304831687_La_moral_institucionalizadaReflexiones_sobre_el_Estado_las_sexualidades_y_la_violencia_en_la_Argentina_del_siglo_XX.

Sippial, Tiffany. *Prostitution, Modernity, and the Making of the Cuban Republic, 1840–1920*. Chapel Hill: University of North Carolina Press, 2013.

Sirvén, Pablo. *Quién te ha visto y quién TV: Historia informal de la televisión argentina*. Buenos Aires: Ediciones de la Flor, 1998.

Sonderéguer, María, and Violeta Correa, eds. *Cuaderno de Trabajo: Análisis de la relación entre violencia sexual, tortura y violación de los derechos humanos.* Buenos Aires: Universidad Nacional de Quilmes, 2008.

Sonderéguer, María, and Violeta Correa. "Género y violencias en el terrorismo de Estado en Argentina." In *Género y poder: Violencias de género en contextos de represión política y conflictos armados,* edited by María Sonderéguer, 289–302. Buenos Aires: Universidad Nacional de Quilmes Editorial, 2012.

Stantic, Lila. "El cine que compartimos." In *María Luisa Bemberg,* edited by Grupo Némenis, 21–23. Buenos Aires: Museo Roca, 2005.

Suárez-Findley, Eileen. *Imposing Decency: The Politics of Sexuality and Race in Puerto Rico, 1870–1920.* Durham, NC: Duke University Press, 1999.

Suriano, Juan, ed. *Nueva Historia Argentina: Dictadura y democracia (1976–2001).* Buenos Aires: Sudamericana, 2005.

Sutton, Barbara. *Surviving State Terror: Women's Testimonies of Repression and Resistance in Argentina.* New York: New York University Press, 2018.

Szot, Liliana. *Educación Sexual.* Rosario: n.p., 1989.

Tarducci, Mónica. "Hitos de la militancia lesbofeminista de Buenos Aires (1984–1995)." In *Feminismo, lesbianismo y maternidad en Buenos Aires,* edited by Mónica Tarducci, 37–59. Buenos Aires: Librería de Mujeres Editoras, 2014.

Taylor, Diana. *Disappearing Acts: Spectacles of Gender and Nationalism in Argentina's Dirty War.* Durham, NC: Duke University Press, 1997.

Taylor, Diana. "Making a Spectacle: The Mothers of Plaza de Mayo." *Journal of the Association for Research on Mothering* 3, no. 2 (2001): 97–109.

Tompkins, Cynthia. "Las *Mujeres alteradas* y *Superadas* de Maitena Burundarena: Feminismo 'Made in Argentina.'" *Studies in Latin American Popular Culture* 22 (2003): 35–60.

Torres Molina, Susana. *Dueña y señora.* Buenos Aires: Ediciones La Campana, 1983.

Torricella, Paula. "Comentarios sobre la experiencia editorial de *Cuaderno de Existencia Lesbiana.*" *Revista Interdisciplinaria de Estudios Sociales,* no. 2 (July–December 2010): 85–107.

Trebisacce, Catalina. "Una batalla sexual en los setenta: Las feministas y los militantes homosexuales apostando a otra economía de placeres." In *Deseo y represión: Sexualidad, género y estado en la historia argentina reciente,* edited by Débora D'Antonio, 43–61. Buenos Aires: Imago Mundi, 2015.

Trebisacce, Catalina. "Historias feministas desde la lente de María Luisa Bemberg." *Revista Nomadías* 18 (November 2013): 19–41.

Trebisacce, Catalina. "Modernización y experiencia feminista en los años setenta en Argentina." In *Hilvanando historias: Mujeres y política en el pasado reciente latinoamericano,* edited by Andrea Andújar, Débora D'Antonio, Karin Grammático, and María Laura Rosa, 63–81. Buenos Aires: Luxemburg, 2010.

Tulchin, Joseph, ed. *The Consolidation of Democracy in Latin America.* Boulder, CO: Lynne Rienner Publishers, 1995.

Tyler May, Elaine. *Homeward Bound: American Families in the Cold War Era.* New York: Basic Books, 2017.

Ulanovsky, Carlos. *Paren las rotativas: Una historia de grandes diarios, revistas y periodistas argentinos*. Buenos Aires: Espasa, 1997.

Ulanovsky, Carlos, Silvia Itkin, and Pablo Sirvén. *Estamos en el aire: Una historia de la televisión en la Argentina*. Buenos Aires: Planeta, 1999.

United Nations Human Rights Office of the High Commissioner. *Reproductive Rights Are Human Rights: A Handbook for National Human Rights Institutions*. New York: United Nations, 2014.

Varea, Fernando. *El cine argentino durante la dictadura militar, 1976/1983*. Rosario: Editorial Municipal de Rosario, 2008.

Varela, Mirta. "Silencio, mordaza y optimismo." *Todo es Historia*, no. 104 (March 2001): 50–63.

Vázquez Lorda, Lilia. "Intervenciones e iniciativas católicas en el ámbito familiar: Las Ligas de Madres y Padres de Familia (Argentina, 1950–1970)." MA thesis, Buenos Aires, Universidad de San Andrés, 2012.

Verbitsky, Horacio. *The Flight: Confessions of an Argentine Dirty Warrior*. New York: New Press, 1996.

Vezzetti, Hugo. *Pasado y presente: Guerra, dictadura y sociedad en la Argentina*. Buenos Aires: Siglo Veintiuno, 2002.

Vila, Pablo, and Pablo Semán. *Troubling Gender: Youth and Cumbia in Argentina's Music Scene*. Philadelphia: Temple University Press, 2011.

Walsh, María Elena. *Desventuras en el país jardín de infantes*. Buenos Aires: Sudamericana, 1994.

Weeks, Jeffrey. "The Sexual Citizen." *Theory, Culture, and Society* 15, nos. 3–4 (1998): 35–52.

Weeks, Jeffrey. "Traps We Set Ourselves." *Sexualities* 2, nos. 1–2 (2008): 27–33.

Whitaker, Sheyla. "Pride and Prejudice: María Luisa Bemberg. Interview with Sheyla Whitaker." In *The Garden of Forking Paths: Argentine Cinema*, edited by John King and Nissa Torrents, 115–21. London: British Film Institute, 1988.

Williams, Linda. *Hard Core: Power, Pleasure, and the "Frenzy of the Visible."* Durham, NC: Duke University Press, 1999.

Williams, Linda. *Screening Sex*. Durham, NC: Duke University Press, 2008.

Willoughby, Brian, and Dean Busby. "In the Eye of the Beholder: Exploring Variations in the Perceptions of Pornography." *Journal of Sex Research* 53, no. 6 (2016): 678–88.

Wolf, Naomi. *The Beauty Myth: How Images of Beauty Are Used against Women*. New York: Harper Perennial, 2002.

World Health Organization. *Education and Treatment in Human Sexuality: The Training of Health Professionals: Report of a WHO Meeting*. Geneva: World Health Organization, 1975.

Wydra, Harald. *Communism and the Emergence of Democracy*. New York: Cambridge University Press, 2007.

Zeno, Ana María. "El grito silencioso y la educación sexual," *Documentos del Centro de Estudios Sociales Rafael Barret*, no. 9 (1986): 2–3.

Zylberman, Lior. "Estrategias narrativas de un cine post dictatorial." *Revista Afuera: Estudios de crítica cultural* 13 (September 2013), http://www.revistaafuera.com/articulo.php?id=280&nro=13.

# INDEX

Note: Page numbers in *italics* refer to figures.